Joseph Gandy

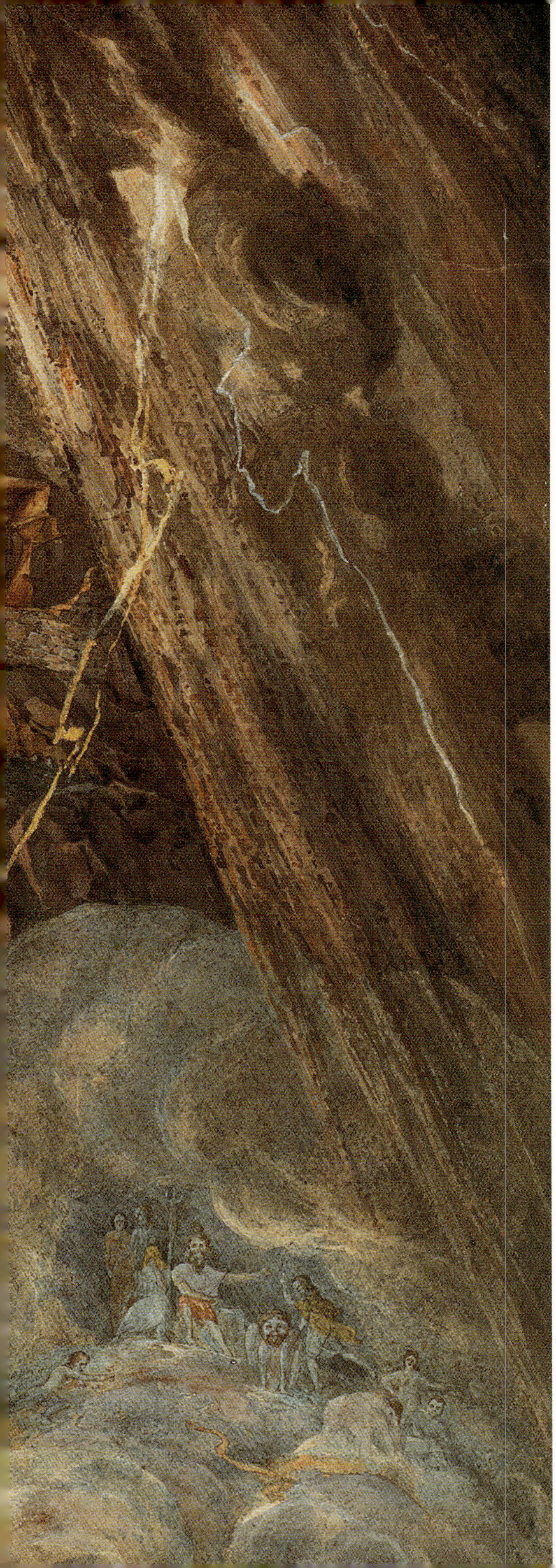

Joseph Gandy

An Architectural Visionary in Georgian England

Brian Lukacher

With 205 illustrations

Frontispiece: Gandy, *Bridge over Chaos* (1833). Detail

© 2006 Brian Lukacher

All Rights Reserved. No part of this publication may be reproduced or transmitted in any form or by any means, electronic or mechanical, including photocopy, recording or any other information storage and retrieval system, without prior permission in writing from the publisher.

First published in 2006 in hardcover in the United States of America by Thames & Hudson Inc., 500 Fifth Avenue, New York, New York 10110

thamesandhudsonusa.com

Library of Congress Catalog Card Number 2005907354

ISBN-13: 978-0-500-34221-3
ISBN-10: 0-500-34221-0

Designed by Anna Perotti

Printed and bound in China by C&C Offset Printing Co Ltd

Contents

Preface and Acknowledgments	6
Introduction: On the Misrepresentation of Architecture	8
I To Rival Antiquity: Gandy's Youthful Dreams	12
II Natural Abodes of Men: Sepulchers and Cottages	32
III Wounded Sensibility, or Fragments of a Career	56
IV Architectural History Painting: Gandy at the Royal Academy	88
V Soane and Gandy at the Fall of Architecture	132
VI Gandy's Later Period: Toward a Mythography of Architecture	168
Conclusion: On the Madness of Architecture	198
Notes	202
Bibliography	211
Sources of Illustrations	216
Index	220

Preface and Acknowledgments

This book is the first monograph devoted to the life, career, and work of the architect and artist Joseph Gandy (1771–1843). First monographs are an inherently flawed and fragile scholarly medium. Confidently vaunted claims to definitiveness in such volumes are by necessity stalked by the shadow of imminent obsolescence. As art and architectural history has become relentlessly self-critical and theoretically informed over the last generation, the "life and times" format of the art-history monograph has fundamentally gone to ground, especially within so-called academic writing. Despite these trends, this book is cautiously yet steadfastly empirical and straightforwardly narrative in its structure and approach. It is in part a documentary biography, in part a descriptive analysis of this artist's remarkable pictures and designs, and in part a cultural and social history of the romantic epoch that was vividly though episodically refracted through Gandy's imagination and experiences. I have sought to recover the cultural and intellectual controversies surrounding Gandy's work and reputation in early nineteenth-century London and to locate the significance of his artistic production and theoretical ideas within the milieu of the most prominent and influential architects, architectural thinkers, painters, antiquarians, and art critics of late Georgian Britain. I have tried to do so in terms and language that would be broadly recognizable to Gandy and his contemporaries. The architectural historian Henry-Russell Hitchcock had remarked of Gandy's imaginary designs, "they are among the most distinguished examples of what could *never* have been built in that period." This would suggest that Gandy's work was strangely and tragically remote from its own historical setting, and thereby made all the more meaningful and relevant to our own. I am not anxious to renounce the prophetic aspects of Gandy's work. However, it is the complicated and revealing historical fabric of Gandy's life, and its resonance in the architectural imagery of his drawings as well as in his mythic and ideological formulations about the larger meaning of architecture and culture, that is the primary concern of this book.

Over the long, rather fitful, period of research for this volume, I have enjoyed and benefited from the support of many individuals. The descendants of Joseph Gandy have been extremely generous and gracious over two decades. I am most grateful to the late Joan Rising, the late John Gandy and his widow Jill Gandy, and the late Rosalie Gandy. They kindly welcomed me into their homes repeatedly to inspect manuscripts and drawings in their possession. I regret deeply that they are not all here to see this book as testimony to the trust and friendship that they extended to me. Barry Saxton was no less helpful in allowing me access to his portfolio of Gandy sketches. Over the last few years, Virginia Novarra has been an unfailing supporter of my project and has helped with many questions about Gandy genealogy and family history.

Sir John Soane's Museum has served as my London research base over the last decade. Curator emeritus Margaret Richardson has lent encouragement and support to my work on Gandy at every stage. I am especially grateful and honored that she gave me the opportunity to share my research on the occasion of the Annual Soane Lecture in the autumn of 2001. Likewise, her dedicated colleagues at the Soane Museum, Helen Dorey, Susan Palmer, and Stephen Astley, never seemed to tire of my endless requests and queries. Their expert assistance in guiding me through the collections and archives of the Soane Museum has been inestimable.

Damie Stillman and Robin Middleton have offered scholarly guidance and advice over the long duration of my search for Gandy. I owe a great deal to both of them for continuously sharing their comprehensive knowledge of eighteenth- and nineteenth-century British and European architecture with me. Other distinguished scholars and colleagues have advanced the efforts of my research in ways too numerous to recount. They are: John Harris, the late Sir John Summerson, Wolfgang Ernst, Stephen Bann, J. Mordaunt Crook, Joseph Rykwert, Nicholas Adams, John McCoubrey, Sam Smiles, Frank Salmon, Alistair Rowan, and Howard Shubert. The longstanding friendship and encouragement of Stephen Eisenman, Franklin Kelly, and Christopher London deserve special mention. I am equally grateful for the support of my colleagues—present and past—in the Department of Art at Vassar College, as well as to colleagues in the Art Library, the Frances Lehman Loeb Art Center, and the Visual Resources and Special Collections divisions of the Vassar College Library.

I would like to thank those private collectors who have generously allowed me to inspect and to secure photographs of drawings by Gandy in their possession and who offered great hospitality and trust in doing so: Peter Brandt, Ray Harryhausen, Walter Chatham, and Herbert Mitchell. For assistance in tracking down Gandy drawings in private hands and through the auction houses, I am most grateful to the late Ben Weinreb, Harriet Drummond of Christie's, London, and Ann Guité of Richard L. Feigen & Co.

The editing of the book manuscript at Thames & Hudson has been expertly and patiently handled by Ian Sutton, who brought clarity and concision to the text. My gratitude also to Anna Perotti who is responsible for the book's elegant and sympathetic design. Alessandra Sauven has been a dedicated picture researcher. I also think of the late Nikos Stangos, who first encouraged me to bring the book to Thames & Hudson.

My brother Ned Lukacher first brought me to things intellectual and cultural, and therefore deserves some of the blame. My wife Joanne Martin Lukacher first put a copy of *Heavenly Mansions* in my hands and took me for the first time in 1975 to Sir John Soane's Museum. None of this would have been possible without her and it is to her that the book is affectionately dedicated.

Funding for research on this book has been granted by the Center for Advanced Studies in the Visual Arts, National Gallery of Art, Washington, D.C. and the Vassar College Faculty Research Committee.

1 *A Trophy and Temple, Leading to a Sepulchral Cavern*, 1821

7

Introduction: On the Misrepresentation of Architecture

"And how often does it fall out," observed the Renaissance architect and humanist Alberti, "that even when we are employed upon other things, we cannot keep our thoughts and imaginations from projecting some edifice?"[1] Joseph Gandy, the subject of the pages that follow, was forever projecting edifices, which involved the translation of his mental images of architecture into pictorial ones. The eminent architectural historian Sir John Summerson, who first brought scholarly attention to the work of Gandy in a series of articles during the 1930s and 1940s, spoke of "an architecture of the mind" in reference to the late eighteenth-century proclivity for creating imaginary buildings on paper. Resorting to a psychological analogy, Summerson speculated that "the introvert architect often tends to express himself in drawings and writings rather than in brick and stone—to produce fantasies like those of Lajoue, Piranesi, Ledoux, or Gandy."[2] Whether all these distinguished architects of an artistic and theoretical bent suffered from introverted character traits is far from certain (Gandy, as we shall see, conformed somewhat to this profile). However, all were progeny of the Enlightenment, especially in the ambitious scope and experimental classicism of their architectural conceptions, and all sought to express their ideas about the history, theory, and design of architecture through visual, or more precisely pictorial, imagery—imagery that both affirmed and contested the architectural possibilities and cultural expectations of the time.

Architectural historian and theorist Manfredo Tafuri has argued that with Piranesi's visionary archaeology of antiquity during the late eighteenth century, "the theme of imagination thus enters into the history of modern architecture in all its ideological significance." Tafuri finds within this Piranesian realm of imaginary architecture "an alternative that departs from actual historical conditions … in order to project into the future the bursting forth of present contradictions."[3]

Building castles (or prisons and ruins) in the air was not merely an exercise of the imagination but could also serve as a dissenting ideological critique. Piranesi and Gandy were probably not eschatological Marxists, avant la lettre, but their relation to society and history, both as experienced in their lives and through the architectural imagery that they created, accords with Tafuri's compelling formulation. This architecture of the mind for Piranesi and Gandy was inspired by a profound engagement with the historical past; by a profound struggle against the limits of their own historical epoch; and by a profound hope for the meaningful endurance of their architectural ideas as pictorial images into an uncertain future.

Although Gandy's work has remained relatively little known, with the exception of the drawings he rendered in his role as the perspectivist for the innovative architect Sir John Soane, this was often not the case within his own lifetime. In recovering the critical reception of Gandy's art, we find that he was characterized by his contemporaries (especially art reviewers who commented on his exhibited drawings at the Royal Academy) as being something of an estranged genius, an unfulfilled architect who applied his exceptional talent to magnificent perspectives of imaginary architecture. Indeed, later in the twentieth century, some of Gandy's pictures would be misattributed to architects and artists of such stature as Karl Friedrich Schinkel and J. M. W. Turner. The vicissitudes of Gandy's career and his disappearance from the history of art and architecture circa 1790 to 1840 can be ascribed in large measure to the divided nature of his artistic output: at once pictorial and architectural, but not fully either. In addition there were the closely guarded tribulations of his life and temperament.

2 Henry Pickersgill, *Portrait of Joseph Gandy*, 1822

Summerson entitled one of his essays "The Strange Case of J. M. Gandy," as though to suggest that the sleuthing and deciphering skills of Conan Doyle and Freud were required to fathom the troubled circumstances of Gandy's career and the defiant quality of his imagination.

As a young student of architecture studying in Rome during the 1790s, Gandy received a letter of advice from the engraver and portraitist William Pether, who counseled him to be "an artist pursuing a quiet path without deviating into disputes and schisms of either religion or politics."[4] This proved impossible for Gandy, the course of whose career was framed roughly by the Napoleonic Wars. He witnessed Napoleon's sacking of Rome as a young man and was later unduly hopeful that he would participate in a post-Waterloo efflorescence of monumental public architecture in Great Britain. To anticipate: Gandy's political and religious leanings were fickle in the extreme, which was perhaps true to the volatile historical period in which he lived. One moment he thinks and writes like a radical deist; and in another, one finds him gripped by the millenarian fervor of evangelical devotion. Educated and reasoned enlightenment was at hand for all of society, Gandy seemed to believe, but so too was the end of the world. At one point, Gandy writes in despair from debtor's prison about the social and economic injustices heaped upon him, citing the editorial opinions of *The Englishman's Whig* to support his political disaffection; and at another, he writes to *The Guardian* arguing vociferously like a Tory royalist that the resources of the nation were not being adequately expended on extravagant palaces for the controversially unpopular monarch George IV. Gandy often dreamt of London's transformation into a new classical capital of unparalleled splendor, but like Wordsworth, Blake, and Shelley, he also reviled the metropolis as an impervious kind of hell.

Whether he suffered from missed opportunities or simply chased opportunity from his door, Gandy resented patronage as desperately as he needed it. Early in his career, he gained commissions from the politically progressive reformer Major John Cartwright, and also from the Tory slave magnate John Bolton—patrons representative of strenuously opposing outlooks. He had also succeeded in attracting the patronage of the wealthy and tasteful connoisseur Thomas Hope, who purchased two pictures from him in 1806. But afterwards, nothing further developed; one can only wonder what might have resulted had Hope enlisted Gandy for the picturesque renovation of his country residence Deepdene. The Royal Academy was in many respects Gandy's professional home, but even there he repeatedly fell out of institutional favor and taxed the patience of its powerful inner circle of academicians. He occasionally alienated those who had most steadfastly looked after his interests, particularly John Soane and the antiquarian topographer John Britton. Even his few patrons were sometimes cursed with the same pecuniary misfortunes that had plagued his own life. The publisher and journalist Alaric Watts commissioned a series of engravings by Gandy in the 1820s and amassed an impressive collection of modern English watercolors (including five important pictures by Gandy), but bankruptcy brought an end to his publishing ventures and forced the auction of his collection in 1832.[5]

The social pressures and commercial challenges of professional practice did not sit easy with Gandy. He nursed his own sense of genius and artistic independence often to the point of self-detriment. Frequently Gandy wrote of his fear of being "degraded" within his professional and social life. Anxious expectations of persecution and feelings of damaged pride alternated in his mind to an almost debilitating extent. Henry Pickersgill's 1822 portrait drawing [2] of him is telling in this respect. Gandy is presented as a gentleman scholar attired in a fur-collared dressing gown and seated in quietude turning the page of a folio volume. The pose and attitude may at first be taken as aloof and disinterested. But his expression is also solicitously alert and lively. The noticeably slack right arm that comes between figure and beholder perhaps hints at a note of despondency and a slight faltering of self-possession. Gandy's fleshy face, tousled hair, and deep-set eyes naturally receive the most delineative detail, accentuated as well by the hatched area of shadow framing the head and upper torso. The active imagination of the portrait subject is thereby strikingly suggested, as Gandy's mind and likeness appears to emerge out of, or perhaps to recede into, its own dark cloud.

Of course, melancholic remoteness was itself a kind of social performance for an architect and artist on public display (the sketch was preparatory for an exhibition portrait at the RA). Whatever combination of fashioned identity and self-disclosure that Gandy and Pickersgill wished to convey, there can be little doubt that Gandy's own artistic production was never very remote from the larger cultural formations of his epoch. No matter how tempting it is to estimate images of architectural fantasy as being "visionary" and "transcendental" in nature, this primary aspect of Gandy's work was fully conversant with the wider visual culture of late Georgian Britain. The explosion of scientific archaeological publications and picturesque landscape watercolor painting; the popularity of eidophusikons, panoramas, and other scenographic spectacles; the sweeping architectural redefinitions of urban and rural environments during and just after the Napoleonic Wars: these were the determining influences and incentives behind Gandy's architectural vision.

For Gandy, architectural rendering was also fundamentally an act of historical imagination. Late in his career, he authored an esoteric architectural treatise that contained the fullest expression of his artistic credo. "If the prejudices against architecture," Gandy wrote, "enrapt it in a cloud of darkness where it has struggled through many ages, in many kinds of mysticity [sic], to unveil its powers in true splendour ought to be the aim of the artist whose hand is the index of his eye, whose eye is the index of his understanding."[6] The turbulent and almost palpable atmospheres that were a hallmark of Gandy's perspectives assume a metaphoric connotation: clouds of history and religious belief mysteriously obscuring, while also giving enhanced significance to, the architecture of the past. In a characteristic watercolor by Gandy, his *Trophy and Temple* of 1821 [1], the antique-inspired monument, sited dramatically on a coastal promontory, is partially enveloped by these mists of time and nature. The commemorative trophy is poised between a Doric temple built into the earth and the azure heavens into which the monument rises. Architecture is framed and determined by topography and atmosphere, and yet these structures also demarcate a sacred space for human reflection and reverence. It is this complex symbiosis between architecture, nature, and historical understanding that Gandy's pictures consistently interrogate.

The pictorial depiction of architecture that became Gandy's singular forte often implied deeper questions about the categorical nature of architecture itself. His perspectives probed the contextual conditions of architecture as an object of knowledge—its relation to landscape, religious and social practices, human memory, and the spatial as well as temporal perspectives from out of which built form can be imagined and comprehended. His pictures always displayed an omnivorous range of knowledge and reference. As architectural historian Emil Kaufmann lamented, "It would be a trying task to trace all the sources, architectural as well as stage designs, which may have inspired Gandy's fantastic drawings."[7] Of course, Gandy's architectural representations were intended to make buildings (whether they be hypothetically drawn from the past or postulated for the future) appear spellbindingly beautiful—almost to the point where the traditional authority of western architecture and its highly developed classical language of geometry and ornament was subsumed by pictorial illusion. The architect George Wightwick, who was briefly Soane's amanuensis, raised this question of the paradoxical status of pictorial architecture. Writing in 1853, he warned: "Even the perspective view—all coloured and enlivened with cloud, tree, and figure—is more like a chimerical prospectus than an honest and bona fide prospect. It lies under the ban of proverbial suspicion. It represents nothing that is: it probably misrepresents what would be the result of its professed realization."[8] This was a pragmatic rebuke of the bewitching power of perspective rendering. As will become evident, admonishments of this kind were not unfamiliar to Gandy. Throughout the post-Renaissance period, the acute verisimilitude and spatial projection of the architectural perspective were seen as generative of and also to some degree compromising of architectural design.[9] This heightened illusionism, furthermore, often yielded its inverse: a commanding dream world of architectural representation (or virtuality, in contemporary nomenclature) that promised to undermine the eventual reception of architectural realities not yet inflicted upon the world of actuality.

Writing about the eighteenth-century spectrum of French and Italian architectural fantasies in the visual arts that was the foundation of Gandy's work, the philosopher and critical theorist Walter Benjamin asserted that, "as regards the images themselves, one cannot say that they *re*-produce architecture. They *produce* it in the first place, a production which less often benefits the reality of architectural planning than it does dreams … a completely new and untouched world of images, which Baudelaire would have ranked higher than all painting."[10] Gandy's perspectives envisioned such a realm of images, which encompassed and negotiated between interior dreams, erudite and often poetical histories of antiquity, and utopian proposals for the future. In mastering and brilliantly demonstrating the art of architectural misrepresentation, his imagery purposively tested the distinctions between architectural fiction and architectural reality for the early nineteenth century. Moreover, Gandy's lifework proposed that architecture was a medium of thought and vision that would hopefully impel the culture of his own time and beyond to consider anew how architectural creation and symbolic investiture in the world were inextricably bound.

1: To Rival Antiquity: Gandy's Youthful Dreams

On December 10, 1790, Sir Joshua Reynolds delivered his valedictory address to the Royal Academy of Arts. Reynolds's final discourse to the institution to which he had devoted much of his professional life betrayed a profound sense of disenchantment over the state of the RA and the political factions and narrow interests that he believed had recently divided its ranks. Early on into the delivery of his address, there was an extraordinary occurrence: a beam in the floor of the lecture hall of Somerset House gave way. The most vivid account of this strange event was provided by the satirist and art critic Anthony Pasquin (a pseudonym for John Williams): "In Sir Joshua Reynolds's Presidency, the floor gave way, and sunk many inches, when Burke, and a few more of the *illuminati*, were eagerly listening to a theme they could not comprehend: the company shrieked, Burke prayed, and the gods suspended their mischief."[1] The terror associated with the Burkean sublime had momentarily interrupted the solemn academic proceedings of England's premier art institution. Reynolds, according to other academicians in attendance, did not even pause in the delivery of his cautionary lecture, though later he was said to have observed that had the entire room collapsed the arts in England would have been set back two hundred years.[2]

Among the witnesses to this singular event was Joseph Gandy, a nineteen-year-old student of architecture at the RA school. Just moments before delivering his last discourse, Reynolds had awarded a gold medal to Gandy for his design of a triumphal arch, the highest honor that the RA granted its diploma students. In his autobiographical notes (written as a third-person narrative), Gandy recalled the mixture of pride and alarm that he felt upon receiving this distinction from Sir Joshua, followed soon after by the shock "when the floor gave way." As in the ironical account given by Pasquin, Gandy also confirmed, quite pointedly, that "amongst the audience was the sublime Burke, who favoured Jos. Gandy's works."[3] There appears to be no other corroboration of Burke's advocacy for the young Gandy's efforts. One can only surmise that Burke might have seen Gandy's student drawings as offering some hope for the future of English architecture (a year later Burke would refer disparagingly to "the foppish Structures of this enlightened age").[4] Gandy's prideful recognition of "the sublime Burke" was predictive of his own lifelong fascination with the architec-

3, 4 *Design in Perspective of Part of the Inside of a Museum*, 1793, with detail (right)

tural sublime. On that morning Gandy enjoyed accolades from some of the most influential and respected figures of the artistic and political elite. But the fact that this propitious triumph was attended by near-disaster was symptomatic. The failure of architecture would come to assume a recurrent and defining significance for him.

Born in Aldgate, London, on September 2, 1771, Joseph Michael was one of twelve children parented by Thomas Gandy and Sophia Adams.[5] Gandy's father was employed by John Martindale, "Master of the House" at White's Club from 1779 until 1797; a fellow student at the RA would refer condescendingly to Gandy as "son of a butler or waiter at Martindale's."[6] White's had earned its reputation as a renowned gaming club and supper-house that served as the unofficial meeting-place for Prime Minister William Pitt and the Tory Party.[7] For servants and assistants employed at the London gentlemen's clubs, there were often serendipitous opportunities for self-advancement and sudden financial reward. Such was the case for Thomas Gandy and his son. In 1787–88, the highly successful and fashionable, though famously dilatory, architect James Wyatt was engaged to refurbish White's.[8] Martindale showed Wyatt some untutored sketches by the sixteen-year-old Gandy and upon this evidence Wyatt took Gandy into his office as a pupil. It was within this Tory enclave of social privilege and political influence that Gandy first found favor. He later wrote, with characteristic immodesty:

> A man self-taught sometimes surpasses in sublimity those who have a university education. Such was a Shakespeare, but whether the subject of this will arrive at a similar honour, who has never had more learning than what a day school afforded him, although always perusing some book or embodying an Idea, remains for his exertions yet to surmount.

He adds, however: "Candidates for fame seldom succeed without Patronage."[9] In his genealogical notes about the family name, he traces its origins back to Norman roots while also finding distinguished ancestors clustered around Devon and Exeter in the seventeenth and early eighteenth centuries. Most significant to this family history was the painter William Gandy (1660–1729), a portraitist whose work had impressed and inspired the young Joshua Reynolds.[10] Joseph characterized William as a temperamental artist whose professional career was unfulfilled and whose life was marked by, as he phrased it, "a singular union of pride and poverty"[11]—a characterization that would soon prove self-descriptive for Joseph Gandy.

Through his early education in Wyatt's office and in the Royal Academy school where he enrolled in 1789, it became clear to Gandy that the architecture student's primary proving ground was the medium of drawing. Although Gandy fancied himself one of Wyatt's favorites (he reported that Wyatt would take him on business excursions and advanced his interests at the RA), his professional apprenticeship most likely kept him close to the drafting table and under the watchful eye of John Dixon. Dixon was Wyatt's chief draftsman and clerk, respected especially for his skills as a topographic artist and architectural renderer. On one occasion when Wyatt praised a new drawing by Gandy, the student recalled that "I made answer to Mr. Wyatt that I had to thank Mr. Dixon for his instruction."[12] It was from Dixon that Gandy would have first learned about the various techniques, conventions, and functions of architectural drawing. The educational regime at the Royal Academy school encountered by Gandy also revolved around the graphic skills of architectural representation: copying plates from archaeological publications and neo-Palladian pattern books, taking lessons from the Instructor of Perspective, who at the time was the topographic watercolorist and history painter Edward Edwards, and studying the elaborate drawings that the Professor of Architecture, Thomas Sandby, displayed to enliven his often dry, though theoretically informed, lectures.[13] Concurrent with his period of study at the RA school, Gandy was submitting drawings to the annual Academy exhibitions, listing his address as "at Mr. Wyatt's." Between 1790 and 1794, the period leading up to his Italian travels, he exhibited perspective views of his designs for mausolea, a museum, an ancient bath, and a public library, among others. These designs involved challenging and monumental building types, some of them for institutional forms of architecture that were just emerging during the late eighteenth century, and presented in the most complicated mode of architectural rendering.

Most of Gandy's prize-winning student work and initial entries at the RA exhibitions are lost, but one early perspective drawing in his hand can be safely dated to this period, his 1793 exhibit, *Design in Perspective of Part of the Inside of a Museum* [3, 4]. Depicting a neo-classical *cortile* and gallery, the drawing was a self-conscious demonstration piece of Gandy's precocious facility. Tightly ruled and outlined, the pen and ink drawing is overlaid with water- and body-color, the sheet achieving a studied balance between the intricate delineation of antique architectural details and the evocative treatment of atmosphere and light. The increasing height of the vaulted bays, as they diminish *enfilade*-like into the distance, is wonderfully conveyed. Alternating vaulting systems are paraded meticulously along the longitudinal axis, encompassing the cyclopean groin vaults, the elegantly coffered saucer domes, and the towering semi-barrel vault that marks the more expansive space of a sculpture court visible beyond the fourth bay. Differently scaled Ionic orders are used throughout the design, most notably in the colonnaded screen that dominates the length of the gallery. The emphatically high cornice of this trabeated continuum supports the massive segmental arches and the more elastic pendentives of the vaulting; this produces a controlled tension between spatial verticality and perspectival depth. Equally striking is the dramatic pattern of illumination created by the diagonal shafts of light entering through the range of windows to the right, as well as through the domed oculi and clerestory in the background. Gandy's drawing makes its effect more through atmospheric mood than through programmatic clarity (note, for example, the subtle terracing of the floor plane in its seemingly infinite recession, suggestive of a processional, ritualized space). Roman-styled statues of philosophers and senators seem merely incidental to the antique-inspired grandeur of the architectural setting.

To make classical antiquity truly knowable and present for the late eighteenth-century student of architecture required a period of study in Italy. With the moral support of James Wyatt [5] and the financial support of John Martindale (at £100 per annum), Gandy embarked from Portsmouth for Rome on April 26, 1794.[14] Because of the survival of Gandy's correspondence with his father during his Italian travels, this seminal period of his early career is the most thoroughly documented of his life.

Among the first letters written soon after his departure from England is a three-page account of a remarkable dream that Gandy had aboard the storm-tossed vessel bound for Italy on the night of May 8. The dream concerned a visitation to Hell. It begins with a Faustian scene of demonic entrapment, the devil appearing in the guise of an elderly and deceivingly beneficent patron who offers Gandy assurance about the courtship of a young woman whose affection he is trying to gain:

so he [the devil] led me away and shew me a vast
number of fine places and things, entertainments, and

presents he gave me most of which I forgot in the confusion of dreams ... but this one appeared more connected than any dream I ever had before. I was determined to write it down as it likewise contained a good moral in it—not to receive favours from that man who is ungrateful afterwards to charge you with the guilt of ingratitude. This is generally seen by those set of gentry, and when once they can play with the temper of a grateful mind they soon debauch it and make you their slave.[15]

The ominous moral extracted so instantaneously from Gandy's dream seems to imply that the dreamer is already enslaved by the guilt of ingratitude, and that the class-conscious resentments about his social station in waking life have permeated his unrefined dreamwork. The tour through Hell that Gandy proceeds to recount is but a subterranean

5 George Dance the Younger, *Portrait of James Wyatt*, 1795

version of mercantile London, with bustling quays, flaming furnaces, and an excess of frustrated and unrewarding human endeavor. He does, however, pause to comment on the imaginative scope of the dreaming process:

> your own reflections must lead you into what sort of place this Hell was that I saw, and for my want of words you must employ an extensive mind. I here saw in one moment more than I shall in twelve months conceive again; after employing myself with the different views of mankind, their pursuits I found was the same as in this world and travelling about as I thought to no purpose under a low dungeon. I saw a light, then again I was in total darkness and was groping my way, and at last I saw daylight peep through a hole above me which appeared to be above a mile high. On my left I saw a room with the Devil drinking with Lawyers, Alderman, &c. ... [then] there was a great many men on a hill, and they seemed piling it up with bottles which the Devil and his companions had emptied, as a trophy of what feats they had performed, and were striving to reach heaven with them.

John Summerson, who first drew attention to the significance of this letter, has convincingly argued that the main narrative of the dream rather transparently allegorizes Gandy's real-life ascent of the hill of bottles which was White's. Hell is reduced to an exclusive gentlemen's club (he particularly notes the absence of women in his pilgrimage through Hell). The professional men of wealth and influence whose respect Gandy hoped to command are here condemned to inebriated pleasures within an infernal dungeon. The dream concludes with Gandy discovering a bottle of "righteousness" that enables him to command the devil to lead him to "the light of the world." Through the careful narration of the dream and in the religious moralizing of its content, Gandy performs a self-defining exercise in psycho-autobiography.

Beyond the array of psychological and social anxieties that this dream fable discloses, there are also prescient glimpses of his later artistic and intellectual preoccupations: the archaeological compression of society and history ("the different views of mankind"), entombed within a cavernous space and cast in a drama of light and shade replete with dizzying perspective.

Gandy's period of study in Italy had a quickening effect on his artistic development. This comes through vividly in a debate he had with his companion and fellow student of architecture C. H. Tatham. Tatham had fled the drudgery of his apprenticeship in S. P. Cockerell's office and found patronage from the architect Henry Holland, who commissioned him to collect and sketch antiquities in Italy. Interestingly, Tatham, like Gandy, would enjoy a promising and ambitious beginning in his search for a more innovative style of neo-classical architecture, though his later professional career would never fulfill this initial promise.[16] As recorded by Gandy in a letter home, Tatham maintained that an ingenious student of architecture could gain mastery of antique models and become an accomplished architect by relying solely on published sources. Gandy disputed this argument by asserting that, "books give not that idea of greatness, grandeur, nor magnitude which the place itself will give and which I conceive an architect should be possessed of."[17] He also insisted that, for the sake of archaeological accuracy, the first-hand inspection of classical monuments was much preferred to dependence on published accounts. Only on the basis of this knowledge could the architect choose, as Gandy put it, "the best flowers ... from every garden the Ancients have left us, and to select them in the mind that they may always be as a mould either to improve upon or follow." The pilgrimage to Rome was considered absolutely essential by Gandy for the assembling of this mental inventory of classical "moulds." In a parenthetical remark that further denies Tatham's position, he off-handedly dismissed published illustrations of architecture as "only a representation." Yet it was only within this realm of mere representation that Gandy would eventually find his own creative role.

The productivity of Gandy's years of study in Italy is indicated by an inventory of his possessions drawn up before he left Rome in May 1797. There he lists "300 studies, drawings in architecture" and "3 Books large and small of sketches & memorandums in architecture," most of which were left behind.[18] In his letters home, Gandy wrote often of his untiring dedication to his studies. With an encyclopedic sense of purpose, he confided that he was "making a series of designs in architecture for every subject I can possibly think on," by which he meant the entire spectrum of building typology. This compendious impulse is visually documented in an architectural *capriccio* from his Roman period [6]. Although the sepia and pen drawing is extremely sketchy and seems rapidly improvised, the sheet assembles an array of classical building types, with Doric peristyle temples, rusticated arcades, and monuments loosely modeled after the Pantheon and the Flavian Amphitheatre. Archaeological excursions and sketching trips away from Rome occupied much of his time: Tivoli and Albano in the autumn of 1794, Palestrina and Frascati in the summer of 1795, and Naples and its environs in May of 1796.[19] His itinerary also included less frequented sites of interest that elicited lengthy descriptions in his letters home: the cyclopean walls at Fondi, the ruins of Cicero's villa near Isola di Sora, and the spectacular mountaintop Benedictine monastery at Monte Cassino. "I travel with stool and book under my arm," Gandy wrote to his father, "[and] when arrived at a good situation, I sit down and make a design."[20] A sheet of elevations for a church design from his Roman period demonstrate how Gandy was habitually assimilating the antique vocabulary of architecture over the course of his travels [7]. The entrance façade is composed of a giant Corinthian hexastyle raised portico flanked at the altar end of the church by austere campanili with blind arches. The side elevation is demarcated by a parade of Diocletian windows. All were meant to impart a distinctly Roman gravity to the relatively unadorned and imposing building. However, among the few surviving drawings from his Italian travels, the majority are studies in sepia and ink of decorative details of ancient Roman monuments: intricate delineations of enriched moldings, coffered panels and other deeply incised ornamentation, in which delicate shadow projections and the subtle recession of patterned surfaces are finely observed and recorded [8, 9].

Residing in lodgings on the Piazza Barberini, Gandy gravitated toward the British colony of art students, collectors, and antiquarians who used the Caffè degli Inglesi in Rome as their social and profes-

6 Roman Capriccio, ca. 1794–95
7 Elevations of a Design for a Church, ca. 1794–95
8 Ceiling of the Arch of the Silversmiths, 1796

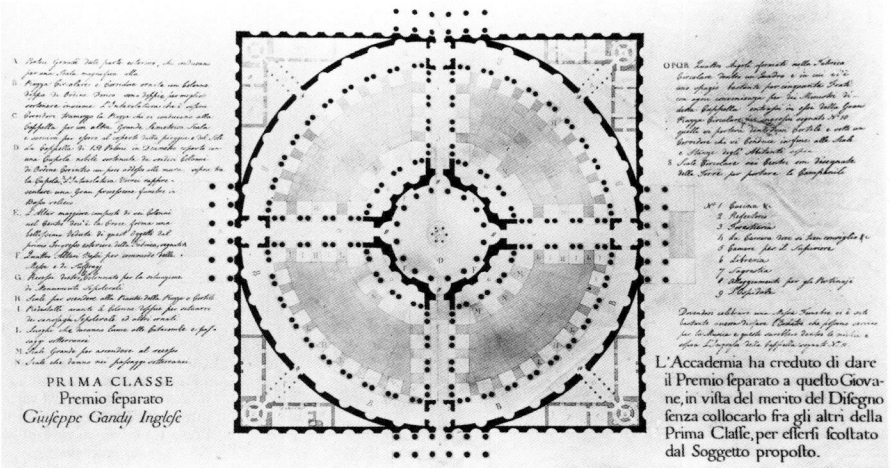

sional center of activity. There his circle of colleagues included his fellow RA student, the sculptor Richard Westmacott, and expatriate history painters and art dealers James Durno and Guy Head, as well as the antiquarian dealer and sculptor John Deare. From his letters it is evident that Gandy engaged, as far as he could afford to, in the trade in spurious artworks and antiquities that had made Rome so popular with British tourists: buying and selling "Etruscan" vases, purchasing so-called Poussins and Rosas at bargain prices, amassing a collection of prints by Piranesi (154 by his own count), and trying to attract commissions from touring gentry. Whether arguing with other architects at the Caffè degli Inglesi over the merit of Wyatt's design for the Oxford Street Pantheon or debating the archaeology and history of the Roman catacombs after a seven-hour tour of its subterranean passages, Gandy took full advantage of the unique cultural and social milieu of the Eternal City. He also wrote often of having to contend with the rampant, violent street crime and late summer fevers that complicated daily life in Rome.

Without question the highlight of Gandy's period of study in Italy was his successful participation in the 1795 *Concorso Clementino* sponsored by the Accademia di San Luca in Rome. He himself referred to winning the competition as "the one thing I wished for, and what I gave so much study to."[21] Since mid-century, English architects studying abroad had yearned for the prestige associated with the honors awarded by the Italian academies; before Gandy, such distinguished talents as Robert Mylne, George Dance the Younger, John Soane, and Thomas Harrison had participated in Italian architectural competitions, pitting their skills against Italian students as well as *pensionnaires* from the Académie de France.[22] It gave young architects the opportunity to flaunt their recently acquired knowledge in grandiloquent compositions on paper.

The subject for the first class in architecture of the 1795 *Concorso Clementino* in which Gandy chose to compete was a sepulchral chapel set within a circular piazza on an elevated site. This building type provided the student architect with the perfect pretext for displaying the more grandiose excesses of the neo-classical sensibility. Because a sepulchral building was short on functional requirements and long on ennobling pretensions, the designer could invoke the grandeur and sobriety of ancient precedents to an appropriately lugubrious extreme.

During his stay in Rome Gandy's mind had often dwelt on sepulchral themes. Like most tourists, he delighted in rummaging around the ruined fragments of tombs and mausolea along the Via Appia. The idea of an avenue of sepulchral monuments preoccupied him. He wrote to his father on several occasions about an ambitious scheme "to raise trophies to past eminent men," a British Appian Way to be situated around either Clapham Common or Kensington Gardens.[23] With naive enthusiasm, he even suggested that this idea for a grand highway lined with monuments honoring national heroes be introduced as a topic for debate in Parliament (as though his father could promote such a scheme from the Tory corridor of power at White's). Gandy was indulging in the late eighteenth-century Enlightenment passion for proposing vast public works of edifying monuments that would commemorate and resurrect an idealized conception of antiquity. Earlier in the century, William Chambers had also imagined the transformation of the British kingdom into a sepulchral garden traversed by magnificent roads and bridges, adorned with triumphal arches and cenotaphs.[24] Both Chambers and Gandy were familiar with the visionary archaeology of the Appian Way that had been presented by Piranesi in his famous frontispiece to the second volume of *Antichità Romane*

9 *Entablature of the Temple of Jupiter Tonans*, 1796
10 *Elevation of Sepulchral Chapel*, 1794–95
11 *Section of Sepulchral Chapel*, 1794–95
12 *Plan of Sepulchral Chapel*, 1794–95
13 G. B. Piranesi, Frontispiece etching of the Appian Way from Vol. II of *Antichità Romane*, 1756

(1756), which illustrated his imaginary reconstruction of the renowned sepulchral avenue as a vast canyon made up of gargantuan funerary urns and telescopic mausoleal towers [13]. In justifying the pictorial exaggeration of scale, perspective, and chiaroscuro that he brought to this kind of provocative amplification of ancient Roman monuments, Piranesi had written of how "speaking ruins have filled my spirit with images ... [and] there seems to be no recourse than for me or some other modern architect to explain his ideas through his drawings."[25]

Gandy worked intermittently on his set of four *concorso* drawings—each almost a meter in breadth—for over eight months. As dictated by the program of the competition, the plan for his sepulchral chapel and piazza is a judicious study in concentric geometry, focused on symmetrical precincts around a centralized structure with the whole ensemble enclosed by a larger superstructure [12]. In emulation of French academic techniques in the planning of cemeteries and sepulchral gardens, Gandy's ground plan negotiates a logical relation between center and periphery, in this case between circle and square.[26] Radial symmetry is established between the circular chapel and the surrounding ring of the piazza, while axial symmetry is formed by the crossing colonnades. Circulation and spatial sequencing is plotted by the corridors of paired columns that also subdivide the quadrants of the piazza. As indicated by Gandy's key to the plan, the four corner spaces between the outermost colonnade and the external fortification wall accommodate monastic quarters, with charnels and burial vaults in the expansive crypt below. The exterior elevation presents the four-square block protecting the sepulchral complex with slightly elevated hexastyle porticoes on the uniform façades [10]. In a Piranesian gesture, Gandy punctuates the elevation with an insistent row of niches housing allegorical sculptures, honorific statues, and rostral columns, some of these monuments reminiscent of the hermetic trophies designed and published by the esoteric *ornemaniste* J.-C. Delafosse in his *Nouvelle iconologie historique* (1768). The pedimented Roman Doric porticoes are majestically aligned with the domed chapel that rises up from behind. Linear striations at stringcourse level and along the parapet accentuate the pronounced severity and starkness of the exterior treatment. The section drawing exhibits a contrasting sensitivity [11]. The chapel interior is a splendid variation on the oft-quoted Roman Pantheon.[27] The monumentality of the domed space is moderated by the careful deployment of decorative flourishes: the enriched ornamental frieze of the Corinthian order, the blind fanlights in the side-altar niches, and the diamond coffering of the entrance bays. A more solemnly epic note is sounded by the large figural frieze around the circumference of the dome, which Gandy described on the plan as depicting "a grand funeral procession in low relief." Amid the pagan and classical ambience of this interior, the liturgical epicenter of the sepulchral chapel is marked by a domed ciborium protecting an altar and crucifix. The domed spatial theme is repeated yet again in the entrance vestibules on the outer ring of the piazza, counteracting the trabeated articulation of the cross-axial colonnades. Gandy carefully observes the most advanced artistic conventions in the technique of section drawing, for instance in the rendering of the serpentine shading lines cutting through the domed interiors and in the raking light across the colonnades.

Perspective drawings were optional for architects competing in the *concorsi*, and Gandy took full advantage of the opportunity to display his strength in this area. The perspective drawing transforms a diagrammed building into a scenic drama. The vantage point in Gandy's drawing is inside the perimeter of the piazza looking toward the circular chapel [14]. The colonnades converging toward the projecting mass of the chapel and the sweeping curvature of the piazza glimpsed in the background involve a spatial dynamism that only the perspective

drawing can convey. The imposing dome and high parapet walls contribute to the characteristically oppressive mood, intensified by the diagonal shafts of light and menacing wedges of shadow. Diminutive figures (the monks who administer the chapel) are included to swell the scale of the surrounding buildings. The only embellishments are the garland swags and bucrania in the Doric frieze and the antique sarcophaghi mounted in front of the paired columns. At the lower center of the drawing, at the foot of the colonnaded chapel, there is a shadowy stairwell and portal leading to the subterranean passages, a slightly macabre motif well suited to the ceremonial dread of the entire sepulchral complex.

Although Gandy conceived and executed these drawings in the cosmopolitan milieu of late eighteenth-century Rome, his *concorso* entry retained distinctive ties to neo-classical architecture back in England. His selection of the paired Roman Doric columns for his design alludes to Chambers's impressive cross-vaulted vestibule off the Strand at Somerset House where the Royal Academy was housed. Even more directly formative was the architecture of James Wyatt. In 1786, the first year of Gandy's apprenticeship, Wyatt began work on the Brocklesby Mausoleum in Lincolnshire [15], a building in many respects prototypical of Gandy's sepulchral chapel. Wyatt's mausoleum, without its balustrade and rusticated basement, serves as a compact model of his student's later design. Their Pantheon-inspired interiors are also quite similar, though the gem-like refinement of Wyatt's building is a far cry from the more severe gravity and untried scale of Gandy's paper project. During his Italian years, Gandy paid homage to Wyatt both in his designs and in the loyal and somewhat misplaced praise for his master's style that he expressed in a letter to his younger brother Michael, who himself had just entered Wyatt's office: "If you ever leave England for Rome, which I hope you may, you will find what I say is true, that Mr. Wyatt's architecture is more truly antique, he may be said to rival the ancients."[28]

Gandy's *concorso* entry, especially the perspective view, is most significant as an architectural essay in the Burkean sublime. With its empiricist and psychological analysis of sensory experience and the esthetics of terror, Burke's influential treatise A Philosophical Enquiry into ... Our Ideas of the Sublime and Beautiful (1757) gave consideration to the formal properties in buildings that could best elicit intimations of the sublime.[29] They entailed dramatic transitions in light and shade, sparse ornamentation, dusky colors, and, most essential, magnitude in scale. Architecture is construed more or less as an arena of overwhelming sensation and subsuming mood. Dismissive of the traditionally Platonic emphasis on matters of proportion and harmony, Burke instead speculates on how something as finite and self-determined as architecture can induce a delirious awareness of the infinite. Two forms are judged most conducive to inspiring a sense of artificial infinitude: vast rotundas and extended colonnades. The uniform succession of these elements (spherical wall surface and repetitive columniation) incites the mind's eye to replicate the sensory data ad infinitum. With the circularity of the piazza and the repeating colonnades directed toward a domed rotunda, Gandy's *concorso* design incorporates these sensorial points of departure for artificial infinitude. The enveloping chiaroscuro and glancing streaks of light in the perspective drawing also conform to the dicta of the Burkean sublime.

14 *Perspective of Sepulchral Chapel and Courtyard*, 1794–95
15 James Wyatt, Brocklesby Mausoleum, Lincolnshire, 1786–94

The Burkean sublime and architectural *terribilità* filtered down quickly into late eighteenth-century theoretical parlance on the design and esthetics of architecture. Chambers's literary excursion into architectural fantasy, his *Dissertation on Oriental Gardening* (1772), presented hypothetical architectural settings as if they were supernatural amusement parks of terrifying splendor. Similarly, Le Camus de Mézières's influential introduction to his *Le Génie de l'architecture, ou l'analogie de cet art avec nos sensations* (1780) urged the architect to study the modulation of sentiment and sensation in the theatrical illusionism of Servandoni in order to realize "*le genre terrible*" of architectural expression.[30] Étienne Boullée and C.-N. Ledoux would carry these suggestions much further.

Burke had confidently asserted, "There is no danger of drawing men into extravagant designs by this rule; it carries its own caution with it."[31] The first-class entries for the 1795 *Concorso Clementino*, however, thoroughly disprove Burke's prognosis. The other prize-winning entries against which Gandy competed were even more extreme than his in their gigantic scale and theatrical sensationalism. In Giorgio Duran's sepulchral complex, the elevation is devoid of archaeological detail and ornamentation [16] except for the use of the primitivizing Greek Doric order. In section, Duran's chapel also reworks the Pantheon, obviously a stock-in-trade motif in the repertoire of student architects; unlike Gandy, however, Duran makes more of the central crypt beneath the chapel, enclosing the space with a shallow coffered dome and enhancing the subterranean tectonics of the design with truncated Doric columns. In contrast, too, with the baroque inflections of Gandy's crossing colonnades, Duran's piazza is a vast denuded space, its expansive circumference contained only by the seemingly endless round of a Doric colonnade. The other prize-winning entry, by Giovanni Campana, sought to achieve an almost scenographic extravagance in his perspective view [17].[32] Campana's chapel is conceived of as a colossal sarcophagus surmounted by a circular temple and flanked by a quadrangle of pyramids, all burdened with a decorative program of cinerary urns, burning altars, and antique sculptural friezes and statuary. However, the forbidding spectacle of the entire composition depends more on the eerie floodlighting, funereal cypresses, and mountainous cascade in the background for its sublime mood. Gandy's perspective seems almost circumspect and dryly academic by comparison. But Campana's shrill theatricality is compromised by the technical limitations of the drawing style. There is a thin clarity in the rendering of the architectural forms, making the proposed monumentality of the scene all the more improbable. The shadow projections defy pictorial logic and the rigid symmetry of the composition imparts a static inertness to the architectural space.

Unlike Duran and Campana, who were both awarded first premiums for their *concorso* entries, Gandy's submission was granted a separate premium. The official reason for this unusual award, as documented in an Accademia inscription on the floor-plan presentation drawing, was because Gandy had departed from the proposed subject of the competition ("*per essersi scostato dal Soggetto proposto*"). Gandy's letters to his father tell a far more complicated tale behind this official pronouncement. The judging procedure was compromised by an accusation of plagiarism directed against Gandy's entry. The charge was made by Giuseppe Barberi, a Roman architect, a prominent member of the Accademia, and one of the *concorso* judges. Barberi was well known

16 Giorgio Duran, *Elevation and Section of Sepulchral Chapel*, 1793–95
17 Giovanni Campana, *Perspective of Sepulchral Chapel*, 1793–95
18 *Plans and Elevations for a Triumphal Arch*, 1795

for his contentious personality, Jacobin political sympathies, and a fluent pen with which he sketched multitudes of architectural and decorative fantasies in the antique manner.[33] He would later find official patronage under Napoleon only to end up working in Francesco Piranesi's Parisian printing shop. Barberi claimed that Gandy's drawings were copied from designs that he had sent to England some years earlier, an accusation for which he had no evidence (he should have tried accusing Gandy of copying Wyatt's designs). Two of Barberi's students were competing in the 1795 *concorso*, one of them being Campana in the first class and his own son in the second class. Conspiratorial favoritism and undisguised nepotism undoubtedly undermined the fair judging of the competitions. Gandy performed admirably on the second part of the competition, the extemporary *prova* examination in which the competing student is given two hours to complete a design on a prescribed subject. It was fortuitous for him that the chosen subject was for the design of a triumphal arch, the same theme on which he had won his RA Gold Medal five years earlier. Perhaps plagiarizing himself, Gandy handily composed a tripartite arch adorned with the Corinthinian order and sculptural trophies situated in an idealized Campagna landscape [18]. Confounded but not vanquished, Barberi intimidated his colleagues on the officiating jury forcefully enough so that they capitulated by awarding Gandy a separate premium, thereby excluding his award from the standard hierarchy of prizes. Throughout the ordeal, Gandy naturally defended the originality and artistic integrity of his designs. He appealed to his countryman the artist and dealer Guy Head and perhaps to the Roman architect and garden designer Antonio Asprucci, who had expressed admiration of Gandy's work, for advice and support. Barberi's true motivations in this affair remain difficult to fathom, though it is possible that he harbored Anglophobic sentiments and that his territorial pride had been offended by the impressive architectural performance of a young English upstart. Aside from the scandalous irregularities of the competition, Gandy relished his newfound notoriety and felt that he had been soundly vindicated, reporting to his father, "such an honour never was conferred before though the Academy has existed two hundred years."[34]

During his period of study in Italy, when not mapping out sepulchral precincts or tracing florid modillions from Roman ruins, Gandy often turned his attention to the Italian landscape. There was good reason for this. With the ascendancy of the picturesque esthetic in the late eighteenth century and its emphasis on the situation of the building within the landscape setting, architectural theorists often noted points of correspondence between the architect and the landscape painter. As early as 1762, James Adam had written: "What is so material an excellence in landscape is not less requisite for composition in architecture, namely the variety of contour, the rise and fall different parts and likewise those great projections and recesses which produce a broad light and shade."[35] The Adam brothers would incorporate this passage in their widely known discussion of "movement" and architectural composition that was published in 1773. By the time of Uvedale Price's *Essay on Architecture* (1798), the parallels between landscape painting and architectural design had become an almost canonical issue; as Price maintained, "the architect should be *architetto-pittore*, for indeed, he ought not only have the mind, but the hand of the painter— not only to be acquainted with the principles, but as far as design goes, with the practice of landscape painting."[36]

In his thirteenth discourse to the Royal Academy, delivered in 1786, Reynolds had already advised the architect to come to terms with the visual drama of architecture by considering its capacity to in his words, "address the imagination."[37] Rejecting the traditional notion of architecture as a non-mimetic art form, Reynolds argued for the shared commonality of architecture, painting, and poetry. By virtue of a building's historical style (and here Reynolds was prophetically eclectic by citing Greek, Gothic, and "Asiatick"), architecture can engender an associative chain of ideas in the mind of the spectator. According to Reynolds, architecture in its massing and "background," or siting, becomes a kind of scenery comparable to ideal landscape painting. The architect should be sensitive to the compositional uses of varied outline and *repoussoir* in the design of a building; John Vanbrugh was singled out as the model architect in this respect. By promoting this concept of architecture as a manipulated landscape with much the same esthetic criteria as painting, Reynolds believed that he was bringing architecture closer to the sphere of artistic invention: "it seems to me that the object and intention of all the arts is ... often to gratify the mind by realizing and embodying what never existed but in the imagination." Moreover, Reynolds's praise for "an Architect who composed like a Painter" must have lent encouragement to an architecture student like Gandy in pursuing his early artistic studies in landscape painting.

An even more immediate cause for his vital interest in landscape art during the Italian years was his contact with "Mr. Wallis," the name that recurs most frequently in Gandy's letters home from 1795 to 1797.[38] George Augustus Wallis was an expatriate British landscapist who had arrived in Italy six years before Gandy, during which time he attracted prestigious patronage as a draftsman from the aristocratic

19 George Augustus Wallis, *Landscape near Rome*, 1794
20 *View of San Fiorenza, Corsica*, 1794

24 JOSEPH GANDY

and wealthy antiquaries/collectors Sir William Hamilton and Thomas Hope. A practitioner of Italianate ideal landscape painting, he specialized in classical imagery of arcadian settings, Greco-Roman cityscapes, and the ruins of the Campagna, as exemplified by his *Landscape near Rome* of 1794 [19]. Like other European landscape artists working in Italy during this period of the late 1780s and '90s, such as Louis Ducros, P.-H. Valenciennes and Philipp Hackert, Wallis combined topographic view painting, precise architectural rendering, and a generic heroic landscape style redolent of Poussin.[39]

Gandy's landscape drawings in Italy functioned not surprisingly as a visual diary and travelogue. Soon after his arrival in Rome, he sent his father a group of drawings of the coast of Corsica recorded during his voyage to Italy in June of 1794. Particularly striking is his sepia drawing of the coastal town and bay of San Fiorenza [20]. The ruins of a Romanesque cathedral and fortifications are situated dramatically between the rough waters along the embracing coastline and what Gandy called "the cloud capt hills" reaching down to the sea. Diagonal slashes of light and gray washes accentuate the turbulence of the day and the inherent wildness and "devastation" (Gandy's wording) of the topographic features. In later sketches from his 1795 tour through the rugged valleys of the Abruzzi, accompanied by Wallis, Gandy approximated the scenery he observed with the aid of familiar recipes in landscape composition: dark foliage framing light-filled mountainous vistas with winding paths directing the eye's movement through receding planes of the view, the architectural landmarks nestled strategically in middle distance or perched on remote hilltops [21, 22]. These rapidly executed pen and pencil drawings were treated to gray monochrome washes to suggest effects of atmospheric perspective. Representative of a classicizing mode of picturesque travel sketching popular among British artists in Rome during the 1790s, they show Gandy striving toward some fluency in the formulaic schema of landscape composition.[40]

One highly finished watercolor from the same period is an apparent composite of several Italian locales—the abbey and Alban hillside town

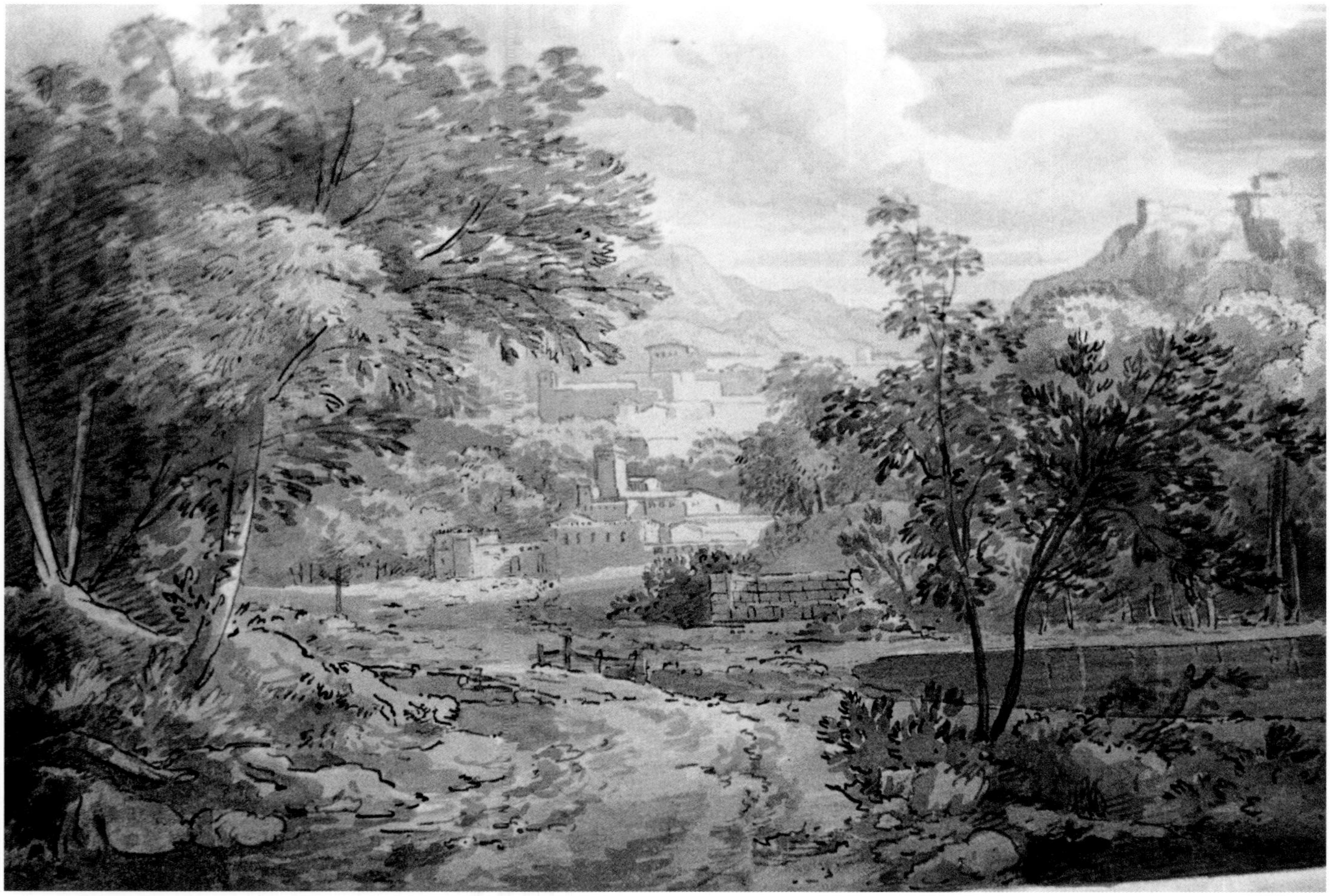

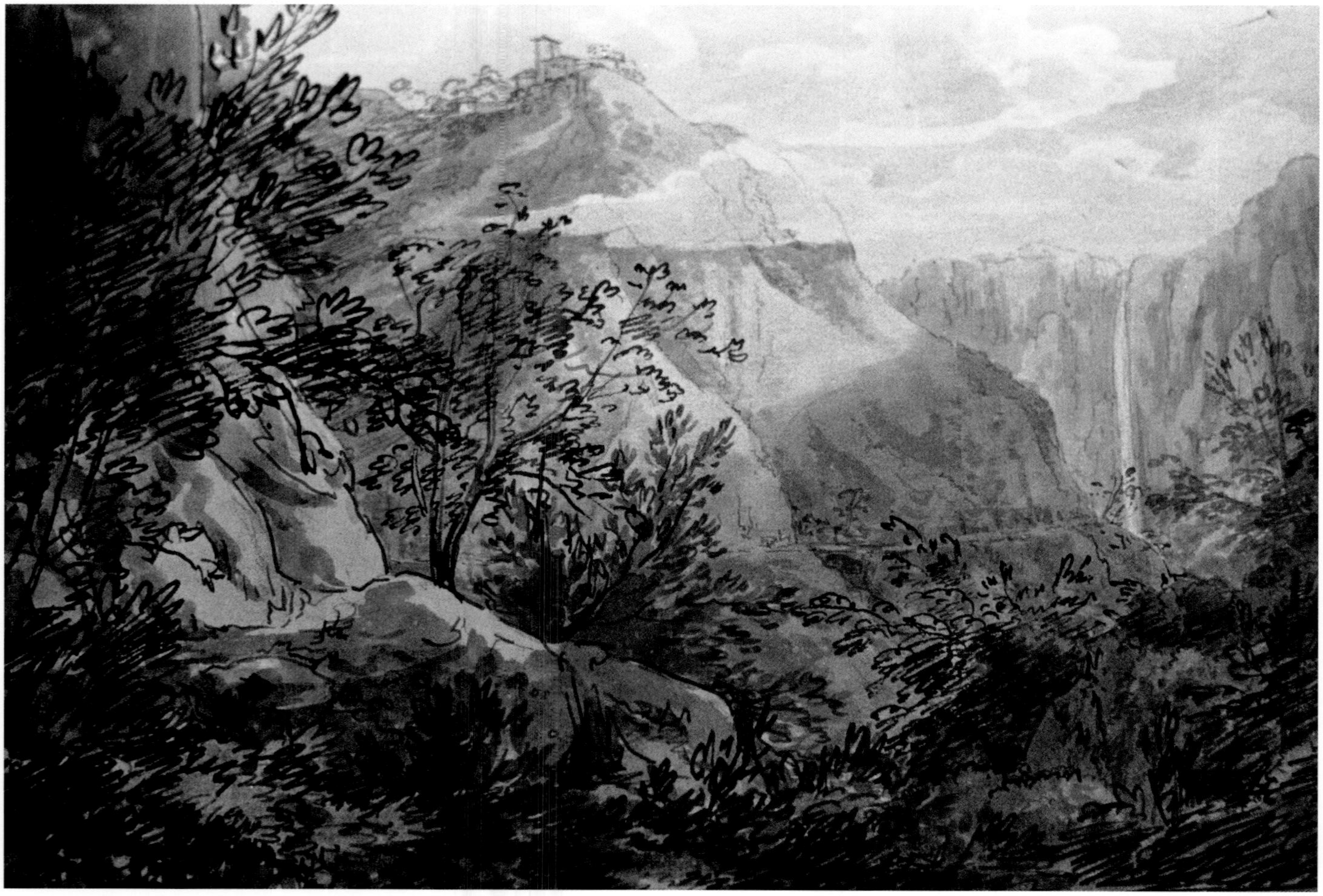

at Grottaferrata with the Castel di Sangro in the Abruzzi [23]. The aggregate geometry of the building façades and monastery fortifications in middle distance mediates between the fertile slopes in the foreground and the towering mountain range beyond. There is a corresponding gradation to the shifting mood of the landscape. It is this striking conjunction of pastoral calm and natural turbulence commonly associated with the Italian landscape that the picture celebrates. Gandy's nuanced treatment of the atmospheric drama of gray-violet clouds and mists, as well as of the variegated textures of pale green foliage and chalky geology, reveals a confident, though carefully detailed, watercolor technique.

Along with these early efforts in landscape painting, Gandy's Italian letters attest to a larger visual and scientific curiosity about natural phenomena. Although he did not visit Naples until 1796, he was stirred by reports of the 1794 eruption of Vesuvius. He sent his father a watercolor copy of L.-J. Desprez's engraving that depicted a moonlit view of the molten destruction of Torre del Greco on the Bay of Naples, accompanied by a transcription of the Duke della Torre's firsthand account of the eruption (embellished with passages from Pliny), in which Gandy had read of "the discharge of lava like liquified glass ... the furfuraceous ashes and electrical kindling in the smoke and air."[41] While speculating on the interconnection between the volcanic geology and verdant lushness of Italy, he cited Joseph Priestley's

21 *Abruzzi Landscape*, 1795
22 *Abruzzi Landscape*, 1795
23 *Italianate Landscape with Castel di Sangro*, 1795–96

TO RIVAL ANTIQUITY: GANDY'S YOUTHFUL DREAMS 27

natural philosophical experiments on vegetable regeneration and atmospheric purity.[42] Like most British tourists visiting Rome, Gandy was equally enthralled with the artificial wonders of explosive lights and spectacular pageantry that he witnessed in Rome during Holy Week. Comparing the eruption of Vesuvius with the celebratory display of fireworks at the Castel Sant'Angelo [24] ("without the terrible emotions"), he momentarily put aside his anti-Catholic sentiments and marveled, "It forms a beautiful fiery circular canopy and overspreads the whole heavens."[43] Gandy's responsiveness to these meteorological and pyrotechnical effects during his Italian travels would find later application in the atmospheric artistry of his architectural perspectives.

Despite the success of his artistic and architectural pursuits during his time in Italy, Gandy grew increasingly anxious over his professional prospects; as he commented in the summer of 1795, "Those hopes and benefits that we receive while young I fear will not be repeated beyond a certain age."[44] Constantly meditating on his own ambitions, he wrote to his father about the lack of likelihood of securing employment upon his return home as a journeyman to an established architect or as a parish surveyor. While in Rome, Gandy naturally tried to cultivate elite patrons who could advance his career upon his return to England. In early 1796, he produced drawings for the well-connected Sir Godfrey [25] and Lady Webster of Battle Abbey, Sussex. Traveling throughout Italy in the 1790s, the Websters lavished commissions on many of the British artists they encountered during their extended stays in Naples, Florence, and Rome. Gandy produced a design in the "Gothic manner" for a commemorative monument to mark the spot where Harold fell against the Norman invaders. A handsome elevation survives that depicts a sleek medievalizing spire under a raking light against a jet black background, the monument treated in a perpendicular Gothic style rather than in a less refined Saxon-Norman idiom that would have been more appropriate [26]. The drawing balances sharp exactitude in the delineation of tracery and pinnacles with the evocative distribution of light and shade, evidenced especially by the dripping double shadows seen in the empty sculpture niches. Although immersed in the world of classical antiquity, Gandy could still resort to a Gothic mode in his efforts to attract patronage from notable English grand tourists. This commission, however, came to nothing, as Sir Godfrey's melancholic temper and compulsive gambling would drive him to suicide in 1800. In brooding over his future options, the worst fear and frustration was that, as Gandy noted, "all my exertions will be in vain to gain any rank in the first line of artists."[45] Gandy hoped for the imminent efflorescence of a national culture back in England; after penning some ruminations on the ruins of Rome, he quickly asserted, "But enough of this. It may be England will shine out as Italy has done, provided it creates Genius in our Island equal to those of Antiquity."[46]

The social and economic conditions awaiting him in England, however, were far from encouraging. Market-controlled grain shortages in the mid-1790s led to widespread famine and rioting throughout England. Repressive measures of censorship and fervid anti-Jacobinism fuelled social unrest and political paranoia. The social historian E. P. Thompson has characterized 1795 as "the climactic year" for the English mobilization of both government repression and public protest in the years following the revolution.[47] A letter written to Gandy from his father in late 1795 captured the crisis-ridden mood of the country: "Petitions are applying, the mobs are raising, the soldiers are parading; everything seems in preparation for some great event. A little time will decide. I hope God will avert his judgements on the nation."[48] While Gandy studied the ruins of antiquity in Italy, planning nationalist sepulchral avenues that were to adorn neo-classical London, civil protest and social dissension were threatening the security of the British capital (the royal carriage was surrounded by incensed crowds of Londoners on several occasions in 1795).

Perhaps because of this historical incongruity, Gandy found some solace in what he described as "the merits of a glorious and rising generation whose plans exceed even in its infancy all other nations."[49] This was obviously not England, but America. In early 1796, Gandy was sent

24 Francesco Panini, *View of Castel Sant'Angelo with Fireworks*, ca. 1780
25 Louis Gauffier, *Sir Godfrey Webster Bt.*, 1794

a copy of Major L'Enfant's urban plan of Washington (most likely the version published by Andrew Elicott in 1792), which he shared with fellow architects in Rome. Returning often to the question of whether any modern civilization would ever rival ancient Rome in its architectural grandeur, he speculated that "the first foundations of Rome were not on that magnificent scale the more enlightened Americans have formed and we must recollect that we are apt to praise and form greater ideas of ruins than we should ... what will Rome be compared to Washington?" Gandy, however, never seems to have considered following the example of his elder contemporary, the architect/engineer Benjamin Henry Latrobe, who had fled the repressive political climate of England in 1795 to search for, as he recalled it, "a sort of dawn of the golden age," which America appeared to herald.[50]

In Gandy's case, such utopian illusions were prematurely undermined by Napoleon Bonaparte's military campaign against the Papal

States. By the summer of 1796 an advance guard of invading troops and French Commissioners had reached Rome. Judging from Gandy's frantic letters, Rome was no longer a cultural haven. Himself a victim of street crime and rumor-mongering, Gandy complained to his father, "I conceive myself in Hell and Rome contains nothing but devils."[51] C. H. Tatham confirmed Gandy's disenchantment with the Eternal City when he reported that "Rome instead of being the quiet repose of the fine arts has now become a Babylon."[52] Gandy's letters describe a world in chaotic dissolution in which public displays of erratic violence and devout piety were met with in cruel succession. He was especially observant of the French sacking of Rome's antiquities and art treasures; as he wrote, with acerbic erudition, in August 1796: "The French Commissioners are now in Rome taking their choice of the best pictures and statues. I wonder they never thought of taking the Egyptian Obelisk which was brought to Rome by the Emperors as trophies to their victories. I cannot help telling you that in the sermons the priests mentioned the taking away of the pictures and statues. 'Rome,' said they, 'will always be Rome, the French cannot carry away the Pantheon or Coliseum.'"[53]

For the dwindling colony of English nationals that remained in Rome, the French occupation bred a climate of political suspicion and uncertainty. The once-convivial setting of the Caffè degli Inglesi became fraught with mistrust, as accusations of espionage and the questioning of loyalties spread among the few remaining English. Gandy's friendship with the landscapist Wallis proved dangerous in this respect, as Wallis was widely suspected of being an informant to the French Commissioners in Rome. Some years later, Joseph Farington recorded gossip about Wallis's "democratick conduct" against the English in Rome, including the anecdotal report that, "in so great detestation was Wallis held, that one day coming into the English Coffee House at Rome, accompanied by Gandy, all who were present rose and retired."[54] For his part, Gandy confessed to his father that the denizens of the Caffè degli Inglesi openly engaged in political disputes and that there were rumors that a list of names of Englishmen who voiced anti-Jacobin opinions had been given to the French ministers in Rome by an informant. Gandy's own uncensored political asides in letters home were far from Jacobin in sympathy. After watching penitent crowds gather in the streets of Rome under the threat of invasion and after a recent assassination attempt on the Pope, he exclaimed in a letter to his father, "I have seen an English mob headed by a Politician, a Fox; I have seen an Italian mob headed by a Priest; there is but one mob more I wish to see, that is a French mob headed by a King."[55] This fierce jab at Charles James Fox, the liberal Whig parliamentarian, would have resonated particularly with Gandy's father, as Fox (ignoring the partisan political affiliations of London's gentlemen's clubs) would often satisfy his renowned gambling compulsion at White's gaming tables.

26 *Gothic Monument for Battle Abbey*, 1796

Despite his admiration for America, Gandy yearned for the imagined stability of monarchical power in the midst of political intrigue, military occupation, and religious frenzy. Ironically, Gandy's father, as revealed in his letters to his son, was more inclined to a radical political position. His frequent reports on domestic government policies and on the economic inequalities of British society in the late 1790s reveal a striking disjunction between his obsequious professional obligations at White's and the private political opinions aired in letters to his son. In the summer of 1796, Thomas Gandy even encouraged Joseph to consider resettling, not in London, but in Paris, to enjoy the growing cultural supremacy of "those victorious Republicans."[56]

Even greater calamity befell Gandy when his patron Martindale began to refuse paying the bills mounting up in Rome. The final blow was dispatched in a letter from his father: "you must have learnt the situation of this country, its credit lost and what is worse for you and me, through some Damn'd disaster, your Patron, my Master, is brought down."[57] While most of the English who were in Rome had already fled to Naples for protection from the French, Gandy remained and was forced to put up his own collectibles and drawings as collateral with a Roman banker. The English collector and art historian William Ottley, a close friend of Wallis, came to Gandy's rescue in June 1797 with a credit note of £50.[58] This enabled Gandy to flee Rome for Florence, where he was fortunate in meeting up with a King's Messenger who conducted him safely back to London.

The inauspicious circumstances surrounding Gandy's return to England appeared to fulfill his prophetic fears. The artistic achievement and intensive labors of his student years abroad were now of little account, the tangible evidence of his studies (his voluminous notebooks and drawings) lost to war-torn Italy. The unfounded accusations and strained relations that clouded both his competition at the Accademia di San Luca and his sense of an artistic community at the Caffè degli Inglesi would make Gandy increasingly wary of patrons and colleagues alike. The almost paranoid protectiveness and prideful solitude about himself and his work that would come to have a prevailing influence on his ill-fated career have their traumatic origins in these Roman experiences. After years of meditating on the monumental remains of Roman architecture and speculating confidently on the future architectural splendor of Great Britain, in which he was hoping to play a decisive role, Gandy was confronted on his return from Rome with a profession severely undermined by the Napoleonic Wars, economic depression, and the subsequent decline in architectural commissions and building activity. Moreover, as one overly sensitive to the precarious vicissitudes of patronage and professional competitiveness, Gandy was not resourceful enough to cope with the exacting responsibilities required for successful independent practice. The profound sense of dejection and loss of purpose that he experienced after his arrival home in London was most decisively and painfully expressed in the fragmentary notes to his third-person autobiography: "but on his return he found himself alone in the greatest metropolis in the world; the ideal Castles, Palaces, and Mansions he had fostered in his mind, and in which he dwelt with so much pleasure on the Continent, and fondly hoped to rear in England, were vanished."[59]

11: Natural Abodes of Men: Sepulchers and Cottages

Gandy's buildings of the mind of course had not vanished. They were simply restricted to the imaginative realm of his architectural renderings. The incommensurable relation between student dreams and professional prospects, between pictorial architecture and commissioned buildings, would perennially haunt Gandy's career. It was not, of course, so unusual. In characterizing the progress of an aspiring architect recently returned from study in Italy, an anonymous early nineteenth-century art critic commented, "He [the young architect] is content for a time to 'build castles in the air', that is, to suspend his imaginings in the atmosphere of the exhibition at the Royal Academy."[1] Gandy would protract what might be called the dreaming phase of his Italian student years in two significant ways: by sustaining his pictorial vision of an antique-inspired sepulchral architecture at the Royal Academy exhibitions around 1800, and by producing two remarkable pattern books of cottage designs in 1805, which were inspired in part by his study of picturesque vernacular architecture in Italy. More importantly, through both his designs for sepulchers and cottages, Gandy addressed the national symbolism and social instrumentality of architecture at the onset of a new century.

Summerson rightly commented that "Gandy's mind ran on obsequies," with no fewer than five RA exhibits devoted to funereal structures between 1797 and 1804.[2] One of these, his *Sepulchral Chamber* of 1800 [27, 28], is a strikingly hallucinatory watercolor depicting a subterranean tomb. Surrounded by sculptural sentinels of seated philosophers and weary lions, the compound sarcophagus is embellished with corner antifixae and relief panels (the lower one depicting a battle scene, the upper one of genii presenting a medallion portrait of the deceased). Incense altars frame the tomb, which is surmounted by a rosette-scrolled pediment, resembling wings atop the otherwise solemnly grounded monument. The heroic tomb is emblazoned by an orb of intense light reverberating within a blue halo, its gleaming brilliance belying its apparent source from the suspended lamp. The frontal symmetry and superimposition of the primary forms of rectangle (tomb), circle (ring of light), and triangle (lamp chain) at the center of the drawing intimates the mystical property of geometry within the perspectival, three-dimensional interior space. Lateral beams of light shine forth to illuminate flanking sculpture niches (also lit from below by their own glowing altars) and the cyclopean masonry of the chamber. The spatial sensation of descent and enclosure is reinforced by the staired approaches to the tomb and by the heavy, shallow barrel-

27, 28 *Sepulchral Chamber*, 1800, with detail (right)

vault that seals the room. A shrouded female figure bearing a torch enters through the Doric colonnade in the background (the Doric order applied with stopped fluting, as at Delos and Pompeii). The sepulchral gloom of this interior is dispelled by the spectral rays of light, which have a transforming effect on the architectural setting: the mute tomb animated into an enormous magic lantern of incandescent stone.

Gandy's compulsive attachment to hallowed sepulchral precincts is also seen in his *Design for a Cenotaph* exhibited in 1804 [29]. In this drawing, the ritualistic props and symbols of classical mourning are accumulated in elaborate detail. The cenotaph, warmly irradiated and spotlit by the fading rays of the sun, is strung with garlands, its steadfast Doric pillars adorned with star-crested pine-cone ornaments. The painting of a shipwreck scene on the monument invokes the memory of the absent corpse to whom this cenotaph is dedicated; likewise, the display of trophied arms, animal skins, and warrior attire serve as honorific reminders of the deceased. The architectural decoration is rife with mythological imagery and pagan motifs emblematic of commemoration, eternity, and the afterlife: anchor and dolphin tridents on the ribs of the vaulting, crescent moon and stars and pegasi in relief on the altar bases, and Apollo's cloud-borne chariot racing across the ceiling painting. To heighten the narrative fiction of the architectural setting, Gandy includes dramatis personae in the form of a gesticulating priest making burnt offerings at an altar and a disconsolate mourner sitting in cloaked despair on the steps of the monument.

29 *Design for a Cenotaph*, 1804
30 Thomas Hope, *Doric Picture Gallery*, 1807
31 *Design for a Temple and a Bridge in a Nobleman's Park*, 1807
32 John Baber, *Design for Interior of Cemetery*, 1809

what Hope himself referred to as "a sepulchral cast."[4] In seeking to unite "visible and intellectual beauty," Hope advocated an enriched decorative vocabulary that was to incorporate "symbolic personages, attributes and insignia of gods and of men, trophies, ... sacrificial implements, civil and military emblems &c. that once gave to every piece of Grecian and Roman furniture so much ... expression and physiognomy."[5] The excessive array of ritualistic articles and symbolic ornament seen in Gandy's picture knowingly accords with Hope's call for an antique symbolic decor in modern design.

A later follower of Hope, the drawing master and architectural writer Richard Brown, argued even more polemically for a revival of a

With its opulent clutter of incense candelabra, cinerary urns, and bronze hanging lamps, Gandy's picture provided a virtual catalogue of Greco-Roman ornamental objects of the kind most favored by the picture's purchaser: the fashionable collector and advanced neo-classical designer Thomas Hope.[3] The lavish sanctuary of cultural refinement that Hope created at his Duchess Street mansion, completed in 1804 and documented in his influential publication entitled *Household Furniture and Interior Decoration* (1807), involved a brilliant museological experiment. The architectural setting of Hope's London house-gallery and the collection of pictures, antiquities, and decorative objects it contained were brought into programmatic harmony. Gandy's *Design for a Cenotaph* would have echoed precisely the design ethos of Hope's Doric picture gallery and mock-columbaria [30], these incipient museum spaces that fused ancient and modern articles of design while retaining

NATURAL ABODES OF MEN: SEPULCHERS AND COTTAGES   35

symbolic decorative system—"ornamented by allusive mythology"—finding that "Beautiful and novel forms may also be observed in the drawings of Gandy, very suitable to cabinet works."[6] The richly decorated sepulchral designs by Gandy were thus valued as inspired source material in the recovery of an expressive and allusive code of symbolic meaning in neo-classical design. The presentation of Gandy's own work from this period also reveals other aspects of Hope's rarefied Greco-Roman esthetic. His *Design for a Temple and a Bridge in a Nobleman's Park* [31], published in 1807, a planimetric elevation of a decorative Doric temple dedicated to Diana, adheres closely to Hope's cultivated taste for "chastity of contour" and "visible elegance."

Gandy's sepulchral projects also entailed an element of illusionistic theatricality. His tutor and teacher of perspective at the RA, Edward Edwards, strongly encouraged student architects to utilize scenographic techniques of perspective rendering, adding that "there are few examples of such artificial effects to be seen in this country except in the theatres."[7] Untried and unknown architects based in London along with Gandy, such as John Baber of Knightsbridge, seemed to follow Edwards's advice by applying dramatic scenographic devices in their Royal Academy submissions. Baber's *Design for Interior of a Cemetery* [32] of 1809 (one of five sepulchral designs exhibited by him between 1807 and 1812) was a majestic exercise in *scena per angolo* set design. With its multiplicity of spatial vistas, raking lights, and well-situated funereal props (the over-scaled cinerary urn in the atrium of the crypt and the statue of a cloaked shade beside the corner cluster of Doric columns), this imposing drawing—just over a meter in height—responded generously to Edwards's recommendation to develop a theatrical bravura in architectural design.

In Gandy's case, the skillful balance of solemnity and opulence achieved in his contemporaneous sepulchral interiors betrayed specifically continental scenographic sources. Both *Sepulchral Chamber* and *Design for a Cenotaph* are indebted to the subterranean Doric crypt in the stage set of *The Tomb of Agamemnon* [33] designed and engraved in 1787 by the cosmopolite architect-artist Louis-Jean Desprez, whose views of Vesuvius Gandy had already copied while in Italy.[8] Gandy's architectural imagery in these sepulchral interiors owes much of its heroic and morbid grandeur to the imaginative prints and drawings of Desprez, as was recognized by the architect George Dance the Younger when in 1803 he spoke of Gandy, in rather disparaging terms, as "not more than a Draughtsman, something of an Imitator of Du Pre [sic] and French artists."[9]

It was precisely because of his pictorial mastery of architectural rendering that Gandy found employment in the office of John Soane. Their shared passion for sepulchral architecture was already evident in Gandy's drafting for Soane immediately after he entered the Soane office in 1798. Concurrent with exhibiting his own mausoleal projects at the Royal Academy, Gandy was employed by Soane to produce exhibition watercolors illustrating and promoting a variety of the latter's sepulchral projects. And there can be little doubt that Soane was impressed by the younger architect's Italian credentials and his passion for sepulchral grandeur. From the outset of his work for Soane, Gandy served as much as a kind of architectural ghostwriter and artistic interpreter as a mere delineator of the elder architect's projects (Soane was Gandy's senior by eighteen years). As Gandy recalled his early devotion to Soane soon after his return from Italy: "for him [Soane], he [Gandy] bent the whole of his genius in that line of direction which forwarded his views."[10] Gandy's phrasing is characteristically awkward and strained, but revealingly so. In bending his genius, which is to say selling his notable skills as a draftsman/architect to Soane, Gandy submitted his artistry to forwarding another's views, this self-sacrificing advancement or advocacy of Soane's architecture appropriately conveyed through the metaphor of perspectival projection. Soane early on employed Gandy to resurrect, from the dead as it were, his own student Italian sepulchral fantasies through the creation of elaborate watercolors destined for the Royal Academy exhibits (under Soane's name, of course).

33 Louis-Jean Desprez, *The Tomb of Agamemnon*, 1787
34 John Soane (rendered by Gandy), *Design for a Mausoleum*, 1800

This tendency in Gandy's drafting for Soane is ideally seen in a landscape watercolor dated 1800 and exhibited at the RA in 1805 as *Design for a Mausoleum* [34]. The monopteral Doric structure is sited in a sequestered glade with a mountainous backdrop and cloud-streaked sky. The irregular verdure and billowing clouds of the landscape *repoussoir*, rather than diverting attention away from the central architectural forms, instead draws the eye toward the rusticated base and heavily arched recesses of the mausoleum. As in Gandy's own sepulchral RA exhibits of this period, this drawing makes no pretense of being a modern monument. Classically robed figures are seen discoursing in the shadow of sepulchral urns on the circular crepidoma, with a funeral procession approaching on a winding path in the distance. Death is not only personified as a skeletal allegorical statue atop the dome but is also present as a gaunt figure with torch in hand greeting mourners at the darkened entry into the realm of the dead. These figurative and narrative devices contribute to the illusionistic fiction of the architectural proposal, removing it from the present or any probable future and instead realizing the design as if it truly belonged to a timeless antique world. This mausoleum originated in earlier student designs by Soane from 1778 and 1784, here refashioned, decades later, into a startling pictorial display.[11]

As Professor of Architecture at the Royal Academy, Soane's attitude to this category of enthusiastic student designs was ambivalent. In the sixth lecture, delivered in 1812, the architect admitted that "Nothing can be more useful to the Student than his own theoretical dreams of magnificent Compositions produced by a warm imagination." But, in tracing the passage of the student architect from youthful imaginings to the less elevated demands of professional practice, Soane pointedly censured the protracted retention of these "theoretical compositions." As he warned, "Here [he] must commit himself with the greatest caution and due mistrust of his own powers."[12] Soane nevertheless did indulge himself in revisiting and recreating his own theoretical designs through Gandy's "bent genius" (so to speak). Soane's public artistic persona at the RA exhibitions was very much dependent on the illusionistic, and illusory, renderings of Gandy. The cautionary polemic of his remarks in his RA lecture contains an elegiac note of loss and self-doubt, in which the architect's imaginative powers are at once celebrated and renounced—a contradiction that Gandy's entire career would eventually come to exemplify.

As Soane's draftsman and landscape scenographer, Gandy was also called upon to visualize buildings and design proposals, sepulchral and otherwise, that were closer to the actuality of Soane's professional practice. Between 1798 and 1800, Gandy executed many topographic views of the villa/country house and outbuildings at Tyringham designed by Soane for the prominent banker William Praed. Among them is a storm-streaked perspective of the gate lodge [35], in which the fading rays of sunlight and rustling foliage dramatically illuminate and frame this elemental, yet suave, specimen of Soane's primitivist classical style, imparting to the structure an aura of sepulchral gravity. As part of the architectural complex at Tyringham, Soane also proposed a monumental sepulchral chapel, a trefoil-plan building with a triad of simplified Doric porches. Gandy's perspectives include a nocturnal scene by moonlight, perhaps identifiable with Soane's 1801 RA entry *Design for a Sepulchral Church at Tyringham* [36, 37]. Here the play of shadows enhances the meditative and reverential mood demanded by the building's program, with the decorative sarcophagi, commemorative tablets, and cinerary urns bathed in a lunar glow. The artificial illumination from within the chapel highlights the Ionic centerpiece of the lantern dome embellished by a self-consuming serpent, a pagan symbol of eternity.

During the first decade of the nineteenth century, Soane would bolster his lifelong fascination with sepulchral architecture through research into antiquarian and archaeological literature on the subject, in large measure as preparation for his RA lectures on architecture that commenced in 1809. In 1806, he acquired and annotated an obscure though intriguing treatise by the antiquary John Gregory entitled *An Account of the Sepulchers of the Antients* (1712), which surveyed the titanic efforts of earliest civilizations and their despotic rulers to perpetuate their memory through ambitious sepulchral works. Gregory drew a parallel between the ancient impulse to erect great sepulchers and the more modern antiquarian project of recreating the long-vanished

35 John Soane (rendered by Gandy), *Tyringham Gate Lodge in a Storm*, 1798–1800

NATURAL ABODES OF MEN: SEPULCHERS AND COTTAGES 39

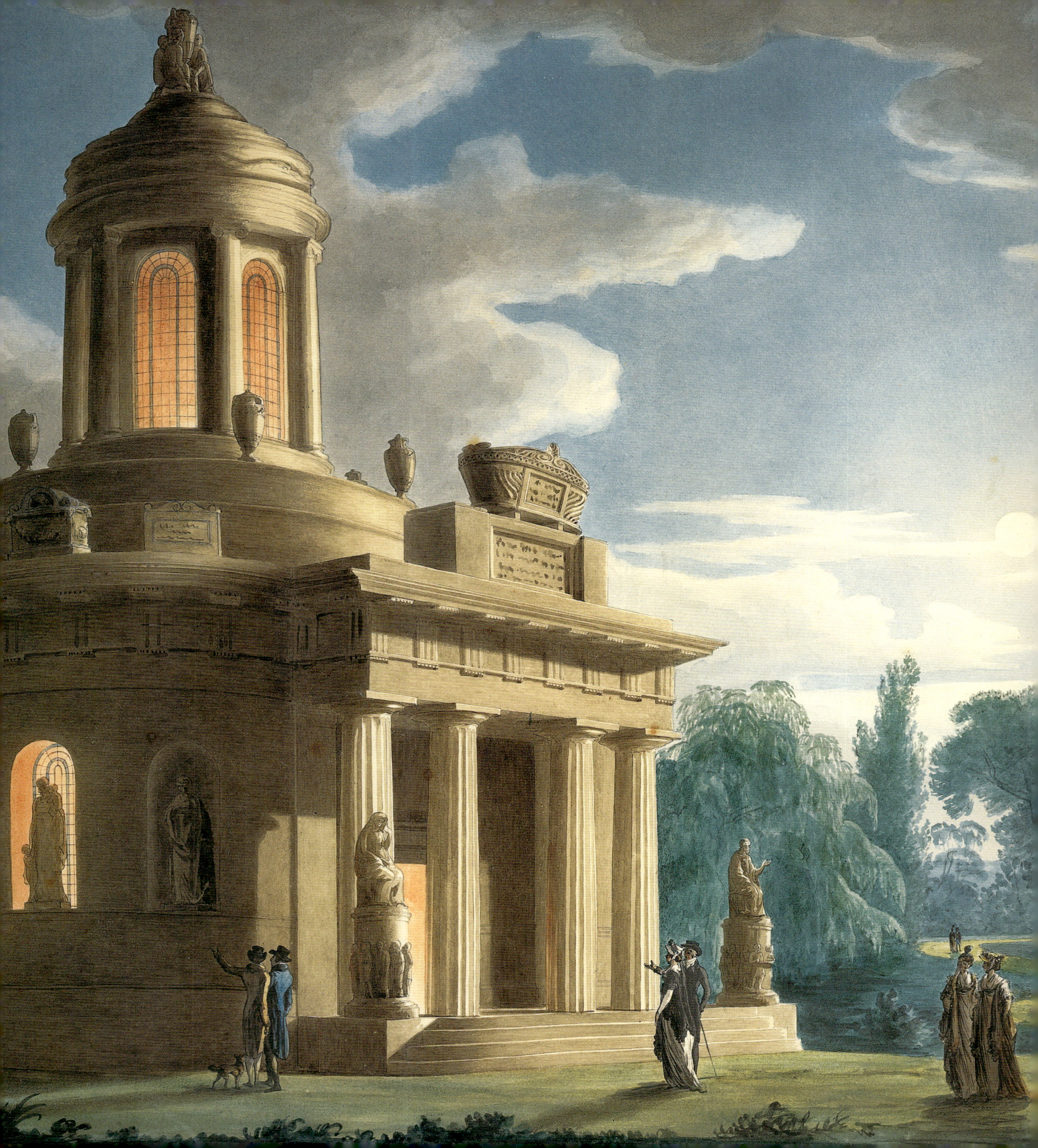

historical past. As Gregory commented on the dialogical relation between past and present that his study implied, "Compounding and Deriving things from their Origins, or First Principles, into what they are Now at this Day, and resolving or tracing them from what they are Now into their Origins."[13] Sepulchral architecture, by virtue of its commemorative function, similarly performs rituals of historic memory, inviting a regenerative return to origins, a theme that would resonate especially in Soane's RA lectures. This part of Gregory's volume was echoed directly in an important section of Soane's fourth lecture, where he condemned the misapplication of hallowed sepulchral forms in modern architecture, the obelisk being cited as the most abused example. This ancient architectural prototype, Soane believed, was frequently corrupted of its solemn meaning and reduced to a decorative device in unhallowed contexts, the kind of transgression that architectural theorists conventionally debated under the rubric of "Propriety" (Soane's contemporaries, it should be noted, often took his own architecture to task on these same grounds). But he went on to issue this stern injunction: "the architect, by close study and unwearied attention, should be ... well informed of the primitive destination and origin of things, and on all occasions be able to trace every invention up to First Principles and Original Causes."[14]

The historical status of sepulchral architecture was a concern not merely of archaeological and theoretical conjecture for Soane, Gandy, and other architects in early nineteenth-century England. With the traumatic testing of England and the rest of Europe during the Napoleonic Wars, public consciousness about historical memory and national identity was defined and debated in often highly speculative political and cultural treatises of the time. Soane, for example, owned a copy of *Essay on Sepulchres* (1809) by the radical political theorist William Godwin. Without broaching the philosophical anarchism and theories of moral utility argued for in his earlier *Political Justice* (1793), Godwin proposed the national establishment of a "Sepulchral Atlas," which would involve not the construction of antique-inspired monuments but rather the erection of diminutive white crosses in designated sepulchral areas of remembrance throughout the English landscape. In defending the pronounced anti-monumentality of his proposal, Godwin wrote, "while pyramids and vast cities shall perish, these simple land-marks shall be regarded as sacred and remain undisturbed witnesses of the most extraordinary revolutions."[15] Without denying the possibility of impending social change and political reform, Godwin conceived of national sepulchral remembrance as a collective incentive toward mystical thought-processes.

Godwin's sepulchral atlas was in many ways a response to patriotic feelings evoked by the Anglo-French Wars.[16] Another English radical reformer who entered into national debate about sepulchral remembrance was Major John Cartwright, and he, like Soane, enlisted Gandy to serve as the delineator and artist of his designs. A retired naval officer hailing from a Nottinghamshire gentry family, Cartwright became renowned as an indefatigable advocate of political reform movements in London during the Napoleonic period. Lord Byron praised him for his devotion to political and parliamentary reform, while the critic William Hazlitt would lampoon him in his essay "On People with One Idea" (1816). Cartwright advocated universal male suffrage.[17] In the hope of generating nationalist sentiments he turned amateur architect and prepared designs for what he called the "Hieronauticon, or Naval Temple." Gathering together a team of Royal Academy artists, including Gandy, the illustrator Thomas Stothard, and the history painter William Hamilton, Cartwright oversaw the creation of forty-six drawings (twenty-six of which were by Gandy) that were exhibited at one of James Christie's galleries on Pall Mall in 1800. This complicated set of drawings—including a seven-and-a-half-feet-square elevation—remains unlocated,[18] though they are described in a checklist of the

36, 37 John Soane (rendered by Gandy), *Design for Sepulchral Church at Tyringham*, 1798

NATURAL ABODES OF MEN: SEPULCHERS AND COTTAGES

drawings and a lengthy textual account by Cartwright, published anonymously as *The Trident* (1802) by the radical printer and bookseller Joseph Johnson.

The Hieronauticon consisted of a massive truncated pyramidal temple surmounted by a triumphal column, the whole embraced by a subsidiary network of terraces and turrets. A newly invented system of ornament and copious sculptural decoration was dedicated to maritime themes, with Cartwright redesigning the classical orders as "Nautico-Doric," "Nautico-Ionic," etc. This symbolic approach to architectural ornament and relief sculpture, as Cartwright phrased it, "emblematically expresses ... the subject to be celebrated."[19] This concern with the emblematic and signifying capacity of architecture would reemerge quite strongly in Gandy's later theoretical writings. Although the foundation of the structure was to house an enormous vaulted cemetery and a sepulchral church, with the upper levels containing commemorative, "moralizing" compartments and corridors of tomb sculptures ("Halls of Emulation"), the program of the Hieronauticon was not exclusively sepulchral. Much of it was to be museological in function: painting and sculpture galleries and displays of naval history and natural history were integral to Cartwright's building program. In an undated elevation drawing that can be assigned to this same period [38], Gandy delineates a truncated pyramidal temple with a colonnade in antis framing a projecting portico. Together these elements form the base of an enormous architectural throne for a statue of Zeus or Neptune in lieu of a triumphal column. The sketch hints at the intimidating scale and monumental profile that the Hieronauticon was to have had. Employing the familiar esthetic language of "grandeur and sublimity," Cartwright hoped "to confer on such an edifice, the power of speaking to the human mind."[20] It was this emphasis on the formative power of architecture on the social body and the collective mind of the British people that made Cartwright's prospectus distinctive.

In its megalomaniacal scale and sweeping cultural mission, the Hieronauticon was meant to overshadow similarly impractical nationalist monuments proposed during this period, such as John Flaxman's arid designs for a colossal statue of Britannia sited in a sepulchral precinct on Greenwich Hill that he published in 1799. These displays of patriotic gigantism were satirized by the Tory caricaturist James Gillray in his *Design for the Naval Pillar* of 1800 [39]. Like Cartwright's scheme, Gillray's was devoted to Britannia's nautical prowess (as the engraving inscription announces in patriotic language identical to that of Cartwright, "the Trident is confirmed"), but the anti-Jacobin spleen generally associated with Gillray's often sadistic caricatures is not entirely suppressed: the ruin of French republicanism is symbolized by tattered Phrygian caps, torn tricolors, and dismembered sans-culotte corpses. Whereas Cartwright's project was conceived as a monument for historical instruction and remembrance, Gillray's is a titanic beacon isolated along a stormy Channel crossing, a heroic and grim challenge to, as the caption of the print tells us, "the regicide Navy of France."

Ironically, Cartwright and members of the London Corresponding Society were being persecuted as revolutionary agitators at the same time as they themselves were encouraging the enlistment of volunteer national guards to protect against fearfully anticipated French landings in the British Isles.[21] Gandy himself was enrolled in the Westminster Regiment in 1803–06, during which time he fractured his leg (not, it should be added, while vigilantly guarding Albion's shores but in horseplay with his fellow volunteers).[22]

Other British artists shared a tradition of patriotic radicalism during the Anglo-French Wars.[23] James Barry, John Opie, and William Blake had variously proposed artistic projects on an epic civic scale that were meant to reconcile progressive "democratick" values with a patriotic stance. Although often at odds with, and even exiled from, the artistic establishment of the Royal Academy, they nourished an ambitious (and perhaps politically naive) hope that a truly public culture of the fine arts could be fostered at this time. To the late twentieth-century observer, this conception of artistic culture as a catalyst for collective nationalism inevitably evokes orchestrated spectacles of modern totalitarianism. Cartwright was alive to this danger himself. "The fine arts," he admitted, "will be full as likely to produce moral and political evil as good, … [but] they may, as I conceive it, be made powerful instruments of moral and political improvement."[24]

Cartwright employed Gandy again later in his career for another sepulchral project, when in 1823–24 he promoted the commission of a monument commemorating the death of General Rafael del Riego. Executed on November 7, 1823 during the repressive purge of liberal constitutionalists when King Ferdinand reclaimed his throne and despotic rule of Spain, Riego was hailed by Cartwright as the noble martyr to Spanish political freedom. Cartwright also implicated the British government for helping to insure the demise of the Spanish liberales. The reformist-minded Duke of Sussex, brother of the Prince Regent and black sheep of the royal family, and Archibald Alison, the Whig associationist philosopher and journalist, also supported the cause of Riego and his émigré family, who took refuge in London after the arrest of the General. If Cartwright's earlier proposal for the Hieronauticon implied an ideal of national solidarity around a monumental site of remembrance, this hypothetical cenotaph was more of a demonstration of political conscience. According to Cartwright's prospectus, it was to combine simplified architectural forms (a series of cubes and

38 *Design for a Temple (Preliminary Sketch for the Hieronauticon)*, ca. 1800–05
39 James Gillray, *Design for the Naval Pillar*, 1800

spheres) with allegorical statuary (the body of Riego cradled by Fame between the secular altars of liberty and eternity). Gandy's drawing for the project is unlocated, but an undated sepia drawing by him, delineating classical sepulchral motifs and moldings [40], may give some idea of its laconic arrangement of enduring geometric elements and its stark iconography. Cartwright's effort to publicize his scheme was thwarted when the drawing by Gandy was rejected for the 1824 Royal Academy exhibition, presumably because of its politically compromising theme. Appeals on Cartwright's behalf by an unnamed academician—perhaps the elderly Henry Fuseli, whom Cartwright had known since the 1770s—to the RA Council (a ruling panel of senior members of the RA) also failed. The Riego design thus fell victim to censorship within the academy, its commemorated subject made to suffer another kind of execution at the hands of a repressive tribunal.[25]

Gandy's association with Cartwright was a continuation of his painful education in the politics of the arts. Farington's diary entries (a main source of knowledge about the RA) suggest that Gandy was considered politically suspect because of his fraternization in Italy with artists such as Wallis, Ottley, and Artaud, all of whom were distrusted by conservative academicians for their democratic sympathies. Gandy's enlistment by the insistently vocal reformer Cartwright must have appeared to confirm this. The projects by Cartwright to which Gandy contributed brought to his attention the political dilemmas that compromised his utopian dreams. Antique-inspired sepulchral meditations could no longer remain insulated from contemporary debates about the national character of the fine arts.

The social instrumentality of architecture was soon tested by Gandy in a different branch of theoretical design. In 1805, he issued two pattern books entitled *Designs for Cottages, Cottage Farms, and Other Rural Buildings* and *The Rural Architect*. Although appearing to signal a marked divergence from the sepulchral monumentality of his recent RA submissions, these two volumes of model cottage designs offered equally speculative architectural schemes. By delving into the lower genres of utilitarian rural architecture, Gandy came to terms with the most important and prevailing concerns in architectural theory circa 1800: the esthetic of the picturesque and the concept of architectural primitivism, both of which posed fundamental questions about the relation of architecture to nature and to social need.

In turning to the pattern book as a published medium for his architectural designs and ideas, Gandy was conforming to a trend that had been escalating since the mid-eighteenth century, when books of designs for villas, cottages, and rural architecture began to proliferate in England. With the Anglo-French Wars and a concomitant decline in building commissions, the incidence of these publishing ventures in pattern books for domestic architecture drastically increased.[26] Gandy's publisher, John Harding, specialized in volumes on agricultural improvement and cottage architecture. The pattern book was the handiest way for architects to disseminate and market their designs. As a commercial strategy, these publications also sought to target, and even create, a new clientele. In 1798, Uvedale Price, the prolific theoretical writer on the picturesque, forecast these new directions in architectural patronage:

> All the splendid effects of architecture, and of assemblages of magnificent buildings, whether in cities, or amidst rural scenery can only be displayed by princes and men of princely revenues. But it is the men of moderate fortune, by means of slight additions and alterations, to produce a very essential change in the appearance of farm buildings, cottages &c. and in the grouping of them in villages; and such effects, though less splendid than those of regular architecture, are not less interesting.[27]

The concept of the picturesque had begun in the late eighteenth century as an esthetic category concerned primarily with the perception of landscape. Under Price and other commentators it acquired a new dimension connected with agricultural improvement, which depended on the patronage of a new middle-class farming interest. It was to this audience that pattern book designers—many of them, like Gandy, struggling young architects looking to advertise their nascent practices —addressed their publications.

The picturesque was a wonderfully and desperately changing concept. It could be taken as a Whig symbol of enlightened liberality and privileged freedom, a Tory claim for time-honored dominion over the rural patrimony of England, a parvenu fashion of consumer tourism enjoyed by a burgeoning urban middle class, or some contradictory hybrid of all of these.[28] One unifying idea, however, surfaces: the natural and the cultural were to efface one another. The artifact of human design was made to seem the work of nature, while simultane-

40 Sepulchral Monument, ca. 1820–25

ously the natural world was made to bear the coded inscriptions of esthetic appropriation, by virtue of its resemblance to pictorial landscape art and through its inducements to philosophical reflection.

From a late twentieth-century perspective, it could be said that the picturesque signaled the inception of the modern, tourist commercialization of the countryside. William Wordsworth's professed antipathy toward the raging fashionability of the picturesque suggests as much. In his 1805 draft of *The Prelude*, Wordsworth condemned the moral insensibility and esthetic relativism of the picturesque and its prescribed tastes for mildly untamed natural scenery, antiquarian debris, and simulated rusticity. The picturesque is summarily dismissed as "a strong infection of the age .../ Bent overmuch on superficial things" (12.121–24).[29] By way of distinguishing himself from the pleasure-seeking tourist trade, Wordsworth sought to establish a poetic identification with the incorrupt rustic laborer, a subject observed and engaged only in passing, but nonetheless refreshingly devoid of picturesque frippery. "Inspect the basis of the social pile," Wordsworth counseled himself. "I chiefly looked (What need to look beyond?)/ Among the natural abodes of men" (13.94–102).

Over the half-century before Wordsworth, architectural writers had inquired into "the natural abodes of men" in their commentaries on the rustic cottage and its relation to Nature. Robert Morris, in his *Rural Architecture* (1750), offered one definition: "just as if the inhabitants had newly started into Being, and were led by Nature and Necessity to form a Fabric for their own Preservation."[30] The polymath and architect/astronomer Thomas Wright of Durham in his *Universal Architecture*

(1755) saw it in terms of rustic arbors, gnarled garden seats, and pre-weathered grottoes sited in overgrown, uncultivated landscapes and safely out of view of one another, "being imagined to please most where they be naturally supposed the Productions of the Age before Building became a Science."[31] This primitivist myth of a first architecture based on the fundamental requirements of human need had its most profound and influential articulation in Marc-Antoine Laugier's *Essai sur l'architecture* (1753). As a *philosophe* arguing for the reform of architecture based on a purifying return to origins, Laugier's almost evangelical emphasis on a design ethos of structural integrity and functional rationale carried with it a moralizing dimension. The elemental simplification of architectural form encouraged by Laugier's theory implies a belief in the power of architecture to remake society.

By the late eighteenth century, the social agency of architecture was often probed through the design typology of rural housing, primed by a generation of agricultural improvement and paternalistic philanthropy in estate management and model farm planning.[32] Representative of this concern was the publication by John Wood the Younger, *A Series of Plans, for Cottages or Habitations of the Labourer* (1781). Like Morris before him, Wood lamented the subhuman degradation of the rural working classes that he had witnessed in his survey of their housing conditions. In descending from the socially elite context of the residential crescents that he had designed in Bath, Wood legitimized the functional mission of his modest cottage designs with this compassionate admission: "in order to make myself master of the subject, it was imperative for me to feel as the cottager himself, for I have always held it as a maxim that no architect can form a convenient plan unless he ideally places himself in the situation of the person for who he designs."[33] Toward the end of the eighteenth century, architects well versed in both the refined and primitivist strains of neo-classicism, such as the innovative Scottish architect James Playfair whose drawings were purchased by Soane in 1804, continued to bring an elemental plain style to the design of rural housing. This leveling of architectural style in the name of social improvement was even promoted in pattern books of designs for more socially respectable classes of dwellings. In the witty treatise *OIKIDIA, or Nutshells* (1785), the architect James Peacock offered a series of plans for diminutive villas and rural retreats aimed at clients of modest wealth that were to be distinguished by their unassuming architectural esthetic. As the lifelong assistant to George Dance and the author of several tracts on philanthropy and the plight of the impoverished, Peacock was closely familiar with both advanced neo-classicism and moral debates about class relations in late eighteenth-century society. Aware of the commercial risks that his minimalist architectural credo might bring upon the provincial builder consulting his treatise, Peacock conceded that the outer shells to these modest villas could be varied according to the preference of the client, thereby predicting the picturesque shuffling of historical styles that was soon to begin in earnest.

The quintessential redefinition of the picturesque cottage appeared in *An Essay on British Cottage Architecture* (1798) by the topographic artist James Malton. Shunning the thatched, wattle-and-daub "hovels" of the working rural landscape, Malton proclaims, "When mention is made of this kind of dwelling called a cottage, I see in my imagination, a small house in the country, of odd irregular form, with various harmonious colours, and the effects of weather, time, and accident, the whole environed by smiling verdure."[34] By this sort of shallow romanticism the cottage was transformed from the real (and uncomfortable) dwelling of the impoverished country man into a crafted structure of artful intimacy aged gently by nature. It could now accommodate a medley of vernacular, Gothic, Tudor, and classical accents [41], a stylistic amalgamation sanctioned by the esthetician and collector Richard Payne Knight in 1805 when he wrote: "The best style of architecture for irregular and picturesque houses, which can now be adopted, is that mixed style ... taken from models, which are built piece-meal, during many successive ages; and by several different nations, it is distinguished by no particular manner of execution, or class of ornaments; but admits of all promiscuously."[35]

This new esthetics of heterogeneity and discontinuity elicited caution and even a strain of social criticism from its own practitioners. The landscape improver Humphry Repton, for example, had grown wary of the polemical and philosophical convolutions of picturesque theorists such as Knight and Price; pictorialist *bricolage* and associationist sentiment threatened to undermine any semblance of cultural authority and a sense of tradition: "we daily see wealth acquired by industry, or by fortunate speculation ... this will often account for the increase of novel or fantastic edifices, and the decrease of those specimens of former grandeur."[36]

This prolonged account of the conflicting social and esthetic claims of the picturesque has been necessary to understand Gandy's *Designs for*

41 James Malton, Model Cottages, in An Essay on British Cottage Architecture (1798)

Cottages. His incentive to turn to the design of rural architecture was provided by the first volume of *Communications to the Board of Agriculture; on Subjects Relative to the Husbandry and Internal Improvement of the Country* (1797). The primary objective of the Board of Agriculture, chartered in 1793 and overseen by Sir John Sinclair on appointment by Prime Minister William Pitt, was to publish an agricultural survey of the British Isles. Central to the Board's mission was the architectural improvement of rural cottages. The volume of *Communications* cited by Gandy in his preface contained two brief articles on model cottage construction by the architect Henry Holland, the first of which dealt with the classification of cottages based upon the hierarchy of occupations among rural workers (from field laborer to the independent farmer) and the second on the French cottage construction method of *pisé*—an economical building material consisting of compressed clay, lime, and earth. While acceding to the wisdom and usefulness of these articles, Gandy indicates that his ambition goes well beyond the mere reform of the living conditions of the rural laborer: his cause is rather "the advancement of Public Taste" (iii). The architectural landscape of rural England, Gandy observes, is injurious to national pride. In order to bring a portentous gravity to the modest building type of the cottage, he conceived of rural architecture as a category of civil architecture—a kind of public works in the countryside.

By way of justifying his calling as both esthetic and social reformer, Gandy ventured into the theoretical domain of, as he put it, "the Moralist and speculative philosopher" (vi). In what is the most interesting passage from the preface to the pattern book, he proposed this foundation for his social psychology of "taste":

> The effect of early impression is well known to every attentive observer of human nature ... the early habit of contemplating fine forms, produces a correspondence in ideas of beauty, and creates a natural good taste;

NATURAL ABODES OF MEN: SEPULCHERS AND COTTAGES 47

whilst, on the contrary, vulgarity and lowness of ideas are acquired, when we are born and educated among objects incapable of exciting any fine impressions. (vi)

With his basic epistemology drawn from Locke and Kames, Gandy privileges first impressions and first sensations. Architecture has the capacity not only to improve the physical conditions of the social environment, but also to mold the sensibilities of those who live and work in it: Beauty set to work for the cultivation of society. The net result, Gandy believes, is that "taste would thus be naturalized." (vii) This naturalization of taste of course implies just the opposite: taste will be a socializing force—an esthetic morality—that will shape the habits and customs of the impressionable, unformed laboring classes. Gandy argues for the social instrumentality of architecture by resorting to sensationalist psychology and by subscribing to "natural" taste that was in fact a cultural predisposition enforced from without.

In support of his arguments for this naturalization of taste and the advancement of society, Gandy cites passages from *Reports of the Society for Bettering the Conditions of the Poor* that were published between 1798 and 1808. Founded by transport magnate turned religious/social activist Sir Thomas Bernard, this philanthropic society encouraged national attention to the plight of the rural poor, a population unprepared for the demands of a manufacturing-based, freemarket economy. Bernard's reports reveal a discouraging view of the rapacious enclosure laws and industrial expansion that characterized modern commercial society in England during the Napoleonic period.[37] While expressing a pastoral nostalgia for a cottage-based economy dependent on the enlightened benevolence of landowners, Bernard hoped that the commodious model cottage, understated in its picturesque aspect, would inspire not only a greater sense of self-respect among the laboring poor, but also a collective, proprietary interest in the welfare of the nation. The improved cottage was potentially the catalyst for the enfranchisement of the rural poor in civil society, similar in many respects to the socially transformative power of architecture that Cartwright ascribed to his imaginary Hieronauticon. The efforts of the Board of Agriculture and the Bettering Society, and the citation of their reports in the pattern books of Gandy and other architects, supported this view.

Correspondents writing in William Cobbett's *Political Register* during this period often debated the ills and virtues of "the agricultural mania"—the label for draconian methods in estate management, the formation of farming monopolies and the dire social consequences of the scientific spirit in agrarian improvement. Paraphrasing the opinions of the Scottish Whig historian and antiquary George Chalmers, one offered this summary: "By consolidating farms to an enormous extent; by forcing cottagers from their hamlets; by pretending to make much profit with little labour; our modern system of agriculture has depopulated the shires wherein it prevails. While peers sink into peasants, and peasants rise to peers, the great body of the people is pining for want."[38] Anxiety about the mutability of classhood in rural England, circa 1800–06, was especially acute because of the shadow of Jacobin and Napoleonic France. Contributors to the *Political Register* returned obsessively to the fear of a peasantry abandoned by market forces and mobilized by revolutionary discontent. There were indeed radical strains of agrarian reform that made such fears not unfounded. The London-based reformer Thomas Spence—a schoolmaster originally heralding from Newcastle—represented the radical-fringe end of the spectrum in these social and political debates about the condition of rural Britain. Major Cartwright's tireless campaign for parliamentary reform seemed like Tory cant when pitted against the millenarian communistic doctrines of "Citizen Spence" and his followers.[39] Spence's tract *The Restorer of Society to Its Natural State* (1801) landed him in prison on charges of sedition, as its fundamental recommendation centered on the abolition of inherited property rights and the nation-wide, communal redistribution of the land. He criticized the efforts of philanthropic societies and agricultural reform movements for their moderate proposals to ease the suffering of the rural poor; these programs, Spence argued, merely protected the moribund traditions of landed paternalism while failing to reverse the ill-gotten fortunes of commercial speculation.

In *Designs for Cottages*, after announcing the broadly social and national mission of his reformist cottage designs, Gandy devotes the majority of his prefatory text to more exclusively esthetic issues of the kind commonly expounded on in picturesque treatises. The picturesque challenge to the classical tradition (picturesque irregularity vanquishing classical uniformity) was promulgated with numbing consistency in the pattern books from this period, and Gandy's was no exception. The varied outline of architectural forms (the "picturesque" skyline of Oxford cited as an example) is deemed by Gandy to have an affective esthetic power, "like the imagery of the Poet" (v). Similarly, the shifting vantage points encouraged by picturesque techniques in architectural composition demands, as Gandy maintains, "the same sort of skill and genius as fine music" (viii). But, not wanting to declare a classical bias and thereby seem contrary to the picturesque fashion, Gandy offers an equivocating compromise on the issue of symmetry/asymmetry in his cottages:

> Most of the following Designs have been studied on this principle of variety, which the Author conceives to be that best adapted for Cottages. Those which are regular may be changed into the picturesque by taking away one wing; and the picturesque or irregular Designs will become regular by selecting a center, and repeating the parts on each side, if the Builder prefers such dull monotony. (ix)

This solution is evasive and hedging but also ingeniously contemporary, implying, as it does, a modular variability of architectural units that may be adjusted to the circumstances, taste, and economy of the reformist patron.

However, after leafing through the plates of Gandy's pattern books, it is evident that the designs often betray a highly sophisticated preference for "such dull monotony." Especially in the many designs for duplex or double cottages, the elevations possess a symmetrical unity that would not feasibly invite the picturesque displacement of one wing [42]. The geometric severity and rectilinear interplay of window and door voids are also in defiance of the picturesque preference for broken contours and irregular profiles. In the preface, Gandy itemizes the building materials for his rural architecture: *pisé* and whitewash walls, thatch and slate roofing, piers and uprights from tree trunks with the bark left intact—all of these fairly typical of the rustic primitivism of materials found in other pattern books of the period. The formal style of architectural rendering in Gandy's plates, however, with their emphasis on stereometric concision and sharp planarity, contradicts the picturesque taste for surface tactility and the organic merging of built form and landscape elements [43–48]. Many of the aquatinted plates in Gandy's volumes are enlivened with cursive landscape vignettes. But in plates such as that for a design of a shepherd's cottage in which landscape and building are compositionally interlocked [43], the rugged sketchiness of the terrain only accentuates the crisp diagrammatic features of the elevation. The picturesque irregularity of the diagonal fracturing of the cubic central block effected by the stair encasement and lean-to wing is at odds with the formal disposition of the building's apertures, creating a subtle level of architectural dissonance that takes it far beyond "picturesque variety."

Gandy's ambivalent relation to the picturesque is also seen in the antiseptic, stark whiteness of his designs for rural architecture. Picturesque theorists such as Uvedale Price generally prized the ruinous foliation of architectural surfaces in which nature and building become indissoluble. But Price also recommended the application of whitewash to rural cottages, writing with almost childish glee: "White ... there is such a look of neatness and gaiety in it, that one cannot be surprised if only one idea should prevail—that of making everything as white as possible."[40] The picturesque cottage as a piquant

42 *A Double Cottage*, from *Designs for Cottages, Cottage Farms, and Other Rural Buildings*, 1805

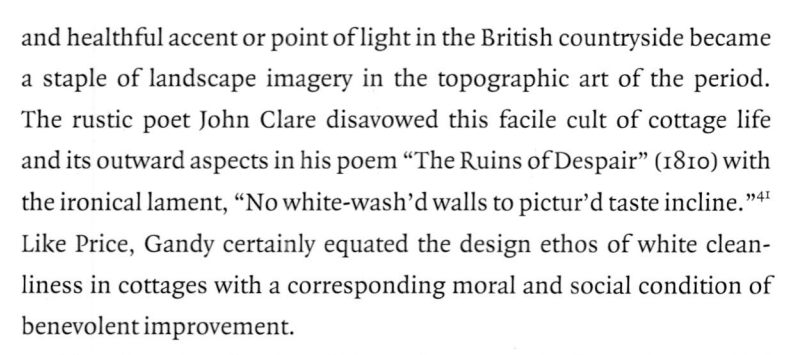

and healthful accent or point of light in the British countryside became a staple of landscape imagery in the topographic art of the period. The rustic poet John Clare disavowed this facile cult of cottage life and its outward aspects in his poem "The Ruins of Despair" (1810) with the ironical lament, "No white-wash'd walls to pictur'd taste incline."[41] Like Price, Gandy certainly equated the design ethos of white cleanliness in cottages with a corresponding moral and social condition of benevolent improvement.

The gleaming façades of Gandy's cottage designs also recalled other architectural lessons from his student sojourn in Italy. While touring the Italian countryside in August of 1795, Gandy wrote to his father, "I get at buildings few other architects visit, and it has led me into a study whereby I am making a series of designs without neglecting the antique, adapting each for the particular parts of the country that I visit. This is a study that no architect has made before and will be absolutely necessary on my return to England."[42] An Italian-period drawing with two elevations of farm buildings and stables gives evidence of this new "study" [49]. The elongated horizontality of these façades, along with the sleek rooflines, overhanging eaves, and strip fenestration, would be reincorporated directly into the 1805 pattern books. Similarly, Italian landscape watercolors from the mid-1790s by Gandy [50] that depict clusters of rural vernacular build-

Top left to bottom right: 43 *A Shepherd's Cottage, and Conveniences*, from *Designs for Cottages, Cottage Farms, and Other Rural Buildings*, 1805
44 *Entrance Gate and Double Lodge*, from *The Rural Architect*, 1805
45 *Plan & Design for a Bath*, from *The Rural Architect*, 1805
46 *A Dairy Farm*, from *The Rural Architect*, 1805
47 *A Labourer's Cottage, Who Keeps Poultry and Pigs for Sale*, from *Designs for Cottages, Cottage Farms, and Other Rural Buildings*, 1805
48 *A Cottage with Conveniences for Keeping Poultry, Pigs, and Pigeons*, from *Designs for Cottages, Cottage Farms, and Other Rural Buildings*, 1805
49 *Elevation of Farm Buildings*, ca. 1795–97

ings nestled in the terrain would inform the more stylized, Mediterranean flavor of his later publications. The dedication of *Designs for Cottages* to the collector and designer Thomas Hope reaffirms this picturesque appropriation of Italianate rural architecture, as Hope's own contemporaneous sketches for country villas with belvederes and prospect towers accord perfectly with Gandy's appropriation of the Italian vernacular.[43] Although Gandy thought that he was a solitary pathfinder in his exploration of non-classical architecture in the Italian countryside, this was surely not the case: the French architect and topographer F.-L. Seheult was surveying Italian rural architecture in the early 1790s and the Florentine architect Giuseppe Pistocchi was producing radical designs for vernacularly inspired farm buildings illustrative of the primitivist architectural theories of Francesco Milizia in the late 1790s.[44] As hinted by Gandy in the letter to his father, the study of vernacular architecture did not necessarily imply that the antique would be forsaken. Instead, the spirit of a submerged classicism was discerned within the simple geometries and unadorned surfaces of this utilitarian architecture.

It is not surprising therefore that Gandy's propensity for the sublime rhetoric of architecture was not entirely suppressed with the designing of the pattern books. The picturesque architecture of social reform could also incorporate startling and imposing elements. Thus, in Gandy's plates, an estate gate lodge is presented as a guardian-like monument composed of solemnly stark pyramids [44]; a farm complex has battered fortification walls and malevolently expressive fenestration; and a sunken bridge and streamlined bath house are treated with a self-consciously constrained sense of monumentality and formal tension [45]. Although many features of the picturesque are at play in many of these plates—compositional asymmetry with visually determined counterpoints between verticals and horizontals, patterning of light and shade to create recession and projection—Gandy maintains a strident lucidity in the overall design esthetic. Indeed, the slightly epic tone to some of these elevations accords with their moral and social agenda. There was also a degree of continuity between the more overtly neo-classical austerity of Gandy's *concorso* project and the stylistic restraint of his rural architecture. One contemporary reviewer noted that the pattern book designs were perhaps exceedingly dour in their architectural character, speculating that "Perhaps Mr. Gandy has given these sepulchral forms in compliance with the taste of a sombre patron."[45]

This anonymous critic from *New Monthly Review* and a journalist writing in *The Annual Review and History of Literature* responded with hostile incredulity to Gandy's pattern books. Although the latter praised Gandy as "an exquisite painter of architectural subjects," the reviewer seized on the unconventional and even aberrant quality of Gandy's designs:

> In a wild pursuit of novelty, he [Gandy] has adopted
> a style of frigid extravagance, disregarding the requisites
> of climate, manners, and convenience, and with a singular
> dereliction, or rather inversion, of usual proportions ...
> Mr. Gandy, however a pupil of the picturesque, seems
> as much embarrassed by his whimsical elevations, as
> by the most rigid symmetry, and has neglected to a strange
> excess the adaptation of his plans to domestic convenience.
> Full little would the farmer or labourer praise the taste
> that should lodge him in these picturesque hovels.[46]

This criticism ignores the tension between the philosophical assumptions of Gandy's "hygienic" formalism and his esthetic desire for picturesque planning. "These are cottages for carnival time," another critic gibed.[47] The reviewer quoted above, however, coined an apt oxymoron in criticizing Gandy's pattern books: "a style of frigid extravagance" approximates both the spartan purification of architectural form and the rarefied artfulness of these designs. Two years later in *The Annual Review*, an anonymous critic employed the very same phrasing to condemn the idiosyncratic poetic language that Wordsworth employed in treating his subjects of rural simplicity.[48]

The charge of "frigid extravagance" leveled against Gandy's rural architecture rings true when examining the more utopian and large-scale projects that are proposed in his pattern books. *The Rural Architect*, for example, included a series of elevations for "A Rural Institute" that entailed monotonous rows of dormitories and lectures halls, along with an experimental teaching farm and a chapel, all of these structures organized around a quadrangular system of vast courtyards [51]. The façades are characteristically minimal in detailing, with repetitive massing and bay divisions distinguished only by expansive arcades and the light/dark rhythm of the fenestration. The inclusion of this proposal for an agrarian college implies a systematic promulgation of architectural and agricultural reform throughout Great Britain, though it also undermines the illusion of casual freedom in nature popularly associated with the picturesque. Gandy's comprehensive agrarian schemes of this kind lapse into a sort of authoritarian conceptualism.

One of the most problematic designs in this utopian vein is "The Cottage of the Winds" from Gandy's *Designs for Cottages*: a proposal for a quasi-communal structure of eight wedge-shaped dwellings forming a unified circular plan [52]. The placement of the initials of wind directions over the door of each cottage was a Vitruvian conceit, imparting to rural architecture a hallowed classical allusion. The elevation is of course very plain, with pedimented porches demarcating the individual units of the multiple dwelling. Garden yard plots for each unit create a concentric strip of green within the circular plan, while the innermost circle houses a ring of privies. The concentric geometry of the design recalls the planning techniques Gandy had first worked through in his sepulchral *concorso* entry: the universality of circular perfection applied equally to the dead and the living. Had this design been built and inhabited, the compartmentalized cottages would have been poorly lit, vertiginously confining, and downright insalubrious. But as a holistic model of improvement born on the drawing board, it must have seemed wonderfully ingenious in its interplay of geometry and social subordination. Gandy even enlarged upon this proposal with what can best be called "The Village of the Winds," a model community of eight cottages of the winds positioned around a centralized church. Here was a systematic plan that could be replicated ad infinitum: expanding circular orbits of rural housing compounds forming a microcosmic plan in which the life, labor, and faith of the rural classes were bought into social and universal order.

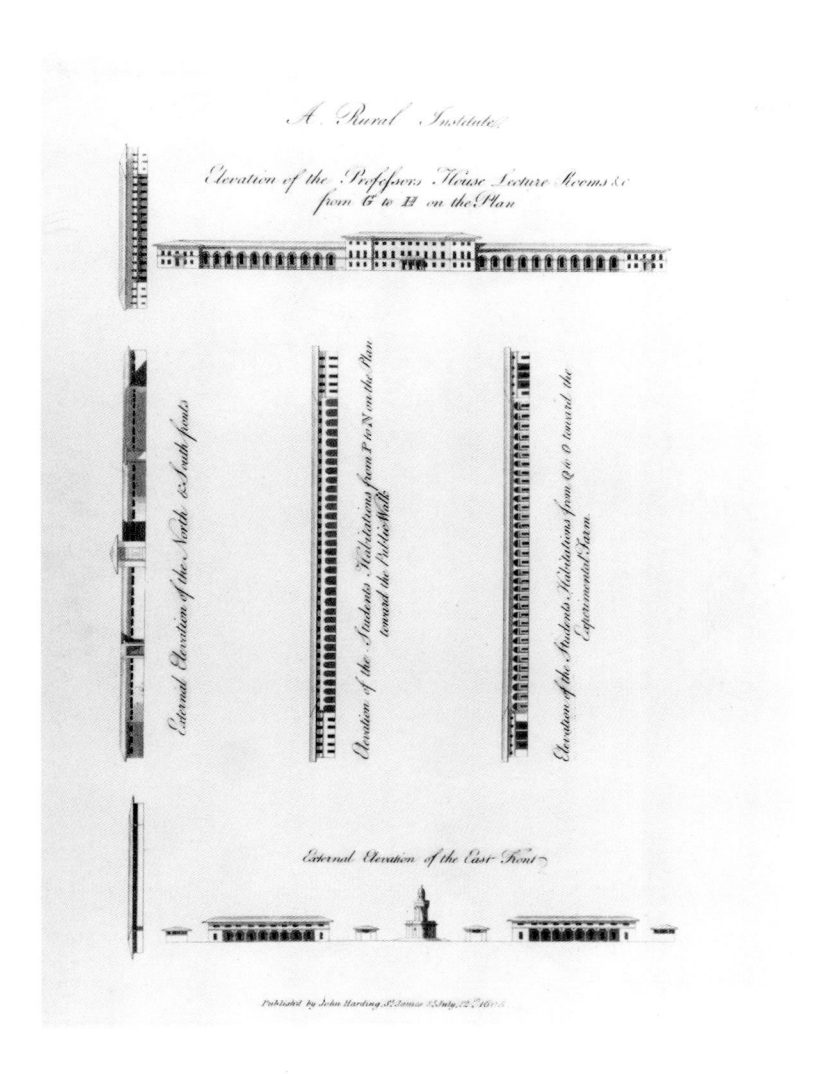

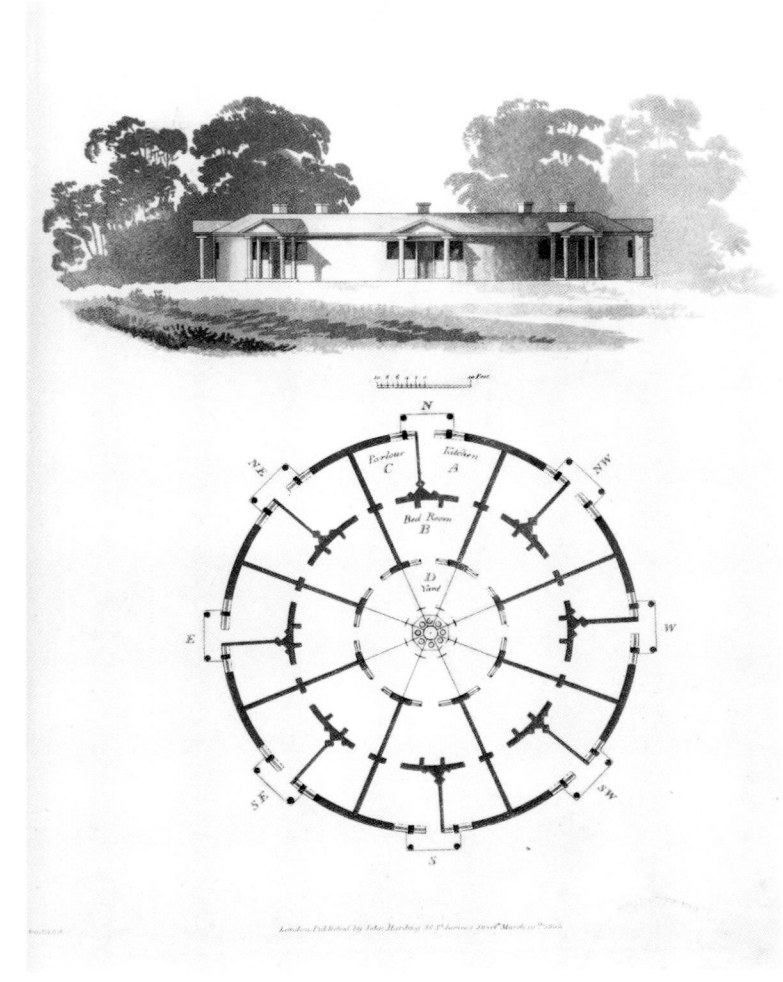

It was this project that the architectural historian Emil Kaufmann had in mind when he ridiculed "Gandy's toys" as being miniaturized

50 *Italian Landscape* (detail), ca. 1795–97
51 *A Rural Institute*, from *The Rural Architect*, 1805
52 *These Cottages Are Supposed to Be Situated near a Wood...*,
from *Designs for Cottages, Cottage Farms, and Other Rural Buildings*, 1805

restatements of the French utopian proposals by C.-N. Ledoux.[49] Gandy's pattern books were preceded the year before by Ledoux's comprehensive and lavishly illustrated treatise on the physiocratic and industrial utopia of Chaux entitled *L'Architecture considérée sous le rapport de l'art, des moeurs et de la législation* (1804). Gandy perhaps consulted the newly issued publication in Soane's library while preparing his own pattern books. Ledoux's spare and elemental designs for granges and cottages [53] may have directly influenced or simply confirmed Gandy's preference for a new architectural esthetic of linear concision and geometric abstraction. Ledoux's treatise expounds the power of architecture to inculcate moral and civil values in society through the clarity and simplicity of its building forms. Repeatedly, Ledoux insists that the acute legibility of a building's outline and the unadorned white surfaces of its façades have a terrific sensory impact that will stimulate and even determine the productive capacities of the human subject.

NATURAL ABODES OF MEN: SEPULCHERS AND COTTAGES

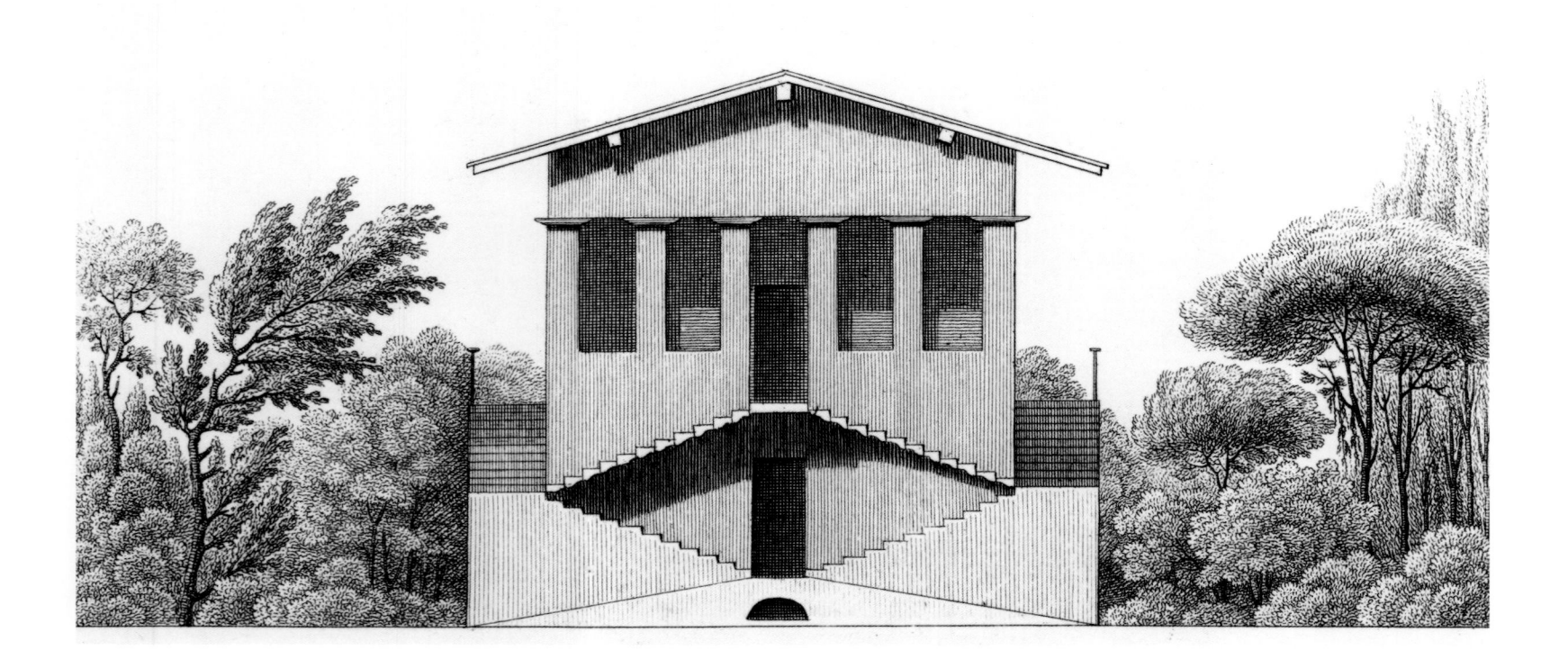

Architecture thus not only externalizes the social compact but may also be said to narrate its society. Certainly the scope of Gandy's rural architecture was not as audacious, formally or theoretically. But, like Ledoux, Gandy postulated that the purified forms and lines of his rural architecture would transmit edifying sensory inscriptions onto the *tabula rasa* of a social class unaccustomed to the esthetic and moral modification of its built environment.

It is instructive, when looking at Gandy's pattern books, to recall his letter about the dream of his descent into the infernal underworld that he wrote while en route to Italy. As already noted, the description of hell was socially specific in its evocation of late eighteenth-century London: "men over the furnaces making all sorts of utensils for the luxuries of life, such as glass, gold, &c., others again dragging heavy cranes up to lift Foreign goods from ships ... racking out his own brains for many luxuries he can do without."[50] Gandy's model cottages may be seen as a rejoinder to this vision of hell. His dream condemns the urban demand for luxury goods and imports, and the dissipation of human invention and industry within a mercantile economy. The picturesque cottage movement drew its urgency and appeal from the urban growth of the period, countering the Stygian nightmare of the industrial metropolis with the idyllic prospect of simplified model cottages set in geometric harmony within the English landscape. Like other disenchanted romantics circa 1800, Gandy conceived of the improved cottage as a refuge from the trials of the city and the political divisions of classhood and nationhood: an architecture of natural reason in which the social and the esthetic are at one. Edmund Bartell, an art critic and pattern book author from Norwich, wrote in his *Hints for Picturesque Improvements* (1804): "The cottage system, I am persuaded, need only be carried to its extent to render England indeed a paradise ... the scheme is not a visionary one."[51]

The designs in Gandy's pattern books were to remain, if not unrealizable, certainly unrealized, but their influence may be detected in subsequent pattern books, such as *Designs for Villas and Other Rural Buildings* (1808) by Edmund Aikin, who likewise dedicated his volume to the cognoscente Hope. In 1807, Gandy exhibited a design for the rebuilding of Ballon Town, Co. Carlow in Ireland, though there is no evidence that the project was actually undertaken.[52] It can be safely supposed that the design was consonant with the rural housing complexes and agrarian institutes advertised in the pattern books.

Starting in 1803, how or why is still unknown, Gandy completed renovations and expansions begun by Thomas Harrison at Lancaster Castle. Here, in the institutional building types that connoted judicial authority and social reform, specifically the county courts and prisons incorporated within the massive castellated shell of the medieval site, one can recognize his preference for hemicyclical and concentric plans.[53] His design for the female penitentiary wing, built between 1817 and 1822, was a variation on the panoptic plan for prison architecture developed in the late eighteenth century by the utilitarian philosopher Jeremy Bentham. The innovative distinction of Bentham's Panopticon was its inspection or surveillance tower around which a circular web of cells or wards was distributed. Gandy's design adopted the concentric geometry of his own Cottage of the Winds—bisected and with an inspection tower replacing the hub of privies. With utilitarian conviction, Gandy explained that "the surrounding cells [were] for promoting the industry of female convicts."[54] Both the model cottage and the panoptic prison thus sought to achieve the administrative ordering and transparent containment of the social body.

Although contemporary reviewers savaged Gandy's cottage publications, they eventually found a more receptive audience in the twentieth century. One can certainly detect a forecast of modernist design features in Gandy's elevations: the sweeping horizontality of projecting rooflines, the staccato repetition of sparse bays, the strip fenestration, and the planimetric compression of architectural shapes. Gandy's pattern books earned him inclusion in the standard architectural history survey book of the mid-twentieth century: Talbot Hamlin's *Architecture Through the Ages*, first published in 1940, in which it is claimed that "the basis of much contemporary architecture already prophetically appears [in Gandy's designs]."[55] By conflating primitivist and picturesque ideas in his pattern books, Gandy at once reexamined and redefined the precepts of architectural style and, in doing so, arrived at design proposals that retained a remarkable familiarity with later architectural developments. His inquiry into the esthetic expression of social utility in the cottage designs led to the radical, if momentary, divestment of historical reference in architecture. Gandy's pattern books belong to a futuristic primitivism, strangely detached from the social reality that presumably called them into being as well as from the stylistic plenum and whimsical relativism intrinsic to the picturesque theory of architecture to which they feigned affiliation.

The conjunction of sepulchral monumentality and experimental minimalism in Gandy's projects between 1800 and 1805 was exceptionally his own but at the same time highly characteristic of the period. Many commentators have alluded to this central paradox in late eighteenth-century European architectural thinking, for instance the Vienna School art historian Hans Sedlmayr: "A curious and somewhat cold-blooded fusion came into being between the ancient and profound on the one hand and the utopian and abstract on the other."[56] Or the literary historian and philosopher Jean Starobinski, who remarked on the contradictory obsession with "functional intentionality and funereal reverie" in the architectural imagination approaching 1800.[57] Gandy's sepulchral projects evoked with sumptuous abandon the aura of classical antiquity and, in doing so, removed the depicted designs from the realm of probability. The purified architecture of the pattern books sought to cast off that burden of antique monumentality and commemorative ritual. Gandy went from creatively mourning the past to reforming, at least hypothetically, the present-day conditions of architecture and society. Despite the ideological contradictions and utopian premises of his pattern books, they posited a radically new social architecture for Great Britain. It was an ambition, however, to which Gandy would never turn again.

53 C.-N. Ledoux, *Elevation of a Grange*, from *L'Architecture considérée sous le rapport de l'art, des moeurs et de la législation*, 1804

III: Wounded Sensibility, or Fragments of a Career

After his hazardous return from Italy and his search for employment as an architect and draftsman in London at the turn of the century, Gandy's biography offers little pronounced drama and only incidental change of scene. References to Gandy by his contemporaries are relatively few and tantalizingly sketchy. He fell into a sort of professional limbo, where he was obliged to undertake other artistic and intellectual pursuits, from antiquarian topography to architectural theory, by way of supplementing his limited achievements as a practicing architect. In the contemporary press he was heralded and lamented as an unacknowledged genius struggling at the margins of his profession and culture. Judging from his own letters and accounts of his behavior recorded by acquaintances, Gandy believed this himself. The melancholy cult of genius to which he subscribed had its disheartening parallel in the troubled life of dispossession and penury that he and his family had to endure.

Married in 1801 to Eleanor Webb, about whom nothing is known, Gandy sired nine children, three of whom died in childhood. The family resided in a series of rented properties in Soho—up and down Greek Street and just north of Oxford Street on Wells and Newman Streets, neighborhoods reputed for their transient populations of artisans and aspiring literary types. The romantic essayist Thomas de Quincey, who had lived in a brick and stucco house later occupied by the Gandys on the corner of Greek Street and Soho Square, noted with some surprise in 1821 that the residence looked more respectable and well-maintained than it had when he lived there himself.[1] Financial distress continually plagued the Gandy household, so much so that on two occasions Gandy was incarcerated for undischarged debts, in 1816 at Fleet Prison and in 1830 at Whitecroft Street Prison.

John Soane was often called upon to aid the Gandy family during these episodes of financial crisis. He was constantly giving loans to Gandy that were surely never repaid. In the journal entries and in the flurry of letters between Soane, Gandy, and Gandy's solicitor, Mr Snow, there are disturbing glimpses into the dire circumstances of the architect and his family. Soane offered guidance and professional advice to Gandy, especially in promoting and advertising his own work with prospective clients. Gandy, however, was unreceptive much of the time. In March 1816, he responded to Soane: "You have made the same remark at different times that others have done, by saying that I am too closed and reserved or not open enough ... a promise that I shall faithfully keep [is] not to let anyone see what is done in my home with respect to drawings &c."[2] That year only got worse for him. Writing to Soane in May 1816 from Lancaster, where he was working temporarily, Gandy confessed that "I never have any idle moment ... to spare from work to keep my family alive, or being destroyed in a sea of trouble," and by the next month he was back in London, "more harassed than usual and confined to my study."[3] Refusing to follow the advice of his solicitor and claim bankruptcy, he confided to Soane, "I felt myself on the threshold of perdition forever."[4] On the day of Gandy's arrest in 1816, Soane coolly recorded in his notebook, "Mrs Gandy called to say her husband had surrendered and they were all starving. Gave her £1.00."[5] From prison, Gandy wrote Soane a passionately worded letter in which exclamations of self-loathing give way to unexpected hubris:

54 *A Sketch of the Arms of Sir John Swinburne Bart. and Part of the Phoenix Office, Charing Cross*, ca. 1805

PHOENIX ✱ FIRE ✱ OFFICE

SEMEL

SEMPER

"If Genius can soar above the orb of man, it must sometimes descend into its own cage and feel for those about it, but when it is forced into a prison like Fleet, it is placed in the lowest sink of vice and depravity, its sensibility is wounded to the utmost and with death it can only pass away."[6] In the remainder of the letter, he makes observations about the distressing mixture of social classes in prison and the painful moral lessons that an architect can learn from the experience. It closes with an archaeological disquisition on the recent discovery of polychromy in ancient Greek statuary and architecture, the passage written with a lively enthusiasm that bears no relation to the querulous tone of the earlier section of the letter, with its dramatic allegorizing of the trials of Genius. After his release from prison, Gandy wrote to Soane on Christmas Day 1816 to take stock of his predicament, at which time he reaffirmed his refusal to seek employment with an established architectural firm: "I should conceive myself a slave and debased below the character of a man ... a non-entity."[7]

Much of this resentment was directed, not so subtly, toward Soane himself. Gandy's letters to his colleague and intermittent employer veer unpredictably from the sycophantic to the indignant. Soane, however, never wavered in his support and continued to give financial relief to the Gandy family for the rest of his life. The sense of dependency that Gandy felt toward Soane bred prideful displays of pique that are copiously documented in the correspondence. Soane seemed more than willing to overlook Gandy's temperamental outbursts, as his own self-regard was that of—to paraphrase from Gandy's letter quoted above—a wounded sensibility. He sympathized with Gandy's damaged pride and shared his acute dread of critical censure from colleagues and competitors. In late 1830, when Gandy again faced financial ruin, Soane offered not only monetary support but also the use of a studio in his Chelsea offices so that Gandy could find refuge from creditors and family pressures. By this time, Gandy had grown completely unmindful of his day-to-day responsibilities, his obliviousness to everything except his art serving as his best means of defense against the world. As the solicitor Snow wrote to Soane just before Gandy was thrown into debtor's prison in October of 1830, "His mind seems fully occupied with about his picture ... I wish I could bring him to a proper sense of his situation in life."[8] One month later Gandy's possessions were put up for public auction, including his library of over 400 volumes, a collection of drawings, and his own paintings (among them, an unfinished Miltonic picture).[9]

When one looks at his relations with the Royal Academy, Gandy's professional and personal struggles come into even greater relief. After the success of his youthful period of study at the RA, he naturally saw the Academy as the central forum for his artistic life and he continuously desired its prestigious recognition. In 1803, he succeeded in gaining election as an Associate of the RA, even though he had not yet secured a single commission as a practicing architect. Joseph Farington's diary recorded the quiet diplomacy, shameless petitioning, and back-stabbing gossip that attended every election, including Gandy's. Opinion before his successful election was mixed: James Wyatt and George Dance thought that he was too inexperienced as an architect to be made an ARA, while Joseph Bonomi and Robert Smirke argued that Gandy merited the promotion on the overwhelming strength of his draftsmanly skills.[10] A week after his election as ARA, Farington and the sculptor John Flaxman were still stirring the pot about Gandy's promotion, evidently dissatisfied with the favorable outcome for the young architect. As Farington recorded:

> Flaxman mentioned that Gandy while canvassing him had spoke of his situation with Soane, which caused Flaxman to ask him some particulars. He said that Soane allowed him £150 a year and behaved well to him. Gandy afterward went to Soane and repeated what had passed in such a way as to cause Soane with his usual irritability to write a warm letter to Flaxman beginning Sir and requiring to know why he put questions relative to him and his engagements &c ... So much for Gandy and a similarity to the Roman account.[11]

Gandy's alliance with the fractious Soane did not sit well with certain cliques at the RA and his rumored reputation for deviousness was therefore unfairly reinforced. Farington and Flaxman's denigration of Gandy's integrity—or particularly of his failure to keep confidences—was of course hypocritical, since their own maneuvering within the Academy relied often on spreading innuendo and divulging confidential opinions. But Farington's chillingly dismissive remark, "So much for Gandy," proved to be not entirely inaccurate. Gandy received no further promotion within the ranks of the RA. He put himself forward for election as a full academician six times between 1809 and 1820, only to receive no more than a handful of votes from his fellow academicians with the tendentious Soane as his only consistent advocate. Aside from his participation at the annual exhibitions, Gandy's other official contact with the RA involved some pleading letters to the Council of senior academicians soliciting advance payments from his pension fund in 1830 and 1831; the reason stated for these requests was "total want of professional employment."[12] The advances were granted.

The landscape painter John Constable was on the Academy Council at the time that Gandy submitted these needful requests. In a letter to his friend and confidant, the American artist C. R. Leslie, Constable addressed the question of Gandy's status within the Academy; it is the most candid of documents respecting Gandy's plight and therefore deserves to be quoted at length:

> I was at the Academy last evening at a Council—& another melancholy letter of poor Gandy's was read. It was very strangely worded—much like a person in distraction. He mentioned his having dreadful symptoms of a discharge of blood from his mouth—sometimes in quantity and always a constant spitting of it—this will I fear dispense you & me of fulfilling our proper attention. I however declared before the Council that I was shocked that such a man should never have been elected an Academician—&c that I could not myself vote for any other architect while he still breathed. This I could well say because of the extraordinary praise of his genius & which Shee, Westmacott &c, bestowed on him.
>
> I walked away with Westmacott—I then asked him if he knew of any positive reason or cause which had ever been urged to his exclusion—no answer that was intelligible. He said he was a "bad-mannerd" man—& was *rude* to any *gentleman* or *nobleman* who *found fault* with his designs— & "that he would not alter his drawings," &c. This has much enhanced Gandy with me!! I told him that I had my suspicions that he was one of the victims of Thompson's caprice—he said there "was something in that," for he added "Thompson was the Devil." ... But I have said too much on a hatefull subject—to us both.[13]

This letter takes us deep into the peculiar micro-politics and conspiratorial factions of the Royal Academy. The subject is so hateful to Constable because he knew full well of the arbitrary power and petty abuses of the Council, even though he was now a party to it. His own election as full academician came too late in his own career to be a source of satisfaction and his letters consistently disclose a profound distrust of the London art world and the fickle social dynamics of its institutions. Horrified by Gandy's intemperate description of his gruesome infirmity and yet gratified by second-hand accounts of his habitual disrespect toward eminent clients, Constable expresses both pity and admiration for this acclaimed genius (though, it should be noted, he makes no judgement of his own about Gandy's work). The remarks of the sculptor Richard Westmacott—whom Gandy had known since student days at the RA school and in Italy—interestingly focus on Gandy's obstinate resistance to moderating his architectural ideas once they were put to paper and on the compromising class frictions that undermined his ability to secure commissions. All of this remains extremely atmospheric, but not as unintelligible as Constable initially finds it. Certainly Westmacott was speaking on some authority, as he would have been reliably familiar with the downward professional trajectory of his old student friend and colleague. The final allusion to the despised Henry Thomson (not Thompson), the Keeper of the RA and an underachieving history painter, is tantalizing. Thomson had been in Rome at the same time as Gandy. When the opportunity arose he was strategically maligning Gandy as a social inferior and a republican spy to Farington just as the time when Gandy was being considered for election as an ARA.[14] The bad blood between them otherwise remains something of a mystery, though Constable and Westmacott were plainly in agreement over the grudging, ruthless nature of Thomson's character and his abuse of authority at the RA. Even before this exchange with Westmacott, Constable had tellingly referred to Gandy as "a man that has been hunted down—& that too, most cruelly and unfairly."[15]

The acclamations of Gandy's genius in Constable's letter were echoed in reviews of Gandy's drawings on display at the annual Royal Academy and British Institution exhibitions. Newspaper and architectural criticism of the day portrayed Gandy as a brilliant artist whose lavishly rendered designs languished year after year on Academy walls, an architect whose unfulfilled career stood as an indictment of a larger failure by society to express the national destiny in architectural form. The following passages from *The Morning Post* and *The Examiner* reviewing the 1808 RA exhibition are the only coverage given to the architectural drawings on display: "In architecture there is nothing very marked, if we except some models of GANDY of imaginary buildings"; "In Architecture, we have several pleasing artists, but little originality, independent of GANDY."[16] By 1819, Gandy's inactivity as a practicing architect became a concern to critics reviewing his perspective drawings; as *The Literary Gazette* reported, "turning from the picture to the man, we feel our sentiment not diminished by the regret that such powers should not have been for many a year called to contribute to the glory of the arts in England."[17] Two years later, *The Guardian*, in a scathing attack on John Soane and what its critic saw as the modern decrepitude of British architecture, offered this backhanded compliment: "We have long ceased to consider the Associate Gandy as an architect; in this case we regret it, in every other we should have rejoiced at it." A week later, the unsigned writer continued: "nothing would give us greater pleasure than to be convinced that his [Gandy's] talents in the 'real' have been as conspicuous and as splendid as they have been in the 'ideal.'"[18]

By the following decade of the 1830s, reviewers of the annual RA exhibitions began to grow fatigued by Gandy's relentless stream of imaginary architectural perspectives. As a critic wrote in 1834, "We really wish GANDY would descend a little from his ultra-classicism, ultra-poetry, and monstrous sublimities, and favor us with something approaching nearer the realities of architecture."[19] Even his sanity would be called into question. A writer for J. C. Loudon's *Architectural Magazine* remarked in 1837 on Gandy's lifelong compulsion to exhibit his architectural fantasies, observing that "Gandy possesses a superabundance of imagination, yet of the most ill-regulated sort, and almost, in fact, to the exclusion of common sense."[20]

The most impassioned and controversial appraisal of Gandy's lifework and reputation appeared in the Whig newspaper the *Morning Chronicle* as part of a review of the 1832 RA exhibition. Without commenting specifically on Gandy's drawings for that year, the critic launched into this lengthy diatribe:

> To say that in this country "everything is a job" is, to use household words, an accepted thing, a submission, and a suffering. Had it been otherwise, Mr Gandy would not in the building mania have been so shamefully overlooked. Modern times has given birth to no such genius in design as this man, as extraordinary in his talent as in the neglect he has experienced; while meaner architects, begging, borrowing, or stealing from him, have risen on the ruins that their barbarous ignorance and misapplication have produced. In truth, Mr Gandy should have lived in other climes during the palmy days of architecture. "Exegi monumentum" would have no vain boast in him; but it was unhappily his lot to fall on an evil soil! England, with all its wealth, never knew how to use it with that classic feeling for grace, beauty, and poetry

which forms the Corinthian capital of all the proudest State can leave behind it. Innumerable have been the designs of this admirable artist—often magnificent, it is true, beyond the means of society to execute, but not beyond the power of the Nashes and others to plunder and profit by. It is grievous to behold the unjust division of the spoils—here we have pieces which no other architect in England could have conceived, or would have attempted to produce.[21]

Gandy's ill-fated career is here elevated to the level of a national disgrace. The metropolitan improvements of London during the 1820s— guided by the entrepreneurial architect and royal favorite John Nash—are symbolic, our critic argues, not of the supremacy of Great Britain after Waterloo but rather of the country's fundamental unworthiness to inherit the classical tradition. Removed from the contemporary venality of his society, Gandy's grandiose visions belong more properly to another epoch and another civilization. His imaginary architecture thus reprimands the depravity of present-day building practices and their diminished cultural status. Gandy must have felt momentarily vindicated by this journalistic clamor.

In the earlier part of his career, Gandy's architectural practice had not been entirely desolate. Although meager in number, his few commissions resulted in accomplished and even original buildings within the context of late Georgian neo-classicism and the Greek Revival. His first was ironically his only prominent work to be erected in London: the Phoenix Fire and Pelican Life Insurance Offices built in 1804–05 at Charing Cross, facing what would become Trafalgar Square [55]. Confined to a narrow urban site, the architect was faced with the difficulty of integrating classical orders into a commercial building façade while also creating some suggestion of architectural projection and recession. The superimposed arrangement of paired orders, surmounted by avian corporate symbols, is applied to the brick and dressed stone façade. It serves as a subdividing classical scaffold set before an otherwise stock Georgian row. But by raising the two sets of paired Doric columns on an oversized plinth and by having above them Ionic members support a heavy blank entablature—surely these are instances of modernizing the antique—Gandy brings both an aggressively tec-

55 Charing Cross elevation of the Phoenix Fire and
Life Insurance Co., London. Built 1805, demolished 1924
56 Spring Gardens elevation of the Phoenix Fire and
Life Insurance Co., London. Built 1805, demolished 1924

tonic severity and a dense sculptural richness to the design of the building. The Spring Gardens elevation [56], on the other hand, tends toward a more suave restraint, its façade etched away in shallow relief with Ionic pilasters and decorative urns framing the central bay mirroring the composition of the commercial frontage. The preference seen here for scored linear window surrounds, blank strip pilasters, and unadorned horizontal panels betrays the influence of John Soane, whose unique style sought to fuse ornament and structure in a novel manner. In 1915, *The Builder* singled out Gandy's first building as an ingenious exception to "the illiterate versions of the Orders" that dominated London architecture.[22] Unfortunately, this praise did not save the building from demolition in 1924. Gandy also gave this design some breathing space in a fanciful watercolor sketch that transfigured the façade of the insurance office into a monumental arcaded screen resembling an aqueduct [54].[23]

Gandy's erudite though unconventional application of the classical orders recurs even more emphatically at the so-called Doric House in Bath, built for the portraitist and landscape painter Thomas Barker. Exhibits at the RA for this project span from 1803 to 1818, in addition to a line engraving published in 1807; the gallery and house were probably built around 1805.[24] Overlooking the Royal Crescent from Sion Hill, the

57 Side and rear elevations of Doric House, Bath, 1803–06
58 Egyptian Revival mantel in the Picture Gallery at Doric House, Bath
59 Cavendish Place elevation of Doric House, Bath, 1803–06

building occupies a steep wedge-shaped site that presented a challenge unto itself. The main elevation facing Cavendish Place comprises a slightly recessed wall behind detached, unfluted Doric columns with an attic story composed of the same colonnade on a smaller scale [57, 59]. This transposition of the interior cella of a Greek temple onto an exterior façade of a contemporary building has been deemed by one architectural historian as "an archaeological joke" at the expense of the Temple of Poseidon at Paestum—the classical, and ruggedly primitivizing, prototype being referenced by Gandy's building.[25] If theoretical purists such as Laugier had been exercised by the conjunction of wall and column in post-classical architecture, Gandy seemed not at all reluctant to turn a temple inside out so as to arrive at a more modern usage of the orders. By introducing a modillioned cornice between the stories and by stripping the Doric frieze of its traditional decoration, the architect disregards both archaeological accuracy and rationalist dogma. As with the Phoenix offices, Gandy explores the visual and tectonic tension between planarity and relief. The pedimented end of the main block housing the gallery has the same linear banding and vertical panels that were Soane's stylistic signatures, even down to the acroterial flourishes. The curvilinear projection of the apsidal drawing room adjacent to the building's main cube sets up a striking juxtaposition of volumetric geometries. The interior treatment is understated with stock moldings and blank walls, although the picture gallery is distinguished by a Hope-style Egyptian Revival fireplace mantle and surround [58]. Despite the modest scale and formal subtlety of Doric House, its overall effect remains extremely sobering, even somewhat forbidding. However, the antiquarian topographer John Britton, whose association with Gandy will be broached shortly, designated Doric House in 1850 as a notable landmark in the architectural history of Bath, applauding it as "this commodious and handsome house on the romantic slope of Sion Hill."[26]

The vanguard application of the Doric order remained Gandy's architectural signature in his work at Storrs Hall on Lake Windermere. From 1804 until 1806, Gandy designed a boat-house and renovated a small octagonal temple at Storrs for the property's first owner, Sir John Legard, and its new purchaser, John Bolton, who acquired the property in 1806.[27] Bolton was a powerful Liverpool merchant with holdings in the slave trade—a proper denizen of Gandy's particular

60 *A Boat-House for Sir J. Legard, Bart., on the Lake Windermere*, 1804
61 Thomas Harwood, *View of Storrs, Windermere Lake*, in W. H. Pyne, *Lancashire Illustrated*, 1831

64 JOSEPH GANDY

hell from his nightmare en route to Italy. The ambitious proposal for the boat-house, never realized as designed, is seen in a dramatic perspective exhibited at the RA in 1804 [60]: a Greek Doric peripteral temple, its stone foundation cut away and its inter-columniation broken to provide a slip for a vessel's shelter. The design is once again a study in architectural primitivism evident in the projecting eaves, exposed roof beams, blank entablature, and truncated entasis of the order. The Temple of Poseidon at Paestum remains the primary model (Gandy's triton sculptures are allusive in this respect), though Inigo Jones's St. Paul's at Covent Garden is also being sampled. The visual impression of the compressive strength of the building is heightened by the turbulent atmosphere of the landscape backdrop: the storm-streaked sky and broken sunlight played against the brutishly emergent forms of classical architecture. The masonry octagonal temple or prospect pavilion at Storrs built by Legard and remodeled by Gandy is a far less adventurous effort. Although it still survives, the structure is best understood in the picturesque context of an early nineteenth-century topographic engraving of Lake Windermere. This "Temple of

WOUNDED SENSIBILITY, OR FRAGMENTS OF A CAREER 65

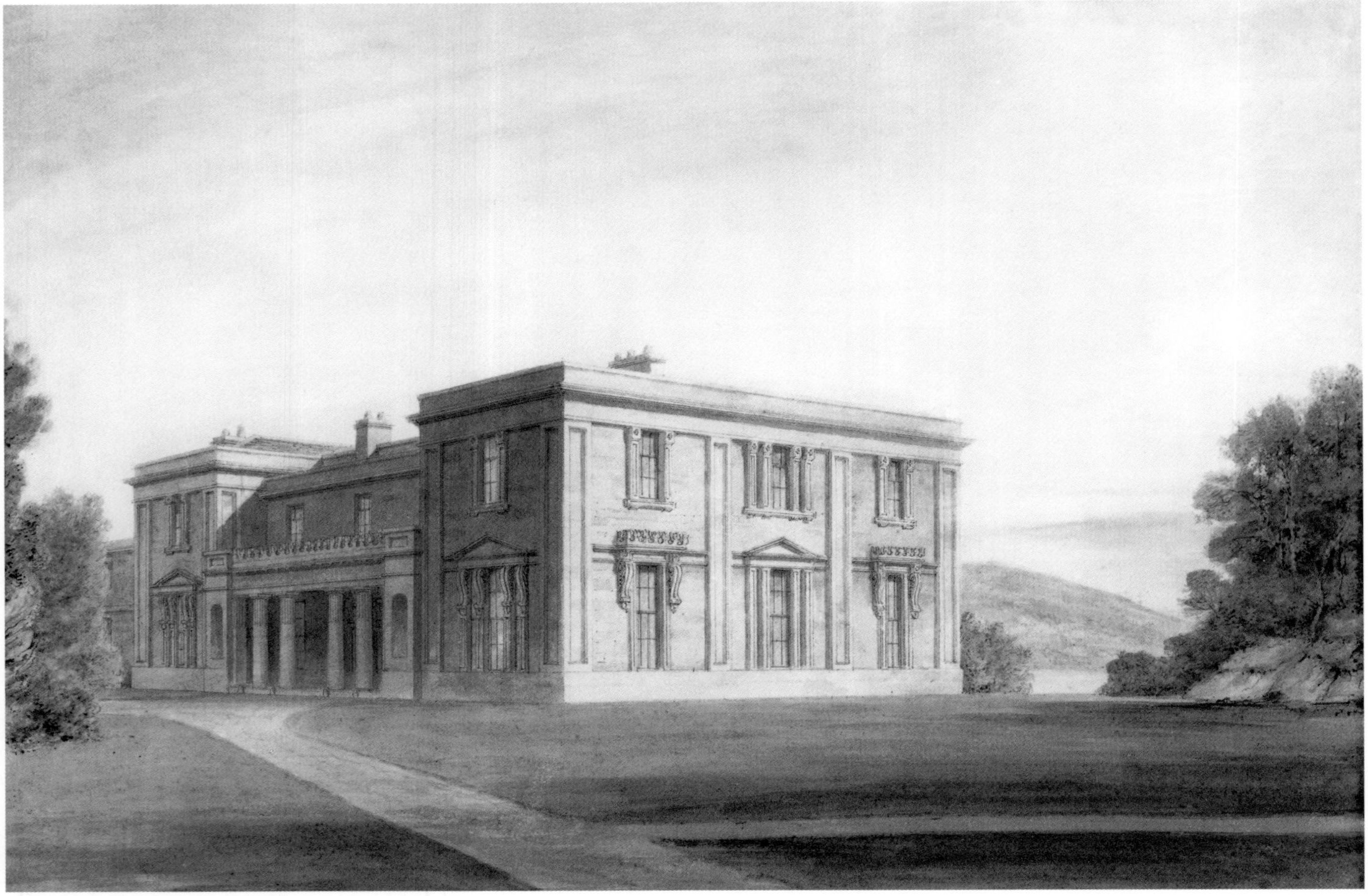

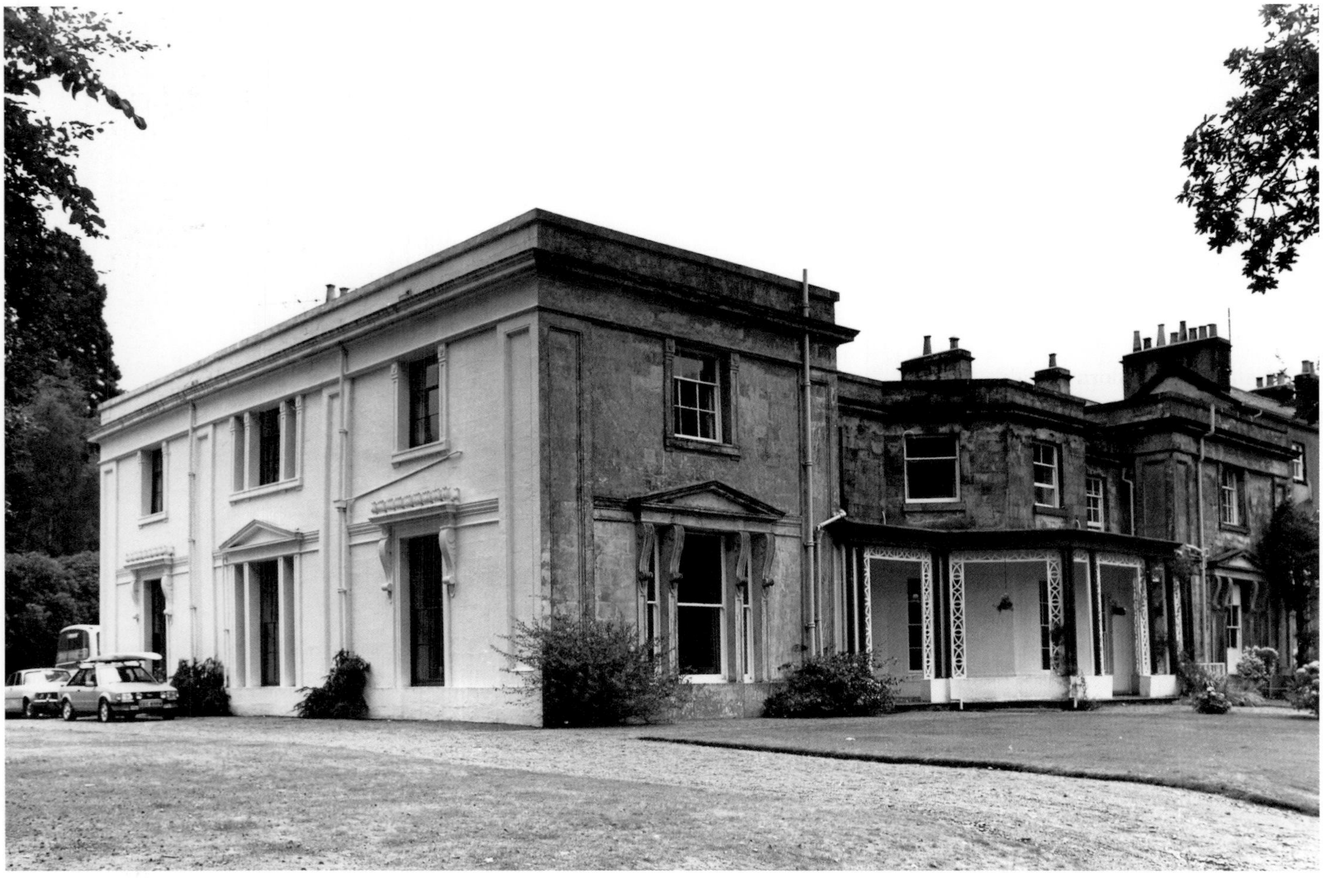

the Heroes" was little more than a pavilion and landing situated at the end of a causeway. Gandy's contribution was a raised parapet to give the temple greater scale and verticality; he was probably responsible for adding the crenellation to the causeway. Dedicated in patriotic honor of the great British admirals of the Napoleonic Wars, this modest undemonstrative building stood in Lilliputian mockery of Gandy's extravagant designs for Cartwright's Hieronauticon. The construction of the "little naval temple" elicited sly protests from the journalist John Wilson, the widely read "Christopher North" from *Blackwood's Magazine*, who authored this doggerel regarding the monument: "Plaything of art, it venture thus to stand/ 'Mid the great forms of Nature. Doth it seem/ A vain intruder in the quiet heart/ Of this majestic lake?"[28] However, for topographers like Thomas Harwood, who rendered the view of Lake Windermere for *Lancashire Illustrated* (1831) [61] reproduced here, the temple, rather than desecrating the placid landscape, gave it greater visual incident of shadow and outline.

From 1806 until 1811, Gandy was engaged by Bolton to remodel and expand the main house.[29] The pristine appearance of Storrs Hall soon after the remodeling is recorded in a topographic watercolor of 1814 by John C. Buckler [62]. Gandy's design survives relatively intact, even though Storrs was converted into a hotel in 1892, which it remains to this day [63]. The entrance façade is demarcated by a Greek Doric loggia, the orders now treated with stopped fluting, a modification of the Doric made familiar through late eighteenth-century engravings of the so-called gladiator's courtyard at Pompeii. Although Storrs in many ways maintained the severity of style already established at Doric House—noticeable especially in the unadorned pilaster strips that turn the corners and in the cubic rectitude of the side wings—there is nevertheless an unexpected attention to ornament, albeit of a slightly bizarre kind. Lotus-blossom antefixae march atop the loggia and also form window hoods on the south elevation, while triple windows are adorned with attenuated scroll brackets and blank pediments. These ornamental accents and window treatments appear over-scaled in relation to the compact reticence of the building's general composition. They also simulate a Gothic intricacy that would have been perceived as giving picturesque variety to the symmetry of the house. The one storey projection on the garden elevation—

later converted to a verandah—likewise has a Gothicizing aspect. The main feature of the interior is a compact though elegant rotunda with a segmental arched entrance, curved doorways with uniform architraves, and a circular balustraded gallery [64]. The scrolled console brackets supporting the gallery echo those used on the exterior window and door surrounds, while the lantern dome is distinguished by intricate polychrome glazing. The space is crisply defined with an unfolding sense of transparency, but the ornamental mouldings retain

62 John Buckler, *Northwest View of Storrs*, 1814
63 Garden elevation of Storrs Hall, Lake Windermere
64 Interior rotunda of Storrs Hall, Lake Windermere

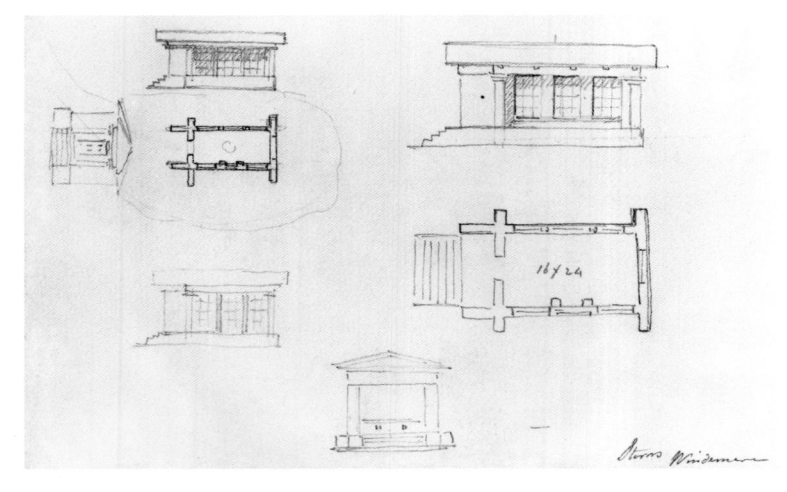

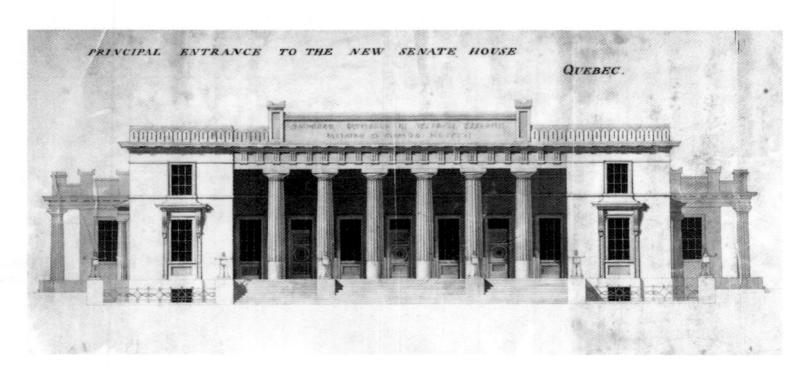

some of the swollen and heavily modeled aspects of the façade's decorative treatment.

A sketchbook by Gandy, dated September 1806, contains designs for a more complicated array of estate buildings and decorative structures for the grounds at Storrs [65, 66], including a miniature Greek temple-like summerhouse, an aedicular garden seat, and "a druidical temple" for a nearby island, none of which came to fruition.[30] A gate lodge survives on the property that bears the hallmarks of Gandy's design. Its corner pilasters with sunken blank panels and its recessed screen of Greek Doric columns (rendered in wood with stopped fluting) carry on the primitivist tendencies of the boat-house design, the pattern book cottages, and the reductive gate lodges of Soane. Storrs Hall was received as a distinctive country seat and show-house of the Lake Country, as Bolton was fond of entertaining Tory politicos such as George Canning and literary celebrities such as Wordsworth and Scott in near-ceremonial splendor. Writing in 1830 about an excursion on Windermere, the opinionated John Wilson now hymned Storrs Hall for its scenic habitude: "let us put about for a fine view of the Grecian edifice. It does honour to the genius of Gandy—and say what people choose of a classic clime, the light of a Westmoreland sky falls beautifully and majestically on that marble-like stone."[31]

Although journalists and reviewers often noted the discrepancy between the profuse magnificence of Gandy's drawings and the paucity of his actual commissions, Storrs Hall was unusual in that it provided the template for other more speculative projects by Gandy. He reapplied the design of Storrs, for example, to his 1811–12 proposal for a new senate house or parliamentary building for Quebec [67].[32] The entrance façade is a monumental restatement of Storrs with the loggia transformed into a full-dress Greek Doric portico in antis. The stylistic tendency toward both archaicizing reduction and decorative animation was revisited for this unexecuted and ambitious design of a civic public building. Similarly, an undated architectural capriccio by Gandy that depicts a piazza and fountain bounded by a sweeping Doric peristyle may also be seen as an imaginative enhancement of the more modest architectural reality of the entrance loggia at Storrs Hall [68].

There were moments in Gandy's troubled career when he sought to galvanize his professional life as a practicing architect. In 1809, he moved to Liverpool to set up office with the cabinet-maker and sculptor George Bullock. Bullock had high expectations about the partnership, describing Gandy as "a clever man ... whose professional abilities and

65 *Storrs Sketchbook with Proposed Summerhouse*, 1806
66 *Storrs Sketchbook with Proposed Druid Temple*, 1806
67 *Design for a New Senate House at Quebec*, 1811
68 *Imaginary Architectural Design Based on Storrs Hall*, ca. 1810–15

WOUNDED SENSIBILITY, OR FRAGMENTS OF A CAREER 69

system of business will enable me to conduct and accomplish everything I wish."³³ Gandy and Bullock shared a passion for the ornamental symbolism of Greco-Roman decor in architecture and interior design. They also saw themselves as cultural advocates for the fine arts in Liverpool and the northwest. Cultivating the support of the Mayor of Liverpool and hoping to attract the patronage of Henry Blundell of Ince Blundell, Gandy and Bullock along with portraitist William Allan and architect John Foster made plans to rejuvenate the Liverpool Academy of the Arts. While in Liverpool, Gandy also had two students articled to him: Richard Elland, who exhibited two designs after him at the RA in 1809–10, and John Soane Jr., the younger, ailing son of Soane, who had nurtured vain hopes that he would spawn a dynasty of architects. The designs produced by Gandy at this time show a penchant for decorative experimentation in both ancient and modern building types. The younger Soane exhibited a design for a public bath at the RA in 1811 that may safely be assumed to be entirely the work of Gandy [69]. The visually dramatic division of light and shade and the application of the massive Doric order—visible in the intervening colonnade between the foreground quadrangle of the outdoor bath and the distant temple courtyard—immediately reveal Gandy's hand; the composition is broadly a throwback to his student *concorso* perspective. The monochrome porphyry of the architecture is enlivened by scored decoration, especially in the elongated Greek fret pattern and abstracted plant

69 John Soane Jr., *Design for a Public Bath*, 1811
70 *Interior of a New Ball and Assembly-room Surrounded by a Promenade, Designed for the Town of Liverpool*, 1810

forms on the piers and buttressing of the atrium. Here Gandy was simulating, almost to the point of exaggeration, the style of the senior Soane, who often brought a complex linear mode of inscribed ornament to the surfaces of his architecture. Although these decorative elements have parallels in the publications by Hope and Tatham of Greco-Roman-styled ornament, Gandy's treatment also anticipates later tendencies in architectural decoration of the French Neo-Grecs and even Art Nouveau.

Gandy's concern with decorative splendor of a more fashionably contemporary kind during this period in Liverpool also distinguishes his 1810 RA exhibit *Interior of a New Ball and Assembly-room Surrounded by a Promenade, Designed for the Town of Liverpool* [70].[34] This design conflates, on a comparatively diminutive scale, two of the most celebrated interiors of public pleasure architecture in mid-eighteenth-century London: the Ranelagh Rotunda, designed by William Jones in the 1740s, and the Oxford Street Pantheon, designed by James Wyatt in 1769–72. Although these metropolitan resorts belonged to the prior generation, Gandy knowingly played upon their notoriety in conceiving of this architectural essay in Regency opulence. His taste for elaborate Greek Revival decor for interior furnishings, in the style of Thomas Hope and Gaetano Landi, was partially realized in designs for cast-iron stoves that equipped the Dining Room Saloon and Assembly Rooms in the Liverpool Town Hall.[35] If he had repeatedly proven himself as an adherent to architectural primitivism, Gandy was also quite capable of producing designs in which the architectural environment was one of sensuous artifice and modish display.

Gandy's relocation to Liverpool proved short-lived, as by early 1811 he and his family had returned to London and were residing back on Greek Street. The younger Soane's apprenticeship was cut short due to the pupil's ill health and intellectual apathy. The partnership with Bullock had reached an impasse over Gandy's refusal to become a member of the Liverpool Academy, which would have necessitated his resignation from the RA in London. Gandy valued the mantle and prestige of the RA over the professional advancement and economic promise of his newly established business enterprise with Bullock. Legal entanglements with Liverpool business investors over payment for designs of the ballroom and a billiard room also troubled him. Apart from the ongoing completion of Thomas Harrison's designs for Lancaster Castle Gaol and County Courts [71], the remainder of Gandy's architectural practice was limited to renovations of Georgian villas and townhouses, small scale and fairly inconsequential projects that were spread out sparsely over the teens and 1820s.[36] After 1830, the RA exhibits by Gandy are bereft of reference to architectural commissions or feasible building proposals.[37]

Despite its pattern of disappointment and wasted potential, Gandy's career had a prevailing influence on the professional aspirations of his own family. His younger brothers Michael and John Peter followed in his footsteps by becoming students and assistants of James Wyatt. Gandy's involvement in his siblings' student training in Wyatt's office and at the RA was at times even compromising in nature. When Michael Gandy submitted a design for the Silver Medal in architecture at the RA in 1797 the drawing was removed from competition by the judges because the elder brother's hand was discerned.[38] Michael Gandy subsequently went into naval service, became a skilled topographic delineator, and spent the majority of his career with the architectural firm of Jeffry Wyatville. John Peter established himself as a proponent of the Greek Revival with credentials both as an archaeological draftsman/researcher and architect. He collaborated with Sir William Gell on definitive scholarly publications on ancient Greek architecture such as *Unedited Antiquities of Attica* (1817) and a more popularizing volume on the excavations at Pompeii entitled *Pompeiana* (1819). While traveling in Asia Minor and Greece in 1812, John Peter wrote to Joseph and described the imposing visual impact of the Athenian acropolis while chastising himself, "How much I hate myself for not drawing so well as you."[39] However, he enjoyed greater success as a practicing architect than did his elder brother, primarily in assisting William Wilkins with the prominent Greek Revival designs of the University Club and College, London. In 1828, he assumed the surname of Deering, after receiving the inheritance and estate of a wealthy friend in Buckinghamshire, and thereafter withdrew from professional life.

71 Lancaster Crown Court and Shire Hall, Castle Park, Lancaster, begun by Thomas Harrison, completed by Joseph Gandy, 1803–10

Regardless of his early retirement from architectural practice, Gandy Deering was promoted to a full RA in 1838, an honor repeatedly and unfairly denied his older brother. An 1850 obituary took note of this injustice, observing with irony, "He [Gandy Deering] was fond of his art, and if he had been a poorer man would have become more distinguished in it."[40]

Joseph Gandy's own children also undertook pursuits in the fine arts. His daughters Celia and Hannah practiced still-life painting, exhibiting works at the RA in the late 1820s and 1830s. Gandy's son Thomas was one of his architecture students along with the miniature painter Charles Woodley during the mid-1820s. He exhibited works after his father's designs at the RA, including a cork model of a sepulchral church in the exhibition of 1824 that was acclaimed in the press. A reviewer for *The European Magazine* cited the lengthy and pedantic title of the exhibit, which included citations from the Book of Kings and Villalpando on the Temple of Solomon, and proclaimed the model to be "impressively grand in the aggregate."[41] Thomas Gandy was also among the team of young artists employed by the topographer and entrepreneur Thomas Hornor to take on the perilous job of painting the enormous panorama of London in the Regent Park Colosseum in 1828–29. This ambitious spectacle, housed in a custom-designed rotunda by Decimus Burton, was plagued by financial and technical difficulties, though contemporary accounts of the state-of-the-art panorama marveled at both the transcriptive accuracy and breathtaking perspective of the metropolitan landscape.[42] Despite this training in architecture and architectural painting, Thomas switched to portrait painting in the 1830s, practicing first in Plymouth and later in London. In the last surviving letters of Joseph Gandy, dated from March to September of 1837 and addressed to Thomas, he encouraged his son to become familiar with political affairs, noting their acute relevance to the fine arts, while also urging him "to write on the theory and practice of painting."[43] Family legend maintains that Thomas Gandy forbade his children from entertaining any artistic ambitions in light of the errant careers that both he and his father had experienced.[44]

Joseph Gandy was compelled, both by need and by inclination, to diversify his own artistic and professional roles. Because of his graphic skills in architectural rendering and landscape watercolor painting, he frequently contributed to the wealth of antiquarian topographic images in British visual culture and publishing during the Napoleonic period. The recovery of the medieval architectural heritage of Great Britain assumed national importance during the historically tumultuous years following the French Revolution and during the Anglo-French Wars. As a commentator in *The Anti-Jacobin Review* argued in 1808, "Works of topography make us better acquainted with every thing which exists in our native land, and are therefore conducive to the progress of real knowledge, to the diffusion of rational patriotism, and to virtuous sentiments."[45] Attuned to both the scientific requirements of antiquarian description and the picturesque modes of landscape representation, Gandy found a commercial market for his skills as a graphic technician of architecture in the rapidly expanding field of antiquarian scholarship. His association with John Britton, the leading proponent of the antiquarian topography of medieval architecture, was especially productive.

As the prime mover in antiquarian research and publishing during the late Georgian and early Victorian periods, Britton brought a commercial eagerness and a democratizing educational mission to the study and documentation of the medieval past.[46] Gandy's early contact with Britton came through two likely routes: Britton acted as a personal advisor and collecting consultant to Soane, and his political affiliations with the radical reformist circle of John Thelwall and the London Corresponding Society brought him into the orbit of Major Cartwright. Britton established an informal antiquarian academy of topographers and architects (including Gandy, Samuel Prout, A. C. Pugin, Frederick Mackenzie, and W. H. Bartlett) in his suburban villa in St. Pancras, London. In 1825, Gandy described the hectic cottage industry in antiquarian publishing at Britton's residence, noting that he had to navigate through "a squadron of six draftsmen operating there." He took the occasion to pose a hypothetical question to the enterprising Britton. "'Let us imagine ourselves travelling in the further parts of Hindoostan amongst the Himalay mountains, if you please, whence the origin of the Hindoo architecture had its rise; what would be the first thing to do if we met with a similarly collected group of antiquities?' Mr B answered, 'Measure and make all the drawings possible and publish them.'"[47] A book reviewer confidently asserted in 1826, "Mr Britton has contributed more than any other person to the illustration of our architectural antiquities," while also forecasting that these publications would justifiably inspire "our national liberality" and spur on a preservation movement devoted to "medieval treasures and national edifices."[48]

Gandy contributed to two of Britton's serial omnium-gatherums of medieval topography, *The Architectural Antiquities of Great Britain* (1807–26) and *The Cathedral Antiquities of England* (1814–35). For the former, Gandy prepared detailed sketches and drawings of the renowned Scottish fifteenth-century architectural landmark of Rosslyn Chapel. The site was steeped in Freemasonic lore and had been celebrated in the final canto of Sir Walter Scott's "The Lay of the Last Minstrel" (1805). Its romantic and mystical associations also made the chapel a popular subject of picturesque travelogues and illusionistic dioramas of the period.[49] Gandy first recorded Rosslyn Chapel in an 1806 sketchbook that contains measured drawings and notations about the building plan and the diversity of ornamental forms that made the chapel so stylistically distinctive in the minds of antiquaries and architectural historians such as Britton, who had noted that the site "awakened the enthusiasm of Mr Gandy's genius, and he did not leave the spot till he had stored his sketch book with all the architectural parts of the chapel as well as general views of the surrounding scenery."[50]

Gandy exhibited two views of Rosslyn at the RA in 1807 and 1809 (with verse citations from Scott's "Lay" in the full titles), neither of which has come to light, though the 1809 interior of the Lady Chapel and the entrance to the crypt survives in a copy by the topographic watercolorist George Shepherd. This interior perspective reappeared in engraved form, along with thirteen other views, plans, and decorative details, in the third volume of Britton's *Architectural Antiquities* (1812) [72–74]. Britton's analysis of Rosslyn focused on the anachronistic uniqueness of the building, as evidenced by its unclassifiable combination of overcharged ornament and primitive solidity. The notable lack of repetition in the carved foliated motifs of column capitals and in the decorative patterns of the pinnacles at Rosslyn was deemed especially significant by Britton in evaluating the exceptionally fanciful and inventive quality of the monument. He cited Gandy's opinion that the stylistic variety of the arches and traceries of the chapel represented "a combination of Egyptian, Grecian, Roman, and Sarasenic styles."[51] Rosslyn, in Gandy's mind, marked the convergence of multiple historical idioms of architecture, as though to redeem it from being merely a late medieval eccentricity that defied the stylistic terms of periodization, which had vexed systematically minded antiquaries and scholars of medieval architecture. In keeping with the empirical zeal of antiquarian topography, Britton's commentary grants little historical cogency to the mystical legends of Freemasonry surrounding Rosslyn but recounts them nonetheless, including the master-mason of the chapel murdering his apprentice in envy over the design of the "apprentice's column"—the distinctive shaft with the serpentine decoration prominently visible in Gandy's view of the chapel. In addition, there is the hallowed lineage of Rosslyn's commissioners, the Lords of Rosslyn and the St. Clairs, who were credited with introducing the mysteries of Freemasonry to Scotland. According to local lore, the night before a St. Clair dies, the chapel appears, as Britton reported, "all in flames, without sustaining any injury."[52] The engravings after Gandy's drawings have a crackling, highly textured chiaroscuro that allows for the close articulation of architectural and sculptural detail requisite of such publications while also affecting a spatial and atmospheric moodiness appropriate to the poetical superstitions and historical legends of the monument.

72 J. Burnett after Gandy, *Rosslyn Chapel, Interior View*, from Britton's Architectural Antiquities, 1812
73 W. Woolnoth after Gandy, *Rosslyn Chapel, View of Buttresses and Pinnacles*, from Britton's Architectural Antiquities, 1812
74 J. Burnett after Gandy, *Rosslyn Chapel, Elevation of Part of the South Side*, from Britton's Architectural Antiquities, 1812

In a testy letter to Britton written while he was working and residing in Liverpool, Gandy complained vociferously about the accuracy and technique of the engravings executed after his drawings of Rosslyn Chapel. Playing the temperamental genius to the hilt, Gandy exhorted his patron about what were, after all, a few book illustrations among many in a multi-volume series: "They would ruin a reputation. If it is possible take my name from them. I am ashamed to see it so much disgraced."[53] In his letters to Britton, Gandy often complained about not receiving more timely or even any replies from the antiquarian, which suggests that Britton often thought it best simply to ignore his prickly correspondent. One wonders whether Britton had Gandy in mind when he wrote to Soane in 1809 about the psychology and character traits of those in the artistic profession, "The croakers, querulous, and discontented ... too many artists are of this description."[54] To be fair, Britton himself conformed to this psychological profile, as A. W. N. Pugin noted unsympathetically in 1834 after meeting with the antiquarian: "[He] complains of want of encouragement, wishes he never had attached himself to Literary pursuits ... with the exclamation of horrid bad times."[55]

Despite Gandy's professed dissatisfaction with his contribution to Britton's *Architectural Antiquities*, their collaboration continued through two decades. Gandy provided drawings of the considerably less refined and less poetical Barfreston Church, Kent, for the fourth volume of *Architectural Antiquities* (1817) and watercolors for the evocative views of

76 JOSEPH GANDY

the choir of Exeter Cathedral [75, 76] that were adapted for an installment of *Cathedral Antiquities* (1826). Gandy's own calling card from the 1820s [78] confirms his affiliation with Britton's publishing empire in medieval antiquities (unprofitable though it may have been), as its design bore the motif of an arch with trefoil and egg-and-dart moldings very similar in treatment to the portals adorning the frontispieces of Britton's volumes [77].

It is telling, however, that for the elaborate frontispiece to Britton's paean to the modern history of British art and architecture, a folio volume entitled *The Fine Arts of the British School* (1812), Gandy produced an imaginary design for a National Institution of Fine Arts that was thoroughly Greco-Roman in style [79]. In the book's introduction, Britton clarified the contemporary historical incentive for this patriotic survey of the fine arts in Britain and its proposal for a new institution of the arts: "In spite of the raging devastations of war, the much regretted

75 *View of Bishop Bronscombe's Monument, Exeter Cathedral*, 1825
76 *East End of South Aisle of Choir at Exeter Cathedral*, 1825
77 J. Le Keux after F. Mackenzie, *Lullington Church, North Doorway*, from Britton's Architectural Antiquities, 1812
78 Joseph Gandy's calling card, ca. 1820

WOUNDED SENSIBILITY, OR FRAGMENTS OF A CAREER 77

cabal of party-politicians, and the serious privations which Englishmen must endure from these joint calamities, the present time is chosen for the commencement of a work devoted to peace, to the refinements of polished life, and to the pleasures of intellect."[56] Although Britton's antiquarian scholarship had perpetuated the ideal of the Gothic as a national British style of architecture, the utopian vision of a new arts academy for Great Britain was here clothed in antique attire. Gandy's Ionic courtyard and cultural acropolis had an immaculate grandeur that was far removed from the musty topography and trying documentation of medieval ruins.

Gandy of course realized that he could ill-afford not to participate in the Gothic Revival. The interior finishing that he brought to Thomas Harrison's civil court at Lancaster Castle from 1803 onward demonstrated a mastery of intricate medieval decoration in the ornate Gothic plasterwork and canopied screen of that impressive chamber, while his 1804–08 renovations for Bolton Abbey, John Bolton's Lancashire country residence, demolished in 1959, featured a castellated Gothic style [80]. While in Liverpool, he produced a set of Gothic Revival church designs entailing cast-iron roof construction and detailing that may have been related to the local ecclesiastical projects of Thomas Rickman and John Foster.[57] There are also hints that Gandy was planning to emulate Britton by assembling his own topographic research on medieval architecture for publication. In 1821, Britton wrote to Gandy announcing his intention of visiting him, "to learn something of your progressive collections for Castles, etc."[58] Gandy was perhaps undertaking a survey of castle ruins for a future topographic volume. A set of watercolors from 1816 documents his sketching campaign at the Norman battlements of Pevensey Castle, Sussex [81, 82]. They range from a dramatic view of the weathered skyline of the tower keep and its adjacent ruins to a tunnel-vision perspective of the massively

78 JOSEPH GANDY

vaulted entry passage of the castle. The on-site sketches have a subdued palette of sandy dun and windswept blue-gray perfectly suited to both the crumbling ruins and the unsettled weather. Similarly, his topographic rendering of Conway Castle [84], printed as an aquatint in Thomas Compton's *The North Cambrian Mountains; or a Tour Through North Wales* (1820), and his 1825 watercolor of Richborough Castle, Kent [83], impart to the feudal sites the epic appearance of labyrinthine earthworks. In an 1816 letter to Soane, Gandy summarized his recent travels throughout Great Britain and gave recommendations for particular sites of commanding interest to the architectural imagination. "I wish I could travel with you," he observed to Soane, "my ready hand, and your mind, would be perhaps useful; but pardon the presumption, I am teaching what I want to be taught."[59] Despite this humbling tone, Gandy's thumbnail travelogue to Soane placed special emphasis on his expert archaeological detection of classical methods of construction at the feudal battlements that he was cataloguing. Conway was remarkable because of "its cyclopian walls, yes cyclopean … as in Greece," while the masonry and tile work at Pevensey was recognized as Roman, thereby making the monument a stratified historical record of both the Roman occupation and the Norman yoke. For Gandy (and in his mind for Soane as well), the medieval architectural vestiges of Great Britain were most fascinating and instructive for the submerged traces of a classical past that could be uncovered or divined. Gandy's sensitivity to landscape and conditions of light and atmosphere was no less important on these travels, for in separate letters to Britton and Soane he wrote of surveying Conway at sunrise and sunset "enraptured … by effects lively, strong, magical," promising that "you will frequently enjoy the sublime."[60]

His acute responsiveness to landscape topography and the transient conditions of nature is also revealed in over 175 small-scale watercolor sketches from the late 1810s and 1820s that have no apparent relation to antiquarian publications.[61] The inscriptions on these drawings allow us to chart Gandy's travels around the outskirts of London, along the Thames, through Sussex, and down to the southeast coast. Some

79 J. Le Keux after Gandy, *Design for a National Institution of the Fine Arts*, from Britton's *The Fine Arts of the British School*, 1812
80 *Entrance Façade of Bolton Abbey, Lancashire*, remodeled by Gandy, ca. 1804–08
81 *Pevensey Castle, Tower Keep*, 1816
82 *Pevensey Castle, Entrance Passage*, 1816
83 *Richborough Castle, Kent*, 1825

sequences of watercolours document an afternoon's worth of topographic sketching. Although many of the landscapes focus on the quintessentially picturesque aspects of English village scenery [85–92], a large number also depict urban, suburban, and industrial topography. The dark London skyline is glimpsed from the rural enclave of Peckham Rye. New suburban estates are recorded along the coastal landscapes between Brighton and Ramsgate. The mines, forges, and kilns of Purfleet and Coalbrookedale—ravaged and worn landscapes—figure prominently in some series of watercolors. Gandy's drawings often bear notations indicating the time of day or night that the view was observed and rendered: a twilit landscape of the enclosed commons at Milton, a late afternoon stormy landscape rent by a flash of lightning, or unidentified nocturnes with distinctive atmospheric phenomena seen in the scarlet dyeing of early evening clouds or in the moon encircled by a hazy pink nimbus. The science and poetry of meteorology is often the primary focus of these optically alert drawings. Antiquarian and landscape topography allowed Gandy to observe and represent the sights around him within diverging frames of time, from depicting architectural remains worn and sculpted by the centuries and altered drastically because of changing religious and political beliefs, to capturing ephemeral and intangible apparitions of light and atmosphere in more prosaic and actively present-day locales. Whatever the larger purpose behind Gandy's topographic sketches of castle ruins and working

84 T. H. Fielding after Gandy, *Conway Castle*, from Thomas Compton's *Northern Cambrian Mountains; or a Tour Through North Wales*, 1820
85 *Epsom*, 1822
86 *Leith Hill, Dorking*, 1822
87 *Brighton*, 1822
88 *View of London from Peckham Rye*, 1822
89 *Purfleet*, 1821
90 *Coalbrookedale*, 1821

WOUNDED SENSIBILITY, OR FRAGMENTS OF A CAREER 81

landscapes around Great Britain, they were never to be incorporated into a systematic publication under his direction.

Gandy's only forays into print, in which he attempted to formulate his ideas about the history and theory of architecture, were concentrated in 1821 with a series of letters addressed to The Guardian and two scholarly epistles published in Britton's short-lived Magazine of the Fine Arts. His letters to The Guardian were written in response to a string of devastating articles about the state of modern British architecture, with particularly harsh criticism directed against Soane and his recent submissions, drawn by Gandy, to the RA exhibition. Soane, true to his paranoid temper, became obsessed with discovering the identity of the articles' authors (they were signed only with a set of three initials). He drew Britton and Gandy into the affair in the hope of unmasking and bringing legal action against the journalists, which only strained the triangulated relationship between the architect, the draftsman, and the antiquary. Their exchange of letters throughout this unfortunate episode is shot through with wary accusations and fretful suspicion.[62] Gandy took it upon himself to assail The Guardian with five disjointed and often ungrammatical "To the Editor" letters, in which he tried to defend his status as a practicing architect, which involved a sociological critique of the condition of architectural knowledge and patronage in Great Britain. Gandy's inveterate flair for malapropism, however, arcane digressions, and irrelevant scholarly quotations plainly compromised his new literary endeavor. Despite The Guardian's expressed wish not to "slay the slain" with regard to the nonsensical quality of Gandy's "unmeaning letters," the newspaper seems to have taken an almost perverse pleasure in giving him the opportunity for this unfortunate showing off. As the architect James Spiller quipped to Soane about Gandy's literary exploits, "I wish something could be done for Mr G. to take away his leisure for writing."[63]

91 *Moon with Nimbus*, 1821
92 *Enclosed Commons at Milton*, 1821

The brief articles entitled "On the Philosophy of Architecture" that appeared in *Magazine of the Fine Arts* begin with a reference to the "ridicule" Gandy suffered at the hands of *The Guardian*'s editors. Claiming a need for greater "interchange of thought" about the meaning and function of architecture from ancient times to the present, Gandy's philosophical, or more properly philological, inquiry sought to correct the viciously opinionated architectural journalism in the popular press. Both *The Guardian* letters and the more measured though still meandering scholarly papers in *Magazine of the Fine Arts* argued for a liberally eclectic outlook on architectural esthetics so as to encourage stylistic authenticity and originality in modern design. Gandy issued a complaint that was not uncommon in academic art theory of the time, "We abound in models, museums, and copies of originals, but have no compositions of our own."[64] For him, familiarity with styles of the past is not a constraint on contemporary originality. On the contrary, he believes, with Piranesi, in the imaginative manipulation of material from a range of sources. "Where is the monstrosity of any architect's novelties or inventions?" Gandy furiously demanded of *The Guardian*'s critics.[65] Endorsing a pluralist dialogue with the history of architecture and its stylistic origins, he proposed that "it seems incumbent on the moderns to prepare a system selected from all tastes, without prepossession for or against any ... the beauties of every clime and age may be selected, by modern art, with taste, judgement, and poetical conception."[66]

These eclectic criteria for modern architectural invention was far from usual in the wake of picturesque and associationist esthetics. Richard Payne Knight coined the term "mixed style" in 1805 to define the modern picturesque approach to architectural design, and lamented that "Architecture, indeed, has been rather too cautious and timid, than too bold in its exertions."[67] Gandy too regretted the Greek versus Gothic controversy—a reductive architectural schism tirelessly and tiresomely debated in political and journalistic settings. "In seeking truth," Gandy sensibly observed, "we fall into sects; one style in architecture, or one religion, is incompatible with the existence of the world or the nature of man."[68] Architects, he thought, should immerse themselves in the sacred lore of ancient architecture throughout the world; the comparative study of speculative archaeology and religious mythology takes up much of Gandy's frantically brief letters and articles. This intellectually ambitious though perhaps fruitless effort to "soar beyond the schools of Vitruvius and Palladio" and reveal the mythic and divine typologies of architectural origins was to absorb Gandy at the close of his career in the 1830s, when he wrote a lengthy unpublished treatise of architectural theory and natural philosophy entitled The Art, Philosophy, and Science of Architecture, the subject of our final chapter.

Central to Gandy's writings on architecture in 1821 was the defense of the architectural imagination in modern metropolitan society and culture. His letters to The Guardian registered considerable anxiety about the unchecked growth of commercial exchange and industrial production, with heated declarations against speculative building practices for quick profit in Georgian London and the debilitating effects of urban pollution. As will be seen, these anti-modern sentiments later informed his proposal for a new royal palace project that recurs throughout his RA exhibits of the 1820s. At a more personal level, Gandy deeply resented being dismissed as an architect whose work was exclusively pictorial in content and form. The Guardian had praised Gandy's "extraordinary powers in pictorial architectural composition" but insisted that this display of "imaginative, impossible architecture" at the RA exhibitions had altogether negated his credentials as an architect.[69] It was this contradiction of what Soane would satirically call "The Pictorial Architect" that shook Gandy to the core.[70] His letters to The Guardian expressed outright indignation over this refusal to recognize his professional identity under the rubric of "architect."

This debate raised the whole question of the status of the pictorial presentation of architectural design during the late eighteenth and early nineteenth centuries. The increased prominence of architectural perspective drawing in public exhibition culture was critically exemplified by Gandy's career.[71] Student academic competitions and the annual RA exhibitions made it imperative that the architect cultivate an artistically appealing drawing style in order to attract the attention of art critics, newspaper reviewers, and prospective clients. In 1814, Ackerman's The Repository of the Arts noted that the architectural entries at the RA suffered from critical neglect and advised architects to adopt "perspective and chiaroscuro" more dramatically in their drawings, adding that "he [the architect] cannot shut himself up in his study and erect palaces."[72] The artistic merit of the perspective drawing would thus raise the level of respect that the architect could command from within the prejudiced ranks of the RA with its institutional favor for history painters, portraitists, and landscapists. As an art journalist commented in 1816 with respect to the predicament of the architect and the academy: "Architects of the present day have arrived under the discouraging idea, that a comparatively short study of landscape and portrait painting will entitle their companions to more flattering notice from the public, & titles from the Academy than they can possibly hope for after drudging in the office and at the drawing board for years."[73] This begs the question as to whether it was professionally advantageous for architects to compete for the kind of academic and public distinction conventionally associated with the fine arts. Responding to the accusations of Gandy's diminished standing as an architect in The Guardian, Britton's Magazine of the Fine Arts put forth a sound counter-argument:

> If the bent and enthusiasm of his mind tempts him to compose architectural pictures, and to produce compositions superior to those of Pannini and Piranesi, we cannot conceive that he thereby lowers his professional reputation. Were our architects, in general better draftsmen, or more accomplished artists, we apprehend that our buildings would rather be improved than injured in style, adaptation, and effect.[74]

But this was not a universally held view.

In 1807, the landscape painter J. M. W. Turner was elected Professor of Perspective at the Royal Academy. Gandy had hoped to compete for the position, but the hierarchical policies of the RA prohibited associate members from serving as professors. Turner's lectures on perspective, delivered between 1811 and 1828, offered critical commentary on the techniques and conventions of architectural drawing. The lectures were illustrated by stunning watercolours, including highly atmospheric architectural interiors depicting an imaginary prison corridor in tenebrous gloom [94] and the domed interior of Wyatt's Brocklesby Mausoleum in mystically filtered light [93]. With his early work as an architectural topographer (producing exhibition watercolors of Wyatt's designs for Fonthill Abbey), a lively friendship with Soane, and his own designs for his London art gallery and his suburban lodge in Twickenham, Turner was a painter who possessed a keen knowledge of matters architectural. In 1816, an art critic titled him "the British Claude with the knowledge of a professed architect."[75] His lecture notes designate perspective as "the colouring of architecture," producing optical data about the sensory experience of architecture. The mathematical rules of perspective, he believed, crumble before the

93 J. M. W. Turner, Interior of Brocklesby Mausoleum, RA lecture diagram, ca. 1810

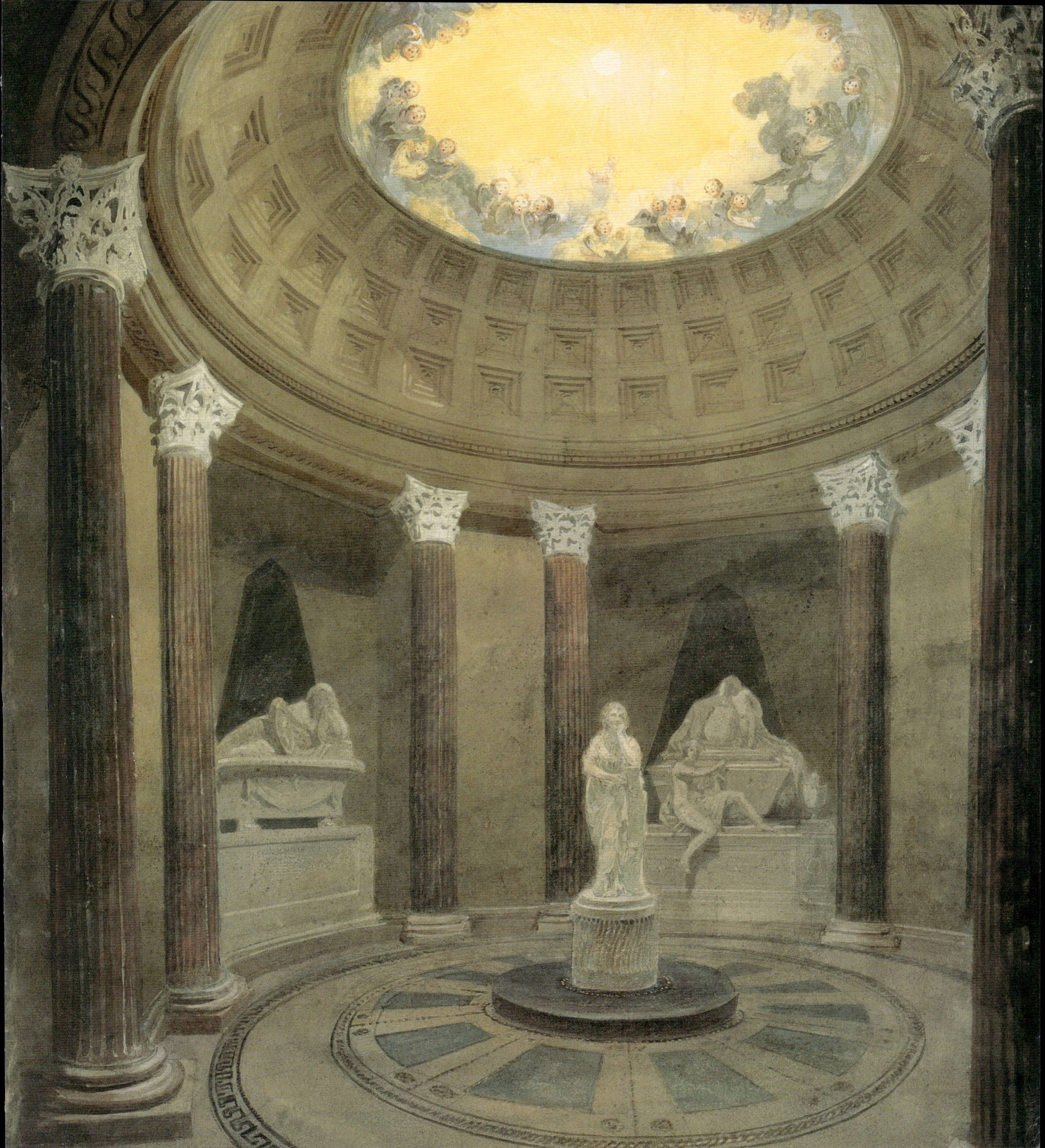

higher metaphysics of the artistic mind fixed on the immeasurable, though he warned young architects over what he characterized as "that far greater fatality for designs of architecture [that] are but splendid drawings when destitute of practicability by an over indulgence of fanciful combinations."[76] One wonders whether he had Gandy in mind.

Turner's friend and colleague Soane extended these warnings in his own lectures on architecture at the RA. In his fifth lecture as Professor of Architecture, first delivered in 1813, Soane paused to praise a mid-eighteenth-century elevation drawing of Salvi's Trevi Fountain rendered by William Chambers, admiring its "chasteness" of technique and style, which he pointedly contrasted to "the present more elaborate mode of treating architectural designs." And he continued in this oft-quoted passage:

A superior manner of drawing is absolutely necessary; indeed, it is impossible not to admire the beauties and almost magical effects in the architectural drawings of a Clérisseau, a Gandy, or a Turner, but few architects can hope to reach the excellency of those artists without devoting to drawing too much of that time which they ought to employ in the attainment of the higher and more essential qualifications of an architect.[77]

Professional survival demanded that the architect forgo the timely pursuit of artistic skills that were superfluous to the art of building. The science of design and its constructive requirements, Soane seems to be saying, were implicitly undermined by the transporting and illusionistic devices of the artistic architectural drawing. Soane's successor as the RA's Professor of Architecture, C. R. Cockerell, made this implicit argument strikingly explicit in his introductory lecture of 1843, which was the year of Gandy's death. While assuring his audience that he subscribed to the double status of architecture as both a science and a fine art, Cockerell repudiated his generation's romance with pictorial architectural rendering. "The illusions of this beautiful art," he observed, "when carried to the point which our modern school has the presumption to aim at, has little to do with the real ends of our science ... pictorial effect takes the place of form, proportion, and design."[78]

Gandy's *Guardian* letters defended architecture as an art form that spoke to the mind and that could hold its place among the other arts within the competitive cultural sphere of the modern exhibition:

> If an Architect, *con amore*, exhibits other works, subordinate but belonging to architecture, as the most pleasing mode of presenting details of that art to the mind, from the knowledge that the dry geometrical, or the calculating part of his science, has no pictorial power to cope with the finished productions of Painting & Sculpture, will he cease to be considered an Architect?[79]

This bold assertion is somewhat qualified by another remark: "I may sometimes be said," he wrote, "to deviate from a strict yet undefineable line that would shackle the mind to one particular department of architecture."[80]

It is tempting to quote a further array of parallel statements by other eminent minds reacting positively to the idea of an architecture that was wholly visionary. George Dance the Younger, as recorded by Farrington: "he derided the prejudice of limiting Designs in Architecture within certain rules, which in fact though held out as laws had never been satisfactorily explained ... in his Opinion Architecture unshackled would afford the greatest genius the greatest opportunities of producing the most powerful efforts of the human mind."[81] Soane, as he rhapsodized in his sixth RA lecture: "the youthful mind, unshackled and unsicklied with the frequent disappointments of professional life, ... [becomes] occupied in the contemplation of the magnificent remains of palaces, temples ... and other interesting objects to the artist, firing his imagination."[82] And James Elmes, who questioned "whether architecture's powers of inventions may be more limited [than its sister arts], whether its artists be more fettered by shackles they dare not throw off, however they may impede their soaring?"[83]

All of these speculations about the predicament of the architectural mind were indebted to Piranesi, who had inveighed against "this shameful yoke" of hidebound architectural traditions that inhibited "a creating Genius."[84] But for Gandy, this proposed liberation of the architectural imagination and the self-definition of his own genius—fueled in part by the rhetoric of his press coverage—only exacerbated the professional impasse that plagued his life and career, especially as he developed and gave definition to a relatively new genre of romantic art: the architectural history painting.

94 J. M. W. Turner, *Interior of a Prison*, RA lecture diagram, ca. 1810

IV: Architectural History Painting: Gandy at the Royal Academy

Between 1789 and 1838, Gandy exhibited 113 works at the Royal Academy, and for the years 1820 and 1821 he submitted fourteen works to the competing British Institution exhibitions. Over one third of these watercolors (only rarely did he exhibit oil paintings) may be classified as architectural history paintings inspired by ancient literary descriptions of classical architecture and by more contemporary English literary texts ranging from John Milton to Horace Walpole. It was this category of imaginative architectural perspectives that had impelled the *Guardian* critics to express regret over Gandy's retreat from the modern realities of architectural practice. For Gandy, the artistic mission of the perspective drawing entailed nothing less than creating a historical vision of architecture: a poetical recovery of the classical past in which both temporal and spatial dimensions would be made startlingly visible. His perspectives are close in spirit to the rumination of Madame de Staël's character Lord Nelvil in her sensational novel *Corinne, or Italy* (1807). After a visit to the ruins of Pompeii, the temperamental Scottish peer extolls the compulsion of the historical imagination, "to delve into the past ... to try to imagine how the world, in its first youth, appeared to the eyes of men ... he [Nelvil] would have found life bearable only in places where historical monuments take the place of present day existence."[1] As will be seen, contemporary art critics often wrote admiringly of Gandy's architectural history paintings in almost identical terms. However, Gandy's perspectives were not merely historical-poetical idylls, for they sought to establish a critical commentary on the cultural significance of architecture in times past, present, and future.

With the rise of archaeological and picturesque surveys of both classical and medieval ruins, topographers and illustrators were inspired to travel back in time to reconstruct the architectural site under inspection. In the lavish serial publication *Voyage pittoresque, ou description des Royaumes de Naples et de Sicile* (1781–86), the Abbé Richard de Saint-Non and Vivant Denon (who was later to become Napoleon's fine arts director) commented on the imaginative latitude of selected illustrations by the *pensionnaire* Desprez, particularly his depiction of a nocturnal ritual at the Temple of Isis at Pompeii [99]:

> His [Desprez's] ready and quick imagination not only restores for us the temple in its entirety, but also represents one of its most solemn ceremonies; and thus this knowledge

95, 96 *The Oracle of Mercury, a Hermes in the Market-place of Patrae*, 1815

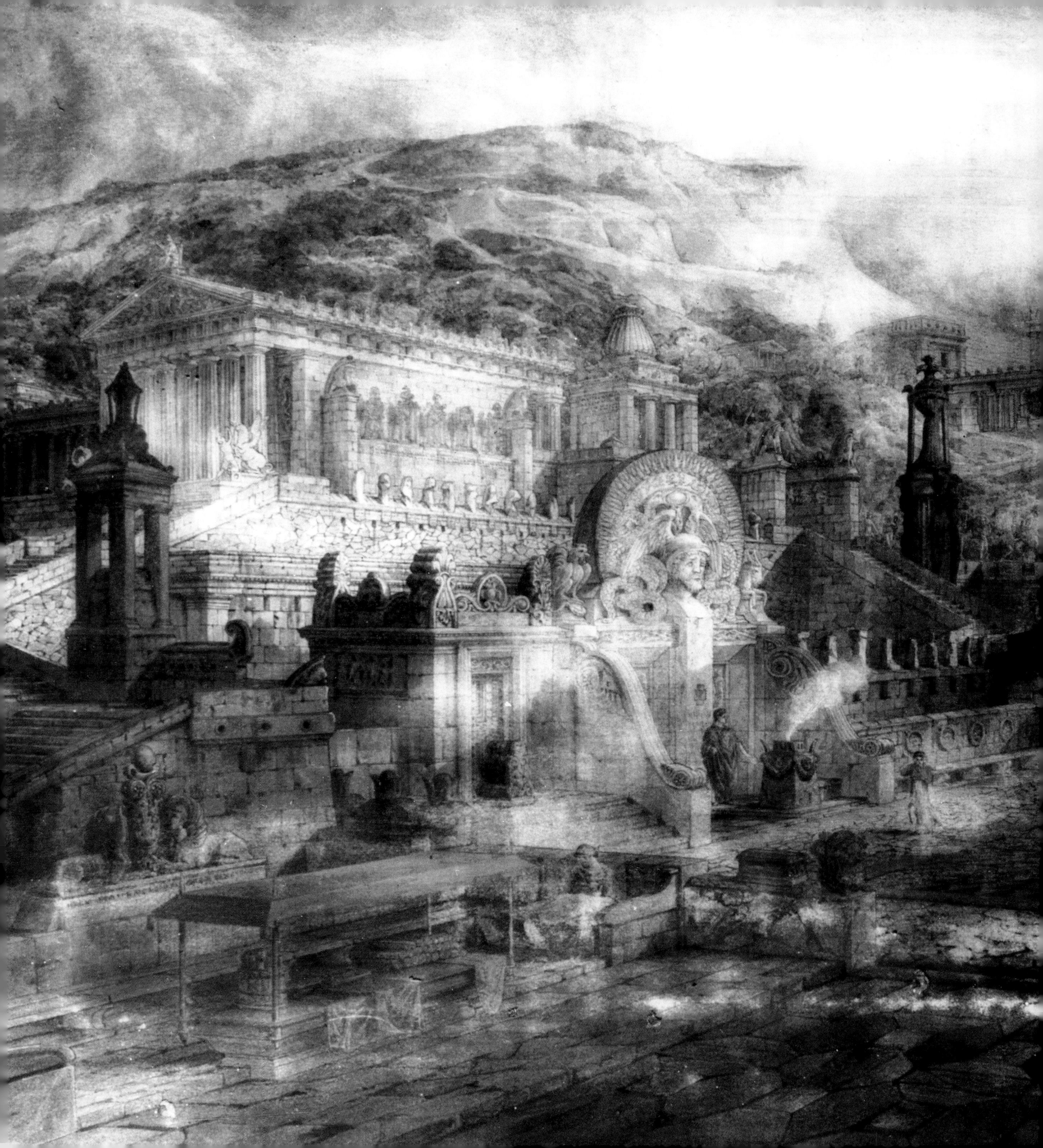

about the different monuments recalls the religious customs of the ancients in the cult of their divinities.[2]

Architectural topography could reveal much more than the transience of a once-thriving civilization: with the reconstructed view, one could witness the vanished religious culture that had first called the now ruined shrines of antiquity into being. The passage quoted above acknowledges the evocative, and therefore slightly deceptive, quality of Desprez's perspectives into the past: "This license in the representation ... makes the monument appear more elevated and vast than it is in truth."[3]

Not everyone had such qualms. In his Élémens de perspective pratique (1799), the neo-classical landscape painter P.-H. Valenciennes instructed artists not to adhere to the topographic conventions of descriptive landscape art, but rather to look beyond the ruins and scenery of immediate reality. They should acquaint themselves with the writings of Pausanias, the second-century Greek who catalogued the architectural landmarks of Roman Greece. This scholarly regression into antiquity is deemed superior to the sad desolation of the topography of ruins: as Valenciennes declared, "The sensitive and philosophical artist, guided by his creative genius, enjoys above all painting the monuments of Greece and Rome at the time of their splendor."[4] These sentiments were echoed in the perspective treatises of contemporary British artists as well. Edward Edwards, Gandy's perspective instructor at the RA, suggested that architects and topographers experiment with "poetic or composite landscapes" to exercise the imagination and pictorial artistry.[5] Not surprisingly, Turner in his perspective lectures at the RA alluded to the creative intersection of history, landscape, and architecture in his accounts of Renaissance and seventeenth-century European art. And in lecture notes marked "to the care of Soane," he wrote of the fundamental importance of "architectural arrangements … to the historical compositions of the present day."[6]

Within the student circle of James Wyatt, other young architects along with Gandy developed a taste for imaginative re-constructions of Greco-Roman architecture. George Hadfield, who was articled to Wyatt from 1784 until 1790, produced impressive drawings of archaeological re-constructions that were often part of academic competitions while in Italy during the early 1790s, including a spectacularly futuristic recreation of the Flavian Amphitheater [97].[7] While simplifying the design, Hadfield depicts the Colosseum equipped with the famous *velaria*, or awning. Diagonal shafts of light spill forth from the glaring oculus of the stadium, with repeated accents of light and shade seen in the rings of apertures and entryways punctuating the curvilinear expanse of the architecture. Hadfield's watercolor achieves a commanding illusion both of perceptual immediacy and spatial remoteness. Sparse groupings of diminutive human figures on the stadium floor and in the viewing stands convey its appropriately inhuman scale and ominous character. Despite its subtle palette of lavender, ocher, and pale blue, the watercolor presents an intimidating and wondrous space where architectural spectacle and ritualistic violence were notoriously conjoined in the service of empire. Another student of Wyatt, his nephew Jeffry Wyatt (later Wyatville), fashioned literary architectural illustrations for the RA exhibitions, from the Homeric *Priam's Palace* (1798) to the Chaucerian *House of Fame* (1804). Although the former is badly damaged and the latter is lost, their imaginative tenor may be seen in a notebook of youthful Wyatville compositions depicting Gothic cloud castles and superposed Greco-Roman fortifications and colonnades [98].[8]

Gandy's exhibition perspectives of classical architecture were justifiably regarded by his contemporaries as erudite though freely conceived reinventions of antiquity with little claim to scientific archaeological accuracy. Critics reviewing his pictorial watercolors of sprawling Greco-Roman cityscapes would characterize them very generally as "a congregated mass of ancient sublimity" or applaud "the poetic charm of the artist's ad-libitum compositions."[9] In accordance with Valenciennes' recommendation [101], Gandy frequently cited Pausanias in the titles of his pictures to give authenticity to his imaginative compositions. He consulted Thomas Taylor's edition of Pausanias' *Description of Greece* with its extensive and provocative neo-Platonic annotations on classical theogony and ancient mystery cults. "The English Pagan" (as Coleridge and others called Taylor) employed this scholarly apparatus to offer a new interpretation of Greek mythology, while at the same time editorializing against the impious and anti-metaphysical mob rule of the French Revolution.[10] Pausanias' descriptions allowed Gandy to function as an imaginary topographer of ancient Greece.

97 George Hadfield, *Imaginary Reconstruction of the Flavian Amphitheatre*, ca. 1790–94
98 Jeffry Wyatville, *Imaginary Architectural Composition* (sketch for *The Palace of Alcinous*), ca. 1797–99
99 L.-J. Desprez, *Temple of Isis, Pompeii*, from J.-C. de Saint Non's *Voyage pittoresque … des royaumes de Naples et Sicile*, 1781–86

Although there is very little precise architectural description in Pausanias' text (for example, the classical orders are never identified or distinguished, though building materials and periods of construction are meticulously differentiated), it does include an abundance of sites and structures of historical and religious significance. Temple precincts, sepulchral monuments, and military and cultic shrines crowd page upon page; sacred myth and heroic ritual inform every physical trace of the past. Sculptures by Phidias and Praxitiles seem to greet his every step. But even in Pausanias' own times these temples or tombs, sometimes described as fire-damaged or in ruins, had acquired elegiac overtones; structures originally dedicated to Greek deities and "ancient heroes" (Pausanias' phrasing) have been rededicated to Roman figures of imperial authority. The mythic topography of Greece is becoming part of secular history.[11]

A representative picture of this kind, with its elaborate descriptive title in the RA catalogue of 1813, is *Architectural Composition, the Vapour Rising from the Miraculous Fountain of Agno to Supply the Earth with Rain in the Mountain of Lycaeus, Agreeably to the Wishes of the Arcadians—Vide*

100 *Architectural Composition ... the Miraculous Fountain of Agno*, 1813
101 Pierre Henri de Valenciennes, *Ancient City of Agrigentum* (detail), 1787

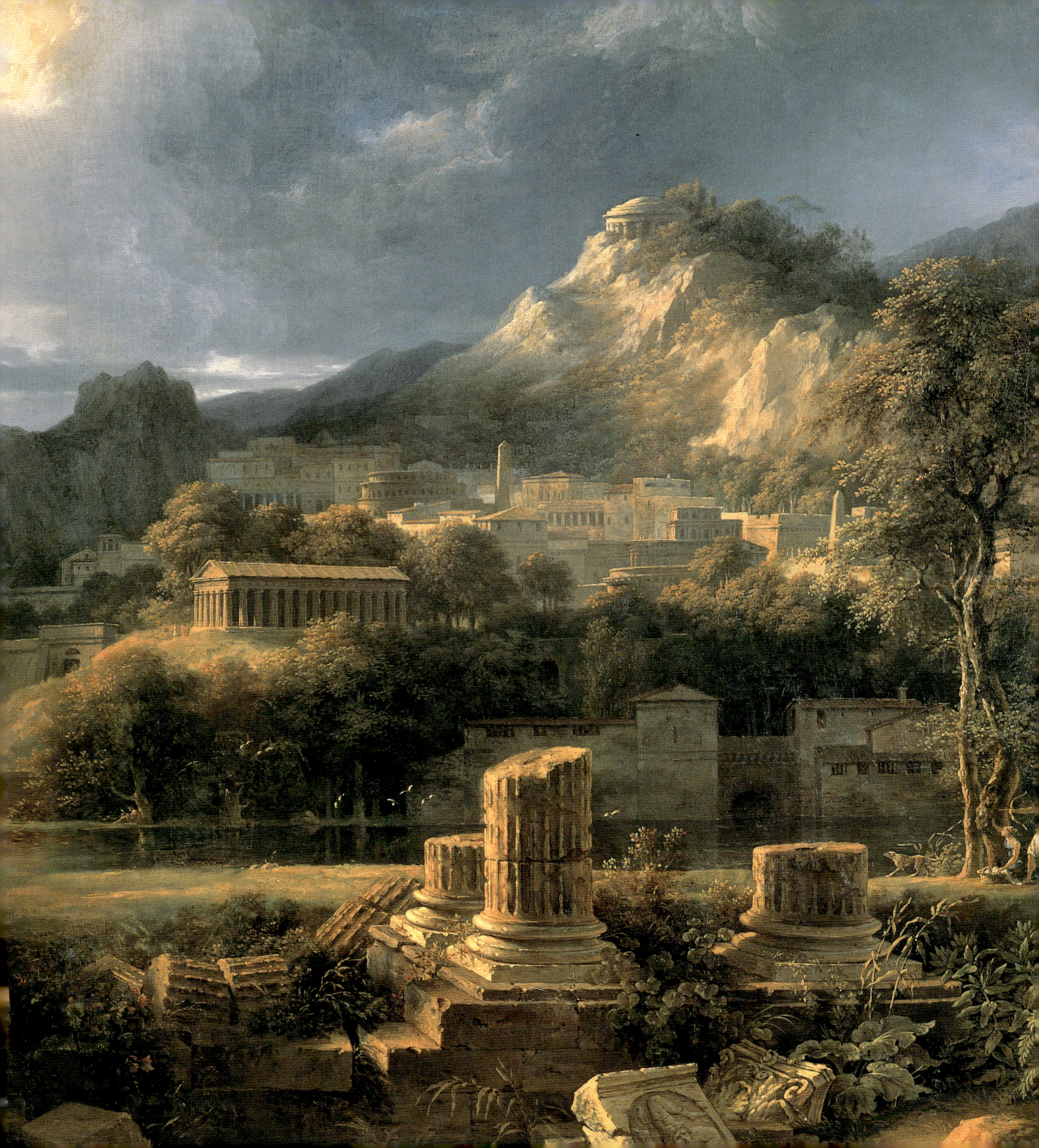

Pausanias b. viii., c.38 [100]. In the left foreground, Gandy depicts the priest of Lycaen Jupiter waving a sacred oak branch over the masonry fountain with a sculpturally decorated altar behind him. Robed figures of the Arcadians, from youthful shepherds to elderly philosophers, supplicate before the ritual (though iconographically significant, Gandy's figurative details are often deficient in technique and rendering). The regenerative vapour of the Fountain of Agno ascends on a drifting diagonal over the colonnaded agora toward a distant acropolis in the mountainous background. An avenue of temples (octagon with tholos lantern, Corinthian prostyle, and other variations) is aligned on a perspectival axis counter to the evaporating path of the fountain mists. Polychromatic marble inlays and warm earthen tones in the foreground monuments cede to a neutral grisaille in the delineation of towered fortifications and palaces in the hillside grove beyond. The thorough integration of architecture and landscape in this picture is at once compositional and symbolic. The architectural setting and its pagan ritual attest to the divine dispensation of the natural order and the symbiotic union of nature, religion, and society in the classical world.

Gandy's working method in architectural landscapes of this kind was analyzed in *The Principles of Practical Perspective* (1815) by the drawing master and architectural writer Richard Brown. "As an architectural painter of edifices of historical celebrity," Brown announced, "Gandy stands unrivalled." However, Brown took issue with Gandy's preference for implementing spherical perspective over linear perspective, a method of pictorial construction more optically than mathematically determined and hence favored by modern artists such as Turner. Spher-

102 *Temple of Minerva Chalinitis, Corinth*, ca. 1815–20
103 *The Landing Place to a Temple*, 1820

ical perspective used an anti-rectilinear bowing of orthogonals and transversals, creating a subtly embracing curvature in the treatment of architectural space that was thought to be more conducive to the parabolic field of vision in human eyesight. Brown consulted with Gandy and gave an account of his technique: "Mr. Gandy only plans the principal or leading buildings in his pictures; the subordinate ones he arranges and proportions by the eye alone. He always uses the curve to obtain his visual rays, but not always to produce the occult lines of the elevation; and as the vanishing points become nearer by this method, he takes a greater distance for the point of view."[2] This is true not only of *Architectural Composition... Fountain of Agno* but also of Gandy's *The Temple of Minerva Chalinitis, Corinth* (c. 1815–20) [102] and *The Landing Place to a Temple* (1820) [103]. All are marked compositionally by the crossing of shallow diagonal axes formed by colonnades, flights of stairs, terraced plazas, and bridges with back-lit monuments in the fore- and middle ground that appear telescopically distorted in perspective. The reliance on *scena per angola* with the superimposition of looming temples over decoratively cluttered forecourts also reflects the conventions of the late eighteenth-century French architectural ruin imagery of C.-L. Clérisseau and Hubert Robert.

Gandy's sublime landscape settings for his temple precincts were no less significant. His RA entries *The Open Temple and Temple Tower of the Greeks, Designed from Various Remarks in Pausanias* (1808) [105] and *Idea of a Bridge and Palace Amongst the Platxenses* [sic], *to Commemorate the Victories by Sea and Land Against the Persians, Vide Pausanias* (1817) [106] brought an epic visual sweep to the conjunction of landscape and architecture. Steep mountainous backdrops and river torrents with splintered rays of sunlight that refract an atmospheric geometry over the landscapes were meant to enhance the splendor and veneration associated with the monuments. The dramatic forms and outlines of the temples and

96

sepulchers even mimic the natural features of the topography: a luminous Doric temple simulates the serpentine outcropping of a distant hillside, while a honeycomb tholos-tomb takes its massive profile from the surrounding mountain crevices. Pausanias alludes frequently to the sacred connotations of mountains, groves, and streams—the landscape of ancient Greece animated with vestigial mythic presence. Architecture and its religious rites commemorate and also perpetuate this haunting of myth in nature. Here, for example, is the passage from Pausanias that inspired Gandy's storm-striven architectural landscape *Idea of Titana from the Pira Grove, Vide Pausanias* (1820) [104]: "In this temple there is an ancient wooden statue of Minerva, which is said to have been struck by lightning. On descending from the eminence on which this temple is built, you will perceive an altar of the Winds, on which in one night every year the priest sacrifices. He also performs certain other arcane ceremonies ... for the purpose of appeasing the rage of the winds, and sings, as they report, the incantations of Medea."[13] The religious sanctuary in Gandy's picture heroically withstands the violent onslaught of nature. Taylor's neo-Platonic annotations to Pausanias interpret the mountain summits and enchanted groves of the ancient Greek landscape as an intermediate zone between the corrupted sublunary world of sensory knowledge and the spiritual world of intellectual wisdom. The architectural landmarks in Gandy's Pausanian compositions may be construed as allegorical signposts in this neo-Platonic pilgrimage from the sublime ferocity of nature in all its mutable beauty to the higher intelligence and illuminated transcendence of the divine soul.

104 *Idea of Titana from the Pira Grove, Vide Pausanias*, 1820
105 *The Open Temple and Temple Tower of the Greeks, Designed from Various Remarks in Pausanias*, 1808
106 *Idea of a Bridge and Palace Amongst the Platxenses*, 1817

Gandy's classical landscapes naturally emphasize the symbolic centrality of architecture within the closely interconnected realms of cultural, religious, and civic life in ancient Greece. His richly detailed pictures *The Great Temple of Ceres at Eleusis, a Composition of Greek Embellishments from Pausanias and Other Authors, and from Discoveries Made on the Spot by the Last Mission of the Dilettanti Society* (1815) [107] and *The Persian Porch and the Place of Consultation of the Lacedemonians* [sic] (1816) [109] recreate the public spaces of ancient Greece as complicated sites of devout ritual, civic pageantry, and artistic display. Gandy's brother John Peter had participated in the Society of Dilettanti's excavations at Eleusis and had exhibited his own reconstructed view of the "mystic" temple at the RA a year earlier [108]. In Gandy's ambitious watercolour of Eleusis, the overall plan of the outer Temple of Diana, the propylaea, and the massive Doric Telesterion, containing the sanctuary dedicated to Ceres where the occult mysteries transpired, owed more to modern archaeology than to Pausanias, whose literary account of Eleusis was uncharacteristically terse, because, as he noted, "I am forbid by a dream from relating the particulars."[14] Taylor's neo-Platonic scholarship and Freemasonic manuals such as William Hutchinson's *The Spirit of Masonry* (1775) delved into the occult mysteries at Eleusis more openly. The antiquarian topographer Hutchinson, noting that the Telesterion was "an edifice so vast and capacious that the most ample theatre did not exceed it," speculated on the occult mysteries within: "Sometimes the place appeared bright and resplendent with light and radiant fire, and then covered with black darkness and horror [with] thunder and lightning."[15] The smoky cloud cover amassing above the Telesterion in Gandy's picture predicts the unfolding of these nocturnal rites and supernatural atmospheres. The ornate agora with its array of sculptures and shrines in the picture's foreground is very much

107 *The Great Temple of Ceres at Eleusis*, 1815
108 John Peter Gandy, *Mystic Temple of Ceres at Eleusis, in Attica*, 1817
109 Overleaf: *The Persian Porch and the Place of Consultation of the Lacedemonians*, 1816

an archaeological fabrication, though the mythological allusions of the statuary and ritual objects were appropriate to the mystery cult at Eleusis. The chariot of Pluto atop the propylaea and the acroterial dogs of the underworld on the corners of the Telesterion refer to Ceres' (or Demeter's) search for her abducted daughter Persephone that led her to Eleusis. Gandy also depicts a procession of the initiates parading vessels of grain in chariots for an agricultural festival of renewal dedicated to Ceres who first brought the art of tillage to the Eleusinians. From a nineteenth-century perspective, this vivid evocation of the ritualistic function of art and architecture in ancient Attica provided a knowing contrast to the museological and commercial applications of artistic culture in modern society. In Gandy's Pausanian pictures, the classical world appears like an inexhaustible outdoor museum of sculptural and architectural masterpieces. But they are also shown as living artifacts, inseparable from the religious and political proceedings of daily life.

In *The Persian Porch* [109], Gandy portrays the forum of Sparta where the building complex encompassed judicial halls, sepulchral monuments, temples, and a marketplace. It is this adjacency and even overlapping of sacred and civic spaces that the picture celebrates, along with the omnipresent public life of art indicated by the cluttered courtyard of mythological sculptures and military trophies. Gandy here diverged from his literary source by failing to incorporate the most noteworthy of monuments cited by Pausanias, including the colonnade of vanquished Persians after which the picture is named. Also absent are tombs and temples that would have signified the diachronic historicity of the city, from the hoary sepulcher of Orestes to a refurbished temple dedicated to Augustus Caesar.[16] Instead, Gandy scatters statues of Neptune, Diana, archaic Egyptian deities, and Spartan athletes among the fountains and urns to capture the polytheistic diversity of sculptural adornment in an ancient metropolis. For his equally congested composition *The Oracle of Mercury, a Hermes in the Market-place of*

100 JOSEPH GANDY

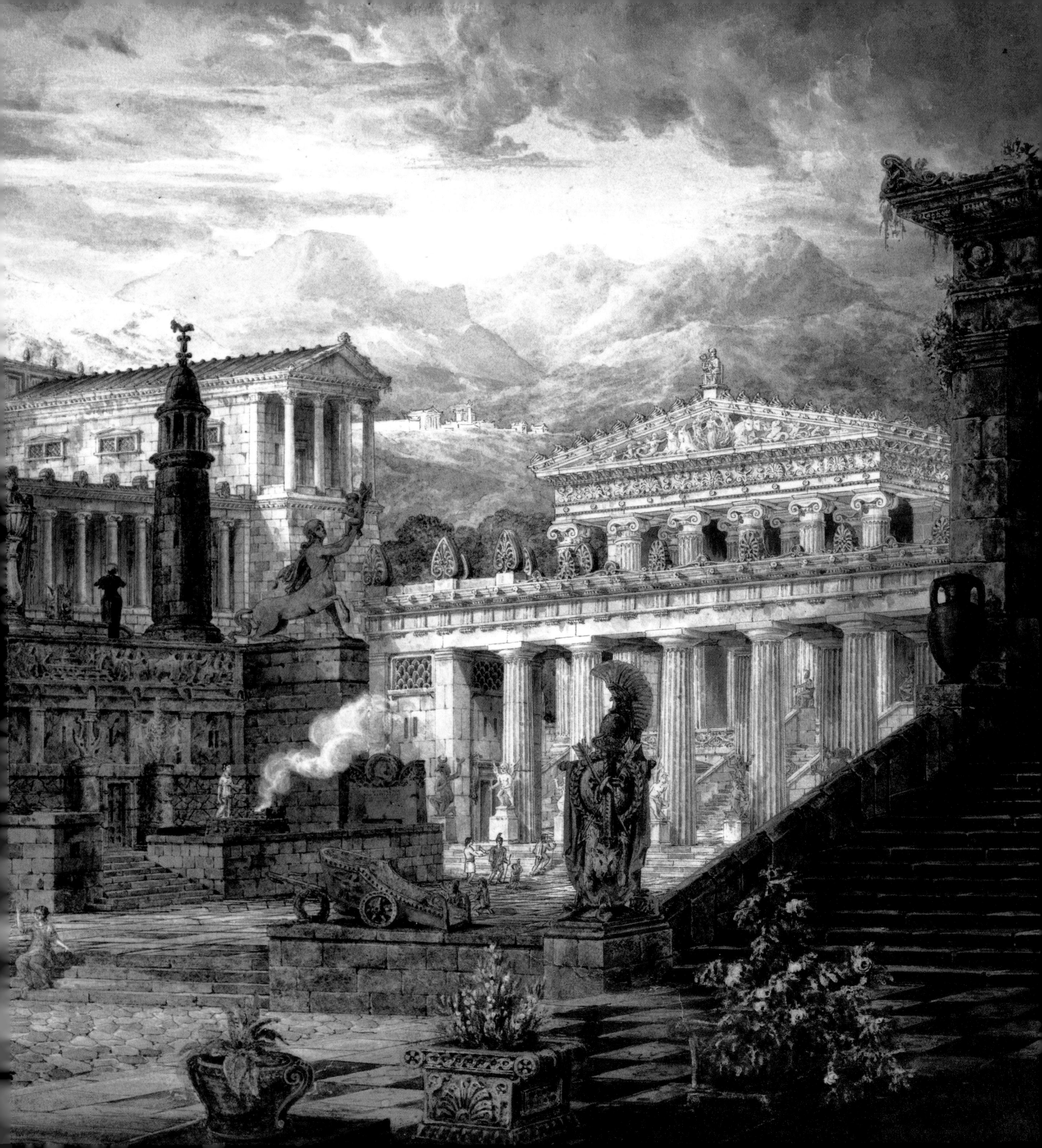

Patrae, Vide Taylor's Pausanias (1815), a similar impression is given of a lavish assemblage of votive shrines, statues, and altars set within the prosperous world of the agora [95, 96]. In this instance, Gandy included very precise iconographic details culled from Pausanias: the tent-cum-altar in the left foreground where lamps and candles were purchased before consulting the oracle and the line of stone fragments installed along the parapets of the temple precinct that recalled earlier religious practices in ancient Greece, as Pausanias explained that "it was formerly the custom with all the Greeks to reverence rude stones in the place of statues of gods."[17] The architectural and sculptural specimens gathered together in this picture thereby visualize an episodic history of Greek religious and civic life in tectonic form. In 1832, an anonymous art critic perceptively compared the excessive accumulation of Greco-Roman temples and sepulchers in Gandy's classical re-constructions to "a kind of architectural congress, to which every class of building has sent its representative."[18]

These Pausanian restorations aspired to the academic status of historical landscape art. Despite his avid defense of his professional credentials as an architect, Gandy, as early as 1813, had suggested to Joseph Farington that his possible candidacy as a senior academician might be considered in painting rather than in architecture.[19] Between 1819 and 1821, he even exhibited large-scale oil paintings of Greco-Roman landscapes at the RA and also at the competing British Institution, perhaps in an effort to attract the patronage of Sir George Beaumont. His exhibits *Idea of Jupiter Pluvius, Ledadea* (1819) [110] and *Landing-place to a Temple of Victory Through the Gate of Minerva, a Composition* (1821) [111] signaled his campaign to establish his credentials not merely as an architectural draftsman and antiquarian watercolorist but as an historical landscape painter. The enormous *Jupiter Pluvius*—almost two meters square—became the object of critical debate in the London art reviews of the 1819 RA exhibition (it was shown again at the British Institution the following year, in part because of its notoriety in the press). An anonymous pamphlet devoted four pages to Gandy's oil painting in which the reviewer carefully compared Pausanias' description of the temple precinct of Jupiter Pluvius, the deity of rainstorms, to its pictorial interpretation. The critic found fault with Gandy's narrative and compositional dispersion of the religious rituals at the imagined site, from the sacred grove and cavern in the shadowy right

110 *Jupiter Pluvius*, 1819
111 *Landing-place to a Temple of Victory Through the Gate of Minerva*, 1821

foreground, where oracular rites of sacrifice and ablution are performed, to the distant Temple of Trophonius seen in the upper center of the mountain prospect. These quadrants of the painting are connected by the religious procession making its way across the bridge and up the terraced approach to the outdoor temple and statue of the winged, enthroned Jupiter. The critic was also perturbed by the fantastical aspect of this sculptural set-piece, whose multiple sources include an engraving of a late Roman relief of Jupiter Pluvius in Bernard de Montfaucon's *Antiquity Explained* (1721) [112] and John Flaxman's outline-engraved illustration from 1793 of the Saturnian Giant King of Crete from the fourteenth canto of Dante's *Inferno* [113]. While acknowledging the pictorial drama of the landscape setting, particularly the torrent of the River Hercyna fed by the oncoming storm blowing in off the towering mountains, the reviewer questioned the picture's topographic fidelity to Pausanias' account. The art critic was certainly correct in noting the repeated liberties that Gandy took with his literary source, though in focusing on the lapsed pedantry of Gandy's picture the writer overlooked the salient theme of this classical landscape. The true attribute of the titanic statue of the Jupiter of storms is in the landscape itself, the polytheistic myths and rituals of ancient Greece conceived of by Gandy as a symbolic refinement of nature worship. Other complaints about the pictorial disregard for temporal unity and the "scattering" of architectural foci across too expansive a canvas were also voiced. The critic was nonetheless insistent in acknowledging Gandy's "genuine talents ... and vast knowledge."[20]

This pamphlet appeared during the first week of the RA exhibition. Gandy took the criticism characteristically to heart by frantically requesting to the RA Council that the picture be withdrawn from the exhibition. Comparing his situation to a pilloried criminal, he urged Soane to act as his advocate on the matter while warning that should the Council deny his request, "I must consider myself degraded to the utmost by them and shall hereafter consider there is more real kindness and attention out of rather than within the walls of the Royal Academy."[21] The Council refused—fortunately, it turns out, for Gandy, as the picture went on to garner extraordinary praise in the weekly press. Robert Hunt in *The Examiner* gave it a lengthy description while favorably comparing the picture to the classical landscapes of Turner for "poetical magnificence and poetic invention."[22] Certainly this comparison was apt in terms of architectural and landscape imagery but not in terms of artistic style, as Gandy's oil painting was stiffly illustrative when compared to the painterly manner of even the most conservative of Turner's exhibition landscapes. The reviewer from *The Literary Gazette* commented enthusiastically and repeatedly on *Jupiter Pluvius* and in doing so broached the cultural and political concerns of the painting that went far beyond artistic merit and scholarly erudition. The critic began, "We observe *Jupiter Pluvius* by J. Gandy, certainly one of the noblest compositions of the year, stuck into the midst of mere designs and architectural drawings in the Library, all of which, indeed, its grand

112 Ancient Roman Relief of Jupiter Pluvius, from
Bernard de Montfaucon's Antiquity Explained, and Represented in Sculptures, 1721
113 T. Piroli after John Flaxman, Saturnian King of Crete,
from Dante's The Divine Comedy, 1802
114 Stage Set for Sophocles, Electra Before the Palace of Aegisthus, ca. 1820–30
115 Stage Set for Euripides, Tomb in Ruins, ca. 1820–30

character and splendid execution cause to look like dirty washings."[23] Here Gandy's peculiar status as neither architect nor painter (or as a compromised hybrid of both) is dramatized within the exhibition space of the RA. That the contemporary sphere of architecture could not adequately accommodate the imagination of Gandy was a pressing issue that received further notice by the same journalist two weeks later:

> No nation of Europe has so few public buildings of value; and if London was to become another Herculaneum, it would not be worth while to disclose its ruins, except for St. Paul's. The picture of which we now speak is the conception of an artist full of the learning of his profession, imbued with the richest memories of Greece, and a man of Genius. Mr. Gandy must have been distinguished wherever his noble art found honour. He would have been eminent in the time of Louis XIV ... in the time of Leo the Tenth ... in the time of Pericles.[24]

Gandy's retrieval of the past—his traveling back in time to see the Greece of Pausanias and his return to the nineteenth century with this idealized vision—is restated by this critic through a marvelous series of rhetorical turns in temporal dislocation. London promises to fail decisively as an edifying future ruin, primarily because Gandy has not been allowed to contribute to the design of its public architecture. Ancient Greece lives in him, but these "memories" will never inhabit the present-day reality of Britain. Gandy's genius flourishes in all great courts and empires and under the direction of all eminent patrons throughout history. Except the present time. Our critic finally conceives of Gandy as embodying the political model of the ancient Greek artist, "whose illustrious works calls us back to republican simplicity." *Jupiter Pluvius* and its poetical gigantism come to stand as an historical utopia against which the present-day culture of art and architecture is merely pitiable.

The anxiety of modern civilization over the historical past and the predicted future implicit in Gandy's Pausanian pictures also informs his stage-set designs for classical and Shakespearean tragedies that were executed intermittently during the 1820s and 1830s [114, 115]. After 1825, several RA exhibition watercolors by Gandy refer to the tragedies of Euripides and Aeschylus in their titles. A large number of preliminary watercolor sketches for stage sets also survive consisting of scenographic proposals Gandy had assembled, most likely for the Covent Garden Theatre where John Grieve and Clarkson Stanfield held sway as scenic designers.[25] The renowned tragedian and theatrical director William Charles Macready recorded in his 1834 diary, "I wrote an answer to Mr. Gandy's critical letter on my performance and costume of Lear," which leads one to wonder whether Gandy had succeeded in alienating another prominent contemporary from whom he was hoping to gain patronage.[26] In many instances, Gandy's stage-set designs were almost indistinguishable in subject and style from his idealized restorations, as in his opulently colored set design for the second scene of Shakespeare's *Titus Andronicus* [116]. A procession led by the future emperor Saturninus enters through the Arch of Septimius Severus and trails through the Forum toward the Capitol, the human drama and imperial ritual plainly upstaged by the architectural canyons of ancient Rome. Like his fellow architects C. R. Cockerell and James Pennethorne who also produced hypothetical restorations of

106

the Roman Forum during the 1820s, Gandy reveled in the opportunity to reconstruct, which also meant to redesign and amplify, the most renowned urban space of antiquity.[27]

Even more captivating to Gandy in his stage designs were ancient Greek episodes of oracular divination, as seen in his *The Temple of Apollo, Delphi* [117], which served both as a proposed set design for the final scene of Euripides' *Ion* and also as an 1827 exhibit at the Old Water-Colour Society where it was shown as part of the recently formed private collection of contemporary British watercolors for the wealthy London patron Mrs. George Haldimand.[28] The architectural elements and ritualistic trappings of this picture rely on Pausanias' account of this most hallowed of temple precincts in ancient Greece. The Pythia—the Delphic oracle—is seated on her outdoor throne before the Doric peristyle Temple of Apollo. She utters prophetic incantations, as Pausanias recounted, "divinely inspired from the vapour of the earth," indicated visually by the veils of mist rising behind her.[29] The Pythian shrines include the legendary tripod of entwined serpents (later to be sacked by Constantine and relocated in the hippodrome of Constantinople) and a polychrome sculpture of a dragon and a lyre (symbolic of Apollonian inspiration triumphing over the chthonic powers of the earth). A colorfully embroidered tent reserved for votive offerings is reminiscent of the first temple dedicated to Apollo at Delphi that was originally constructed from laurel trees, a sprig of which is held by the Pythia. To the left is the Castalian Spring that flows from Mount Parnassus, another source of poetic prophecy, as are the white birds diving above the sanctuary, for, as Pausanias noted, "prophecy by the flight of birds was invented by Parnassus." The supplicants before the Pythia are Queen Kreousa of Athens, who had been raped by Apollo in her youth, and their son Ion, who was abandoned at birth and reared by the Pythia. To prove to Queen Kreousa that Ion is her son, the Pythia reveals the woven basket in which the Queen had placed her infant at birth. Athena appears at the conclusion of Euripides' play to encourage the reconciliation between mother and son and thus ensure the royal succession for the rule of Athens. Here the mystic temple precinct is presented as a site of revelation, prophecy, and restoration. In Gandy's contemporaneous stage design for the opening scene of Sophocles' *Oedipus at Colonus* the architectural setting is associated with the human conditions of guilt, expiation, and exile [120]. Gandy depicts the blind, aged Oedipus with his daughter Antigone seeking rest in the Grove of the Eumenides, or Furies, in the outskirts of Athens. In 1811, a literary critic remarked about the fateful setting, "No sooner does Oedipus arrive at the grove of the Furies in Attica than he immediately recognizes it as the spot on which an oracle had foretold that he would perish."[30] The play's opening scene was intended to create a mood of malignant trepidation and uncertainty, and thus Gandy frames the set design with a wild wood of roots and branches metamorphosing into the coiled serpentine shapes of a winged dragon. The text of the play makes no mention of a Temple of the Furies (and Pausanias makes only passing reference to two temples dedicated to the Furies and Orestes), so

116 *Ancient Rome: A Stage Set for Titus Andronicus, I, ii*, ca. 1825–30
117 *The Temple of Apollo at Delphi*, 1827
118 A. B. Clayton, *Design for a Temple in Memory of Pericles*, 1825
119 A. B. Clayton, *Design for a Water Entrance to an Ancient City*, 1823

Gandy's invention of a compact temple in which the furies are put to work as mortifying caryatids has no textual authority.[31] The benign and pale architectural features of a distant Athens glimpsed beyond the untamed landscape only accentuate the luridly detailed decoration of the Temple of the Furies, which defies all architectural decorum—appropriately so for a monument devoted to the paranoiac and morbid specters of Greek myth.

Gandy's imaginary re-constructions of Greco-Roman antiquity had considerable influence on the artistic ambitions of other late Georgian architects whose careers were also divided between the architectural profession and the visual arts. The Greek Revival designer Alfred B. Clayton listed himself as "Painter and Architect" in the Royal Academy exhibition catalogues, showing elaborate watercolors of narrative architectural scenes and imaginary restorations that clearly betray the impact of Gandy's Pausanian pictures. His RA entries *Design for a Temple Dedicated to the Memory of Pericles* (1825) and *Design for a Water Entrance to an Ancient City* (1823) [118, 119]—grandiose vistas onto Greco-Roman cityscapes in which large-scale sculptural ensembles are often highlighted—are distinguished by a planimetric frontality in the composition. Like Gandy, Clayton set out to redesign the ancient world, imagining his architectural visions not in modern but in antique

120 *Temple of the Furies, Oedipus and Antigone*, 1827
121 George Maddox, *Part of Orchomenus, from Pausanias*, 1832

contexts. However, the insistent attention to military commemorative monuments and maritime cities in this classical architectural imagery did have a modern, if unspoken, parallel in the post-Waterloo supremacy of Great Britain. Another rival to Gandy in the production of fictive scenes of antiquity was the architect and drawing master George Maddox. Employed in the office of S. P. Cockerell (after a brief interlude with the tyrannical Soane), Maddox instructed a generation of young architects including Decimus Burton and Gilbert Scott in architectural drawing, while also exhibiting over thirty watercolors of Greco-Roman cityscapes and ancient ruins at the Royal Society of British Artists between 1824 and 1843. His compositions *Ruins of a Greek City in the Time of Pausanias* (1827) [122] and *Part of Orchomenus, from Pausanias* (1832) are indebted to Gandy in the visual maze of temples, terraces, and sepulchers that crowd them.[32] Maddox's watercolor technique, however, is quite distinct from Gandy's, revealing a more diaphanous and suffused application of the medium. The classically draped figures of priestesses and Roman tourists have a ghostly frailty. Without pretending to archaeological precision, Maddox invents highly embellished variations on the classical orders, as in the modified Doric portico of the Temple of the Graces, singled out by Pausanias for its venerable opulence, situated in the right foreground of his resplendently golden view of the sacred precinct of Orchomenus [121]. As a contemporary critic remarked, "The many very beautiful compositions for capitals we have seen by Mr. G. Maddox prove to us the possibility of deviating considerably from all existing examples of the antique without losing any of its spirit."[33] True to the historical sense of fading grandeur in Pausanias' account, Maddox's pictures also include conspicuous areas of ruin with temples in disrepair and covered partially by drapery and with foliage encroaching upon and cushioning dislodged urns and relief sculptures. The ideal recreation of antiquity is visualized as being reclaimed by nature and temporality. William Hazlitt observed in 1821 that "there is no such thing as antiquity ... Whatever is or has been, while it is passing, must be modern."[34] The classical reconstructions of Gandy, Clayton, and Maddox enact these speculative inventions of the historical past in which modernity and antiquity are constantly in a dialectical condition of "passing."

Contemporary critics often described Gandy's architectural watercolors as "poetical." Thus, for example, *The Examiner* claimed that his pictures typically "unite a poetical feeling with architectural science."[35] This poetical aspect of Gandy's art was self-consciously demonstrated in his Miltonic and other literary exhibition pictures that challenged the hierarchies of both genre and medium at the Royal Academy during the early nineteenth century. As with the Pausanian pictures, these watercolors often had the scale and finish of historical landscape paintings and also entailed an array of atmospheric and visual effects calculated to command attention at Somerset House. As early as 1796, writing from occupied Rome, Gandy informed his father, "I made two sketches lately, or rather architectural designs, from Milton which I intend exhibiting and engraving when I arrive in England."[36] He quoted those passages from *Paradise Lost* that had especially seized his imagination: the contrasting scenes of the infernal construction of Pandemonium and the heavenly vision of the temple and throne of God. As a young architect with artistic and commercial ambitions who saw himself as a

122 George Maddox, *Ruins of a Greek City in the Time of Pausanias*, 1827
123 Edward Burney, *A View of Philip James de Loutherbourg's "Eidophusikon,"* ca. 1782
124 L.-J. Desprez after De Wailly, *Miltonic Theatre Design*, ca. 1775

disciple of Edmund Burke, Gandy laid claim to the Miltonic sublime from an architectural vantage—a kind of parallel to the nationalist strain in figurative historical art in late eighteenth-century London promoted in the paintings and prints of James Barry and Henry Fuseli.[37] Furthermore, Miltonic imagery had also been incorporated into the program of the popular and sensational Eidophusikon, a mechanical display of scenic illusionism devised by the painter and scenographer Philippe Jacques de Loutherbourg.[38] This phantasmagoric spectacle, which had London venues in 1782, 1786, and 1793, recreated the Miltonic episode of Satan's raising of Pandemonium through the technical magic of colored transparencies with musical accompaniment, as seen in Edward Burney's contemporary depiction of this proto-cinematic viewing chamber [123]. It is very possible that Gandy saw the Eidophusikon the year before he traveled to Italy and that he remembered the glowing transparencies and shifting images of the Pandemonium tableau. Before Gandy, the French neo-classical architect Charles De Wailly exhibited a design for the interior decoration of a theater at the Salon of 1771 that referred to the infernal and celestial kingdoms from *Paradise Lost* [124]. Desprez's etching of this scene could be mistaken for a seventeenth-century miraculous apotheosis, with its Solomonic baldacchino ascending out of smoky, angel-laced chiaroscuro. De Wailly's Miltonic illustration betrayed its author's training in the studio of the scenographer Servandoni and the heady world of theatrical machinery, and must have influenced de Loutherbourg's satanic architecture a decade later. De Wailly's artistic submissions to the Salon unfortunately met with discouragement from Diderot, who considered them the inappropriately amateurish forays of "a painter-architect ... the Salon demands something more."[39]

Gandy provided that something, though it was not until 1805 that he exhibited his first Miltonic picture at the Royal Academy, *Pandemonium, or Part of the High Capital of Satan and His Peers* [125]. Of his extant exhibition watercolors, this work is certainly his most accomplished and original, and deserves recognition as an exceptionally innovative contribution to British romantic art. Here Gandy created an incomparable panorama of an otherworldly architectural landscape. With truly tectonic malevolence, the battlements of Hell rise above the convulsed terrain of the infernal realm. Aqueducts and peristyle Doric temples stretch interminably across a seething landscape of volcanic chasms and sulfurous lakes. Enormous domed temples and ancillary turrets emit streams of light from gaping oculi, the skyline streaked with fiery searchlights. Thunderbolts and meteoric flashes of light break through the cloudy obscurity of the eternal night, forming pyramidal shapes in the irradiated atmosphere, a satanic cityscape wonderfully poised between the collision of earth and sky. The cataclysmic imagery of geological and meteorological fury in the picture is true to its Miltonic source.[40] The construction of Pandemonium is analogous to a geological catastrophe: "Anon out of the earth a fabric huge/ Rose like an exhalation" (1.710–11). The poetic image of glaring light, volcanic exhaust, and unstable molten matter solidifying into architectonic mass is marvelously visualized by Gandy. As Milton commented on the architectural vanity of great empires:

And here let those
Who boast in mortal things, and wondering tell
Of Babel and the works of Memphian kings
Learn how their greatest monuments of fame,
And strength and art are easily outdone
By spirits reprobate, and in an hour
What in an age they with incessant toil
And hands innumerable scarce perform. (1.692–99)

The architectural features of *Pandemonium*, however, have their own identifiable origins in archaeological source material. The terraced arcades and scissor ramps in the upper reaches of the infernal palace allude to the extensive hillside setting of the Temple of Fortuna at Palestrina, which Gandy recollected in a sketch for Soane in an 1813 letter. The lines of temples and turrets that give *Pandemonium* its illusion of infinitude are borrowed from Piranesi's reconstruction of the Campo Marzio. The enormous domed circular Doric palaces most prominent in Gandy's picture recall the Roman *concorso*, both his own design for a sepulchral chapel and more pointedly that of his competitor Duran, especially for its Doric severity and gargantuan scale.

Gandy's picture also elicits a powerful association with the modern landscape of the Industrial Revolution. For this idea, he very likely looked to the example of the industrial architectural utopia in Ledoux's treatise *L'architecture considérée* of 1804, which concluded with an imaginary aerial view of a cannon foundry for the ideal city of Chaux [126].

125 *Pandemonium, or Part of the High Capital of Satan and His Peers*, 1805
126 C.-N. Ledoux, *Imaginary Aerial View of Cannon Foundry at Chaux*, from *L'architecture*, 1804

In this dramatic engraving, the foundry's quadrangle of pyramids releases burning columns of light and billowing smoke, a productive energy harnessed to the most ancient of architectural forms. Ledoux's industrial inferno does not disrupt the social order of the model commune, as the civic temples and public colonnades stand calmly in the shadow of the sepulchral-looking factory. Ledoux's textual commentary for the cannon foundry design is a bizarre farrago of natural philosophy and mythic allegory in which he reflects on the perpetual cycles of self-destruction in human history fed by the never-ending conflict between religion and science. To grasp the essence of the law of violence in nature and humanity, Ledoux descends into the center of the earth to study geological formations and to converse with infernal deities. Writing with a Miltonic fervor that anticipated the visual effects of Gandy's picture, he imagines "sulfuric domes concentrated within the vitriolic tumults of the earth." And within this subterranean landscape, as he wrote, "I advance in the shadows and I discover, aided by an accidental beam of light, the enormous stone covering the bloody chasm of Pandemonium."[41] But it was Gandy who revealed what lay beneath, a nocturnal vista of satanic architecture, clothed in a grandiloquent though distorted antique style and glowing like foundries and furnaces across a volcanic landscape.

The Miltonic imagery of Pandemonium seems to have permeated cultural and political parlance during the 1790s and early nineteenth century. Burke had famously appropriated the language of satanic disorder and sublime inversions of power in his anti-Jacobin *Reflections on the Revolution in France* (1790). British pamphleteers across the political spectrum characterized the social conditions and ideological struggles of their country and Europe as a disturbingly mundane incarnation of the state of Pandemonium.[42] The architect John Papworth used the image to describe the 1789 night fire that destroyed Wyatt's ornate pleasure building, the Oxford Street Pantheon: "The successive crashing and falling of different portions of the building furnished to the mind a more lively representation of Pandemonium than the imagination alone could possible supply."[43] In rhapsodizing over the ceaseless building activity at night during the construction of Fonthill Abbey in 1808, its patron William Beckford wrote with his distinctive blend of megalomania and self-abasement: "When I stand under the countless completed arches of the tribunes I hear the echoing voices ... as if drawn from the depths of a mine, and from deep below the curses of hell itself and the hymns of Pandemonium."[44] Picturesque travelogues of Great Britain that paused to remark over industrial scenery—either with censorious regret or cautious amazement—often resorted to satanic and demoniacal analogies to describe the atmospheric vapor and eerie illumination of the factory or foundry setting.

Gandy's Pandemonium pays imaginative witness not only to the changing face of industrial England, but also to its religious controversies during the Anglo-French Wars. In the lower right corner of the watercolor, there is an unusually inspired passage, depicting winged demons tormenting the coiled bodies of the damned, lest the viewer become swayed by the irresistible architectural grandeur of the infernal kingdom. A small gouache sketch for this area of Pandemonium also shows the spirited attention that Gandy brought to these demonic figures and lost souls [127]. In his Philosophical Enquiry into ... the Sublime and Beautiful, Burke argued for the supremacy of literature over the visual arts, especially in treating the sublimity of hell and the torments of the damned. "I have been at a loss," Burke confessed, "in all the pictures I have seen of hell, whether the painter did not intend something ludicrous."[45] Gandy wished to prove otherwise with Pandemonium and thereby demonstrate his unprecedented mastery of the Burkean sublime. But in doing so he may have also taken the picture into the realm of religious enthusiasm. Among Gandy's few autobiographical papers and letters are diary entries that date from the very period when Pandemonium was on show at the RA, in May and June of 1805.[46] The entries focus on Gandy's reactions to the sermons and scriptural readings of a nonconformist evangelical preacher, perhaps of a Methodist sect. While in Rome, Gandy received news from his father about parliamentary hearings on Richard Brothers, a radical millenarian prophet arrested for treason and confined to a lunatic asylum where he would later draw up plans for transforming London into the New Jerusalem.[47] This does not necessarily make Gandy and his father followers of the controversial Brothers, but it does show the family's concern with the growing chiliasm spawned from the social unrest during the revolutionary and Napoleonic periods. Gandy's 1805 diary entries dwell explicitly on "these times of trouble," as the dissenting preacher to whom he is listening makes topical reference to the invasion scares, parliamentary debate on the rights of Roman Catholics, and the propagation of false hope among the working-class miners. His evangelical delirium leads him once more to the airing of class resentment and fantasies of vengeance from a higher power, a continuum in many ways of the Bunyanesque parable of his Italian dream:

> Those frequenters of theatres and fashions, if they come
> to a place of worship its out of civility, its too demure &c
> neither can they like the company of those that frequent a
> House of Worship they are uneasy so much are they taken
> up with the world ... but the road to destruction many went,
> it was wide and broad.

This denunciation of worldliness and social elitism could not have served Gandy's professional ambitions very well. Less than a decade earlier, the polymath poet of natural history Erasmus Darwin wrote about a widespread affliction of the English people that he diagnosed as "orci timor, the fear of hell." In his Zoonomia, or the Laws of Organic Life (1796), Darwin ascribed this mania or "terror" to the theatrical appeal of Methodist preachers and to the political anxiety over the post-revolutionary fortunes of France.[48] The historical and religious constitution of Gandy from 1796 until 1805 virtually makes him a post-facto case study of Darwin's psychosocial pathology of Great Britain. Gandy's Pandemonium first emerges as a sketch done in Rome under Napoleonic

127 Sketch for Pandemonium, ca. 1804–05
128 The Mount of Congregation (detail of oil version), ca. 1818–30

occupation. Its daring visual translation of the sublime esthetic is subsequently fired by evangelical zeal. His terrifying vision of an industrialized classical hellscape matches his utopian proposals for the remaking of rural England put forth in the cottage pattern books. Enlightened reform and spiritual catharsis are held in tremulously creative balance.

Whatever degree of populist millenarianism may have contributed to Gandy's *Pandemonium*, its cultural appeal as a refined artistic statement remained intact. The fashionable collector Hope purchased the picture. Press accounts applauded it as an intrepid visualization of the Burkean sublime from a rising architect-artist of as yet unknown stature. Leigh Hunt recalled the impact of the picture in an essay of 1811 that also took stock of the condition of the fine arts in England:

The architect with the greatest appearance of genius is Mr. Gandy, but he has not exhibited this genius in any new mode of building, though it is possible he might do so, had he a proper opportunity. What gave the public a high idea of his taste and imagination was the drawing of *Pandemonium* exhibited a few years since—a most poetical production certainly, and glowing with preternatural fire of the original; but did the building in itself display invention, abstracted from its poetical circumstances, the extent, the burning ground, and the ghastly illumination?[49]

The pattern of critical opinion about Gandy remains consistent. There is the claim for his under-appreciated genius that is equal only to his lack of patronage, incurring the failure or inability to convert pictorial architectural spectacle into building practice. Consequently, some concern arises that the inspired display of scenic and poetical effect in Gandy's art perhaps hinders or dissembles the possibility of architectural invention anywhere beyond the picture frame of his RA exhibit.

Despite this critical questioning of the relevance of such imaginative and poetical interventions into the field of architecture, Gandy remained committed to the Miltonic project of architectural history painting. The heavenly pendant to *Pandemonium* would not make its appearance at the Royal Academy until 1818 when he exhibited his large watercolor *The Mount of Congregation*, which was also executed in oil, though the canvas has suffered severe damage [128, 129]. In the page-long RA catalogue entry for the picture, Gandy anthologized thirty disparate lines from *Paradise Lost* to serve as a textual guide to his picture. The architectural subject was at once a vision of paradise and "that high mount of God" (5.644) where the coming of the Messiah is foretold. Gandy drew his imagery primarily from the fifth book of Milton's epic. "Pavilions numberless, and sudden reared,/ Celestial tabernacles" (5.653–54), "High on a hill, far blazing, as a mount/ Raised on a mount, with pyramids and towers" (5. 757–58). The celestial kingdom in Gandy's picture encompasses an archetypal history of world architecture, with allusions to such legendary monuments as the Temple of Solomon and the Mausoleum of Augustus. At the base of the fortifications to heaven, Egyptian pylons and truncated pyramids, as well as Hindu colonnades and ramparts, encircle the ascending terraces and temple tiers of the sacred mountain. This microcosm of ancient architecture around the base of the mount is also seen in a verdant landscape study for the picture [130]. The architectural features

129 *The Mount of Congregation*, 1818
130 Landscape study for *The Mount of Congregation*, ca. 1817–18

become increasingly classical and even baroque as the eye follows the tapering heights of the monument, terminating with the redemptive *amortissement* of a glowing cross. As with the architecture of *Pandemonium*, the closest prototype for this Miltonic building is the Temple of Fortuna at Palestrina; the only difference, it seems, between heaven and hell in Gandy's architectural worldview was in the climate and air quality. The composition of Gandy's *Mount of Congregation* is modeled directly after Desprez's idealized re-construction of the Roman temple of Palestrina drawn during the 1780s [131]. Gandy may have seen a copy of the drawing in Wyatt's office (Desprez visited London in 1789) or more likely in copies circulating in Rome during his student sojourn. In transferring the speculative archaeological dimension of Desprez's sheet to the Miltonic beatitude of *The Mount of Congregation*, Gandy merged architectural history with religious vision, a tendency that would be elaborated more comprehensively in his later theories about the origins of human culture and the architectural imagination.

The divine monument in Gandy's picture is viewed in iconic symmetry, an Edenic landscape of palms and flowerbeds stretching before it, the entire scene framed by curtain swags as though the beholder were situated under one of the arboreal tents seen on the left hillside. A flock of angels hovers above a convex, globular censer fountain, the incense clouds filling the vista. Parhelic circles of light shine forth from the mount, echoing the expanding concentricity of the architectural plan of the sacred mountain. The luminous atmospheric effects of spiritual radiance counterbalance the sulfuric fumes and incinerating flares in the earlier *Pandemonium*. The shifting gradations of light in *The Mount of*

Congregation is particularly faithful to the Miltonic verse, as Gandy's catalogue entry cited from the opening of the sixth book, describing the mystery of temporal cycles in heaven: "Where light and darkness in perpetual round/ Lodge and dislodge by turns, which makes through heaven/ Grateful vicissitude, like night and day" (6.6–8). This constantly changing equipoise between night and day in heaven is suggested in Gandy's picture by the astral spheres and stellar rays that burst out of the opposing light and dark corners of the composition. These cosmological motifs recur in another Miltonic passage quoted by Gandy, in which the airborne movement of the angels assumes an astronomical logic, "That day ... they spent/ In song and dance about the sacred hill,/ Mystical dance, which yonder starry sphere/ Of planets and of fixed in all her wheels/ Resembles nearest" (5.618–22).

Gandy may have also looked to other literary sources for his architectural conception of the paradisiacal realm. The Sturm und Drang philosopher and poet J. J. Bodmer—a German translator of Milton and an early supporter of Henry Fuseli—offered his own visionary account of the mount of heaven in his epic prose poem *Noah* (1765). Gandy, as will be discussed later, was obsessed with the figure of Noah as a divinely inspired architect and was certainly familiar with this *Noachide* saga. The amalgamation of landscape and architecture in Gandy's picture corresponds in part to the episode of the storming of paradise by primitive giants in Bodmer's *Noah*: "The stupendous structure erected with steps to enter Paradise was rais'd on the side of the mountain ... a towering pyramid of enormous size, steps parallel extending along the huge pile, and on its top was a platform level with the blooming groves in the terraces of the sacred mountain."[50] Another likely guide to the spiritual topography of the infernal and heavenly realms was Emanuel Swedenborg's *Heaven and Hell* (1778), a mystical religious treatise read by artists and academicians such as William Blake and John Flaxman, who were affiliated with London Swedenborgian congregations during the late eighteenth century. Swedenborg's tract is

131 L.-J. Desprez, *The Temple of Fortuna*, ca. 1785

rife with generic visions of light-filled palaces, airborne colonnades, and crystal pavilions, but more significant are his reflections on space and distance in the empyrean state. The perception of spatial movement through the architectural splendors of heaven is experienced by angelic souls through interiority of vision resulting from the affective correspondence between mind and eye. As Swedenborg tried to explain the paradoxical condition of inner vision, "no notion or idea of space can enter their [angels'] thought, although there are spaces with them equally as in the world ... their sight acts as one with their thought and their thought as one with their affection."[51] In Gandy's *Mount of Congregation*, the concentric bands of light emanating from the monument have a distinctly ocular appearance—an omnipotent mind's eye reflected in the image. The picture returns your gaze. The pupil of this light-diffused eye becomes the medium through which the divine image of heaven is transmitted. As an exercise in Swedenborgian correspondence, Gandy's picture represents this envisioning of interior vision.

One contemporary reviewer at the RA exhibition was understandably mystified by this question of visionary transmission in Gandy's *Mount of Congregation*. The confounded critic astutely and somewhat wryly addressed the picture by way of optical experimentation, paranormal rapture, and electrical attraction. "Gandy has an extraordinary thing, as he says from Paradise Lost, but we are of the opinion it is from a Kaleidoscope found: it is utterly inexplicable, unless the artist has submitted to be magnetized, and this is a copy of one of his beatific visions."[52] The visual intricacy and reflective lighting effects of Gandy's picture elicited this scientifically topical sequence of references. First there is the recently invented Kaleidoscope of the Scottish scientist and natural philosopher David Brewster, whose handy optical device of shifting abstract patterns viewed within a mirrored tube embodied the modern marriage of art and science in the name of visual entertainment, mechanical efficiency, and blinding reverie.[53] The critic's allusion to Gandy being magnetized in order to create his picture has twofold implications. It refers to the spurious practices of mesmerists and magnetists—a hangover from the late Enlightenment shadow world of occult natural philosophy—who believed that trance-induced relaxation could restore body and soul while also invoking current scientific experiments into electromagnetism and the visualization of force fields undertaken by the scientist Humphry Davy and his brilliant apprentice Michael Faraday.[54] The intersection of science, mysticism, and optical invention in this critic's satirical account of Gandy's picture suggests how the reception and epistemological conditions of his art exceeded the literary and religious pretexts of its self-avowedly visionary content. A glimpse of heaven leads headway into the mysteries of mind and matter, involving contemporary explorations of ocular spirals in a novel optic toy, of hypnotic out-of-body experiences, and of electrically charged atmospheres harnessed in laboratory experiments.

Other architects joined Gandy in his effort to create mystically evocative literary pictures of architectural subjects. The Royal Academy exhibition catalogues are littered with entries for as yet untraced pictures of poetical edifices rendered by professional architects. W. F. Pocock exhibited his *Temple of Fame* in 1806, inspired by Alexander Pope's poem in which an allegorical temple whose four façades are adorned in different architectural styles swells to Miltonic proportions: "The growing tow'rs like exhalations rise,/ And the huge columns heave into the skies."[55] The cottage and villa architect John Papworth hoped to rival Gandy's *Pandemonium* with his 1807 RA drawing entitled *The Hall of Hela, Regions of Eternal Punishment, Vide Scandinavian Mythology*. The architectural writer and designer Richard Brown, who paid many compliments to Gandy in his architectural criticism, did so as well in his art by exhibiting *The Sepulchre of Rosicrucius* in 1821, a work depicting a magical automaton guarding the mystic's tomb as reported in Joseph Addison's *Spectator* papers. Many of these literary architectural paintings were medievalizing or Gothicizing in both theme and style, in keeping with the literary and antiquarian craze for the medieval past. Among Gandy's missing drawings in this voguish medieval vein is an RA exhibit of 1812, *Composition of Gothic Architecture*, which illustrated the melodramatic conclusion of Walpole's *The Castle of Otranto*. Nocturnal views of Rosslyn and Melrose from this same decade are also recorded but remain undiscovered. A "gothick" crescendo was attained with a surviving picture, *The Tomb of Merlin*, exhibited in 1815 [134]. Here was a medieval version of the numinous sepulchral interiors that Gandy had rendered earlier in an antique Greco-Roman idiom. The copious text of the catalogue entry for *The Tomb of Merlin* designated both the literary source of the picture—Ariosto's epic poem *Orlando Furioso*—and the historical program of its architectural setting:

> The drawing is a composition from the School
> of Constantinople, where the adoption of early
> Christian emblems began, giving rise to a new
> style of architecture—vide Eusebius, and other

ecclesiastical writers, also medals, and a description of the temple of Apostles which held Constantine's tomb.

> The very marble was so clear and bright,
> That though the sun no light unto it gave,
> The tomb itself did lighten all the cave.
> Vide Harrington's Orlando Furioso[56]

The oracular powers of prophecy, voices of the living dead lingering in baleful light, and the architectural expression of a nascent religion: these were just some of the concerns that Gandy united in *The Tomb of Merlin*. Following Ariosto's narrative, Bradamante, a female knight, has discovered a richly decorated chapel within a secret cavern—she is shown kneeling before a crucifix-mandorla. The small figure entering from the left in Gandy's picture is the Lady of the Lake, the sorceress who had entrapped and murdered Merlin within a crypt so as to claim his magical powers. The glowing tomb contains the corpse of the magus as well as his enduring spirit, the light issuing from it signifying the voice of Merlin that foretells the royal lineage destined to spring from Bradamante. The internally lit monument emits a necromantic aura—the tomb speaks to us from death about the future. Merlin's prophetic powers were also intimately tied to the early histories of Britain and Christianity itself. As Thomas Heywood asserted in his early seventeenth-century *The Life of Merlin*, "how truly Merlin spoke according to the prophetical, evangelical, and apostolical traditions."[57] Merlin was ancient Britain's Delphic oracle and Gandy wished to connect the haunting episode from Ariosto's refashioned version of the Arthurian legend with the early history of Christian architecture and its symbolic forms of worship.

The imagery of sentient tombs and self-illuminating symbols of religious faith had both pagan and Christian antecedents in Gandy's mind. There was the Sepulcher of King David that flamed forth with mystical lightening when violated by Herod's soldiers, as pictured in Maynard's 1800 folio edition of the historical writings of Josephus, which Gandy had consulted [132].[58] As noted earlier, while a student in Rome, he was infatuated with the stunning ephemera of Catholic ceremony. Although like many grand tourists from Protestant countries he frequently ridiculed the pageantry of Catholicism in letters home, Gandy nevertheless confessed to experiencing a momentary conversion while witnessing the papal benediction at St. Peter's. The viewing of the illumination of the cross inspired him to write to his father, "the effect is I suppose that the sun would have were it to issue from the sky in the dead of night."[59] This quasi-theurgic spectacle was recorded, not surprisingly, in Desprez's Roman *vedute* [133]. His interior perspective of the nave of St. Peter's depicting the illumination of the cross confirms Gandy's impression of radiance from a surrogate sun exploding within a shadowy architectural space—a sensate mysticism that was later re-staged in *The Tomb of Merlin* [134]. This eerie conceit of internal lighting also figured in a lost composition by Gandy representing a subterranean Greek temple dedicated to infernal deities. Gandy's RA catalogue entry for the missing picture of 1802 explained its mystical lighting: "The centre, which gives the light, and is fancied to be of a transparent material, receives its luminous appearance from a sub-adytum or from the infernal region itself."[60] Whether emanating from

132 J. Grainger after T. West, *Breaking Open the Royal Sepulcher of King David*, from George Henry Maynard's *The Complete Works of Flavius Josephus*, 1800
133 L.-J. Desprez, *Illumination of Cross at St. Peter's*, 1784
134 *The Tomb of Merlin*, 1815

the pagan underworld or from the imprisoned spirit of Merlin, these spectral lights marked the supernatural habitation of architectural space. In both the earlier *Sepulchral Chamber* and *The Tomb of Merlin*, the central motif of the tomb is complemented by the fitting of an elaborate lamp, which to Gandy also held sacred and occult connotations. In a preparatory drawing for *The Tomb of Merlin* [135] Gandy placed greater emphasis on the prominent oval shape and white glow from the hanging lamp. In Taylor's edition of Pausanias that Gandy often cited in his RA picture titles, the neo-Platonic scholar devoted several pages of endnotes to the archaeology and symbolism of ancient lamps. Taylor proposed that "the ancients possessed the art of constructing lamps that would burn for many ages without supply."[61] These "perpetual fires" were properly associated with the quest for immortality, the protection and veneration of the dead, and the accession of sacred wisdom. In 1784, Taylor lectured at the Freemasonic Tavern in London on the properties of light in which he attempted demonstrations of phosphorus-burning lamps.[62] As neo-Platonic metaphors, the lamps of sepulchral adyta, according to Taylor, signaled to the initiate that the descent into the realm of the dead was simultaneously an ascent into "the temple of intellectual illumination." English archeological and local antiquarian reports during the eighteenth century also recorded discoveries of iridescent lamps in underground tombs and excavations that were of course based entirely on occult legends and literary traditions.[63] That Gandy was attuned to the decorative symbolism of lamps is also seen in a sketchbook of richly colored and luminously transparent lamp designs, very much in the manner of and contemporaneous to Thomas Hope's interior furnishings and dating most likely from 1805–10. The ornamental patterns and outlined shapes of the lamps incorporate astral, lunar, and igneous motifs—crescents and flames of transcendent illumination [136].

The life-after-death narrative of *The Tomb of Merlin* informs the antiquarian spirit of the picture as well. The imaginary burial chamber-chapel of Merlin retains some features of the engraved illustration of the subject from the 1591 Harrington translation of *Orlando Furioso*, which was executed by the Italian engraver and illustrator Girolamo Porro [137]. The kneeling figure of Bradamante and the distinctive motif of the hanging lamp were clearly carried over by Gandy into his version, though their architectural features diverge considerably. Gandy's antiquarian topographic work for John Britton was recycled for the architectural setting of *The Tomb of Merlin*, as aspects of the decorated vaulting and the wreath entwined column are borrowed from his interior view of Rosslyn Chapel [72]. As noted in Chapter III, the Freemasonic legend of Rosslyn told of how the chapel's master-mason traveled to Rome to study an architectural motif for the design of the ornate columns at Rosslyn. Returning from his journey, he discovered that his apprentice had ingeniously designed and executed a wonderful column in his absence and out of envy slew the upstart student. Both the late medieval Masonic legend of Rosslyn and Ariosto's retelling of Merlin's fate center around the usurpation of authority and knowledge followed by ritual murder that haunts an architectural setting. Also recall that another legend of the St. Clair family of Rosslyn, who were reputed to have introduced the mysteries of Freemasonry to Scotland, revolved around the apparition of a fire appearing within the chapel the night before a member of the clan was to die. Such a prophetic though unconsuming flame, a fateful radiance from the realm of the dead, must have resonated in Gandy's mind with the spectral glow from Merlin's oracular tomb.

The translucent sepulcher of Merlin allows for its tracery and intricate decoration to remain legible despite the refulgent lighting. The arcaded monument is an unusual amalgam of a gigantic medieval reliquary and a crystal garden folly. The cluttered plethora of relics, fonts, altars, sepulchral crosses, hermetic banners, and ceiling paintings (most notably of Elijah in the flaming chariot, a motif rife with cabalis-

135 *Sketch for "The Tomb of Merlin,"* 1814–15
136 *Lamp Design*, ca. 1805–10
137 Girolamo Porro, *Illustration of Merlin's Tomb*, from Harrington's *Orlando Furioso*, 1591

tic overtones) throughout the haunted chamber was meant to suggest the urgent self-glorification of the new Christian faith, as Gandy noted, "giving rise to a new style of architecture." By encrusting the massive pillars and vaulted arches of this imaginary crypt with an almost hectic variety of chevrons, crestings, and moldings, Gandy was inventing what might best be called a decorated Norman style rather than reconstructing an early Christian and Byzantine style from the reign of Constantine, as mentioned in the text of the picture's title. The citation of Eusebius, the fourth-century ecclesiastical historian and neo-Platonic philosopher, was not mere discursive pedantry on Gandy's part. In his account of Constantine's funeral in the Church of the Holy Apostles, Eusebius commented on the first Christian emperor's marble coffin, "it dazzled their eyes who beheld it ... as if reverberating the Rays of the Sun."[64] Similarly in John Ball's *A Description of the City of Constantinople* (1729), Gandy's literary source on "the School of Constantinople," the funerary setting was described as being bathed in "a beautiful lustre from top to bottom."[65] Eusebius had also explained the spiritual properties of certain architectural and decorative materials, noting that "the sight of transparent bodies such as crystal, Parian marble, and even ivory recalls the idea of divine light."[66]

The light from Gandy's picture refracts a syncretic array of historical, religious, and poetical allusions. The sepulcher lit from within reconciles the material and the immaterial, the incandescence of the tomb bridging the gulf between the living and the dead and interconnecting its manifold referents across history and legend, from Merlin to Constantine to the Rosslyn clan. The mystical traditions converging

ARCHITECTURAL HISTORY PAINTING: GANDY AT THE ROYAL ACADEMY 123

around *The Tomb of Merlin* destroy the boundaries between the occult and the sacred, its illumination seeming both cursed and ethereal. In this respect, the picture's inquiry into an eclectic spirituality redolent of forbidden and esoteric knowledge has many analogies in the literary romanticism of the epoch. William Blake had imagined being imprisoned in "This Cabinet ... form'd of Gold/ And pearl and crystal shining bright."[67] Coleridge ventured into a dreamt temple of abstract religion where "the walls were brought to the eyes by a number of self-luminous inscriptions of pale sepulchral light."[68] And when in 1839 Edgar Allan Poe described "one of the phantasmagoric conceptions" of his deranged protagonist Roderick Usher, he unknowingly made his character into an artistic pupil of Gandy. Usher's painting of a mysteriously illuminated crypt was distinguished by "a flood of rays [that] rolled throughout, and bathed the whole in a ghastly and inappropriate splendor."[69] The conditions of imprisonment, delirium, and transgression insinuate these luminous revelations—a spiritual or occult quest evolves into the psychological trial of the romantic imagination.

The haunted luminosity of *The Tomb of Merlin* and its literary sources and analogues is also found in the late Georgian visual culture of eidophusikons, illuminated transparencies, and phantasmagoric theaters that flourished especially in London.[70] Loutherbourg's production of Pandemonium discussed earlier led the way in this lively metropolitan commerce in "special effects" entertainment. Irrespective of the scholarly apparatus and poetical tag for *The Tomb of Merlin*, Gandy's image of the lamp-like tomb lurking within a deep pocket of shadow would have reminded spectators of magic lantern projections and other mechanical illusions of the supernatural. The nighttime spectacle of a monument aglow from within was often the theatrical centerpiece on occasions of national celebration in wartime Britain. To mark the centenary of the Hanoverian dynasty, John Nash and Sir William

Congreve designed and staged an ephemeral architectural display in Green Park on the evening of August 1, 1814.[71] An illuminated Gothic castle, with fireworks behind it, underwent a transfiguration into the neo-classical Temple of Concord decorated with allegorical transparencies of the Triumph of Britain, the entire structure slowly rotating on axis. Gandy appears to have been on hand for the event, as he was stirred to execute a memorable atmospheric nocturne in watercolor of the entire spectacle that captured the tremendous effects of light [138]. By the following year, this orchestrated ritual of patriotic nationalism and the architectural showmanship of its crystalline monument would be buried deep within *The Tomb of Merlin*.

During the 1820s, Gandy sought to diversify his literary architectural perspectives by bringing orientalist and Ossianic themes into play. Between 1819 and 1822, there were four RA exhibits inspired by the eighteenth-century poet William Collins' *Persian Eclogues*. The watercolors are lost, but the imagery of the poetry—fortifications and palaces in twilit and nocturnal desert landscapes—plainly appealed to Gandy. Equally, he may been have attracted to Collins because of the poet's historical reputation as an unacknowledged, somewhat errant, genius whose life ended in madness and neglect. In 1828, Gandy produced a suite of watercolor sketches illustrating James MacPherson's controversial and sensationally popular Ossian poems. He was in fact coming somewhat late to the romantic mania for these Celtic mythic fables. The Ossianic poems posed a particular challenge to an architectural illustrator, and that was the absence of any elaborate edifices in the imagery of the verse. But Gandy's artistic proclivity for atmospheric drama was sufficiently engaged by the spirit mists and warring cloudbursts that dominate the climate of Ossian's mournful songs. In his rapidly executed drawings, Gandy washed in cloud-borne ghosts hovering over moonlit battlefields and sketched craggy coastlines with blasted trees and rainbows arcing through leaden skies [139, 140]. The only architectural landmarks were of course primitive and sepulchral—dolmens and cairns virtually indistinguishable from the savagely weathered landscapes. Here Gandy contrasted a primordial architecture of the earth with an atectonic atmosphere of swirling fog and apparitional light.

138 *Nocturnal View of the Temple of Concord in Green Park*, 1814
139 *Grave of Caithbat (from Ossian)*, 1828
140 *Ghosts in Moonlight (from Ossian)*, 1828
141 Thomas Cole, *The Voyage of Life: Youth*, 1840

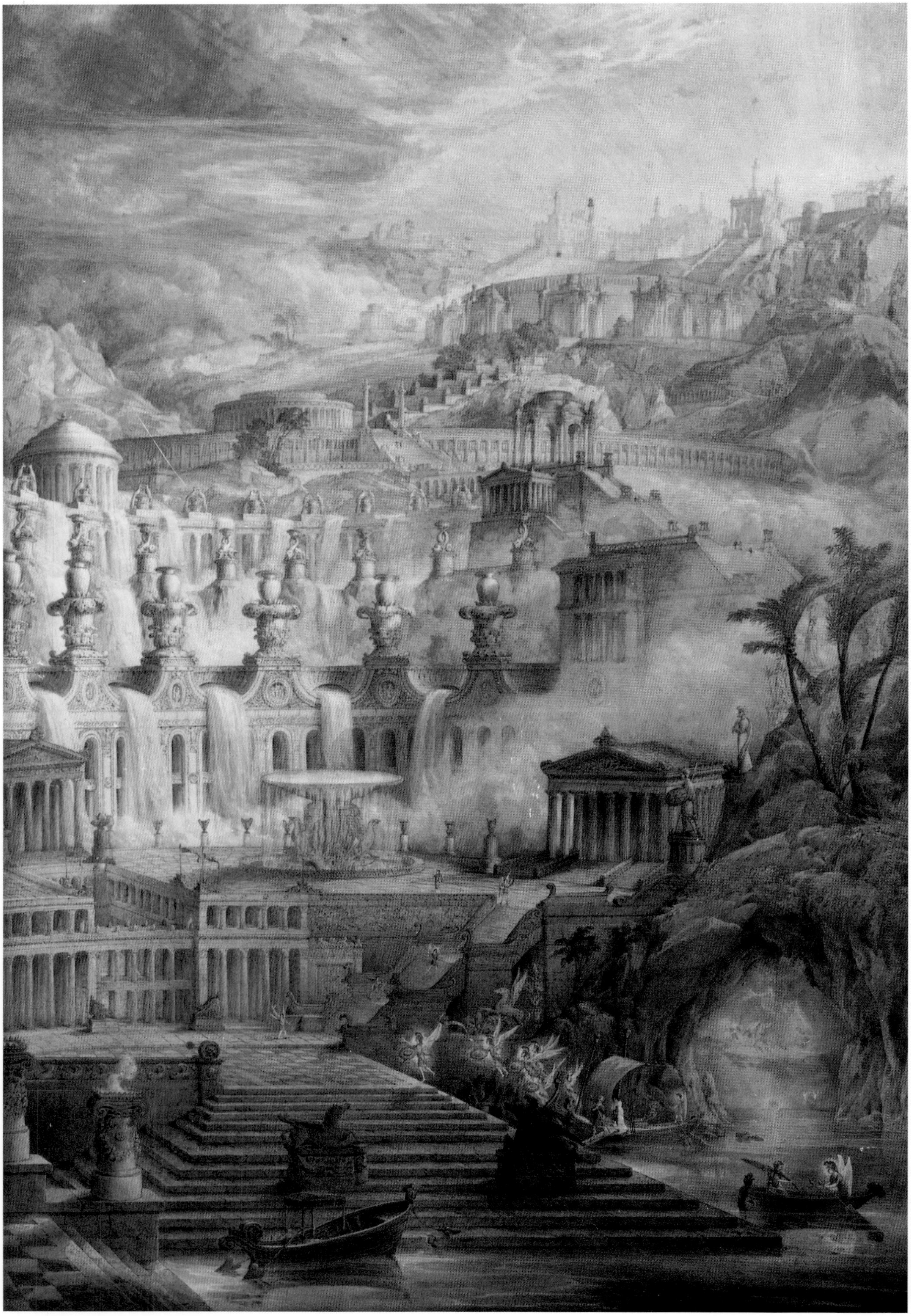

The early 1830s witnessed Gandy's return to Miltonic architectural painting with a vengeance. In successive RA exhibitions of 1832 and 1833, he showed the Miltonic pendants *The Staircase Leading to the Gates of Heaven* and *Bridge over Chaos*, architectural history paintings that were in many ways his most ambitious and most flawed works. Both pictures were arranged on a vertical axis with the architectural elements scaling up the picture plane and closely impacted with restricted depth perspective. Milton had warned that the architecture of heaven and hell was "inimitable on earth/ By model, or by shading pencil drawn" (3.508–09). Gandy was now struggling desperately against this defiance of visualizing the Miltonic sublime. In *The Gates of Heaven* [142], the architecture of heaven is clothed in a Hellenistic baroque style. The piled terraces of temples and pavilions, of courtyards and colonnades, adjoin the ascending levels of the staircase, which leads toward the glare of divine light dissolving the apex of the mountain. The upward progression of the eye, or the soul, through these architectural staging areas en route to heaven is answered by the descending movement of "the waters above the firmament" (3.1), the miraculous hydraulics of heaven channeling the cascades over enormous arcuated wall fountains. These massive waterworks turn the Miltonic scene into a celestial Tivoli adorned with gigantic Piranesian *vasi*. In the lower right corner, guardian angels assist the heaven-bound souls, who disembark from vessels after emerging from a cavernous waterway into the afterlife. Gandy's picture is finally concerned with this architectural mediation of spiritual passage, delineating the journey of the soul from darkness to light, from the nethermost grotto to the threshold of the empyrean.

John Summerson was correct, however: here the Miltonic vision tends perilously toward religious bathos.[72] Contemporary reviewers thought much the same. Gandy had abused poetic license. "Undoubtedly, it is quite unlike any earthly staircase," one critic noted, "but if intended to illustrate Milton's poetical description, and to represent to the eye what he has adumbrated forth to the imagination, we think it an egregious failure."[73] Another reviewer alighted upon the picture's bizarre shifts in scale, its lack of spatial coherence, and its diminution of grandeur brought about by its frantic concatenation of architectural elements: "The last scene of a pantomime would have served his purpose as well as Paradise Lost. When Young says, "He builds too low, who builds beneath the sky," he certainly did not address himself to architects whose poetical ideas are adapted only for our little planet."[74] Gone was the customary declaration of Gandy's under recognized genius; the pictorial crowding of his imaginary architecture was merely likened to childish entertainment. However, the allegorical sentimentality of *The Gates of Heaven* belongs to an important strain of romantic landscape art devoted to the religious topos of the journey of the soul. Turner's fantastically busy illustrative vignette for Bunyan's *Pilgrim's Progress* (1836) [143] and Thomas Cole's allegorical landscape cycle *The Voyage of Life* (1840) [141] further developed this visionary Christian interpretation of nature and architecture.[75]

142 *The Staircase Leading to the Gates of Heaven*, 1832
143 W. Humphrys after J. M. W. Turner, title vignette for John Bunyan's *Pilgrim's Progress*, 1836

Gandy's heart and soul, it appeared, were more truly in hell, at least if the disturbing and remarkable *Bridge over Chaos* is any indication. In Book 10 of *Paradise Lost* [144, 146], Satan returns to Pandemonium after his successful diversion in the Garden of Eden, his arduous journey across chaos expedited by "this new wondrous pontifice" engineered by Sin and Death (10.348). Gandy now locates the infernal capital embedded within a geological chasm. The Doric hypostyle hall has cyclopean retaining walls and a complicated domed portal (almost like a Byzantine-*chinoise* moon gate) flanked by Pompeiian aedicules. The presentation of Pandemonium with its massive piers encased in a gaping cavern recalls the Indian cave temples of Salsette and Elephanta, views of which were widely reproduced in the topographic aquatints of the Daniell Brothers in *Antiquities of India* (1793–99) [145]. In his introductory lecture on architecture at the RA, Soane illustrated these Indian temples and described them as if he were predicting Gandy's later picture: "The quantity, the masses, the gloom, the breaks of light and shade, must altogether produce a most awful and sublime effect."[76] Once again, Gandy's admixture of historical styles and world topographies (Pandemonium as a reworking of the Doric temples of Paestum interred in India) was meant to evoke a malevolent architecture of inestimable prehistory. The bridge spanning the cloudy gulf of chaos winds its way up through the composition, its rudely formed geological foundations supporting a double-story Roman aqueduct. Along the parapet of the bridge are gallows, torture wheels, sacrificial slabs, rocking stones, and granite needle pillars, forming a macabre gallery of implements of primitive religious ritual and torture. Gandy was at great pains to demonstrate his closely detailed reading of Milton and therefore included a number of figurative vignettes that are almost lost to view within the animated landscape. Damned souls are tormented by rebel angels who have themselves suffered from their recent metamorphosis into winged serpents, divine punishment for Satan's deception in Eden. Emblems of worldly power (swords, crowns, and jewels) are seen falling into "the foaming deep" (10.301), as Satan had promised to deliver to the damned "Thrones, dominations, princedoms" (10.460). Satan is twice present: as a vulture in flight above the bridge (he is compared to "ravenous fowl" [10.274]) and as a sea-serpent in the waters of chaos (with God's curse, Satan becomes "dragon grown" [10.529]). In

144, 146 *Bridge over Chaos*, 1833, with detail (right)
145 T. Bensley after Thomas and William Daniell, *Part of the Interior of the Elephanta*, from *Antiquities of India*, 1793–99

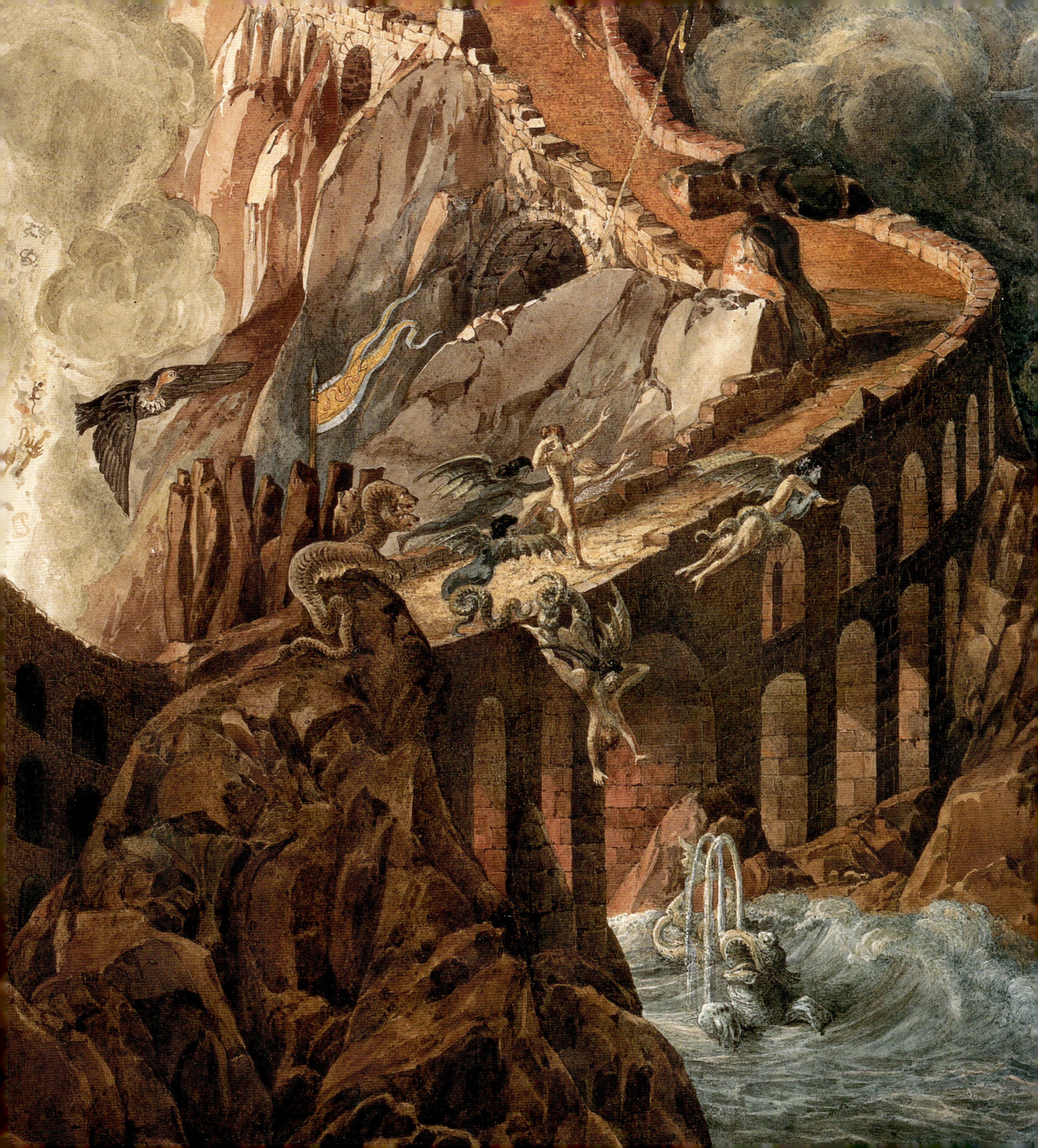

the cloud bank, a council of Greek gods looks on, referring to the serpent Ophion's thwarted plot to rule Mt. Olympus, a pagan variation on Satan's insurgency (10.580–84).

Quite apart from the Miltonic subject matter and these miniature figurative and emblematic details, *Bridge over Chaos*, like *Pandemonium* before it, is one of Gandy's finest efforts in imaginative landscape art. The precipitous cascade of fire and water that strengthens the treacherously vertical bias of the composition is shot through with flashes of lightning. The sharp transition in the chromatic temperature of the cavernous scenery captures the Miltonic phrase, "many a frozen, many a fiery alp" (2.620). Geological surfaces have a faceted and variegated quality, imbued with a pale iridescence of icy blue and soiled mauve. The bridge is of course serpentine in its movement, the built landscape of hell transformed into an architectural manifestation of Satan, "punished in the shape he sinned" (10.516). As it snakes through the quarried abyss, the bridge veers drastically upward into the left foreground, its roughly hewn spandrel looming unexpectedly above the spectator. The perspective brought to this sweeping approach of the bridge is anamorphically distorted, requiring a viewing angle from off to the left of the picture to restore any semblance of perspectival continuity to the aqueduct. The rock formations in the picture also have a delusional aspect. Skeletal patterns and skull-like shapes emerge throughout the subterranean landscape, leaving traces of an agonized geology of the damned. The infernal landscape produces a condition of disorientation and cognitive uncertainty. The dissolution of fundamental sensory polarities (outside/inside, near/far, hot/cold, animate/inanimate) is effected by the teeming surface and vertical compression of Gandy's picture. He was searching for a visual analogy to the highest praise that Edmund Burke had granted to the terrific impact of *Paradise Lost*: "The mind is carried out of itself by a crowd of great and confused images."[77]

These later Miltonic exhibits by Gandy were rendered in the shadow of the popular cataclysmic landscape artist and printmaker John Martin. Although Gandy first thought of engraving Miltonic illustrations for profit while in Rome, it was Martin who made a fortune by marketing his large mezzotints of scenes from *Paradise Lost* in 1825–27. He popularized catastrophic architectural vistas of lost empires and

147 John Martin, *The Courts of Heaven*, from *Paradise Lost*, 1826
148 John Martin, *Bridge over Chaos*, from *Paradise Lost*, 1826
149 *Tomb of Nitocris, Babylon*, ca. 1830

spiritual kingdoms, succeeding outside the academic art world while Gandy was still struggling for recognition. After the premiere of Martin's breakthrough painting *Belshazzar's Feast* at the 1821 British Institution exhibition, one unusually skeptical reviewer (Hazlitt perhaps) wrote, "I would just as soon have Gandy's *Mount of Judgement* which he exhibited several years agone as Martin's *Belshazzar*."[78] Art critics were aware that Martin had an unacknowledged precursor in the person of Gandy; as one reviewer commented in 1834 regarding Martin's much-acclaimed originality:

> The only novelty is in his original idea of accumulating an immensity of stupendous objects by means of perspective, and heightening the most obvious and palpable sources of the sublime. It is a grand and striking idea, but much better adapted to the stage than to a picture. It was an improvement upon Gandy's architectural visions of Pandemonium, &c.—strange aggregations of enormous structures; castles in air with geometrical plans and elevations, each a nightmare to the fancy. Martin cut up and set up in the foil of effect, the rough gem which Gandy had dug up.[79]

Martin's mezzotints of *The Courts of Heaven* and *The Bridge over Chaos* relied on drastically receding orthogonals in expansive vacuums of darkness [147, 148]. The abyssal depth of the celestial stadium in his illustration was framed by a rectilinear colonnade; his mining tunnel through hell is pictured telescoping incisively toward a distant pinpoint of light. In contrast, the vertical pictorial format and the frantically multiplied levels of architecture and landscape in Gandy's Miltonic exhibits of the early 1830s resisted a unified and readily grasped perspective. Gandy was absolutely intent on distinguishing these compositions from Martin's graphically memorable and widely known illustrations. However, in a preliminary sketch from the same period for a historical composition of the tomb of Nitocris in the portal to Babylon [149], Gandy shows that he was already more than familiar with the formulaic techniques that Martin had perfected in his ancient Middle Eastern architectural landscapes.

To Gandy, the irony must have seemed cruelly predictable. When he first exhibited *Pandemonium* in 1805, Martin was looking for work as a decorative coach and china painter; a couple of decades later he was overtaking Gandy. The affinity between them was also noted after the fact in 1852 by George Wightwick, who observed, "I ever lamented that Martin had not been 'apprenticed' to Sir John Soane, because he might then, with legitimate pretension, have even more than rivaled the beautiful illustrations which poor Gandy used to give of Soane's architectural imaginings."[80] The artistic aspirations and poetical resonance that Gandy had brought to his architectural history paintings were not all forsaken, as we shall see, in his "imaginings" for Sir John Soane.

v: Soane and Gandy at the Fall of Architecture

Lecturing at the Royal Academy in 1815 on the lost splendors of Greece and Byzantium, Professor Soane deemed it necessary to burst any pipe dreams that his historical reflections might inspire in the minds of his students:

> Instead of seeing these magnificent examples of rich fancy and bold imagination; instead of those flights of powerful mind and magical genius realized in this country, the artists of our days must, I fear, be more moderate in their expectations. In the great metropolis of this mighty empire, to whom Europe owes its choicest blessings, we in most cases can only contemplate a prodigious extent of buildings of various descriptions formed without any general plan of beauty and convenience and with an almost total disregard for national grandeur.[1]

Soane returns frequently to this sorrowful and resentful lament regarding the impoverished circumstances of modern architecture in Great Britain, and more particularly in London. Through his actual buildings, and even more through his unbuilt projects, Soane sought to fashion a sort of alternative history of contemporary architecture, an idealized vision that transcended the sordid reality. And he depended on Gandy to give these projects an epic scope. Both Gandy and Soane recoiled from the conditions of modernity, and their combined efforts in the field of architectural representation served as a cultural reprimand to the denigration that architecture was suffering in modern society. As Soane woefully declaimed, "O, Architecture! ... how art thou fallen, fallen, fallen!"[2]

From 1798 until 1801, Gandy worked in Soane's office as his draftsman, the office daybooks documenting the schedule of tasks that occupied him. He prepared drawings that would be exhibited under Soane's name at the RA and would also travel to construction sites to record topographic views of buildings (or proposed buildings) at different times of day and in diverse weather conditions. After March of 1801, when Gandy embarked on his own architectural practice, he returned to Soane's office when called upon, which was frequently. Unfortunately, the letters between Soane and Gandy do not tell us much about their working relationship. During the early years, Gandy would communicate with Soane about specific points of concern regarding the content and arrangement of his drawings. In preparing the 1803 RA perspective of Soane's own library at Pitzhanger Manor [151], Gandy requested clarification on the selection of folios and drawings that would appear on the library table (a Piranesi volume and Soane's plan for the Bank of England), adding that "the mirror is large and will have its share of the reflected perspective."[3] However, this letter does not prepare one for the drawing's stylishly somber ambiance with its gloomily draped proscenium and reverberating circle of sunlight. Later that same year, Gandy writes to Soane for clearance on introducing naval flags and globes into the interior perspective of the design for Lord Bridport's library at Cricket Lodge [152]. He begins the letter with the general observation that "pictures of architecture may avoid the repetition of parts of a uniform design, so that it informs the spectator of the Architect's whole intent."[4] Light and landscape remained essential

150 John Soane (rendered by Gandy), *View of the Dome of the Soane Museum at Night*, 1811

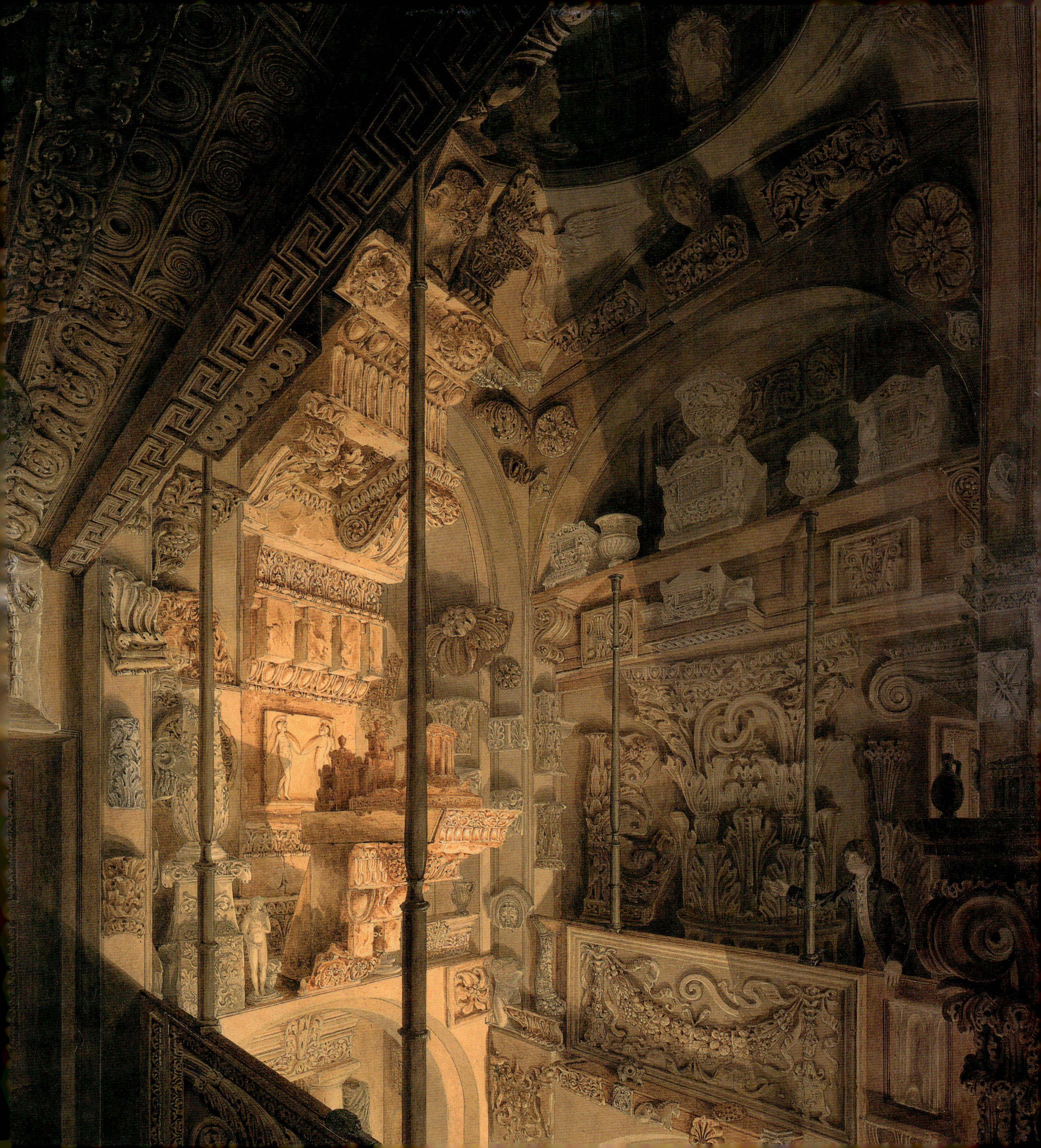

in visualizing this "whole intent." In Gandy's unfinished watercolor view of this library, twilit shafts of light burst into the interior space at a low angle of entry with the distant hills and the sea visible through the window. The linear incised pendentive dome and sail vaults that were Soane's architectural hallmark in demarcating space seem to be actively shaped by the sunbeams. The fanning tunnel of light appears to push the taut domed enclosure into place.

It is extremely difficult to judge the degree to which Gandy's visualizing skills had a determining influence on Soane's experimental approach to spatial form and his unique conflation of Greek and Gothic idioms of architecture. Soane's architectural style was already defined by the time that Gandy entered the office. But for well over a quarter of a century, Gandy's pictorial manipulation of Soane's designs induced and catalyzed the elder architect's ever-increasing sensitivity to the poetical disembodiment of architecture. Gandy is often seen as having a liberating influence on the demanding and repressive Soane. As Gillian Darley wrote of their symbiotic artistic relationship, "It is as if Soane's architecture had been waiting for someone to translate his buildings from pleasing fair copies into a continuous narrative—a visual argument with which to confront a critical world."[5] Gandy was indeed made responsible for presenting Soane's public face at the RA exhibitions, which on occasion led to ill will between them over the question of the creative responsibility for these exhibits. During *The Guardian*'s series of attacks on Soane's architecture in 1821, the anonymous authors had remarked that Soane's exhibit of a proposed

151 John Soane (rendered by Gandy), *Library of Pitzhanger*, 1803
152 John Soane (rendered by Gandy), *Interior of Cricket Lodge*, 1803

national palace was a marvelous drawing but a rotten design. As discussed earlier, the intrigue over *The Guardian* articles elicited what Gandy called "boiling words" between himself, Soane, and Britton. Soane must have dressed down Gandy over the journalistic suggestion that the artistry of the drawing exceeded the ingenuity of the architectural design it represented. With alarm and unwarranted contrition, Gandy wrote to Soane, "The idea of my projecting your designs is absurd; in no way but with malignants [sic] would I get credit for them ... did I not respect you beyond myself?"[6] Gandy's fancifully atmospheric perspectives for Soane may have also inspired some of the critical scorn visited upon Soane in the press, as when *Fraser's Magazine* claimed in a review of the 1832 RA exhibition, "It is, in architecture, the same kind of monstrous thing that Turner's are in painting."[7] During the last eleven years of Gandy's work for Soane, the question of his ghostdrawing Soane's designs was complicated by the aging architect's failing eyesight. As C. R. Leslie recalled:

> He [Gandy] was much employed by Soane in making drawings; and I remember an exhibition at Somerset House, in which the architectural room was made (what is rarely the case) as attractive as any other, by his drawings alone; though his name was not in the catalogue! They were a series of magnificent designs, to which Sir John Soane's name was attached, though Soane was then entirely blind! How far they were suggested to Gandy by him it is impossible to say; but it may be doubted whether anything exhibited by Soane before his blindness equaled them.[8]

This would have been in 1829 or 1830, when Gandy uncharacteristically had no exhibits under his own name at the RA. Gandy of course came to depend financially upon these commissions from Soane, despite the fact that they implied an erasure, as it were, of his own artistic identity.[9] As noted earlier, their relationship was often fraught with barely restrained rancor and also unspoken sympathy. There were even times when Gandy reserved the most innovative techniques in architectural representation that were at his disposal for the rendering of Soane's work.

Gandy correctly recognized in Soane a self-commemorating impulse to secure the historical memory of his architectural creations. Soane's contemporaries saw this trait in him as well, and dismissed it as vanity. Gandy's most elaborate drawings in honor of Soane's work often functioned as allegorical commentaries on the nature of architectural representation itself. In 1818, Gandy exhibited a pictorial tribute to Soane under his own name and direction, which was entitled *A Selection of Parts of Buildings, Public and Private, Erected from the Designs of John Soane, Esq, R.A. in the Metropolis and Other Places in the United Kingdom Between the Years 1780 and 1815* [154, 155]. This elaborate and painstakingly executed picture pays homage to Soane's career while also recording the many renderings that Gandy had produced for him over the prior two decades. The setting is a large studio chamber without windows, intimating that the room is strangely removed from the world of the commonplace. Its architectural features bear Soane's style with a canopied saucer dome adorned with elongated Greek frets and winged victories; an Ionic screen with giant orders is partially visible. Otherwise the interior is covered with models and pictures of Soane's architecture, the space brimming over with one hundred or so architectural vistas and variously scaled replicas of the architect's lifework. The Bank of England with Tivoli Corner and the Dulwich Picture Gallery and Mausoleum are granted pride of place elevated in middle ground, though less grand if no less ingeniously designed buildings such as the primitivizing lodges, gatehouses, and stables from Tyringham, Hamels Park, and Bagshot are also fairly prominent. Soane's personal architectural landmarks, from the understated elevation of his house-museum in Lincoln's Inn Fields to the lugubriously draped Soane family tomb, introduce the private themes of the architect's life into the picture, centered around his habitual collecting of antiquities and artworks and his protracted mourning over the death of his wife in 1815. The majority of the framed pictures within the picture capture the distinctive spatial experiences of Soane's top-lit interiors. There is also an implied *paragone* here between the painted illusion of a watercolor perspective and the three-dimensional illusion of an architectural model. Both are perforce fragmentary and metonymic with respect to the built referent, whether conceptually or perceptually considered. The relative merits of the model and the drawing in architectural practice was a question touched on by Soane in his final RA lecture, in which

153 Daniel Maclise, Portrait Caricature of John Soane, 1834
154 Preliminary Sketch for "A Selection of ... Designs of John Soane," 1818
155 A Selection of Parts of buildings, Public and Private,
Erected from the Designs of John Soane, 1818

SOANE AND GANDY AT THE FALL OF ARCHITECTURE 137

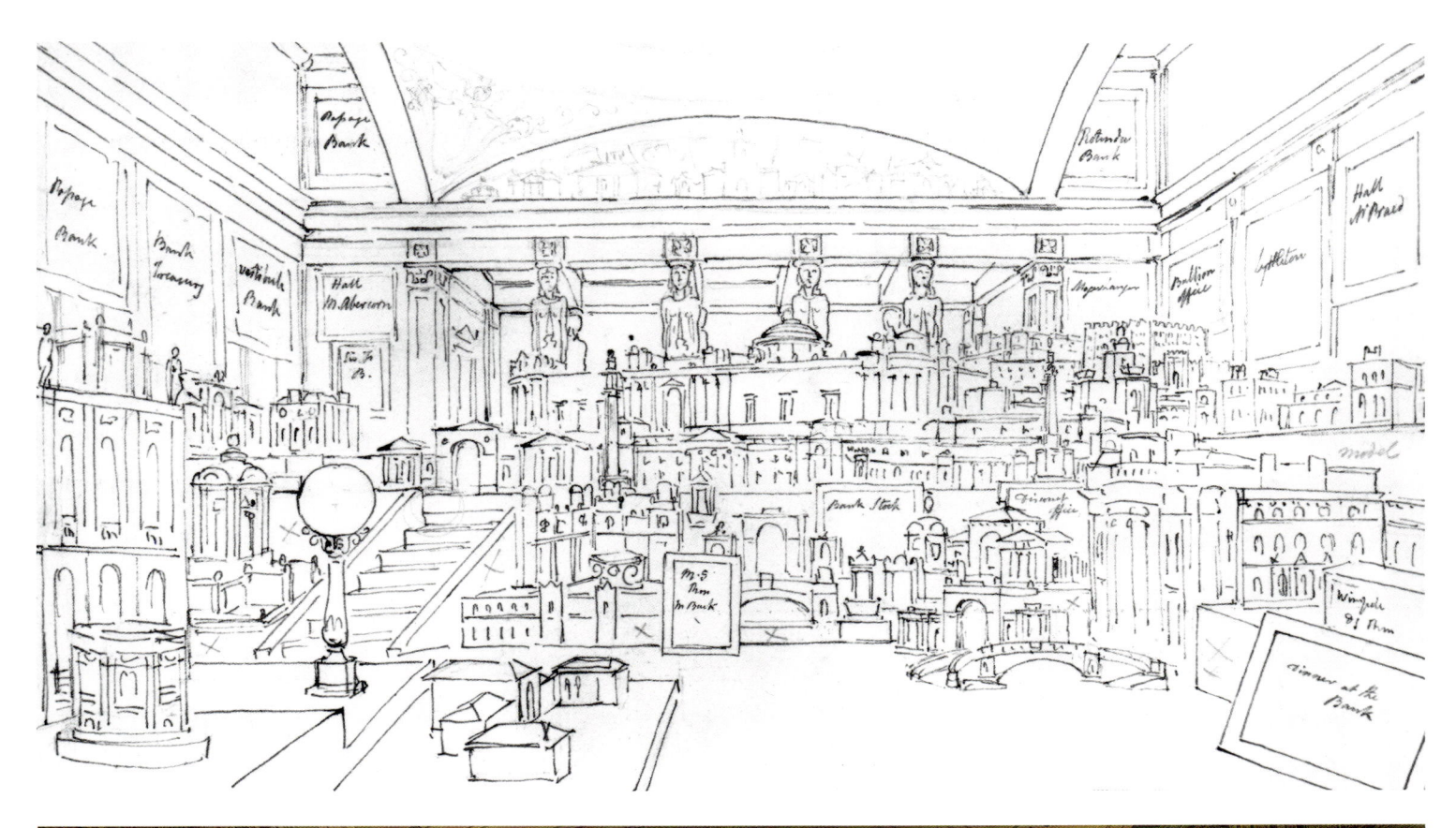

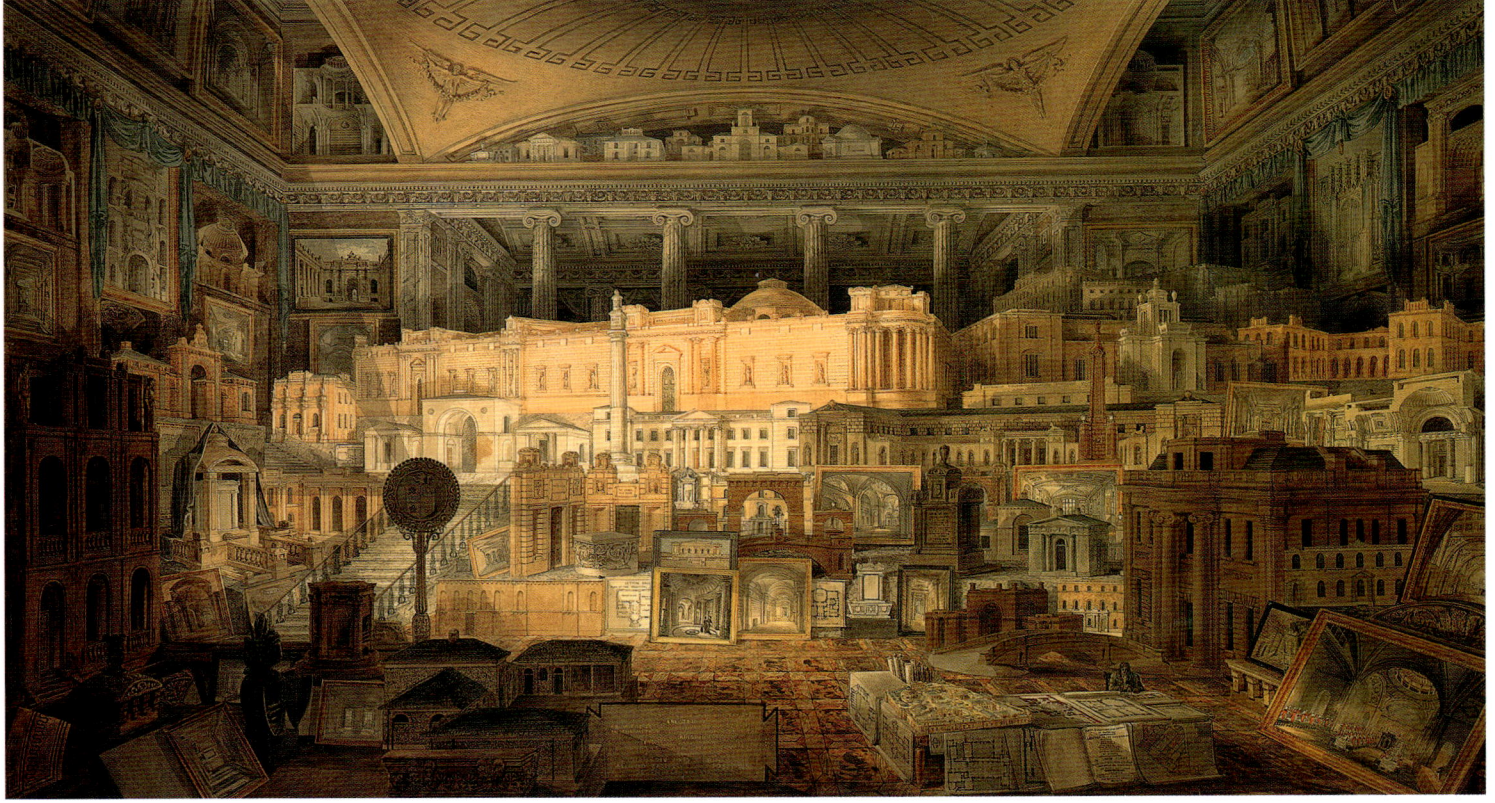

he quoted the opinion of the architect James Peacock from his treatise *OIKIDIA, or Nutshells* (1785). With no-nonsense practicality, Peacock had advised that "when the person who wishes to build is possessed of a design ... his next step should be to have made, not a gaudy eye-trap, to dazzle and confound, ... but a complete plain model."[10] Gandy was if anything a master of the gaudy eye-trap, but here the eye-trap subsumes while also emboldening the surrealistically amplified and miniaturized models of architecture. The picture nods slyly to the conventions of Flemish Baroque *Kunstkammer* painting and to the eighteenth-century Roman gallery paintings of Panini and Robert. In place of the taxonomies of art, nature, and antiquity Gandy collects the architectural corpus of Soane, assembled as a treasure trove of constructed figures of the mind.

This watercolor is a complicated masterwork of artificial lighting and shadow projection. The interior is illuminated by a studio lamp with reflectors, the splintered rays of light breaking through the tenebrous space to reveal multiplying scenes of architecture. Although this reflective lamp is decorated with the concocted heraldry of the Soane family arms, it is more accurate to say that the lamp represents Gandy, who is also shown as physically present in the right foreground working at a table covered with floor plans and a model of the Bank of England complex. Like an eclipsed sun in a penumbral world, the mirror and lamp flood the studio interior with a mystical and rarefied aura, transforming Soane's buildings into artistic mementos. In a letter to Soane written perhaps while he was working on this sheet, Gandy praised him for demonstrating that "architecture is an inventive art whose models must be formed in the mind."[11] He was in fact paraphrasing from Soane's own RA lecture in which it was asserted that "invention is the most painful and the most difficult exercise of the human mind."[12] Soane and Gandy agreed that architectural invention was a mental exercise divorced from the laws of imitation that governed the other arts, but they nonetheless wished to legitimize architectural invention through analogies with poetry and painting. Soane's theoretical notes on the interdependence of architecture and the arts suggest as much. "Like poetry, it [architecture] presents a succession of varied pictures," and elsewhere he wrote, "Architecture can form pictures of the most sublime kind, aye and produce and create a fiction or tell a story and affect the mind with its varied passions."[13] Through this anthology of Soane's work, Gandy visualized this pictorial and narrative range of architecture. Detached from the prosaic reality of commissioned buildings, architecture is represented as a reservoir of what Soane would describe as "intellectual delights and mental gratifications."[14] As so much of the reality of Soane's architecture has been lost to history one may say that Gandy's pictorial illusion has, after all, won out. Many of Soane's most ambitious buildings endure only within the fictive spaces of Gandy's perspectives.

Gandy thus gave pictorial life to buildings by Soane that were never to be brought to architectural reality. The same approach informs the watercolor that he prepared for Soane's 1820 RA exhibit, which bore the elegiac title *Architectural Visions of Early Fancy, in the Gay Morning of Youth; and Dreams in the Evening of Life* [156]. The mountainous scenery and turbulent atmosphere of this allegorical landscape had been seen frequently in Gandy's Pausanian re-constructions. But now the architectural objects of restoration were being constructed anew, or at least their speculative archaeology belonged to the mind and recollections of Soane and not to an ancient source. The picture is a retrospective inventory of grandiose building types that had been favored by the young Soane and other late eighteenth-century architects during their formative period of study: triumphal bridges and ceremonial arches, senate houses and casinos, mausolea and sepulchral chapels. Architectural subjects of this kind, Soane cautioned in his RA lectures, were to be treated "as theoretical visions, as pleasing pictures, as mere portfolio designs."[15] But taken together, they were meant to represent what the architectural landscape of Great Britain could have been had Soane had his way. In the spot-lit middle ground of the landscape, Soane had Gandy place the oldest and the most recent of his unbuilt architectural projects, his student design for a national senate house and the 1818 design for a national monument to memorialize the victories and sacrifices of the Anglo-French Wars. The picture also collects failed architectural competitions for less august building types, including Soane's designs for St. Luke's Hospital and a male penitentiary which are recessed into the distant hills. While youthful figures fish, boat, and explore the architectural scenery of ruins and cemeteries in the picture's foreground, a military funeral procession makes its way up the hill toward the mountain peaks crowned with sepulchral monuments. The palette of the watercolor is marked by the gradual transition from the earthy warmth of the proximate "morning" of the composition to the ethereal blue "evening" of the distant landscape. The resurrection of Soane's unrealized designs yields an architectural Valhalla that is both redemptive and remorseful in mood.

The picture's melancholic grandeur is of course carefully staged, though it remains no less expressive of, as Summerson phrased it, "Soane's self-tormenting mind."[16]

Critical opinion was divided over the narrative and autobiographical tone of this pretentious and imaginative RA exhibit. A reviewer for *Annals of the Fine Arts* judged it "a grand poetical composition of the best of Mr. Soane's designs ... floating in aerial clouds, an architectural vision of real and vivid fancy."[17] This critic also wished Soane happy dreams in the evening of his life. Other reviewers were not so solicitous. A writer for *The Englishman* complained: "Mr. Soane has sent his sketches of recollections of youth and dreams of age; but they are merely chimerical groups of porticoes and temples, huddled together, without any point of practical design. We have never known the architectural part of the Royal Exhibition [to be] worse, [although] architecture has not been so interesting as now, when we are making new streets and projecting grand improvements."[18] Such commentary obviously piqued Soane, though he had seen, and would see, much worse in his press coverage. The reference to John Nash's urban renovations of London's commercial and residential districts was especially galling. Nash was often the unspoken target of Soane's more spectacular proposals for public edifices, which were put forth as epic though largely irrelevant challenges to the royal commissions garnered by his colleague in the Office of the King's Works. Our reviewer quite reasonably questioned the contemporary relevance of the classical civic building types mournfully ennobled in *Architectural Visions*. This skepticism about the durability of classical architecture in the modern metropolis was also voiced elsewhere.

As early as 1800, the anonymous author of *Domestic Union, or London As It Should Be* lampooned the new generation of architects that would presume to stamp a classical imprint onto the unmanageable form of the metropolis:

> I am not going to venture upon so rash a flight as you imagine—to you I leave the sublime study of raising "temples worthier of the Gods"—of Palaces more adequate to the dignity of the Sovereign ... I shall not invade your province by decorating our Squares and Areas with triumphal arches, with obelisks, or with statues—my pursuit is of a different type: the magnificence which flows from public convenience and utility.[19]

Soane and Gandy were soon disseminating designs for palaces that were ruefully illustrative of this urban pragmatist's diatribe. If the English recovery of the architectural grandeur of antiquity was ever to be undertaken, the historical moment after Waterloo, when nationalistic fervor fed cultural expectations for public architecture, was seemingly the perfect time. The popular press and fine arts journals were filled with acclamations for commemorative monuments and public civic architecture. Even while arguing that the commissioning of honorific war monuments was "a wanton waste of national wealth," the practically minded art critic "Publius" had to admit that a Waterloo monument would ideally serve as "an edifice dedicated to the record of national virtue, its exterior exhibiting the history of our freedom."[20] The Scottish associationist philosopher and journalist Archibald Alison petitioned vigorously for national monuments (preferably in the form of Doric temples) throughout the capital cities of the British Isles. As he reasoned in his essay on the topic in 1819:

> To those who have not been in the habit of attending to the influence of animating recollections upon the development of every thing that is generous in human character, it may appear that the effects we anticipate from such structures are visionary and chimerical ... Upon people so disposed, it is difficult to estimate the effects which splendid edifices filled with monuments to the greatest men whom their respective countries can boast may ultimately produce. It will give stability and consistence to the national pride, a feeling, which, when properly directed, is the surest foundation of national eminence.[21]

These expressions of philosophical nationalism and patriotic enfranchisement were not so different from those found earlier in Major Cartwright's plan for the Hieronauticon. Hypothesizing urban space for public rituals of commemoration was deemed fundamental to sustaining a collective spirit of post-war nationalism, especially as economic crises and social dissension between classes began to tarnish the glory of post-Waterloo Britain. The commercial and industrial growth of London had to be balanced by the more reflective

156 Overleaf: John Soane (rendered by Gandy), *Architectural Visions of Early Fancy ...*, 1820

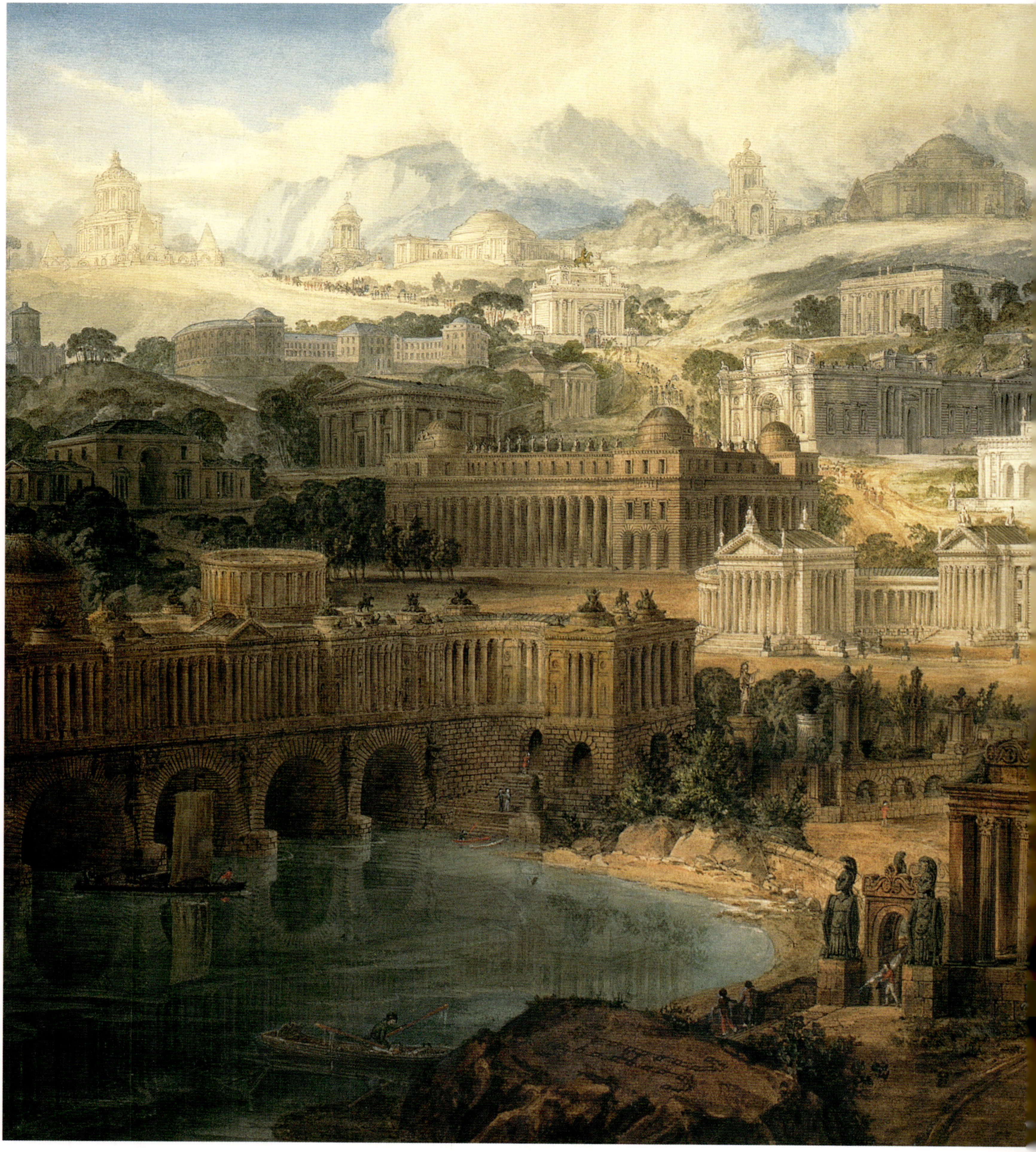

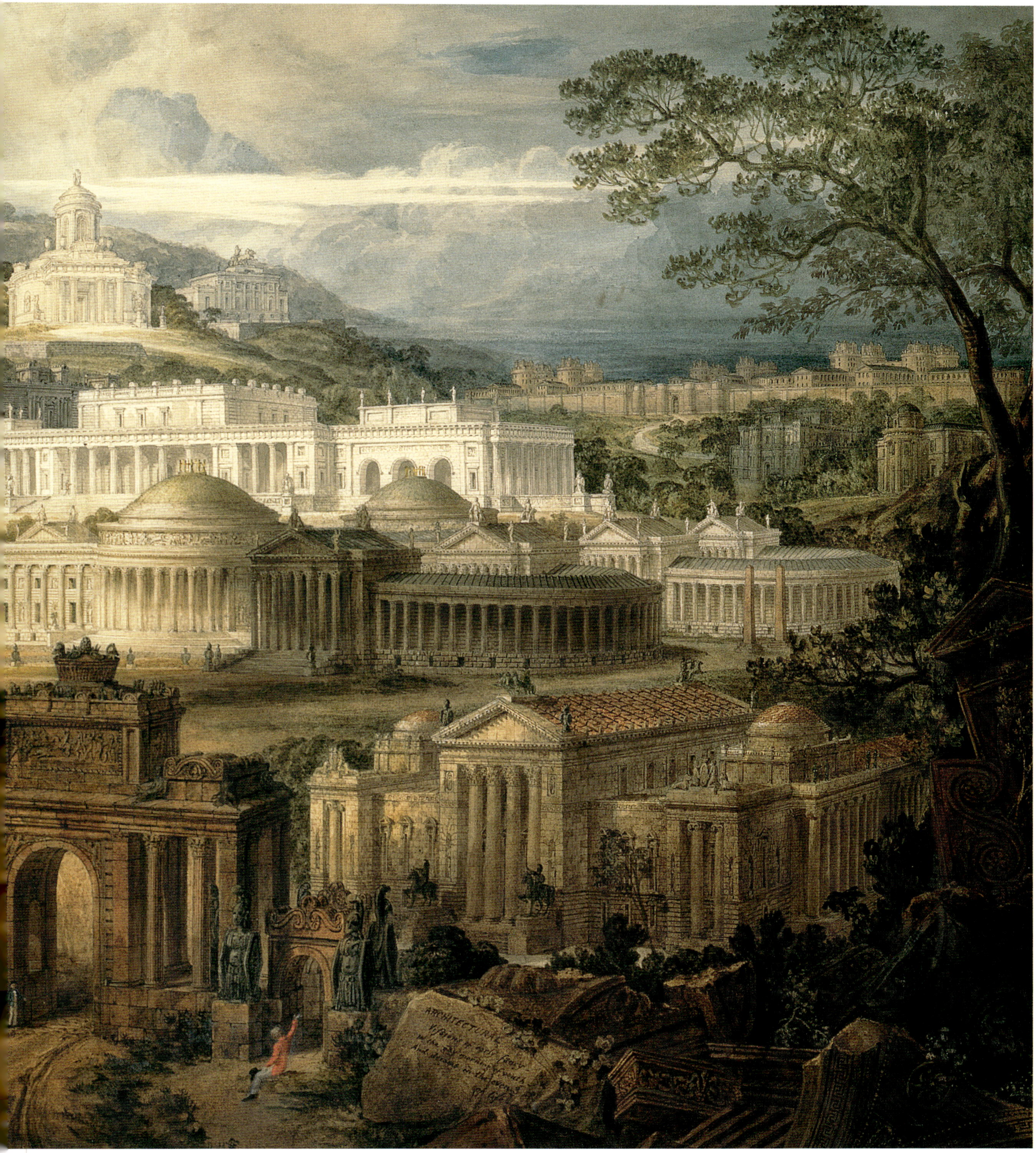

cultivation of the metropolis as a national landscape in which time-honored military power and royal authority could be venerated and re-affirmed.[22]

Throughout the 1820s, Gandy delineated for Soane a series of aerial perspectives of royal palace designs that were proposed as symbolic landmarks in this national metropolis. Soane would have agreed heartily with the sentiments of an art critic who in 1833 wrote, "The palace is an heirloom presented by an enlightened people to future ages. If flimsy piles are to rise and fall at the nod of caprice, farewell to the dream of antiquity!"[23] Other journalists encouraged artists to step forward to contribute to the architectural adornment of post-Waterloo London. John Martin was a likely candidate for the job, as one writer pleaded: "London is but a city of brick-stacks, compared with the meanest city on which the painter has laid his brush. We wish he would make a design for a British palace—we might then hope to see something worthy of the island."[24] This journalistic outcry in support of grandiloquent architectural proposals for royal palaces was answered by the series of designs exhibited by Soane, who was especially anxious to steal the favor of George IV away from Nash. In his RA exhibits and a series of publications during the 1820s and early 1830s, Soane promoted his ambitious "public improvements" including triumphal entrances into the metropolis and ceremonial routes through the parks of London that would connect a new royal palace to the renovated and enhanced building complex at Westminster.[25] As the likelihood that these commissions would ever be realized grew more remote, the tenor of the drawings and proposals grew more shrilly grandiose and vociferous. Passionate futility was dear to both Gandy and Soane. The *Bird's-Eye View of a Design for a Royal Residence* [157], exhibited in 1821, and *Design for a Royal Residence*, exhibited in 1827, were variations on Soane's recurrent obsession with a sprawling palace on Constitution Hill. The first was more Greek, the second more Roman. The first was planned around looping hemi-cycles with quadrangles enclosed within, the second was exclusively quadrangular with an expansive forecourt and projecting wings. Triumphal arches and equestrian military statues as roof ornaments were common to both. *The Guardian* found the 1821 design too funereal, noting that the deeply recessed entry arches along the façades and the ground-hugging extensiveness of the palace gave it the air of a necropolis. The bird's-eye view employed by Gandy allowed the designs more than enough breathing space, with the surrounding parklands and curtains of mists insulating the palaces from the barely discernible skylines of London. The aerial perspective was meant to clarify the site plan of the palace within its urban context while also making it appear like a newly created antique city unto itself. Through the interventions of John Britton, Gandy and his colleague in antiquarian topography Frederick Mackenzie were employed in 1828 to prepare drawings for a publication on the panorama of London at the Regent's Park Colosseum, where Gandy's son had worked as a painter [158]. The sweeping vistas and descriptive precision of these aquatints accord with the bird's-eye perspectives that Gandy had often used for Soane's projects.[26] In an 1821 editorial on "Architectural Portraiture," a London art critic complained of the taste for bird's-eye perspectives and illusions of spatial distance bred by panoramas and topographic prints. "An incorrect and deceitful mode of representation in viewing the metropolis," the critic complained. "It is hoped too that the spectator will not again be compelled to look down into instead of gazing up with admiration at a portico."[27]

Gandy could handily manage both vantages for Soane's imaginary palaces. In successive RA exhibits of 1827 and 1828, he rendered Soane's design for a triangular palace from the admiring point of view beneath a looming portico as favored by the critic cited above and also as an exhilarating aerial panorama. The rendering of the palace's Corinthian portico with its high colonnaded dome and profusion of sculptural decoration is given a spatially activated composition [159].

157 John Soane (rendered by Gandy), *Bird's-Eye View of a Design for a Royal Residence*, 1821
158 After J. Gandy and F. Mackenzie, *Bird's-Eye View from the Staircase and the Upper Part of the Pavillion, in the Colosseum, Regents Park...*, 1829

The acute angle of the palace cuts a dynamic swathe toward the spectator, the billowing clouds rising behind it as if to hasten the relentless advance of the architecture. The illusion of the building's forward surge is arrested by the foreground ridge, which displays a plan of the palace etched on a stone, a model of the entire project, and another framed perspective of one of the palace's interior courtyards. The palace's visual impact was meant to inspire prideful awe in the spectator, but the compositional rhythm of the picture also encourages the projected movement of the eye along and through the elliptical carriage approach that would otherwise be enjoyed only by the royal family and retinue of George IV. The aerial view [160] affords a tally of the palace's three courtyards, eight entrance porticoes, and multiple sequences of domed spaces. The blue-gray tints of the palace rooftops are reflected in the sky and in the distant landscape (with the faded silhouette of St.

Paul's just visible), while the burnt gold of the domes is picked up in the autumn foliage of the surrounding park. Soane commented often (with both enthusiasm and dejection) about this design, maintaining that it originated in his youthful period of study in Rome and thus incorporated a medley of ancient and Renaissance Roman prototypes. The central Pantheon of the palace was especially significant, as he described it as housing a multi-shelled dome that would filter and diffuse the light within. As he further explained: "The decoration of this interior dome, by aid of appropriate machinery, is designed to form a complete representation of the solar system."[28] The cosmic breadth of Gandy's aerial perspective is suggestive of this harmony of the spheres that unite architecture and astronomy, forming an orderly symbolic rejoinder to the piecemeal and disintegrative urban expansion of modern London. The intoxicating urgency and overreaching sublimity of the design was also a riposte to the more circumspect architectural reality of Nash's contemporaneous rebuilding of Buckingham House [161], which Soane had decried as "this mass of building called Buckingham Palace, a most heterogenous work, disgraceful to the nation."[29]

Independent of Soane, Gandy had also participated in the post-Waterloo architectural nationalism and patriotic palace sweepstakes. A Committee on Taste, with members including Richard Payne Knight and George Beaumont, sponsored by the Lord Commissioner of His Majesty's Treasury, requested "plans or designs which any gentleman

159 John Soane (rendered by Gandy), *View in the Portico for a Royal Residence*, 1827
160 John Soane (rendered by Gandy), *Bird's-Eye View of a Design for a Royal Palace*, 1828

SOANE AND GANDY AT THE FALL OF ARCHITECTURE 145

of the Royal Academy may be disposed to offer" for a Waterloo victory monument and a Duke of Wellington palace.[30] This notice was issued in early 1816, though architects in Gandy's circle such as Thomas Harrison and C. H. Tatham had already been producing ambitious designs in this nationalist vein. James Wyatt's eldest son, Benjamin Dean, held the inside track on the commission for a magnificent palace for the Duke of Wellington—a modern Blenheim, though even his elaborate project drawings of 1815–16 came to nothing.[31] With his 1816 RA exhibit, *A Proposed Town Residence for the Duke of Wellington to Commemorate the Battle of Waterloo* [162], Gandy tried to capitalize on the self-congratulatory mood of the country as well as on the unresolved commission for a Wellington palace and the growing debate over the development of the Marylebone Park estate, recently renamed Regent's Park. As the complete text of Gandy's catalogue entry explained, his design conformed to an 1809 plan for the estate by the surveyor John White whose son republicized it in 1815, after his father's death, in an effort to stem the ambitions of Nash and the Crown Lands Commissioners. It was the younger Mr. White who first proposed erecting a splendid mansion for the Duke of Wellington fronted by a garden with commemorative monuments—"to gratify our national feelings"—along a grand crescent in a residential park.[32] Gandy composed his perspective of this project as a sweeping landscape roughly divided into three receding zones: the landscape of history and memory—the garden of ruins and triumphal remembrance cast in foreground shadow; the built landscape of society and accomplishment—the monumental residence itself cast in providential light; and the landscape of nature—the perimeter of the park dotted with picturesque villas, the rising heath beyond skirted by clouds and sheets of rain. The somewhat conventional ordonnance and massing of the palace has a Corinthian hexastyle portico and a shallow dome ringed by caryatids as its focal point. The central pavilions crowned by a quadrangle of turrets betray a Tudor aspect appropriate to the national theme of the palace. Otherwise, the

161 W. Wallis after A. C. Pugin, *The Entrance Front of Buckingham Palace, Designed by John Nash*, 1829. Engraving.
162 *A Proposed Town Residence for the Duke of Wellington to Commemorate the Battle of Waterloo*, 1816

design is dominated by a virtual menagerie of sculptural decoration: winged victories applied to the flanking entry and corner bays, dragons and unicorns atop the porticoes, rearing pegasi on the Doric propylaea connecting the wings of the palace to the residential crescents, and exotic statues of elephants and camels guarding the entryways into the palace courtyard and the commemorative garden. The nondescript core of the palace is animated by a complex program of statuary and figurative emblems, leading one contemporary critic to state a preference for Gandy's architectural idiom over "the cold Romanized style of Mr. Nash which we fondly hoped had been sent to its deserved oblivion."[33] This contrast between the unrewarded Gandy and the well-patronized Nash was restated often in the press, as when another journalist wished that "Mr. Gandy's ideas had been taken for our New Street."[34]

Most distinctive about Gandy's palace design for the Duke of Wellington is the sepulchral garden in the foreground that surrounds the military column bearing a statue of the Iron Duke. Intact urns, canopied tombs, and cone-shaped cenotaphs give way to the litter of broken column bases and detached capitals. An antique sandalled foot sheared off from what would have been a massive sculpture is frozen in mid-step (a cast of this ancient Roman sculptural fragment also adorned the Venetian garden of Antonio Canova). Egyptian antiquities crowd the right foreground with canopic jars, toppled obelisks, and emptied sarcophagi scattered pell-mell to make up an outdoor museum of ruins. Since Gandy had witnessed the Napoleonic plundering of Italy, this preponderance of Egyptian fragments very likely alludes to the former French domination of the archaeology and museology of antiquity and ancient art under the Empire. This would have been especially appropriate in light of the Duke of Wellington's strong advocacy for the restitution of art objects from the Louvre and French imperial households that had been plundered during wartime to their original collections throughout Europe. The ruinous garden in Gandy's picture melancholically undermines the celebratory nationalism otherwise expected from such a design. Gandy's related designs for commemorative monuments, or "trophaeal towers" as he called them, are fitted, as one would expect, with the symbolic trappings of military and ecclesiastical authority [163]. The cloudy atmospheric backgrounds of the elevations were intended to highlight the enduring legacy of the monuments, despite the precarious superposed arrangement of tempiettos that compose them.

In his letters to *The Guardian* of 1821, Gandy entered into the public debate about the national palace as a symbolic building type for post-Waterloo Britain. Lamenting the absence of monumental architecture in London, he accused "commercial economy and the diffusion of property" of checking the progress of contemporary architecture. Like Soane, Gandy railed against the mercenary influence of speculative building practices in London (Nash was once again the notorious representative of this profitable trend) and the resulting corruption of the architectural profession by what Gandy called "Fabricators, or fabrick-caterers." As he declared over the prospect of designing and raising a royal palace of appropriate scale and magnificence:

> In England, monarchy is sheltered in hovels, while poverty reigns in palaces; we decorate our children beyond ourselves. When shall we hail the approach of wealth and exalt ourselves by enshrining our King in a throne worthy the victories of the nation? His palace must combine a trophaeal temple of religion, war, and commerce, where his heroes may exult beyond any ideal restorations or copies of antiquity. Whether this will be the operation of one mind, or the many, after a long research and secret study, is in the soil or seeds of time.[35]

This project had little to do with the immediate contingencies of royal patronage, parliamentary funding, and the political machinations of metropolitan improvements. To Gandy, it was more a matter of historical inevitability. But antiquity could be surpassed, the royal palace conceived of more as a nationalist temple than a serviceable residence for the monarchy. Gandy's role was that of a dejected mastermind with his eye set on futurity, as he wrote to *The Guardian*: "while Genius is neglected, he broods, soars, and waits another generation."

Another theme in his editorial missives concerned the industrial and urban destruction of nature. The challenge of exceeding the architectural grandeur of antiquity was compromised by the ecological changes wrought by urban society. "England's canals facilitate the carriage of manure and profits, little to the glory and splendour of her sovereigns," Gandy wrote; "her atmosphere is immersed in fog; her metropolis in carbon smoke that dyes all things of one colour."[36] Gandy's poetical re-constructions of classical architecture were wreathed in the sacred mists of temple fountains and oracular vapors that brought human and divine affairs into concert. The choking skies and effluvia of the modern metropolis held no such messages from the gods. In his Pausanian picture of a temple complex of Minerva, Gandy decorated the prominent bridge leading to the temple of Bellerophon

163 *Commemorative Monument*, ca. 1816–20
164 *A Geometrical Elevation of Part of One of the Fronts of an Idea for an Imperial Palace for the Sovereigns of the British Empire*, 1824
165 Overleaf: *Perspective Sketch of a Trophal Entrance to Part of the Front of a Design for a Palace*, 1826

with the inscription "APRAGMON ISTHI," which was an entreaty to remove oneself from the active life of the city.³⁷ Predicting Ruskin's paranoia about the poisoned climate of the metropolis, Gandy warned the elderly Soane in 1836 to avoid "the smoke of London, and its mephitic impurities, inhaled by life and vegetation within its vortex, [which] suffocates, or dwindles away the most robust constitutions."³⁸

Despite these discouraging conditions, Gandy continued his campaign with a series of five RA exhibits for *An Imperial Palace for the Sovereigns of the British Empire* shown between 1824 and 1828. An elevation of the palace [164, 165] and subsequent perspectives of detailed parts of the extensive building competed with, while also complementing, the palace renderings for Soane from the same period. The lengthy catalogue descriptions for Gandy's serial palace design laid out the required building materials as well as cost estimates and a timetable: £3,000,000 over a ten-year construction period. A critic for the Whig *European Magazine* immediately lit into the social and political miscalculations of the scheme:

But really—three millions of money proposed to be expended on a single edifice, while so many things are left undone both in Ireland and England ... At present we shall only add that we cannot bring ourselves to be pleased with the turgid style in which this work is publicly announced. "Imperial Palace," "British Empire," every correct thinker and writer knows that this is not an empire, but a kingdom of which the sovereignty is in the people.³⁹

To Gandy, such political quibbling must have seemed shortsighted. This palace was to be a lasting testimony to Britain's post-Napoleonic supremacy that transcended the immediate social and economic requirements of the nation. The catalogue entries for the pictures extracted passages from Ball's *Constantinople*, Johnson's *Rasselas*, and Thomson's *Seasons*, along with some of Gandy's own verses, their combined effect meant to convince the spectator of the future certainty and eventual preeminence of the palace. The perspective of "the

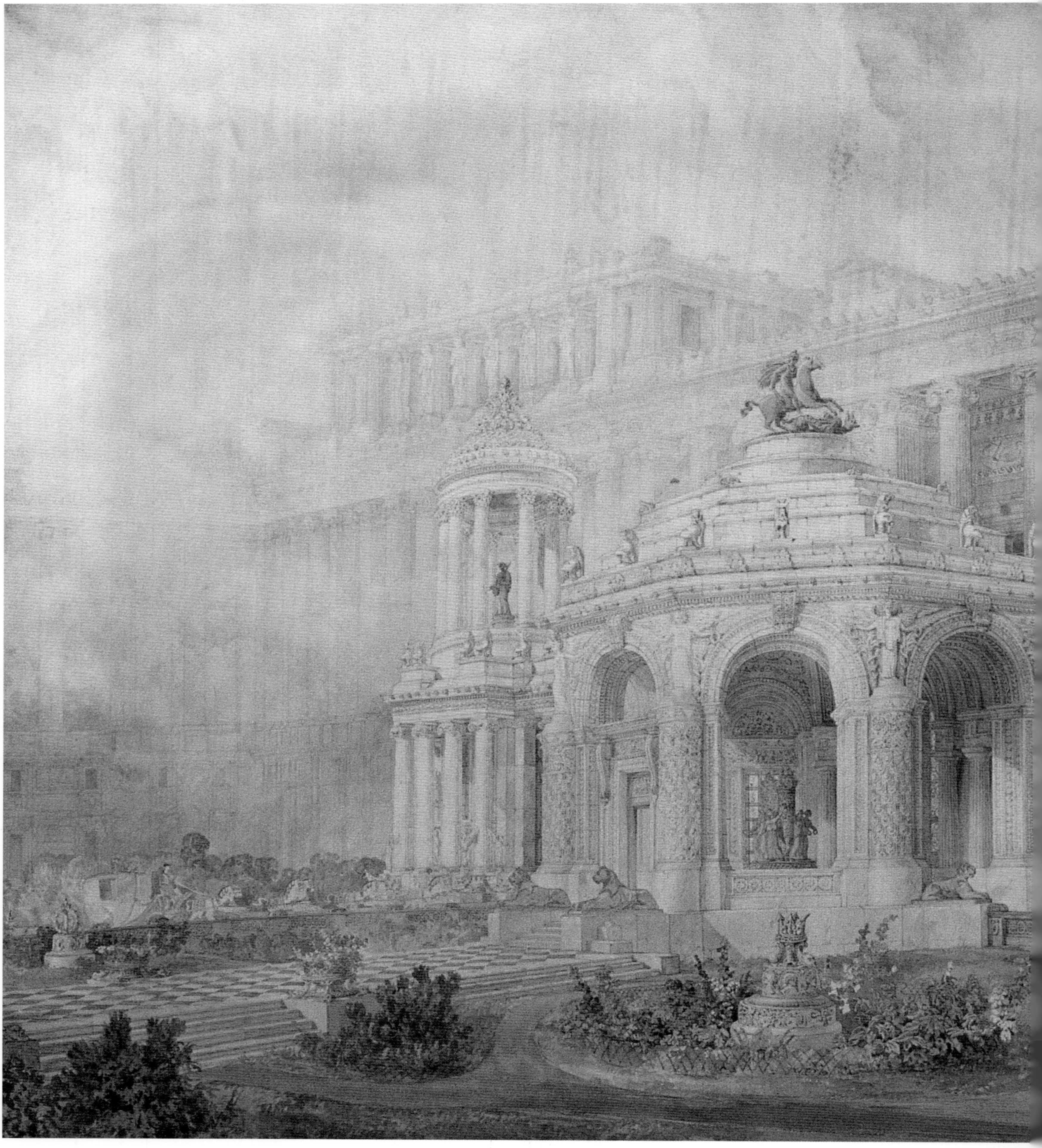

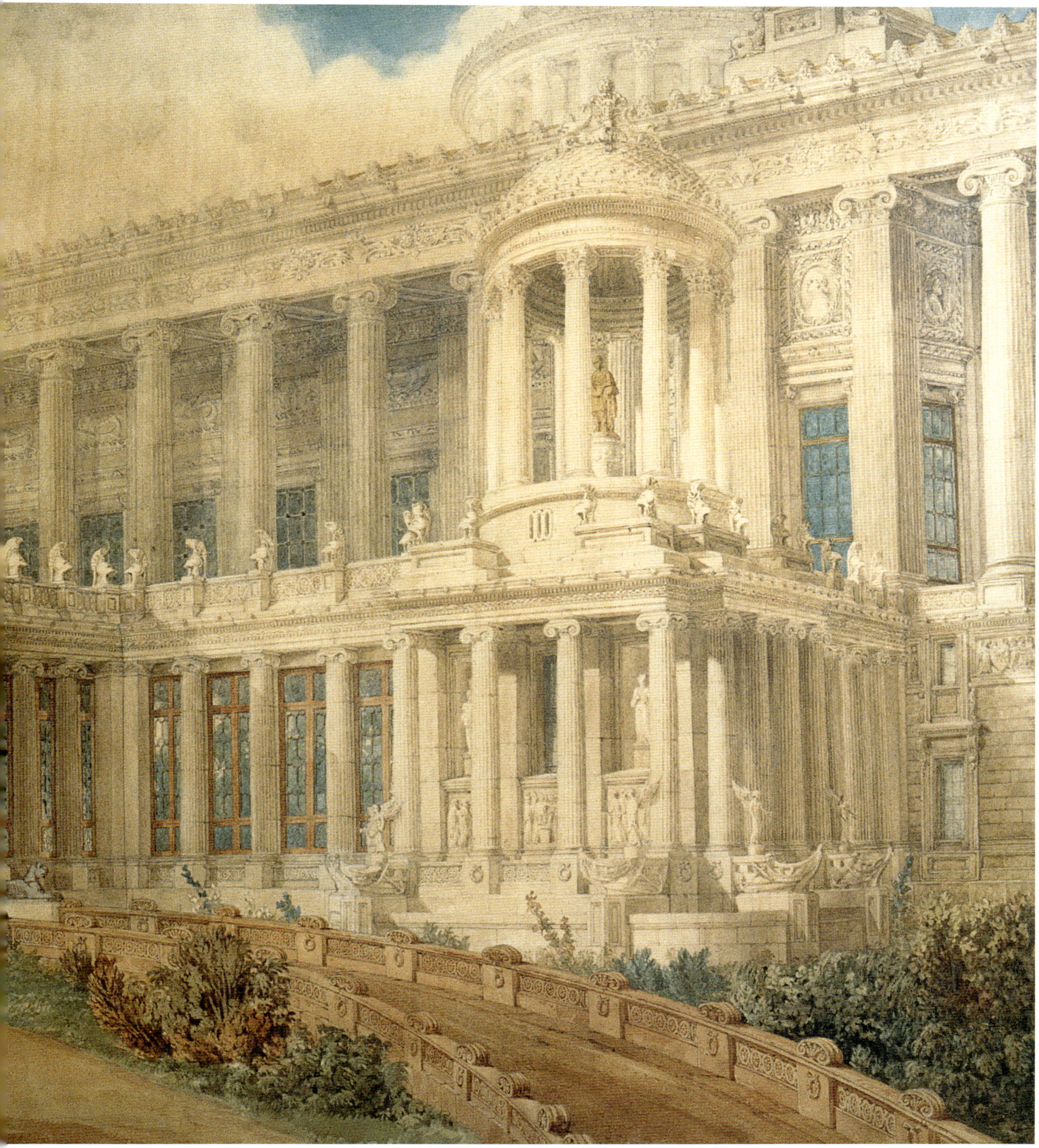

trophal entrance" to the palace was, as the catalogue text explained, "imagined to be erected in Hyde Park, and seen AD 2500."[40]

Critical notices of the series emphasized Gandy's divergence from the Greek idiom of his poetical-historical reconstructions and the adoption of "a fertile florid style."[41] The porte-cochere perspective, similar in its bounding visual cadence to his rendering of Soane's Ionic carriage portico, has such a complex elaboration of projections that it is difficult to ascertain the plane of elevation for the palace's central block. Building surfaces are riddled with ornamental foliation while sculptural motifs mark every juncture of the façade, taxing the limits of description: ships' prows, winged victories, antique helmet antefixae and royal portrait medallions only start the list. As if to suggest the limitless extent of the structure, Gandy surmounted the palace with caryatid adorned pavilions and a colonnaded tower with saw-tooth crenellations. This self-replicating, additive quality of the design is confirmed by Gandy's poetic gloss that trumpets, "Your princely form/ Soars ... / Arch upon arch and tow'r upon tow'r upreared."[42] The over-application of sculptural and ornamental form, treating the architectural surface as an enriched site of textured inscription and modeled relief, prevails as well in the designs of the interior courtyards for the palace [166, 167]. Both perspectives have a strong concavity to the pictorial space, with curving colonnades and arcades defining the foregrounds; the built vistas ascend in graduated stages of ornamental refinement into the turbulent clouds. The decorative program for the circular courtyard leading to the Doric-Ionic royal chapel combines pagan, occult, and Christian symbolism: self-consuming serpents, pagan shades, and river gods on the exterior stairwells, a cosmological sunburst on the courtyard paving, praying apostles as herm pilasters along the second-story arcade, and angelic statues guarding the chapel itself. The pedimental sculpture is difficult to decipher but it appears to depict an enthroned personification of Night—a shrouded female figure ministering to supplicants fleeing from serpents uncoiled at the

166 *Perspective Sketch of a Chapel Viewed from the Basement Court, Part of a Design for a Palace, 1827*
167 *One of the Interior Courts of a Design for a Palace, Exhibited in 1824, 1825*

corners of the pediment. This syncretic mythopoeic iconography certainly tests the boundaries of religious decorum for an Anglican royal chapel. The relative propriety of Gandy's sculptural decor for the royal palace series was even more in question for the other courtyard perspective, "viewed from an audience chamber" as the catalogue text noted. Here Gandy's fascination with figurative architecture is fully realized, the porticoes and screened colonnades all supported by canephorae and Persians. In his third RA lecture on the architectural orders, Soane examined the ancient usage of Persians and caryatids as columns, addressing in particular their propagandistic significance for national security in ancient Greece: "They [the Greeks] in this manner terrified their enemies with the idea of their power, and at the same time inspired their citizens with a love of glory and made them more animated in the defence of their liberties."[43] Gandy would have found this application of architecture as an arena of display for national power perfectly appropriate to his proposed courtyard of figurative columns. Soane, however, had reservations about their deployment in contemporary architecture, observing that "nothing can be more noble or magnificent and at the same time more absurd." A critic for The Literary Gazette agreed on this point with respect to Gandy's RA exhibit. While appreciative of the design's scenic novelty and its "fertile invention," he ascribed a political impropriety to the dominant presence of columnar statues: "It is a departure from the principles of good taste to employ statues in the habit of captives and slaves as the general supporters of a building intended for the residence of a sovereign at the head of a free government."[44]

In this courtyard design, contemporary figures—subjects of "a free government" or of "the British Empire"—are pictured ambling among gigantic fragments of architectural capitals of newly invented orders. They seem like tourists in an archaeological amusement park. The center of the courtyard has balustrades and staircases that descend to an unseen level of the palace, perhaps to a sunken garden of military trophies. In the lengthy poetic caption to this picture, Gandy multiplies the vistas of the palace further by demanding that the building come to life and describe its environs, as if Merlin's voice now haunted this royal residence:

A British Monarch rear'd yon stately pile,
Whence the rapt vision in its hurried glance
The broad interminable feature scans
Of yonder wide expanse—what see'st thou? Speak!
Beneath me lies the world's metropolis,
As some dark giant's slumbering limbs—beyond
Turret and temple, palace, fane, and tow'r,
Recede in slow succession; further yet
In all the blooming witchery of life
Nature's extended beauty, plain and grave;
Garden and landscape burst upon the sight.[45]

Not content with the stationary view of the perspective (singly or serially), Gandy appends these verses to the design so as to expand the temporal and spatial coordinates of the imagined building. The monument's scale defies visual comprehension from without. The building therefore becomes its own agent of vision and casts its gaze over the surrounding urban disorder, its prospect directed toward the admonishing presence of the natural world. The building's sight is refreshed by the landscape that answers from a distance its eminent position above the city. The poetic lines for the porte-cochere perspective evoke the dissipation of the city's "mephitic vapours" so that "the bright emblem of Britannia's pow'r" may illumine the world.

Gandy and Soane's palace designs of the 1820s shared an argument. Britain had been victorious in the Napoleonic Wars, but its capital city had failed to reflect the magnitude and historical stature of this victory. Soane claimed that London was a century behind Paris in its architectural achievement. The post-Waterloo epoch of nationalist euphoria had been wasted. Moreover, their hypothetical palaces were not really designed for the king, but more in place of a king. George IV, suffering from ill health because of obesity and asthma, was rarely seen in public after 1825 (his reign ended with his death in 1830). The costly renovations for Buckingham Palace precipitated parliamentary inquiries into financial irregularities that brought the very public career of Nash to a sudden and ignominious end. The palace designs of Soane and Gandy were left to drift between the mists of time and the polluted air of the metropolis of the world. In 1830, an unknown architect named G. J. Robinson exhibited at the RA an aerial view of a metropolitan palace with the following caption: "An attempt to design a building sufficiently splendid for a royal residence, without verging into such visionary extravagances as to preclude its erection."[46] Plainly, this was a well-timed barb directed at the imperial palaces and royal residences that had graced the walls of the RA by Gandy and Soane over the prior decade. The fustian and burdensome accumulation of sculptural decoration and imperial architectural forms seen, for example in Gandy's view of Soane's *Design for a National Entrance into the Metropolis* (1826) [168] also distinguished the former's imperial palace designs and

168 John Soane (rendered by Gandy), *Design for a National Entrance into the Metropolis*, 1826
169 *Sketch for New Senate Houses*, 1835

would recur less than a decade later in his *Sketch for a new Senate House* (1835). This proposal was exhibited in the wake of the recent destruction by fire of the Houses of Commons and Lords, which is pictured as an atmospheric vignette in the upper left corner [169]. The worm's-eye perspective of the composition, the foreground rubble and foliage bearing an inscribed floor plan, the cloud-rending sky, and the ceremonial pageantry in the perspective of this design were all devices employed over the years by Gandy in his renderings for Soane. Gandy's palatine Greco-Roman fortress could have been plucked from Soane's "dreams" and "visions" compendium of 1820. Loudon's *Architectural Magazine* reviewed the design only to discern a self-defeating air of magnificence and classical obsolescence: "Gandy's proposal is a most flaming affair, altogether so extravagant that its author seems to have been more than anxious to furnish a certain, yet not humiliating, reason for its rejection in toto than to bring forward an idea whose feasibility would recommend it."[47]

The modern urban resistance to monumental architecture of imperial splendor that so troubled Gandy and Soane (the latter bewailing "the too manifest neglect and decay of our architecture") was recognized by other architectural commentators as well. Robert Mudie, a naturalist and urban critic, penned some of the most lively architectural criticism of the period in his volumes on London, entitled (perhaps with a debt to John Martin) *Babylon the Great* (1825) and *Second Judgement of Babylon the Great* (1829). These mock-guidebooks played continuously upon the social trope of the restlessness of the metropolis; as Mudie complains, "there is no keeping up with reality ... fields are palaces, palaces heaps."[48] After surveying the classical bias of recent London architecture by Smirke, Nash, and Soane, Mudie warns of the historical curse that the architecture of a classical revival entails:

> with those monumental remains constantly before our eyes, with our kings and counsellors, and all those to whom we look with respect, packed up as it were in the coffins of nations—and of nations too which have perished of corruption and disease, how can we avoid dreading that the infection may be caught, that we too may become corrupt and perish?[49]

Architecture inspired by or measured against that of antiquity is inherently sepulchral and predisposed to ruination. Mudie deplores the insidious acceptance of classical historicism even within the modern metropolis where its cultural authority would be most severely tested by the unstable commercial interests and social inequalities of urban life. His progressive critique of architectural tradition may be pitted against an unsigned article on "The British School of Architecture" from 1836, in which many of the anxieties about the architecture of modern London voiced by Soane and Gandy were given even more forceful expression. The author (perhaps *Blackwood's* conservative art critic John Eagles, whose ferocious criticism of Turner's landscapes made Ruskin into an art critic) reiterated the damning contrast between the architectural contributions of Paris and London, which had been a virtual leitmotif in Soane's RA lectures: "Future generations will then as now look with undiminished interest on the splendid monuments of Paris ... what will London have to show, to stand in comparison? What will the conquering nation have to exhibit to rival the trophies of the vanquished?"[50] Unlike Soane, however, this writer was receptive to the urban picturesque style of John Nash, while as the same time associating its scenic classicism with "the impatience of the democratic [and] the selfishness of the mercantile spirit." The ephemeral demands of democracy and mercantilism, telltale signs of modernity, jeopardized the shelf life of contemporary architecture. This critic, like Gandy and Soane, yearned for an enlightened autocracy that would ensure the lasting survival of the nation's coffins.

The period after the French Revolution saw a new perception of the role of architecture in history. The cult of ruins, the new urban-industrial forms of modernity, and the infatuation with progress and futurity converged.[51] It was in his renderings of Soane's evolving house-museum that Gandy elaborated on the historical fate of architecture from within this temporalized perspective of the early nineteenth century. The planning, design, and installation of Soane's house-museum in Lincoln's Inn Fields spanned from 1807 until the architect's death.[52] It was designed primarily as an architectural gallery housing Soane's ever-growing collection of antiquities, drawings, and models. Its purported pedagogical function was to offer students of architecture from the Royal Academy a place of study and reflection, an architectural academy that nonetheless bore the inimitable creative stamp of its progenitor. Like Thomas Hope's Duchess Street Mansion and Gallery and its rural counterpart Deepdene and William Beckford's Fonthill Abbey, Soane's house-museum transposed the picturesque taste for modulating vistas and scenic contemplation from the exterior landscape into the artistic interior. John Britton, who wrote sycophantically flattering accounts of all of these artistically experimental private museums of the late Georgian period, characterized Soane's as "a succession of rich, varied, and striking architectural scenery."[53] Behind this scenery, however, lay Soane's psycho-pathological compulsions, which may be attributable in large part to the architect's family disappointments and tragedies, particularly the failure of his two sons to fulfill their father's dynastic dreams in the architectural profession and the death of Mrs. Soane. Soane's caustic melancholy complicated his professional life as well, and like Gandy he nursed an increasingly anxious sense of persecution and alienation. The contemporary press often targeted Soane's unfortunate blend of self-pity and egomania for attack, branding the architect, as one journalist did, for "his perversity of temper."[54] Soane's museum truly merged public and private space to remarkable effect. On one hand, it was to be admired as a memorable repository of antiquities, a proto-museological space of cultural reverence and national heritage. On the other, it was a solipsistic space where the architect's most personal crises of self and sentiment were commemorated, resulting in a strangely confessional architecture of painful conscience, excessive self-reflection, and searching artistic invention. That Soane's museum transcended the contemporary conventions of artistic display and fashionable culture to achieve a psychologically charged exposition of the architect's mental life and creative temperament was noted by the museologist G. F. Waagen, who wrote in 1838, a year after Soane's death: "Passing over the curiosities which fill the apartments, I observe that the whole, notwithstanding the picturesque, fantastic charm, which cannot be denied, has in consequence of this arbitrary mixture of heterogeneous objects, something of the unpleasant effect of a feverish dream."[55]

Gandy's views of Soane's museum capture the dream-like microcosm of antiquity enclosed within the architect's urban residence. His vertiginous perspectives of the narrow multi-tiered gallery known as the Dome, drawn in 1811, accentuate both the sepulchral quietude and the eerie vibrancy of the spaces described [150, 170]. In these watercolours, Gandy focuses on the light well that forms a dramatic vertical shaft through the crypt up to the pendentive rim of the dome in the antiquarian gallery. Architectural and sculptural fragments—some originals, though most plaster casts—climb and line the wall and ceiling surfaces, precariously suspended from or melded to the architectural supports. The sense of *horror vacui* that informed Soane's Piranesian idea of museum installation is thoroughly conveyed. Indeed, although Soane censured "the Architectural Blasphemy of Piranesi" in his RA lectures, the design and pictorial record of his museum alludes often to the imagery of animate ruin and imaginative space found in Piranesi's graphic art. Soane made this connection himself in his tragicomical manuscript about the history of his museum, written in 1812, in which the narrative voice was that of a future antiquary inspecting the mysterious ruins of the building.[56] This literary conceit has its forerunner in L.-S. Mercier's *Le Tableau de Paris* (1781–88), which contained a digression on Paris as a future ruin surveyed by the narrator and also in the scholar-traveler musing on Palmyra's valley of sepulchers in the opening chapter of the Comte de Volney's widely-read treatise *Les Ruines*

(1792). Soane's fictive antiquary offered the following deduction about the ruined townhouse-museum: "I am aware it has been supposed that this very space, if a staircase, could only have been one of those Carcerian dark staircases represented in some of Piranesi's ingenious dreams for prisons."[57] The architectural setting of Soane's museum is comparable only to a pictorial antecedent—Piranesi's etching cycle of the *Carceri*—which is itself construed as the byproduct of a dream. The reality of architecture is thrice removed, lost within this web of literary and artistic

170 John Soane (rendered by Joseph Gandy), *View of the Dome of the Soane Museum*, 1811

projections. Gandy translated the violently diagonal striations and fragmented spatial sections of Piranesi's prints into the watercolour renderings of Soane's crypt and Dome. These sheets also document the experiments in lighting conducted in the museum that intrigued both the architect and his perspectivist. The full-length view of the Dome is illuminated by two hidden lanterns, one placed behind a sepulchre at the end of the catacomb-like enfilade at basement level and the other situated behind the gravity-defying *bricolage* of ancient Roman architectural moldings that supports a cork model of the Temple of Vesta at Tivoli. Disjunction of scale and inversion of proportion were prized effects in the interior distribution of the Dome. The other view from the side tribune of the Dome is even more dramatically lit from an unseen source in the crypt [150]. The strobe-like beam of light turns the narrow antiquarian passage into a yawning space. The Piranesian ramparts are pried open by the intrusive burst of illumination, the delicate colonnettes seemingly strained and stretched by the shaft of light. The architectural surfaces crawl with garland swags and Greek frets, lucidly delineated even though sunk in shadow. The figure of Soane's son John Jr. can barely be seen emerging from the thick transparency of darkness that was truly the symbolic space of the father, who had vainly hoped that his didactic and evocative museum would spawn "a race of artists."[58]

Paraphrasing in translation the late eighteenth-century architectural theory of Le Camus de Mézières, Soane had written, "How much more sensible it would be if we united Architecture, Painting, & Sculpture. Who could then resist this triple magic whose illusions make the mind feel almost every sensation which is known?"[59] This synesthetic approach to architectural design was enacted over two decades within Soane's domestic museum. Gandy represented the unfolding "triple magic" of the museum in two complicated RA exhibits of 1822 that made ingenious use of composite or multiple views within each sheet. The first, generically inscribed "The plan and interior of the ground floor of a town house," emphasizes the elegant domestic space of the integrated library and dining room, in which Gandy's framed perspec-

171 John Soane (rendered by Gandy), *Interior of a Town House*, 1822
172, 173 John Soane (rendered by Gandy), *Multiple Views of Soane Museum* (details), 1822

158 JOSEPH GANDY

tives of Soane's architecture were prominently displayed [171]. The cramped though orderly arrangement of the exterior monument court, which was the epicenter of the museum site, is recorded in the vertical inset on the left, while the breakfast room (the definitive Soane interior with its intricate recessed lighting and vista onto the aforementioned courtyard) is rendered in the lower right. A trompe-l'oeil effect is given of the represented drawing's upper left corner having come loose from the picture plane, the flap of the sheet playfully emulative of the subtle elasticity of the floating canopy dome within the depicted room. It is as though one could peel away the incised surface of the shallow lantern dome that hovers over and defines the interior space of the breakfast room. The other montage-like drawing focuses on the antiquarian fragment and picture galleries and adjacent corridors—the exhibition space proper—along the northern edge of the three properties that Soane had purchased in Lincoln's Inn Fields [172, 173]. Here again, a trompe-l'oeil overlay technique is used, a clever contrivance perfectly suited to the spatial ambiguity and shifting planes and levels of the various chambers and passageways stocked with antiquities, models, and perspectives. The year before, Soane had acquired a collection of antique fragments that Tatham, Gandy's traveling companion to Rome, had purchased from the remnants of Piranesi's studio for the architect Henry Holland. Some of the fictive sheets that comprise the drawing are shaped to resemble arched vistas down the top-lit aisles and along the skeletal walls of the museum. The rectangular drawings to the right of the central area of the colonnade and the Dome depict the student's room, a mezzanine studio virtually suspended within the narrow quarters of the museum and equipped with drafting tables, drawings, and casts; and below is the Picture-Room with its moveable hinged display panels and canopied vaulting with conservatory side lights. These sheets are also made to seem insecurely attached to the entire watercolor, as if to suggest the fragmentary esthetic and experimental mutability of the entire museum. To complicate matters further, the central oval panel is neither a feigned vista into space nor a drawing of a drawing, but a burnished mirror image of the museum interior. The entire watercolor does not merely supply a visual description of these multifarious spaces, but rather offers a pictorial equivalent to the architectural innovations of the museum—its dizzying and cluttered vistas, its dematerialization of the logical forms of architecture, and its mediation of vision through moving planes and catoptric reflection.

Soane's museum aggressively resisted narrative and pedagogical clarity. It had precious few clean sight lines. History was not organized, chronologies and epochs were not defined, the distinctions between original works of art and copies, or even between the artificial and the natural, were not made explicit. Objects and forms were denied independence; they were taken out of themselves and transformed into unexpected accretions of history and architectural-sculptural ensembles that blurred categories of cultures and styles. Active processes of seeing came up against the sepulchral density of antiquity. The past, however, was not simply past—it was reflected and distorted, constantly coming under divergent angles of vision. To enter into the past here incurred the ducking of one's head and the watching of one's step. The museum not only encouraged a heightened awareness of subjective perception, it also took over the subject's capacity for vision; through its broken illumination (refracted in places through colored or tinted glass), fluttering planes, and mirrored doublings of reality, the building seemed to see you. The associative meanings of things in the collection, the sentiments of its objects, were certainly there, some more recognizable than others—Napoleonic memorabilia, the Shakespeare shrine, and a family pet memorial were not difficult to fathom. After 1824, when Soane purchased his prize Egyptian antiquity, the alabaster sarcophagus of Seti I, and began work in the basement on the mock-medieval Monk's Parlor, the connotations became somewhat more private and recondite (the aging architect sardonically reincarnated from the past as despotic pharaoh and reclusive monk). These were humorous and pathetic identifications to amuse Soane and his closest colleagues and friends, but painful truths about his growing sense of isolation and his compulsive desire to take possession of and perpetuate his own creative legacy lurked in the shadows of these antiquarian spoofs. Summerson was unforgiving on this matter, judging it as "senile play-acting in the scene of his own approaching death."[60] The critic Peter Conrad rightly noted that Soane's museum looked backward and forward, it was "a reconstruction of his past and a premonition of the posthumous life he confidently expects."[61] This anticipated immortality was, however, strangely encrypted, the spatial experience of the museum inviting imagined disinterments, and communions with the dead. Because of its insistent refusal to be apologetically instructive or didactically entertaining in accordance with any historical science of the time, Soane's museum confounded many a contemporary observer: "A Kaleidoscope of rich materials," "a sort of architectural *bijouterie*," "a mere broker's shop arrangement of odds and ends ... a raree-show," "a pattern card of the most diverse styles of architecture," "a quaint piece of coxcombry and gimcrackery."[62] Optical disorientation, manic acquisitiveness, bejeweled diminution, squinting vision (a raree-show was a vulgar peepshow), historical compression, and desperate self-display: These were the qualities, most of them pejoratively invoked, that had come to mind. It was not received as a modern version of a *studiolo*, *Wunderkammer*, or memory theater. Instead, the tawdry visual entertainment of the street and the disorderly trade of the pawnshop seeped into the critical perception of Soane's museum.

Of course those close to Soane, such as the belletrist Isaac D'Israeli, claimed that with the creation of his museum the architect "had built a Poem."[63] After attending a gala event in 1825 at Soane's museum in which the Seti sarcophagus was illuminated from within by lanterns (a realization more or less of Gandy's sepulchral interiors), the history painter B. R. Haydon (a friend of Soane, who like Gandy had accepted many "loans" from the architect) declared that the museum was "a perfect Cretan labyrinth."[64] John Britton's fawning but often insightful guide to the museum, *The Union of Architecture, Sculpture, and Painting* (1827), extolled Soane as "not merely the imaginative architect, but the poet."[65] Soane was not satisfied with Britton's volume and published his own three years later, in which this conception of his museum as a specimen of poetical architecture was reiterated. In what is the most famous passage of all Soane's writings on architecture, he observed of the museum's Breakfast Room: "the mirrors in the ceiling and the looking-glasses, combined with the variety of outline and general arrangement in the design and decoration of this limited space, present a succession of those fanciful effects which constitute the poetry of architecture."[66] This was an architecture of fluctuating visibility and mental apprehension, in which the materiality of building is supplanted by an ineffable edifice of sheer "effect." The very language of Soane's description recalls a letter that Gandy wrote to the architect in 1814 about an account of the mirrored dressing room and bath of the Hôtel de Beauharnais in Paris, perhaps the most opulent interior of the Empire; Gandy marveled, "This complete catoptic [sic] room from its reververating [sic] reflections produced a wonderful effect of artificial space, the columns were reflected to infinity (the sublime of Burke) in each direction. The mind fancied a fairy hall and an enchantment."[67] This idea that space can be transformed into the artifice of reflection, into an intangible image that belies architectural reality, may be taken as one of the ruling principles of Soane's museum. The picturesque orchestration of architectural vistas becomes for Soane and Gandy an almost metaphysical project, which may best be described as the dissolution of architecture. In a watercolor sketch of the museum by Gandy of 1825 that depicts a view looking up toward the Picture Room from the Monk's Parlor [174], the effect given is that of an apotheosis-like vision, of being lifted from the medieval detritus and antiquarian morass of the basement cell up toward the dissolving enclosures of the moveable picture planes with framed perspectives above stacked like architectonic steps toward the light. Over a decade later, after receiving a copy of Soane's revised edition of his museum description, Gandy responded with an excitedly composed accolade about the transcendental stimulation of the museum's sundry inventions: "receiving dioptric light from unseen sources, the number of revolving pictures and curved walls, folding doorlike, valve within valve, grading from shade to light the many semblances of departed worth, recalling us to human life, leaves our mind oscillating between heaven and earth."[68] Soane's museum here becomes a paranormal instrument, a strangely sentient though automatistic device that shapes sensations so as to dissolve the boundaries not only between architecture and image or between consciousness and environment but also between mortality and immortality. The museum was meant to serve as a kind of architectural medium through which the presences of past, present, and future were encouraged to commingle.

Soane's preoccupation both with the anticipatory ruination and occult transcendence of his own architecture was also made explicit in the perspectives he had commissioned from Gandy that depict the Bank of England in ruin.[69] For the 1830 RA exhibition, Gandy prepared *A Bird's-Eye View of the Bank of England* [175], a watercolor that successfully conflated several techniques of architectural rendering within one image. Is this an aerial section drawing, or a floor plan in perspective? Is it an imaginary ruin composition, or an imaginary construction document? The sheet allows for a comprehensive survey of the three-acre Bank complex, its roof cut away to disclose its maze-like complexity, thereby divulging the scope of Soane's ambitious building works spanning his forty-five year tenure as Architect to the Bank of England. For all of the technical data that is conveyed about Soane's ingenious

174 John Soane (rendered by Gandy), *View from Monk's Parlor*, 1825

application of hollow cone vaulting, his spatial sequencing of the immense domed offices around the Rotunda, and his interior distribution of colonnaded courtyards, the overall impact of the drawing remains that of a Piranesian ruinscape. Much of the Threadneedle Street façade is left intact, lest the exterior treatment of this economic fortress be overlooked. But even here, slashing clouds overshadow the surviving sections of this monumental enclave, the street itself fallen away and uncovering the Bank's foundation vaults. In 1852, the Pre-Raphaelite artist George Boyce and Victorian sculptor Charles Smith recalled the singular impression of this Soane RA exhibit and attributed the watercolor to Turner because of its atmospheric fury and geological imagery.[70] Architectural fragments and vegetation crowd close to the picture plane in the lower right corner, disrupting the aerial distance and spatial remoteness of the larger composition. The illusionistic magnitude of the perspective, however, tends toward contraction, so that the urban footprint of the enormous excavation, with its sheared columns, jagged walls, and bare brick arches, appears like a damaged version of a model replica of the Bank of England (this model was seen intact in Gandy's earlier compendium of Soane's lifework of 1818). In the catalogue text for the picture, Soane quoted (and amended) a passage from Le Sage's eighteenth-century comic novel *Le Diable Boiteux*, in which the devil, while winging his way over the city, lifts the rooftops off the houses to scorn the puny lives conducted within: "Je vais enlever les toits de ce superbe édifice national … le dedans va se découvrir à vos yeux de meme qu'on voit le dedans d'un pâté dont on vient d'ôter la croûte. [I am going to remove the roofs of this proud national edifice … so that what is within will be revealed to your eyes, like seeing the inside of a pie whose crust has been removed.]"[71] Soane, then, was demonically wreaking havoc with his most renowned London monument.

In doing so, Gandy was once again fulfilling his brief as an architect/artist of the Burkean sublime. In his analysis of tragedy and empathy, Burke speculated on the human reaction to natural cata-

175 John Soane (rendered by Gandy), *A Bird's-Eye View of the Bank of England*, 1830
176 John Soane (rendered by Gandy), *Architectural Ruins—a Vision (Bank of England in Ruins)*, 1798–1832

strophes, citing as an example the aftermath of an earthquake striking London: "But suppose such a fatal accident to have happened, what numbers from all parts would crowd to behold the ruins, and amongst them many who would have been content never to have seen London in its glory."[72] Soane enlisted Gandy to visualize the sublime potential of his lifelong work for the Bank of England, the scale and extent of which had long been the subject of controversy in the press. *The Examiner*, for example, remarked sarcastically in 1808 "that the structure has become already the ninth wonder of the world, it astonishes the citizens and utterly confounds the good people of the West."[73] However, for all of the critics cited earlier who had complained that London in ruins would afford few Piranesian pleasures, Soane's Bank represented a worthy exception. James Elmes came to Soane's defense with this encomium: "The Bank of England by Mr. Soane possesses many noble and tasteful halls. Its exterior is massive and noble … When London is fallen, 'And such as Memphis is, shall London be!' *Old Play*, this building, with those of Wren and the bridges, will be almost the only ruins left to indicate its present greatness."[74] By making the Bank of England the object of an imaginary archaeological inquiry, Soane was reserving a place for his own architecture in the history of an antiquity that had not yet come to pass.

Soane and Gandy returned to this theme two years later with the 1832 RA exhibit *Architectural Ruins—a Vision*, a view of the Bank of England Rotunda fallen into ruin [176]. Although exhibited during the twilight of Soane's career, this watercolor had been executed by Gandy in June 1798 soon after he entered Soane's office, along with a view of the newly renovated Rotunda in pristine condition [177]. They originally formed complementary images of the same structure in contrasting temporal states, demonstrating, as Margaret Richardson has written, "the fine line that divides ruin from construction."[75] By exhibiting a 1798 sheet in 1832, Soane was also reckoning with the duration of his own

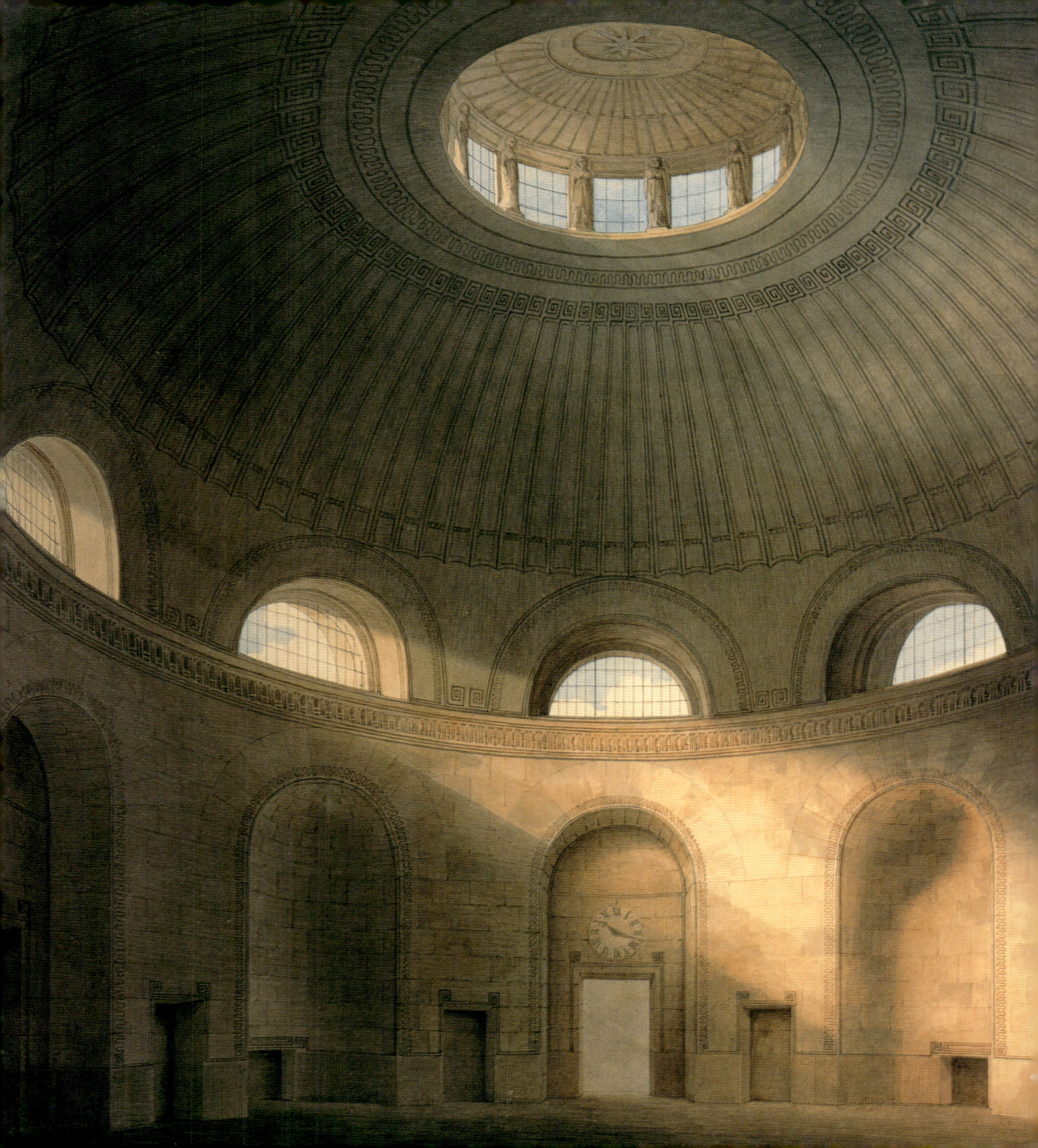

career and lifetime. The historical perplexity of the future ruin motif in *Architectural Ruins—a Vision* is marked by irony and resignation. The building's decaying architectural hallmarks remain identifiably Soanean: caryatids silhouetted around the lantern dome of the Rotunda, the skeletal pendentives and segmental arches of the adjacent Consols Office pierced by streams of fading light, and the broken piers with scored fretwork heaped in the foreground rubble. The masonry shell of the Rotunda, infiltrated with moss and foliage, protects only an encampment of treasure hunters. In Gandy's matching perspective of the freshly completed Rotunda, the archway of the central passage contains a clock that will measure the commercial schedule of the building. In the vision of future ruin, time itself has been torn from the building, the image allegorizing its own temporal disorder.

When Soane exhibited *Architectural Ruin—a Vision*, he included these famous lines from Shakespeare's *The Tempest* in the catalogue entry: "The cloud-cap't towers, the gorgeous palaces,/ The solemn temples, the great globe itself,/ Yea, all which it inherit, shall dissolve."[76] Soane was much taken with this passage, quoting it twice in his RA lectures while ruminating on "the ravages of all devouring time and the convulsions of Empire."[77] He probably saw himself as an architectural Prospero, the weary magician and the figure exiled for his poetical imagination. Prospero delivers these lines as a dream-like masque that he has conjured fades into nothingness—"the baseless fabric of this vision," as Prospero declared, which provided Soane with the subtitle for his future ruin composition. The elderly Soane, one year away from resigning as Architect to the Bank of England, was envisioning—with his eyesight failing—the vainglorious demise of his own creation. Prospero's admission that "my old brain is troubled" (IV.i.159) would have also found a chorus with Soane.

It is very likely, however, that this future ruin leitmotif in Soane's Bank of England exhibits was also responsive to the present-day experience of history in Great Britain during the early 1830s. Soane had grown increasingly paranoid about the salient institutions of modern

177 John Soane (rendered by Gandy), *View of the Bank of England Rotunda as Built*, 1798
178 John Soane (rendered by Gandy), *Interior of the Edifice Devoted Exclusively to Freemasonry ... an Evening View*, 1832

life: a commercial press trading in slander and criticism, parliamentary commissions and government boards meddling in architectural affairs, and political factionalism at the RA had driven him to distraction. The redistribution of political representation in favor of middle-class and industrial interests, the increased enfranchisement of the male population, and the reconsideration of inheritance rights were all Reform Bill red rags to a Pittite Tory like Soane. He kept a scrapbook of press clippings relating to the vicissitudes of the Reform Bill debate. Anonymous pamphlets such as *A Leaf from the Future History of England on the Subject of Reform in Parliament* (1831) also envisioned a state of future ruin with the architectural landmarks of London reduced to rubble as a consequence of democratic mob rule. An editorial notice in *The Sun* spoke of the Reform Bill crisis in profoundly architectural terms: "In this tottering condition of a fabric which once was perfect ... the Reformers step in. They see that the pillars are shaken. That the timbers have got dry rot ... is the temple to be suffered to go to decay?"[78] The pictorial language of the picturesque and the sublime that Gandy and Soane had consolidated in the future ruin imagery of the Bank of England was potentially fraught with political and social topicality. The fall of architecture and the fall of England had become synonymous concerns in 1830–32.

The same year Soane exhibited *Architectural Ruins—a Vision* he also showed Gandy's splendid interior perspective (in an "evening view") of his design for the Council Chamber of the Freemason's Hall, a renovation that had just been completed in 1831 [178].[79] These two pictures of Soane's architecture at the 1832 RA exhibition can be construed in significant ways as symbolic pendants. Both were representative of the architect's long association with the respective institutions (Soane had been a member of the Grand Master's Lodge since 1813, though admittedly he was already sixty years old by that time). Whereas one was a corporate institution that had financed the war machine against Napoleon and was devoted to national economic prosperity, the other was a private sect dedicated to peaceful philanthropy, fraternal exchange, and gentlemanly mysticism. In one, a public yet highly protected monument is pictured as worn away by nature and history; in the other, a Masonic sanctuary is seen in unspoiled splendor, presented as a nocturnal revelation. The proscenium frame and curtain, suggesting that the viewers were witnesses to a secret unveiling, had been used by Gandy in other views of Soane's buildings, but it was also a device often employed in contemporary Freemasonic engravings of Lodge rituals and their symbolic articles. The fulcrum of architectural and visual fascination in this rendering is the canopied vault with pendant dome and glazed lantern (decorated with astrological signs). This distinctive feature of Soane's architectural style was often the subject of critical derision in the press. The elaborately scornful article on Soane entitled "On the Sixth, or Bœotian Order of Architecture" that appeared in an 1824 installment of *Knight's Quarterly* compared his pendant domes and canopied vaults to "the distention of the umbrella ... like a stuffed crocodile on the ceiling of a museum." The critic also had recourse to a familiar Shakespearean allusion, adding "he [Soane] has suspended an infinite series of these 'baseless fabricks.'"[80] The eerie sense of magical levitation and claustrophobic enclosure that permeates this design is highly characteristic of Soane's refined late style, an aspect of which Summerson addressed in his merciless psycho-spatial critique of Soanean architecture: "There is always a temperamental factor, expressing itself in a sense of deflation, as if all *mass* [Summerson's emphasis] had been exhausted from the design ... This deflationary tendency belongs peculiarly to Soane and makes his buildings, for all their feeling and invention, slightly subhuman. His architecture never commands; it shrinks into itself and nervously defines the spaces which it encloses."[81] Gandy's intervention into this nervously articulated space of Soane's designs, even one as ceremoniously orchestrated as the Freemasonic interior, was once more through the agency of light. The preternaturally bright ellipse of moonlight fights off the oppressive weight of the domed lid and segmental vaults in this chamber. *Knight's Quarterly* and Summerson notwithstanding, this space as depicted by Gandy was meant to seem unviolated in its ritualistic promise and cultic *esprit*. The Masonic ark, also designed by Soane, on the central pedestal-desk with a Corinthian candle stand, receives the cascade of light under the glazed zodiac lantern, an illumination staged for the initiate-viewer who dwells in the foreground shadow.

The romantic essayist Thomas de Quincey compared modern Freemasonic rituals to ancient Eleusinian mysteries, as both relied greatly on the nocturnal delusion of the senses. They were also equally "hoaxes" to de Quincey. In considering the relation of English Freemasonry to the historical temper and social climate of the time, de Quincey noted that "English clubs, I admit, are accustomed to harmonize in their political principles."[82] Soane's Freemasonic Hall is presented as a refuge that stands apart from the political controversies of the Great

Reform Bill, though it should be noted that his closest Freemasonic associates and friends—the newspaper editor James Perry, the antiquarian Britton, and the Lodge's Grand Master the Duke of Sussex—were all liberal Whigs. They certainly harmonized politically, though not with Soane. But the ostensible ideology of the Freemasonic lodges was to rise above contesting political positions and sectarian beliefs. The endurance of masonic craft depended on its universalizing appeal to enlightened benevolence and the tolerant reconciliation of disparate creeds. Among his collection of books on Freemasonry, Soane possessed an 1812 volume of Masonic songs, poems, and toasts that included the following verses:

> The solemn temple's cloud capt towers,
> The aspiring domes are works of ours ...
> No storms, nor tempests now are fear'd.
>
> When stately palaces arise,
> When columns grace the hall,
> When tow'rs and spires salute the skies,
> We owe to masons all.[83]

This was a doggerel reworking of Prospero's famous speech, which Soane had appended to the Rotunda-in-ruins perspective. Resistant to the transient influences of nature and history, the mason's craft, unlike the commercial fortress of the Bank of England, transcends earthly decay, an illusion that Soane and Gandy put forth in their portrayal of the Freemasons' Hall as a mystical sanctum.

In 1830, *Fraser's Magazine*, which would rarely miss an opportunity to lampoon Soane, ran an article with a mock description of the election of the magazine's new editor. The literati of London were invited to an open meeting at the Freemasons' Tavern, which was under renovation by Soane. Finding these quarters uninhabitable, this congregation of writers and editors decides to meet at Lincoln's Inn Fields in front of Soane's museum. With spiteful delight, the article lauded Soane's "well-known attachment to artists, authors, and actors." This gibe referred to the many libel suits that Soane had unsuccessfully brought against the press and also to his strained relations with his younger son, George, who had slandered his father in print and who had pursued a fitful literary career as a Drury Lane hack. Soane was one among many to be ridiculed in the article, which took satirical aim at an impromptu congress of noted writers and prominent politicians who found themselves implicated in this journalistic farce (William Cobbett heckling from the Dome of Soane's museum, Horace Twiss declaring martial law out in the square to control the crowd). Cast in the role of the doyen of the gathering was S. T. Coleridge, who recites some improvised verses about Soane's museum: "All then around was dusky twilight dim,/ Made out of shadows most fantastical,/ The unsubstantial progeny of light/ Shining on singularities of art." Observing the statues and fragments crammed into the museum interior, the unauthorized Coleridge divines them to be "stupendous spirits,/ That mock the pride of man, and people space/ With life and mystical predominance."[84]

The parody was very much on the mark. The mystical disembodiment of architecture, the past haunting the future, the substitution of the dead for the living and its sensational correlative of shadows struggling with luminosity: these were the prevailing tropes for the architectural imagination that Soane and Gandy had so evocatively explored in their RA perspectives. Although Soane was obviously fixated on securing the future memory of his own achievement, he held out little hope for the future of architecture. In his jaded and cathartic memoirs of 1835, which were little more than a distended professional complaint, Soane predicted that aspiring architects would read his words and be compelled, as he put it, "to leave the practice of the profession to the ignorant mechanic, the deceptive contractor, the speculative builder, and the fanciful draughtsman."[85] Why, Gandy would have wondered, was he being included among this list of architectural miscreants? Aside from Soane's temperamental passion for personal and professional renunciations, the elderly architect retained a profound suspicion about what he himself had many times called "theoretical architecture." Despite his increasing reliance on Gandy during the 1830s for the presentation of his work at the RA, Soane knew that his fanciful draftsman had truly left architecture behind. The fake Coleridge had spoken of "mystical predominance" in Soane's museum. For Gandy, the mystical effects of architecture required an historical exegesis—a comprehensive theory of human culture that would unify the spheres of nature, architecture, and mythology. It was this project that absorbed him over the last decade of his life.

VI: Gandy's Later Period: Toward a Mythography of Architecture

During the 1830s, Gandy maintained little pretence to conducting a career in the architectural profession. He had not enjoyed a commission since 1825, when he designed a row of semi-detached villas in Vauxhall.[1] In 1833, he and his family fled the suffocating atmosphere and cholera epidemics of central London and relocated to Chiswick, in Grove Terrace near Kew Bridge. For the remainder of his life, Gandy focused his attention on scholarly pursuits, by continuing his collection of drawings and archaeological research on English castles, and by writing a voluminous manuscript of architectural theory and history that he believed would clarify the artistic and intellectual ambitions of his life's work in imaginative architectural rendering. He also embarked on an unwieldy project of illustrating a world history of architecture that began and concluded with a group of extremely complex pictures that would constitute his final series of exhibits at the Royal Academy from 1836 until 1838. After thirty years of exhibiting his works at the Royal Academy, Gandy wished to establish the didactic significance of his pictorial architecture and to demonstrate that, far from being merely alienated fantasies, his pictures could be received as architectural paradigms of historical and philosophical instruction. Through theoretical inquiries in both word and image, he hoped to reveal the primary interconnections between the evolution of architecture and the formation of myth and language. In a period when social utilitarianism and nationalist polemics around the Gothic Revival were dominating architectural thought, Gandy strove to take architectural theory into realms of mysticism, metaphysics, and even science fantasy. His ambition, unrealizable as always, was to arrive at a transcendent resolution that would invest architecture in the coming nineteenth century with heightened meaning and historical significance.

As noted in Chapter III, Gandy first displayed his theoretical and scholarly turn of mind in his 1821 articles "On the Philosophy of Architecture." His notion of "philosophy" was largely a haphazard though erudite mixture of antiquarian research, picturesque esthetic theory, comparative philology, and universal history. The urgent need to formulate this philosophy of architecture arose from the failure of contemporary architecture to embody what Gandy called "a general characteristic." The academic concept of "character" that prevailed in much of eighteenth-century French and English architectural theory derived from the idea that every building should express its program and function and by extension the defined qualities of its culture or nation; "character" also entailed the sensate and affective power of architecture to engender a mood or sentiment through its style, materials, and relation to site and landscape. Soane addressed these connotations of architectural character in his RA lectures as filtered through the French architectural writings of Boffrand, Blondel, and Quatremère de Quincy. For Gandy, "characteristic" in architecture ranged from specific constructive techniques to the architectural declaration of a society's religious, moral, and cultural practices and ideals. The centrality of architecture to religious and civic ritual in the ancient world had already been demonstrated in his Pausanian reconstructions, while the Miltonic pictures portrayed an architecture of spiritual absolutes from within a Christian worldview. His inquiry into the absence of "characteristic" in the architecture of his own time led him to speculate on the signifying

179 *Architectural Assemblage*, 1821

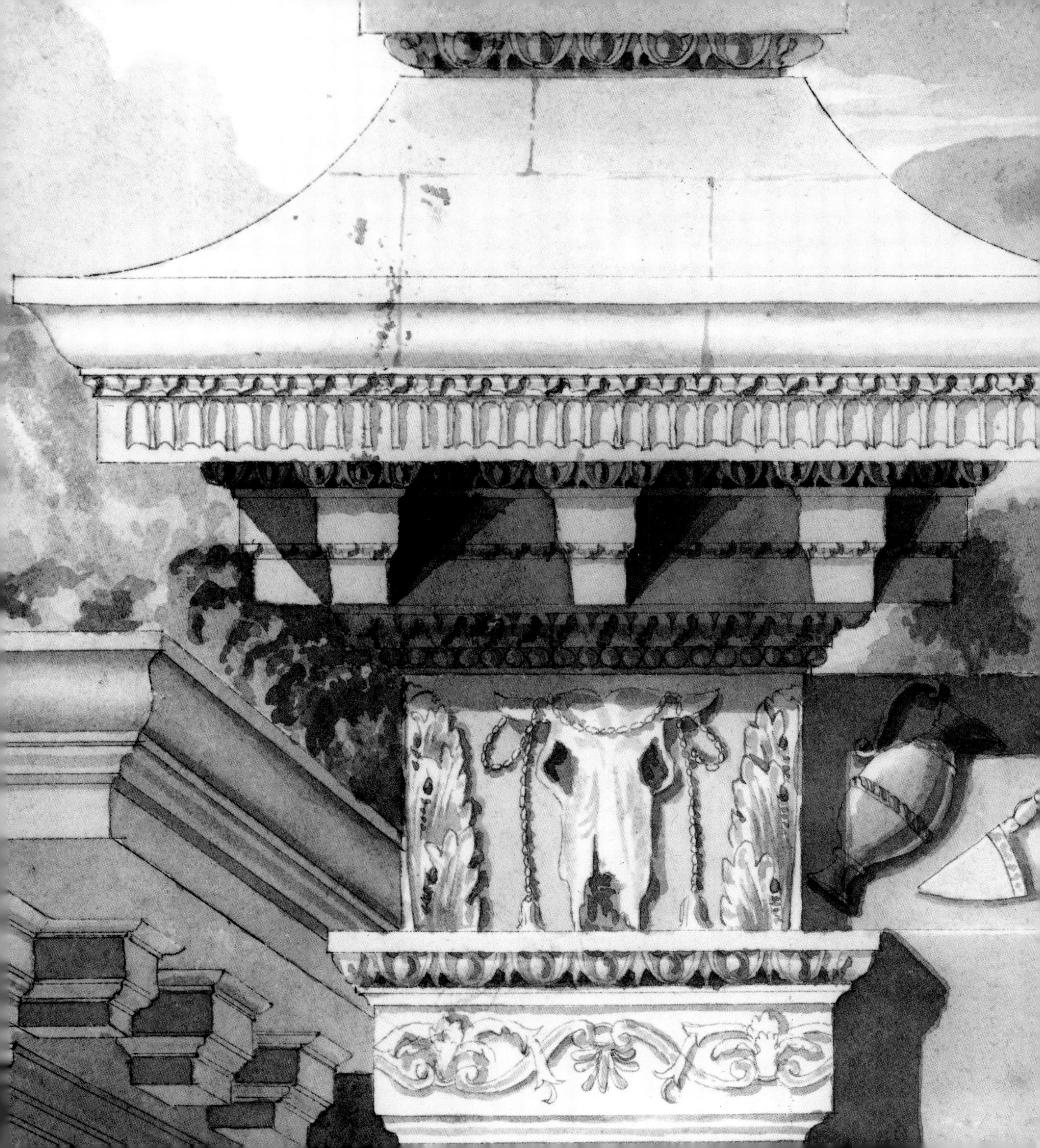

and representational origins of architecture in the ancient world. As Gandy introduced the problem in his 1821 articles:

> Resuming the subject of architecture from the first dawn of its existence, in order to develop each peculiar characteristic which it assumed amongst the nations of antiquity, we are warranted by reason and authority in asserting that all ornaments in architecture are derived from intellectual sources and represent certain ideas in emblematical forms.[2]

By conceiving of architectural ornament as a variable semiotic system, Gandy hoped to recover the lost and occult meaning of ancient architecture. Architectural style was to Gandy a veiled language that spoke of the religious and scientific functions of built form in the ancient world. In tracing the sacred lore of ancient architecture, he seized on two determining elements: the first was the building of Noah's ark as the original prototype for all architecture ("a sacred model and a traditionary image"); the second was the decisive transition in primitive religion from Sabaism (the primitive worship of the stars and the sun) to polytheism. He surveyed through travel literature and antiquarian reports the pyramidal temples of Babylon, India, and Mexico, as well as the Druid barrows and tumuli of Britain, and judged them all to be architectonic recollections of the ark resting on Ararat. The geographic and religious diversity of ancient architecture is consolidated under the sign of the ark, the morphology of architecture traceable to a divinely-inspired origin. Like many Enlightenment historiographers and antiquarians, Gandy interpreted the history of religion as the dispersal of a primitive mystical purity, in which the incorrupt worship of the sun and astral bodies cedes to the manipulative rituals of mystery cults and stately priest crafts. But it was within this historical transition in the ancient world that architecture became the bearer of signs, which is why Gandy became preoccupied with, as he wrote, "all the decorations, consisting of historical and astronomical figures, placed on and about buildings, whether models of the ark, palaces, or religious fanes."[3]

Quite plainly, Gandy's philosophy of architecture had little foundation in the classical traditions of architectural theory. Nor was it merely the eccentric offspring of a fanciful draftsman with time on his hands. His conjectures belonged to a tradition of antiquarian and mythographic scholarship that had flourished since the Enlightenment. In his monumental publication *Indian Antiquities* (1793–1800), Thomas Maurice argued that the architectural evidence relating to the syncretic study of ancient mythology and religion had been largely overlooked. After imagining a world survey of ancient architecture including the Hindu cavern temples of Salsette, the fire-temples of Zoroastrian Persia, and the Pantheon of Rome, Maurice asserted that "from every region, accumulated proofs arise of how much more extensively than is generally imagined the designs of the ancients in architecture were affected by their speculations in astronomy and their wild mythological reveries."[4] Similarly, in his later volume *Observations Connected with Astronomy and Ancient History* (1816), the monuments of the ancient world were interpreted by Maurice as symbolic totems that secretly recorded the transformation of "Sabian superstition" into the earliest institutions of religion and kingship. Gandy's own investigations into "the system of polytheism arising out of the progressive studies of astronomy, polity, and art" followed Maurice's challenge to study the history of architecture as a repository of science and myth in ancient societies. In doing so Gandy's articles touched on burial practices in Ethiopia, the relation between sculpture and hieroglyphics in Egypt and Greece, the significance of scientific characters imprinted on bricks in the walls of Babylon, and Plato's commentary on the fate of the Atlantides. And this was only the beginning.

Some time after 1832, Gandy incorporated and expanded his 1821 articles into an enormous seven-volume, 2500-page manuscript entitled "The Art, Philosophy, and Science of Architecture." The surviving fragments of the manuscript document Gandy's complete immersion in the mythographic study of world architecture and the interconnected origins of building, nature, religion, ornament, and writing.[5] The first volume, or book as Gandy refers to them, contains an extensive table of contents that provides an overview of the ambitious scope of the treatise. Book I presents an outline of the history of the origins of architecture, followed by discussions of the beginnings of astronomy, religion, and writing. Interpolations on the evolution of serpent worship and a descriptive atlas of caverns around the world are also included. The following two volumes surveyed the history of architecture by civilization, nation, and region, succeeded by two volumes that addressed the craft and techniques of architecture (from bricklaying to geometry) and the constituent parts of building (the orders, doors, interior furnishings). This past volume also contained sections on esthetic theory (harmony, the sublime, the picturesque) and compact histories of painting and sculpture. The final two volumes catalogued and analyzed the typologies of architecture, ranging from cottages to museums, bridges to catacombs. In the volumes that have survived (Books I, V, and VI), there are also extended passages of mystical ruminations and anxious sociological commentary. Lacking, as it does, a measured intelligibility, consistent syntax, and developed argument, Gandy's treatise was plainly unpublishable. It was, as Gandy himself noted on the title-page of his manuscript, essentially a compendium of research carried out by antiquarians, natural philosophers, travel writers, early ethnographers, and architectural theorists among others. In describing the intellectual milieu and tributaries of influence around Coleridge's poetry, the literary historian J. L. Lowes wrote, "Ancient cults and primitive religions, Neoplatonic speculations, ethnology, and oxygen and electricity were all seething together in men's minds."[6] A similar constellation of heterodox interests permeates Gandy's treatise, though with a recurrent focus on the question of architectural meaning throughout history.

There was an abiding utopian impulse behind Gandy's tireless undertaking—as he announced in the opening inscription, "To imitate the works of God & create a new world it is necessary to comprehend the pansophy of the one we live in." And in a letter to his son, he asserted that "I seek to know the religion of all countries."[7] This pansophic enterprise was a prelude to the formation of a new utopia. It is telling that among his treatise's list of "books to consult" were Francis Bacon's *New Atlantis* and Tommaso Campanella's *City of the Sun*, both important utopian treatises of early seventeenth-century pansophic theory.[8] The Baconian dream of reconciling pagan philosophy, Christian mysticism and modern science within a model community, in which architecture would serve as a virtual billboard of universal knowledge, was part of Gandy's concern for reanimating the signifying power of architecture. The intellectual scope of his research, as documented in his bibliography of over five hundred publications, indicates that he was not at all doctrinaire or narrow-minded in his readings. The majority of books cited date from the late seventeenth century onward—the references to Bacon and Campanella (and More's *Utopia*), along with citations to early seventeenth-century treatises on the Temple of Solomon, were exceptional in this respect. Many of the volumes were connected to other facets of his career; thus, a large number of pattern books of rural architecture and perspective treatises are inventoried. Picturesque voyage literature and local natural history surveys also figure prominently in his list. Archaeological and topographic publications on ancient Roman and medieval English architecture along with theoretical texts about the origins of the Gothic style that peaked between 1780 and 1820 are prevalent as well. While canonical architectural treatises by Alberti, Palladio, Perrault, Campbell, Fischer von Erlach, Blondel, Piranesi, Chambers, and Milizia are included in Gandy's list, much more revealing are his references to the early eighteenth-century speculative antiquarian deist writings of John Toland and William Whiston, and also to the near-contemporary scholarship of the judicial millenarian polymath Edward King, whose *Munimenta Antiqua* (1799–1806) proposed that English feudal castles and cathedrals of the medieval period were patterned after divine models of architecture from the Bible.

Utopian philosophy, mythographic research, and mystical archaeology consumed Gandy's thoughts. He also wished to develop a visual mode of architectural history. Gandy stated his intention of illustrating all the major monuments and architectural styles discussed in the treatise. His list of "drawings to be made" for his manuscript included perspectives from throughout his career that could find new applications. Gandy was in effect bringing his life's work into alignment with the theoretical concerns of his later years. In 1836, he announced his plan in the Royal Academy exhibition catalogue to execute 1000 drawings that would form a world history of architecture known as *Comparative Architecture*. Gandy, however, would exhibit at the RA for only another two years, by which time he had displayed a mere five works belonging to his ambitious scheme (of these only three are extant). The catalogue introduced the first drawing as "one of series of subjects intended to illustrate essays on its divine origin, and natural model, to contrast ancient emblematic fabrics with the undesigned aspect of modern buildings; to place in opposition the mannerism of many builders with each other, and to show the progress of edifices in chronological epochs, displaying the detail of practical, philosophical, and scientific constructions."[9] This visual mapping of architecture throughout the ages was indebted to the contemporary projects and writings of Gandy's closest colleagues who had likewise undertaken comprehensive pan-historical surveys of architecture.

Soane concluded his RA lectures on architecture, the final series delivered in 1833, with a call for the exhibition of drawings and models to accompany lectures on "comparative architecture," giving direct incentive to Gandy's mission.[10] Soane's phrasing was borrowed from the natural sciences, particularly the rise of comparative anatomy,

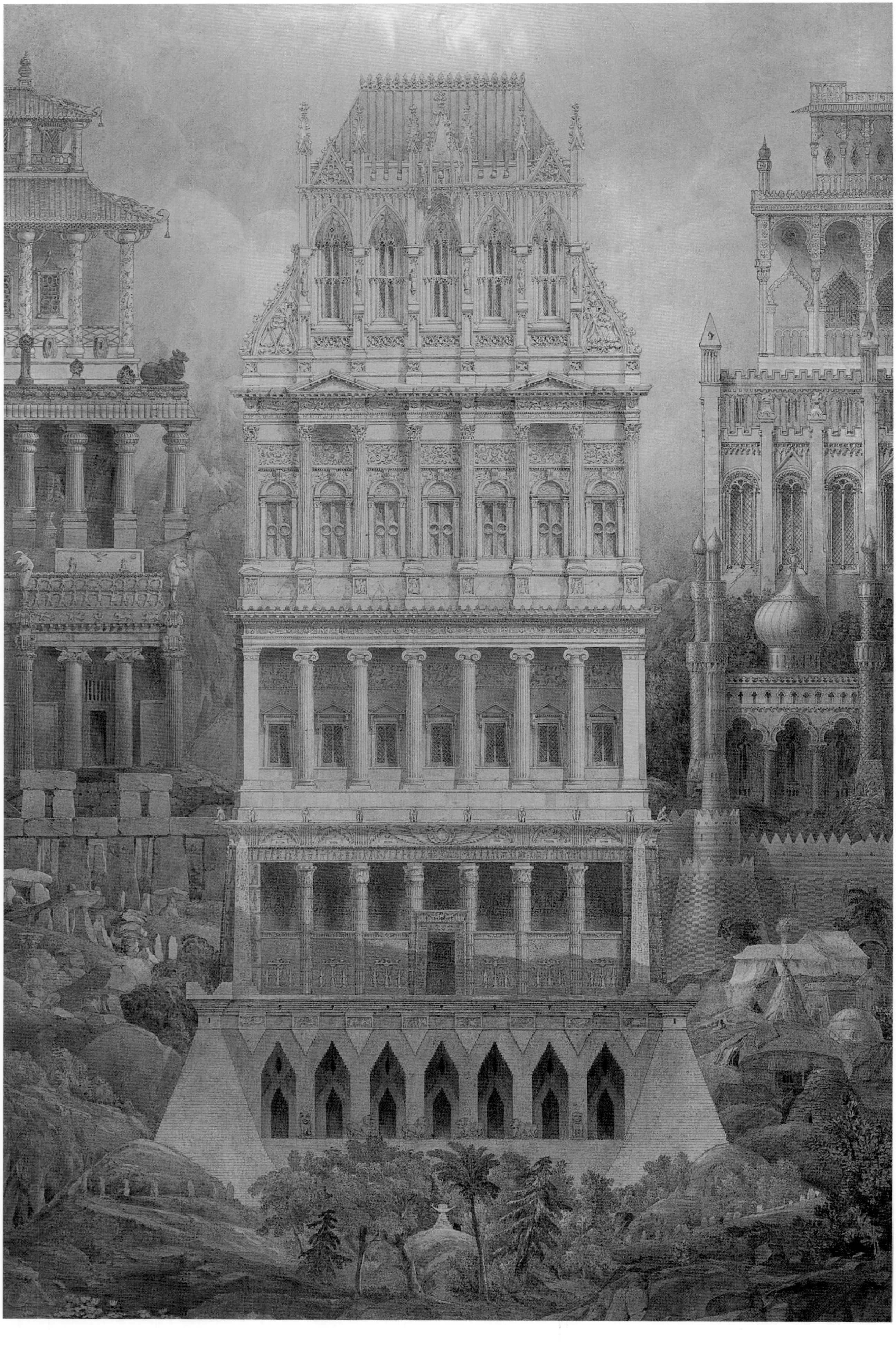

which was the subject of heated debate during the 1820s and '30s at the Royal College of Surgeons located in Lincoln's Inn Fields across from Soane's house-museum. Soane, Gandy, and Turner were familiar with the lectures on anatomy delivered by Sir Anthony Carlisle at the RA. Carlisle's conservative theories of natural history and anatomical science, predicated on the religious doctrine of divine providence, were being undermined by the importation of the comparative anatomical theories of Georges Cuvier, whose revisionist ideas about the adaptive functionalism of animal species and the system of classification in natural history galvanized medical, political, and religious opinion in late Georgian London.[11] Soane clipped newspaper accounts of Cuvier's "Cabinet of Comparative Anatomy" in Paris and of his final "leçon" on the distinctions between historical revolution and animal morphology delivered just before his death in 1832. Soon after the naturalist's death, Soane acquired a portrait bust of Cuvier and installed it in his Monk's Parlor amid the subterranean display of medieval architectural fragments and geological specimens. In employing the term "comparative architecture," Soane and Gandy were bringing a modern scientific nomenclature to the study of architectural form, perhaps in an effort to counteract the insular nationalist polemics of Gothic revivalism for which they had so little sympathy. Even the antiquarian and medievalist proselytizer John Britton was taking a wider view of the history of architecture. Throughout the 1830s he toured the town halls and athenaeums of British cities delivering a lecture series on the "Architectural Antiquities of All Nations," presenting his own visual survey of world monuments with more than 300 drawings.[12] Gandy's old patron Thomas Hope was also turning to the metaphysical and historical analysis of architecture and humanity at this time. Hope's *Essay on the Origins and Prospects of Man* (1831), a three-volume medley of outdated natural philosophy and conservative cultural criticism, argued for a unifying theory of all forms of life and art—"that unbroken connexion between the different parts of the universe of matter and of mind."[13] Much more sensible was his posthumously published *Historical Essay on Architecture* (1835), which, much like Gandy's treatise, conceived of ancient architecture as a religious and scientific instrument. In addressing the longevity and transference of architectural traditions throughout history and across diverse cultures, Hope interpreted "this universal propensity to retrace" as evidence of a fundamental recollective desire in the human race, "reminding a nation of its past origin ... and the first scenes of divine revelation, with the first sanctuaries and places of worship, with all that could produce association of ideas, most interesting and most powerful."[14] Both Hope and Gandy believed that hidden within the history of architecture were the traces of an original encounter with divine power that had sparked the inception of human understanding, religion, and culture.

For Gandy the question remained about how best to communicate these mystical ideas about the history of architecture through a visual medium. An art critic writing in 1832 noted the deficiency of English architectural education in comparison to the French system and recommended the creation of a visually captivating architectural gallery to stimulate the historical imagination of student architects. "For a comparative study," this writer proposed, "there might be one room with models upon the same scale of some of the most remarkable specimens of each style ... the now scattered rays of Architecture would be capable of quickening the most sluggish sensibility into something like perception of the powers of this art."[15] This suggestion for a modular treatment of architectural history in which the diverse styles of building were collected as sample specimens informed Gandy's first exhibit for *Comparative Architecture* entitled *Comparative Characteristics of Thirteen Selected Styles of Architecture* [180]. The drawing accumulates its richly detailed architectural data within vertical planes of iconic symmetry, assimilating successive styles into a single complex building. Architectural history is not traversed spatially, but diagrammatically, through the stacked elevations of the three towering monuments on display. The central five-story structure, and its succession of styles, ascends in epochal sequence and in levels of ornamental refinement: rising from Babylonian brick pylons and arches, followed by the three stages of Mediterranean civilization (Egyptian, Greek, Roman), and terminating with an elaborate Gothic roofline. Somewhat surprisingly, the Greek order is represented by the Ionic rather than the Doric, which was always Gandy's favored order. With its graduated tiers of structural, sculptural, and decorative complexity, and its vertical continuity of stilophily and fenestration, this compendious building retains its hieratic unity. The distinctive features of the world's architectural styles are respected and yet also subsumed within the uniformity of the monument. On either side of it, further multi-styled towers are partially visible, more exotic and remote in geographical or chronological origin, and therefore rendered, at once literally and figuratively, as

180 *Comparative Characteristics of Thirteen Selected Styles of Architecture*, 1836

more marginal to the world history of architecture. To the left, an assemblage of Druid monuments—dolmens, rocking stones, and a restored Stonehenge—provide a foundation for the Persian, Indian, and Chinese elevations, the rudely-formed geology of the Druid base in striking distinction to the ornate insubstantiality of the Chinese pavilion above. The mountainous backdrop intrudes around the Persian and Hindu colonnades, since both monumental styles (from Persepolis and Elephanta) were renowned for their excavated features. To the right are gathered prehistoric tumuli and groups of primitive huts and tents, representing the tribal prelude to an architectural civilization; Saracenic fortifications, minarets, and palace arcades next support Romanesque and Moorish stories, alluding to the interconnection between the culture of Islam and the development of medieval Christian architecture (a much-contended issue in early nineteenth-century archaeological and architectural scholarship). As Gandy noted in the catalogue text, this regimented synthesis of architectural styles is framed by the divine signs of Christianity: an arkite shrine in a sacred grove at the foot of the central tower and a glowing cross hovering on axis above the Gothic pinnacles.

Gandy's visual synopsis of world architecture began in an 1825 sketchbook inscribed "illustrating various style of architecture upon one elevation." From a Persian palace copied from Le Bruyn to a Greek Doric mystery temple described by Pausanius, the historical specimen was submitted to a uniform scale and *parti*, a method of abstractly consolidating and inventorying the history of architecture that was employed in a variety of architectural publications during the early nineteenth century: from J.-N.-L. Durand's *Recueil et parallèle des édifices de tous genres* (1801), with its illustrated taxonomic tables of architectural monuments, to J. C. Loudon's *Encyclopedia of Cottage, Farm, and Villa Architecture* (1833), with its cavalcade of architectural styles applied to a simplified model cottage. Gandy's idea of superimposing the strata of architectural history, creating the congested verticality of his *Comparative Architecture* exhibit, has its most immediate point of reference in Soane's house-museum, and more particularly one of the stranger monuments assembled from out of its collection of architectural fragments. Installed in the Monument Court was an "Architectural Pasticcio" (erected in 1819, dismantled in 1896 and re-erected in 2004) [181], a towering collage of Greco-Roman, Gothic, Indian, and Soanic fragments. The eclectic column was meant to have appeared like an invented antiquity of unknown origin, visible from the breakfast and dining rooms as it arose from out of the courtyard; it also testified to its architect's fiercely acerbic idea of fanciful invention. Here was Payne Knight's "mixed style" run amok. Soane was satirizing the heteroclite novelty with which his own architectural style was so often associated

181 John Soane (rendered by E. Foxhall), *Architectural Pasticcio*, 1819
182, 183 *Designs ... Illustrating Various Styles of Architecture Upon One Elevation (Greek Doric Temple and Persian Palace)*, 1825

GANDY'S LATER PERIOD: TOWARD A MYTHOGRAPHY OF ARCHITECTURE 175

by unreceptive critics. In a series of drawings from 1821 most likely executed in response to Soane's architectural pasticcio, Gandy also experimented with unconventional arrangements of architectural elements stacked upon one another in a seemingly random fashion [179, 184–85]. Over-decorated friezes with sacrificial and Bacchic motifs are contrasted with stark concatenations of moldings. The ornaments recall ritual observances of lost religions. Shadow projections lend ambiguity to the otherwise forthright elevations. In some designs, the spiky irregularity of a tree branch is set against the stratified artifice of human invention. Soane and Gandy were improvising with the established forms of classical ornament, submitting them to operations of chance fragmentation so as to arrive upon a new idiom of design. Although Gandy's amalgamated towers for Comparative Architecture seem systematically logical in their composition when compared to Soane's Babel-like column of architectural dejecta, both works, in their different media, functioned as imaginary and distorted abbreviations of architectural history.

As Gandy indicated in the catalogue entry for this picture, one of his purposes for initiating the Comparative Architecture series was "to contrast ancient emblematic fabrics with the undesigned aspect of modern buildings." It was this "emblematical," or signifying, inadequacy of contemporary design that Gandy hoped to rectify by charting the intertwined tenets of architecture and religious myth. Thus, the first illustration with its monuments of architectural history was followed in 1837 by Comparative Architecture Continued, an Emblematic Sketch, an encyclopedic image of world religions for which Gandy unfortunately did not provide a gloss in the RA exhibition catalogue [186]. The extensive manuscript of his treatise, and the traditions of mythographic scholarship on which it relies, provides the only textual source for this complex picture and its astonishing array of symbolic motifs.

The composition of Gandy's *Emblematic Sketch* is itself "emblematic" with the primary spiritual symbols arranged on a central vertical axis. At the top, a translucent solar disk is encircled by a fluted band of crystalline light adorned with the signs of the zodiac. Underneath the central figure of Aries the ram, the first sign of the zodiac, is an Egyptian winged globe with self-consuming serpents (a symbol of eternity, while also alluding to the caduceus of Hermes as well as to the staff of Moses). To the sides of the zodiac ring are winged Mithraic chimera. Gandy wrote of "the triple Mithras," the godhead flanked by the heads of a lion and an eagle personifying celestial fire and the dominion of the heavens (1:133; here and subsequently references are to the volume and page number of Gandy's manuscript). Just below and virtually suspended from the serpentine tail is the crescent emblem of Noah's ark, which occupies and defines the symbolic center of the picture. It is portrayed as an enormous model woven from straw and hemp, for the ark was venerated in the ancient world because of its associations with agricultural cycles and the seeding or renewal of the world. Astrological medallions of Aries and Taurus are attached to the tapering ends of the ark. Gandy had credited Noah with inventing and regulating astrological science; these signs of the zodiac also connote the postdiluvian rebirth that inaugurates the spring season (1:53). The ark is poised on the rocking mount of Ararat, which marks the separation between the astral and the terrestrial zones of the picture. In front of Mt. Ararat and repeating its form is a stepped pyramid populated with the hierophants and priests of the world's religions. Brahma is seated at the apex with the dove of the holy spirit and a glowing crucifix underneath, triumphing over the symbols of death and corruption: a winged skull and coiled serpent surmounting three globes that allude to sacred sites such as the omphalos at Delphi and the Mount of Golgotha. Flanking this pyramid are cavernous recesses and sacred groves, the first places of worship before the rise of temple architecture. Geological formations in the interior of caves are seen as votive objects of ancient devotion, while further up the hillside on the left stands the tent of Abraham, the sacred antetype to the Holy Tabernacle, which itself is displayed on the opposing summit. Both sides of the landscape are adorned with serpent-entwined trees, an archetypal symbol of destruction and renewal in myth and legend that had been alluded to in Gandy's earlier depictions of the Delphic tripod, the grove of the Eumenides, and Rosslyn's Apprentice Pillar. Animal personifications are also assembled, most of them relating to creation myths and cosmic allegory. Most prominent is the motif of the generative bull breaking the egg of Chaos to produce the two halves of space and time (from ancient Japanese fable and Orphic mysticism). This primordial symbol of the cosmic egg, or mundane shell, recurs in Gandy's writings and art. It appears in his contemporaneous still life of lavish decorative urns and services, among which there is an overturned goblet with a fractured egg, the tumultuous arrangement of ornamen-

184 Architectural Assemblage, 1821
185 Architectural Assemblage, 1821

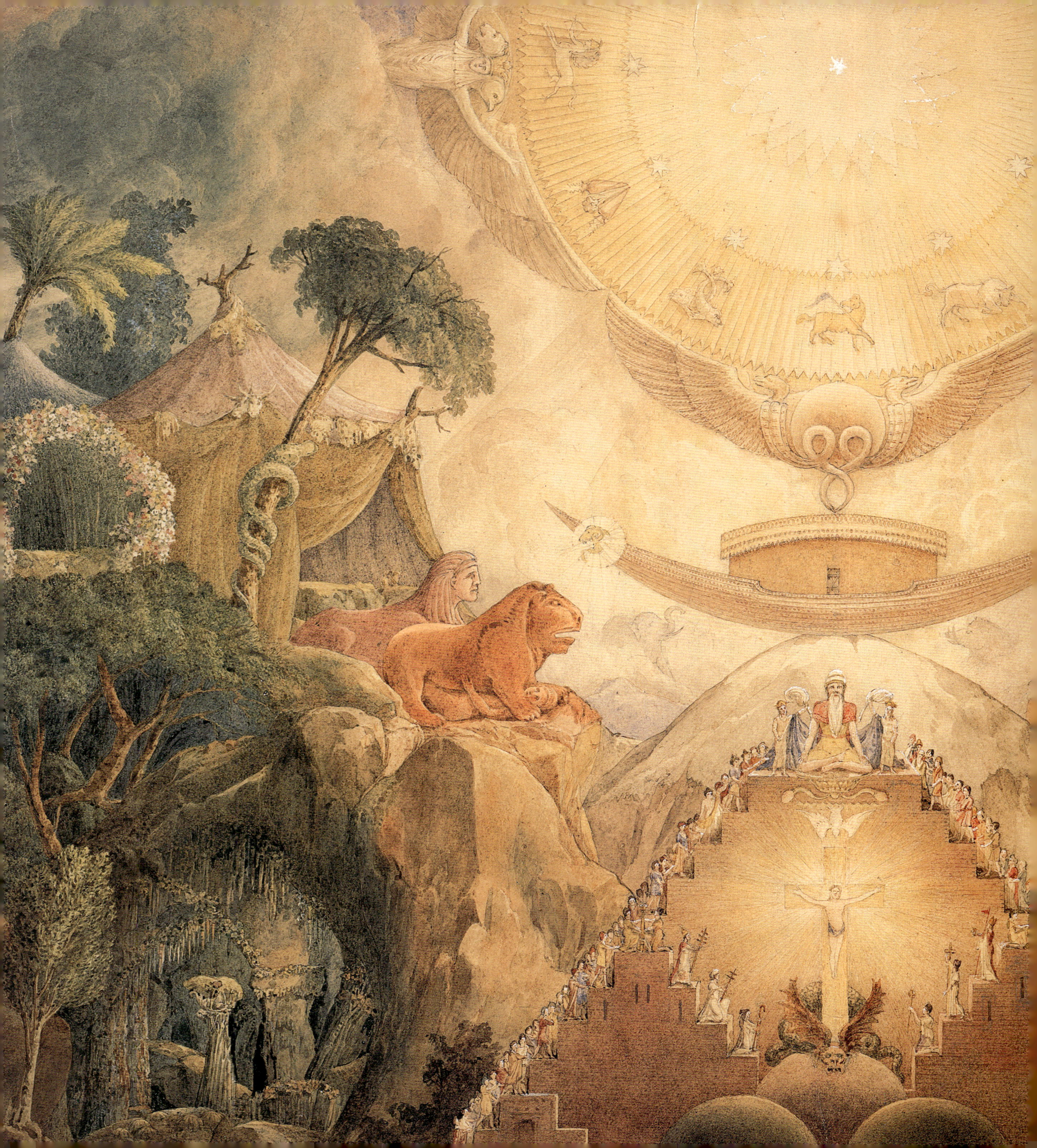

186 Comparative Architecture Continued, an Emblematic Sketch, 1837

tal objects exemplifying the cosmic struggle between chaos and design [187]. The *Emblematic Sketch* also depicts the Zoroastrian lion—at once procreative and destructive—in coitus with a human figure, and the boar Vara, an avatar of Vishnu who spears the world from out of the waters of chaos. Despite the distracting accumulation of symbolic motifs in the picture, its composition nevertheless has a schematic legibility. In his manuscript, Gandy experimented with the idea that the entire chronology of universal history could be indicated by three geometric signs placed on axis: the circle or oval signifying the creation, the crescent for the deluge, and the cross for the advent of Christianity (1:220); this tendency to configure a comprehensive graph of the spiritual history of humanity is fully elaborated in the revelatory spectacle of Gandy's picture.

The significance and centrality of the ark of Noah in the *Emblematic Sketch* was confirmed by Gandy's inquiry into architectural origins in his theoretical writings. The ark embodied the architectural juncture of divine and human purpose, of all known mythologies and faiths, and of the chronology of the world. In claiming that the ark of Noah was the sacred model for all ancient temples, Gandy acceded to scholarly opinion, noting "so says Bryant" (1:2), in reference to Jacob Bryant's influential treatise *A New System, or, An Analysis of Ancient Mythology* (1774). Bryant's work represented a conservative though persistent strain in British mythographic scholarship, one in which oriental and pagan mythologies were tirelessly interpreted as symbolic and allegorical corruptions of the Scriptures. The plotting of the shared genealogies of Mosaic law and of the diverse bodies of "heathen" mythologies determined the course of mythographic studies more contemporary to Gandy, multi-volume exhaustive works such as William Drummond's *The Oedipus Judaicus* (1811), G. S. Faber's *The Origins of Pagan Idolatry* (1816), and Godfrey Higgins's *Anacalypsis ... or an Inquiry into the Origin of Languages, Nations, and Religions* (1836).[16] Gandy's writings bear a closer relationship to these mythographic expositions of universal arkite symbolism than to any classically based traditions of architectural theory. These mythographic currents in intellectual history survived through the romantic and into the Victorian periods, as evidenced by the grim character of Mr. Casaubon from George

Eliot's *Middlemarch* (1871). Set in the midst of the Reform Bill crisis of the early 1830s, Eliot's novel gave a merciless portrayal of the obscurantist scholar who abjures all engagement with the realm of the living in favor of the dark convolutions of mythographic theories. Casaubon's definitive volume that he was forever preparing and that aspired to decipher "all the mythical systems or erratic mythical fragments in the world" could have aptly used Gandy's *Emblematic Sketch* as its prospective frontispiece.[17]

If Bryant had maintained that "the ark was certainly looked upon as the womb of nature," Gandy similarly conceived of the ark as the womb of architecture.[18] Tectonic form and spatial consciousness have their primal beginnings within the lost memory of the ark. In explaining why the first generations of postdiluvian tribes retired to mountainous cavities as places of sacred dread, Gandy theorized about the inception of architectural sublimity: "Stupendous excavations instilled awful and sublime notions of architecture which gave principles for buildings afterwards. In these stony habitations, they always remembered and imitated the interior of the ark" (1:7). This conjunction of the sacred and the sublime, the aura of the divine model fading into numinous and fearful sensations, would also affect the evolution of other ancient building types, particularly mystery temples and sepulchers. In his imagined account of early Greek adyta, Gandy sought to evoke how the postdiluvian excavations had been refined into fantastic sanctuaries: "The temples for mysteries were so constructed as to favour the artifices of the priesthood. The fanes were subterranean apartments [with] the succession of light and shade ... and scenes of Tartarus and Elysium which made deep impressions on the initiated" (1:29). The collective memory of the ark had yielded to what Gandy called "the rhapsodies of myth" and to the ritualistic cults of pagan religion (1:94). The mythographer Faber had referred to the ark as "the transmigrating compound" to the history of architecture, and his comic strip-like illustration [188], showing arkite shrines, primitive excavations, and sacred groves as central to the morphology of ancient pyramids and pylons, was refined and amplified by Gandy in the *Comparative Architecture* exhibits.[19]

Other aspects of Gandy's *Emblematic Sketch* reveal his familiarity with the more radical religious skepticism of revolutionary French mythographic research. The pyramid supporting representatives of the world's religions in Gandy's picture is extrapolated from a visionary scene in the Comte de Volney's *Les Ruines de l'empire* (1791), a book well known to Jacobin sympathizers and to English romantic writers. Coleridge read the text repeatedly so as to refute its atheistic internationalism. Soane kept transcriptions from Volney's writings, which undoubtedly fortified the architect's stern resistance to the solaces of Christianity. The treatise was popularly cited and excerpted by Chartist reformers and progressive intellectuals well into the 1830s. This belated topicality of Volney's book in early Victorian political and religious controversies may explain why Gandy found it still relevant as a source of inspiration.[20] After reflecting on the cycles of despotic tyranny in human history, Volney imagined "a general assembly of the nations" around "the pyramid of natural law"; the omnipotent "legisla-

187 *Still Life with Urns and Goblets*, ca. 1836–37
188 *The Rise and Progress of Temple Architecture*, from G. S. Faber's *The Origins of Pagan Idolatry*, 1816

tor" overseeing this global congress announces, "Let each system of religion, and each particular sect, erect its proper distinctive standard," the communal gathering of world religions illustrated in the foreground of Gandy's Emblematic Sketch.[21] In a footnote about "this immense congress," Volney proposed that a gallery in the Louvre be reserved for the comparative study of costumes and religious artifacts of races and nations worldwide, observing that "it might truly be stiled the science of man!"[22] Gandy was advancing this proposal through the compilation of world religious imagery in these final RA exhibits. Moreover, Gandy, like Volney, speculated endlessly on the original commonality of religious symbols and architectural styles from seemingly disparate cultures. To convince the representatives of the world's religions that their faiths were all descended from the primitive veneration of "the metamorphoses of the sun," Volney's enlightened legislator offered this circular argument: "People of Japan, your Bull which breaks the mundane Egg, is only the Bull of the zodiac, which in former times opened the seasons, the age of creation, the vernal equinox. It is the same Bull Apis which Egypt adored; and which your ancestors, Jewish Rabbins, worshipped in the golden calf. This is still your bull of Zoroaster, sacrificed in the symbolic mysteries of Mithra, which poured out his blood and fertilized the world. And ye Christians, your Bull of the Apocalypse with his wings, symbol of the air, has no other origin; and your Lamb of God, sacrificed like the bull of Mithras, is only the same sun in the sign of the celestial ram."[23] The predominance of the luminous celestial circle and its astrological signs in Emblematic Sketch accords with the emphasis Volney placed on the shared filiation of all myths and faiths in the primitive worship of the sun and stars, and on the intersection of oriental, pagan, and Christian mythic figures and symbols that could be detected in zodiacal constellations.

Gandy's treatise explores this mythographic reduction of the pantheon of world religions to a comprehensive solar and astronomic myth through the study of ancient etymologies and astrological calendars. Drawing on the work of Volney's colleague, Charles Dupuis's *Origine de tous les cultes, ou la religion universelle* (1794), Gandy postulated how the natural religion of "planetary worship" gave way to the development of "hieroglyphical personification" and "allegorical language" created by "the first race of Astronomers, Poets, Priests, and Bards" as implements of religious and civil power in the control of knowledge (1:64–65). To strike through the trappings of mythic allegory and religious mystery was also to return to the doctrine of emanations, the mystical key to the origins of all systems of belief. Gandy's theoretical writings often drift into metaphysical rapture over the declension of the divine from out of the numinous illumination of pure spirit, as in this characteristic passage: "The systems of emanations partaking of the divine presence pervades all nature or the universe; the invisible God supreme and the visible Gods—the Sun, Moon, and Stars—are emanations of a superior order" (1:217). "Emanation" was the mythographer's neo-Platonic and deistic mantra, particularly when delving into the prehistory of religion. Thus, Dupuis could write that "light was the first divinity ... an emanation of the creator of all things"; and further on, "all of nature and the universe ... were seen as emanations of a supreme, universal intelligence."[24] Without citing the esthetic terminology of the sublime and picturesque, Dupuis spoke of "the theory of two principles, light and darkness," as the sensational origin of "the grand fables and fundamental fictions of all ancient religions."[25] This Manichaean duality in the human imagination applied equally to the pictorial form and theoretical argument of Gandy's lifework. The Emblematic Sketch visualized what the mythographer Higgens had referred to as "the sublime doctrine of emanations," in which all of the world's mythologies interpenetrate and are returned to the undifferentiated monism from which they emerged at the dawn of history when the human race first conceived of and witnessed the spiritual in the light of nature.[26] Judging from the list of drawings in Gandy's treatise that were projected for *Comparative Architecture*, several pictures were to entail ritualistic scenes of luminary worship and mystical revelation: views of an Indian cavern temple with an avatar of Vishnu exploding from a glowing column, and of the initiated waiting for the light of dawn outside the mountainous temples of Persepolis.

Gandy's subscription to the doctrine of emanations in the history of ancient religion intersected with his passionate study of meteorology and optics. Under the heading of "perspective" in his treatise, there were lengthy descriptions of meteorological effects and natural catastrophes, after which Gandy concluded: "All the foregoing phenomena astonish and dazzle the spectator ... the representation of the ideal beauties of the poets, whose descriptions of heaven, hell, &c. are borrowed from these and many other appearances of nature" (5:1603). The visionary and the scientific are thus reconciled in Gandy's mind. The spectacular effects of atmosphere and light in the Miltonic pictures are

189 Landscape with Parhelion, 1827

here given an empirical foundation. Infernal exhalations and illuminated pyramids in the clouds indicate the phlogistic combustion of unstable volcanic surfaces and the luminous refraction of meteors entering into the earth's atmosphere. Even the illumination of Merlin's tomb has its basis in natural philosophy: the spectral light results from the glow of putrefying matter, as Gandy notes, "places of burial have a kind of dew which produces light like phosphorus" (5:1579). Parhelia, coronas, ignis fatuus, aurora borealis, waterspouts, and whirlwinds were catalogued and described by Gandy, who relied not only on the natural philosophical writings of Joseph Priestley and David Brewster but also on his first-hand observations of these fugitive atmospheres. The northern lights, he wrote, "first appear about twilight of a dim yellow, then streaming out into columns and changing into an infinity of shapes or varying colour after covering the whole atmosphere, skimming the heavens, and instantly vanishing" (5:1584). And in describing a cloudy moonrise, a quiet prose nocturne unfolded, "the iris faded, the dense cloud dissolved in mist, and the moon appeared like a lamp in a paper lantern" (5:1602). This romantic notation of observable phenomena in the skies was certainly not unique to Gandy. The vaporous crepuscules of Turner's sketchbooks and the lunar vigils of Coleridge's notebooks are renowned instances of a journalistic meteorology in which the optical and the imaginary imperceptibly merge. Gandy at times united visual and verbal description of his atmospheric sightings, as on the morning of March 3, 1827, when he recorded, "on looking toward the sun, the eye in the zenith, there appeared upon a superstrata of clouds the above parhelion. This parhelion was an inverted iris, its colours vivid and pure." The accompanying watercolor depicts the nimbus sun resplendent with the inverted rainbow arc above [189]. The deictic function of the drawing is at once affirmed and undermined by the unerring symmetry and vertical axis of the wondrous atmospheric phenomena. Could they really have presented themselves in so orderly a manner? Gandy brings an attitude of revelation to what he witnessed. Nature is made truly emblematic, a decade before the *Emblematic Sketch*. Perhaps he felt himself to be like the first worshippers of astral bodies and the sun, imparting symbolic permanence to marvelous fluctuations of atmosphere and light.

Gandy's interleaving of architecture, cosmology, and myth perpetuated the symbolically oriented interpretations of the art and architecture of antiquity found in the esoteric research of late eighteenth-century writers. Baron d'Hancarville's *Recherches sur l'origine, l'esprit, et le progrès des arts de la Grèce ... sur les monumens antiques de l'Inde, de la Perse, du reste de l'Asie, de l'Europe et de l'Égypte* (1785) was most renowned for its comparative approach to "generative" symbolism in ancient art, unveiling what the antiquarian referred to as "this emblematical spirit" in primitive theology that determined the sexual and cosmological imagery of sculpture, engraved gems, totemic idols, and temple decorations worldwide. Some of the esoteric motifs in Gandy's *Emblematic Sketch*—such as the aforementioned inclusion of the generative bull creating the material world by breaking the egg of chaos, the sculptural ensemble seen perched on its rocking stone—were lifted from the engravings in d'Hancarville's volumes. D'Hancarville's emphasis on the "common origins" and "first principles" [190] of ancient art and culture, as decoded from the often obscure and obscene symbolism of antiquarian fragments, stimulated Gandy's own insistent belief in "the emblematical language of ancient art" (1:217). Similar ideas were pursued in the realm of architectural theory by J.-L. Viel de Saint-Maux's *Lettres sur l'architecture ... développe le génie symbolique qui présida aux monumens de l'antiquité* (1787), a book which interpreted ancient temple architecture as systematically expressive of agricultural cults and cosmogonic myths from remotest antiquity. Relying almost exclusively on literary evidence—metaphysical writings of late antiquity, speculative archaeological publications, and descriptive travelogues—Viel conceived of architecture as giving shape to, and being shaped by, ancient worldviews in religion and science. These "symbolic types" of architecture proposed by Viel, from sepulchral grottoes to hypaethral solar and zodiacal temples, also influenced the cosmological architectural themes of Boullée and his followers.[27] Gandy's observation that "Astronomy and caverns have given the origin of all ideas in architecture" (1:163) has its own origin in Viel's theory of ancient architecture as the mystical locus for the earliest human comprehension of the cosmic expansiveness of the heavens and the sepulchral enclosure of the earth. The ideal of an architecture encoded with astronomical and cosmological data might also be extended into the modern age, Gandy argued; he advised architects to consult the contemporary astronomical discoveries of William and John Herschel to enliven the form and ornament of their designs (1:168).

The transmission of late eighteenth-century French hypotheses on the symbolic origins of art and architecture into English scholarship consulted by Gandy is most apparent in the controversial writings of the esthetician and connoisseur Richard Payne Knight. Knight's *The Symbolical Language of Ancient Art and Mythology* (1818) brought mythographic parallelism closest to the interpretive study of world antiquities, through which, as Knight noted, "we find traces of the same simple principles and fanciful superstructures, from the shores of the Baltic to the banks of the Ganges."[28] For Knight, ancient art and architecture mediated symbolically between an elemental sensuality and a recondite spirituality in earliest civilizations. Architectural forms in antiquity, such as obelisks, spires, and all columnar members, could thus be interpreted as solar and astronomical emblems with phallic and procreative connotations. The instinctive libido of the ancient world was channeled into architectural forms that strained heavenward. Knight's designating of the orders of architecture—whether Indian, Egyptian, or Greek—as "symbolical compositions" influenced Gandy's own account of the evolution of columns and pillars as "astral and generative symbols" (1:165). The litany of creation myths, mystery religions, and chimerical personifications of cosmic and natural forces that consumes much of Gandy's treatise was very dependent on Knight's avid concern with the symbolizing properties of the religious and artistic imagination in the ancient world. Yet again, behind the analogous structures of world mythologies, Knight also discerned "the system of Emanations ... the operation of one plastic spirit universally diffused and expanded."[29]

In delving into these emblematic and cosmological aspects of ancient art and architecture, Gandy wanted to lay the foundation for a modern revision of an architectural language and its decorative symbolism. In 1838, one of his two *Comparative Architecture* entries at the Academy included a design for a library ceiling adorned with an array of signs, emblems, and symbols relative to what Gandy described in the catalogue caption as "the origin of all ornaments." This drawing remains unlocated, but many of the ideas with which it dealt are treated at some length in his theoretical writings. The evolution of ancient scripts and letters—demotic and sacred, mimetic and abstract—offered, according to Gandy, the basis for a new graphic language of architectural ornament. He assembled comparative alphabetical charts, transcribed hieroglyphs from Soane's prize Egyptian antiquity, the Belzoni sarcophagus of Seti I, and collected examples of ancient votive inscriptions and pictographic signs (many of them traced from the pages of his favorite scholarly journal, *Archaeologia*). Intrigued by the signifying concentration of elements associated with the invention of letters in ancient Ethiopia ("the manner of expressing symbols of celestial constellations" [1:18]), as well as with Chaldean cuneiform ("language on the bricks of Babylon" [1:179]), Chinese calligraphy ("every single mark they use significant of an idea ... a metaphorical application of character" [1:197]), and Egyptian hieroglyphs ("beauti-

190 *The Breaking of the Mundane Shell*, from Pierre d'Hancarville's *Recherches sur l'origine, l'espirit et le progrès des arts de la Grèce*, 1785

ful and more copious than any other writing, teaching sound and the forms of natural history on the mind at one sight" [1:196]), Gandy wanted to recover a mystical semiotic for architectural ornamentation. In interpreting a graphic sign that conflated the Hindu lingam with the Egyptian ankh, he decoded the economical symbolism of this ideographic geometry as "the key that unlocks all propositions and the elements of the arts and sciences, belonging to divine nature and the capacity of human understanding" (1:207).

The conception of architecture as a comprehensive mnemonic sign, as a visible index to knowledge, impelled Gandy to speculate on the signifying conjunction of ornament and writing in architectural design. He was stirred by legendary accounts of the antediluvian columns of Seth, which were renowned for having been inscribed with all scientific, historic, and sacred learning known to humanity, bridging the two epochs separated by the Deluge (1:171). Likewise, the ark of Noah, Gandy imagined, was decorated with "emblems of the universe, hieroglyphical remembrances of a prior state which recorded deeds of heroic warriors and legislators of the social order" (1:18). After encouraging architects to find inspiration in letters and scripts for architectural decoration (citing the Moorish style as an example), Gandy suggested: "The emblems, symbols, and signs of religion, law and other arts and sciences of the present day are infinite and would be more appropriate than the mere idleness of introducing on all occasions the inventive gusto of pagan institutions that marks the utmost poverty of genius of a modern artist" (1:loose leaf). Although intent on charting the migration of languages in the ancient world and cataloguing alphabetic tables, astrological signs, and animal and plant emblems, Gandy ultimately cherished the idea of a universal alphabet and sign language that could be resurrected from out of the linguistic and glyphic fragments of world history. And so he speculated, "a universal or philosophical character may be invented to be read by all people" (1:178), maintaining that "the Symbolic system should be a perfect, durable, and universal language" (1:219). This dream of a universal grammar, potentially modeled after scientific and mathematical notations, had been proposed throughout the eighteenth century by philosophers and ideologues, from Leibniz to Condorcet, and was made known in artistic circles of the Royal Academy through the writings of the scientific poet Erasmus Darwin. In the explanatory notes to his poem The Temple of Nature, or the Origin of Society (1803), Darwin speculated that "a universal visible language in the sciences ... could be introduced into practice which might constitute a more comprehensive language for painters, architects, or the other arts."[30]

Gandy's call for the utopian renovation of architectural language was still predicated on the historical examples of ancient architecture. The symbolic cogency of the earliest architecture had been diminished throughout the course of history; as Gandy recalled the didactic and expressive significance of ornament in antiquity:

> The heathen mythology is one continual allegory, the only means of conveying information to a multitude without books and but few manuscripts. These allegories were the ornaments of every kind of architecture and sculpture ... Ornament is the poem of the wall, the language of stone, the picture of the type and use of a building. They are actual records and authenticate history. (1:217)

Gandy's rhetoric of architecture—buildings as tectonic repositories of meaning—borrows freely from the writings of the French antiquarian/art theorist Quatremère de Quincy, particularly his De l'Architecture égyptienne (1803). Quatremère developed this analogy between language and architecture in characterizing the monuments of ancient Egypt, with their hieroglyphed surfaces and complex sculptural programs, as being encumbered by "chains of symbolic writing," the buildings functioning metaphorically as "public libraries, their ornaments as legends."[31] Soane, who had translated sections of Quatremère's study of Egyptian architecture in preparing for his Royal Academy lectures, also spoke of how the decorative systems of ancient architecture were intimately related to "the symbolical representations of their divinities, to their religious ceremonies and sacrifices, [and] their fabulous histories."[32] Moreover, articles from Quatremère's Encyclopédie méthodique: Architecture (1788–1825) were being translated and published in J. C. Loudon's Architectural Magazine during 1836–37, including the essay "On the Use of Allegory in Architecture." Here Quatremère examined hermetic and figurative modes of decoration in ancient architecture, using the occasion to refute the overzealous theories of Viel de Saint-Maux who had postulated earlier that, as Quatremère summarized the argument, "all architecture might be ... clothed in an emblematic veil."[33] These late Enlightenment debates about the ancient emergence and modern renewal of the symbolic language of architecture were thus sustained into the early Victorian period.

Perhaps the most specific example of a graphic signifying system or a decorative language that Gandy introduced into his library ceiling design and discussed in his theoretical writings was that of heraldry. His interest in these medieval motifs dates back to his friendship with the miniaturist and fellow ARA Ozias Humphry, who had entertained a scholarly and artistic passion for heraldry. When Humphry died in 1810, Gandy prepared a design for his tombstone that incorporated heraldic patterns and allegorical attributes.[34] Gandy thought of heraldry as the Christian equivalent to ancient pagan symbology, calling it "an acknowledged hieroglyphic, an abbreviated language, an algebraic concatenation of historical fact and remote pedigree" (1:218).

His manuscript treatise presented, ad nauseam, an historical survey of the sepulchral, priestly, and military applications of heraldry, accompanied by extensive diagrams on the marshalling and blazoning of heraldic signs, patterns, and attributes. The received conventions, and possible permutations, of heraldry appealed to Gandy as a graphic language of commemorative genealogy, as a visual condensation of history. He argued that new heraldic formulas need not be restricted to medieval revival buildings: tinctured masonry and polychromatic fluting could be deployed more liberally, contributing to a symbolic approach to constructive color in all architectural styles (1:274). Gandy's approval of heraldic ornamentation as a method of enhancing architectural meaning exemplifies what the art historian E. H. Gombrich referred to as "the interaction between signs and design."[35]

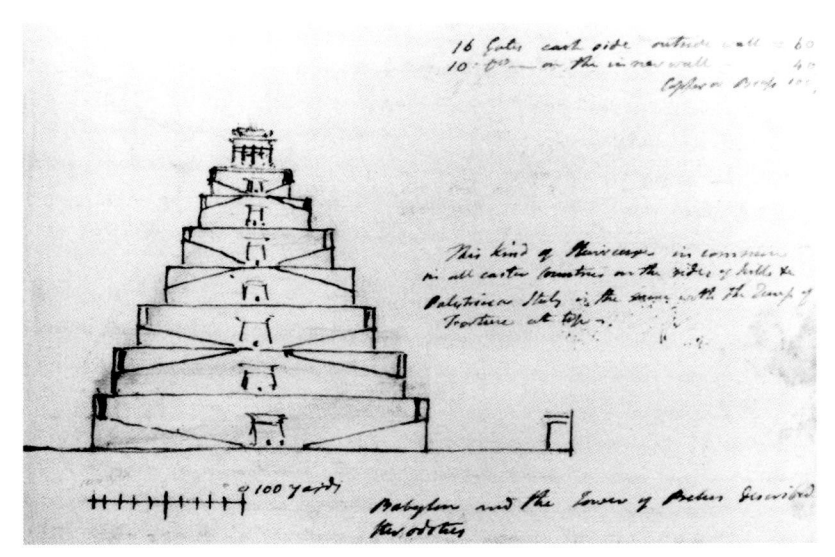

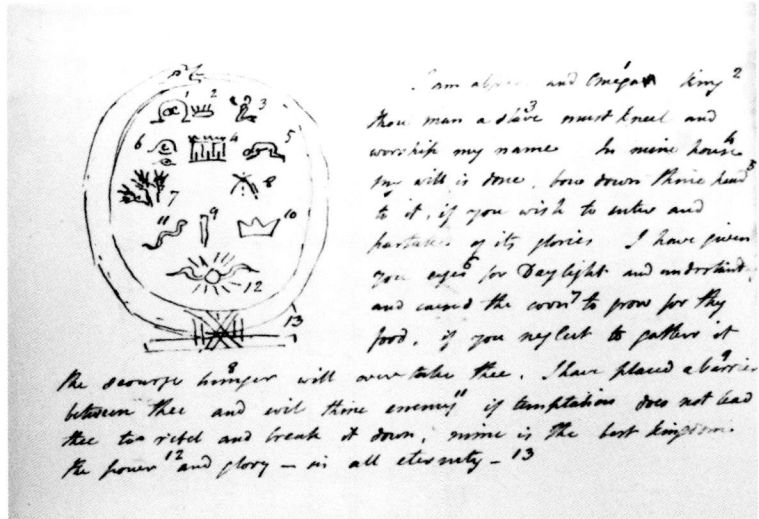

191–95 Drawings from "The Art, Philosophy, and Science of Architecture": Elevation of Temple of Belus; Diagram of Self-Consuming Serpent; Signs and Emblems of Human Knowledge; Comparative Table of Alphabets; Diagram of Heraldry

Amid all of the alphabetic, astrological, and heraldic charts collected by Gandy, there were only occasional attempts on his part to formulate a new sign language for modern architecture [191–95]. On a loose-leaf sheet at the back of the first volume of his treatise, Gandy scribbled down a series of schematic signs denoting the arts and sciences, e.g., a quill for belles-lettres, a sundial for chronology, a jagged arrow for electricity. This pasigraphic experiment represents at best a tentative solution to the insurmountable challenge of inventing a visible language for architectural ornament. The limitations of an inscriptive architecture, irrespective of its universal transparency of meaning, were recognized by Gandy, as when he complained about the insufficient degree of esthetic affectivity in contemporary architecture:

GANDY'S LATER PERIOD: TOWARD A MYTHOGRAPHY OF ARCHITECTURE 187

"Alas! Modern works require names to be written on them to excite any emotion" (5:1490). The only instance in which Gandy tried to codify the communicative language of design in compositional terms, in the massing and *parti* of architecture and not in its ornamental writing and glyphic cryptograms, occurs in his theoretical discussion of domestic buildings. Here Gandy endorsed a strict typology in the scaled formal arrangement of dwellings—the number of columns, bays, and projections of a design determined by the social distinction of the building's inhabitant: as he wrote, "The idea of forming villas into classes and to fixed absolute rules to mark the rank of the occupier appears utopian, but it is the practice of several eastern nations" (6:2055). The architect and art critic James Elmes had already praised the reportedly despotic building codes of oriental architecture (the decoration and size of dwellings closely sanctioned by social and political status) in his published *Lectures on Architecture* (1821), an important sourcebook for Gandy's treatise.[36] With this regulated formalism—a utopian import from the east as well as being an exaggeration of French academic architectural theories of character and propriety—architectural composition becomes a manifestly signifying agent of social hierarchy, its ordained marshalling of façades, as Gandy commented, "necessary to the well being of society" (6:2056).

Having proposed, in his *Comparative Architecture* exhibits, visions of world architecture that attested to the revealed religions and symbolic languages of comparative mythography, it only remained for Gandy to return architecture to the undiluted forces of nature. His final surviving picture for the *Comparative Architecture* series was *Architecture; Its Natural Model* [196], a panoramic watercolor that ironically treated the subject of primeval beginnings while simultaneously marking the close of Gandy's exhibition history at the Royal Academy. In the *Emblematic Sketch*, Gandy had already depicted numinous caverns and lush groves as the primitive sites of natural religion, and the stratification of architectural styles seen in the first exhibit for *Comparative Architecture* also suggested a geological analogy. But now the incipient architecture of the natural world stretched across an expansive landscape, unrestrained by the mythographic iconicity of the preceding pictures. The catalogue entry for *Architecture; Its Natural Model* ran to four long paragraphs, itemizing all of the geological formations, animal constructions, and primitive dwellings derived from nature and collected for this natural historical fantasy.[37] The economy of the natural world had devised architectonic systems that prefigured and determined the course of human invention; as Gandy explained in the opening invocation to his treatise: "Men who traverse this earth and examine the animal, mineral, or vegetable kingdoms find a succession of models for his artificial fabricks ... The philosophy of architecture is the sketchbook from nature." Distinct from the mimetic, developmental impulses of the human mind, Gandy believed, was the constancy of natural processes of design and the unreflective, yet inflexible, principles of animal instinct.

This deistic reverence for the self-generative design of nature had also pervaded architectural and esthetic theory over the prior century. The neo-Palladian architect Robert Morris, in his *Lectures on Architecture* (1736), marveled at the scale of natural creation, "the amazing structure of the whole Animal and Vegetable World, [which] fills us with noble Ideas of the Power which such Proportions have on the Mind."[38] This natural philosophy of esthetics was also addressed by Turner in one of his Royal Academy lectures on perspective of 1818, in which he paraphrased from the writings of Erasmus Darwin to observe that "the vegetable and mineral formation, from the cell of the Bee and the Bysaltic mass, display like Geometric form."[39] In a similar vein, the London literary press reported on the esthetic theories of the Dutch philosopher and artist Humbert de Superville, whose writings and lectures explicated, as one journalist summarized it, "the physiology of architecture ... not only the architecture of every country, but its animals and natural history."[40] It was this multiformity of crafted shapes from the earth and its animal species that contributed to the profusely scenic landscape of Gandy's *Architecture; Its Natural Model*.

Human invention, or at least proto-human invention, was not forsaken by Gandy in this architectural landscape, for in the right foreground he depicted a simian nuclear family taking up residence in a primitive hut at the base of a palm tree, an anthropological paradise that set the clock back on Laugier's primal scene of architecture.[41] The picture's catalogue entry credited the orang-utan of Sierra Leone for its commodious dwellings, but Gandy was thinking most probably of this notorious passage from Lord Monboddo's philological treatise *Of the Origin and Progress of Language* (1774), in which primates were given their assigned place in the development of human culture: "The Orang Outangs have not only invented the art of building huts ... but also have contrived a way of communicating to the absent, and recording ideas by the method of painting or drawing, as practiced by many barbarous nations."[42] Gandy was also using the primate as a humorously conventional trope for artistic imitation—for aping nature—appropriately so, since the overriding thesis of the picture concerns the status of architecture as a mimetic art form observant of the readymade designs of the natural world. Gandy, however, was not being entirely charitable with this anthropoid missing link: while the primate has copied his hut after the grove of trees in the left corner of the picture and is seen twisting vines together to strengthen his building material, in emulation of the creeping vines on the palm tree behind him, he remains unaware of the almost columnar perfection of the basaltic fragment on which he is seated, the faceted and monumental ruins of this classicizing geology spilling all around him. The dramatic view of Fingal's Cave—a geological tourist attraction in Gandy's time regarded as nature's cathedral—seen looming behind the fragile hut conveys the same message: the future history of architecture was already written in the landscape, merely waiting for human civilization to catch up.

Although Gandy compiled a worldwide survey of tribal huts in his manuscript, he was somewhat disdainful of "the Savage State" and what he took to be its primitivist episodes of architectural invention varied only by geography and climate (6:1880). This is why he turned to the instinctual order of the animal kingdom, the authority of natural law that superseded the more restless and undirected course of human history. The engineering wonders of animal habitats, from honeycombs to beaver lodges, were well in advance of human progress in constructive techniques. In his novel *Headlong Hall* (1816), the romantic satirist Thomas Peacock disparaged such comparisons between human and animal faculties by having his fictional phrenologist, the expert Dr. Cranium, analyze the marked similarities between the skull of Christopher Wren and that of a beaver! Nevertheless, Gandy's picture prominently features the domed and turreted constructions of ants and termites, entomological monuments that seemed to embody a civil and social purpose beyond the reach of humankind. As Gandy commented wryly about the enviable state of insect civilization: "With the good order of their subterranean cities, they are foremost in industry and government" (6:1816).

Well beyond the architectural ingenuity of animal species, *Architecture; Its Natural Model* extolls the scenic and structural operations of geology. Gandy's treatise reveals him to have been an enthusiastic armchair traveler and natural historian, vicariously inspecting the natural monuments of the earth through scientific and tourist travelogues and engravings.[43] Caverns, natural bridges, and mountainous excavations were most prized by Gandy, ranging from the grotto of Antiparos, the mines of Maastricht, and the Mammoth Cave of Kentucky, to more local landmarks like Pool's Hole in Derbyshire and the coastal caves of Staffa (1:296–332). His amateur scientific inquiry into the eclectic variety of geologic formations—advertised in the picture's extended catalogue entry—did not lessen his mythographic devotion to the type of the ark and the centrality of the deluge to universal history. After recording his survey of caverns throughout the world, Gandy concluded, "It is not in mines or natural caves nor in graves that we must search for the origin of architecture ... it is to the ark, the first object of the second world and the last of the first" (1:332). The significance of the geological vista in *Architecture; Its Natural Model* lies in the fact that it is specifically a postdiluvian landscape, indicated by the discreet presence of Noah's ark, barely visible atop the central and highest summit in the picture. Gandy was not reluctant to reconcile the biblical with the natural historical, his picture implicitly addressing many of the physico-theological debates over a scriptural geology and the age of the earth that had been raging for a century and a half, from Thomas Burnet's *The Sacred Theory of the Earth* (1684) to William Buckland's *Reliquiae Diluvianae* (1823).[44] If an apocalyptic landscapist like John Martin—with whom, as we have seen, Gandy was often compared—could incorporate elements of catastrophist geology into his spectacles of diluvian destruction, Gandy could envision the rebirth of the world after the subsiding of the Great Flood, the geologic ruins of the earth transformed into, as Gandy noted in the catalogue gloss, "objects of veneration" by the postdiluvian vestiges of civilization. The mythographer Faber had expounded at some length on the sacred connotations of mountain summits, caverns, and all kinds of earthworks in world religion, all traceable to, in his words, "the place where the Ark rested after the deluge ... the Paradisiacal mountain of the Ark."[45] Thus, in Gandy's picture, Mt. Ararat guards over the panoply of geological specimens revealed after the deluge.

This mystical deference to sacred history did not assuage the delirious sense of visual discovery and the vitalistic interpretation of nature that characterize *Architecture; Its Natural Model*. The landscape is protean and diverse in its natural processes, from the glacial ocean and misty cataracts descending from the alpine skyline, to the quiescent volcanic forces that had produced the basaltic cliffs of the Giant's Causeway

196 Architecture; Its Natural Model, 1838

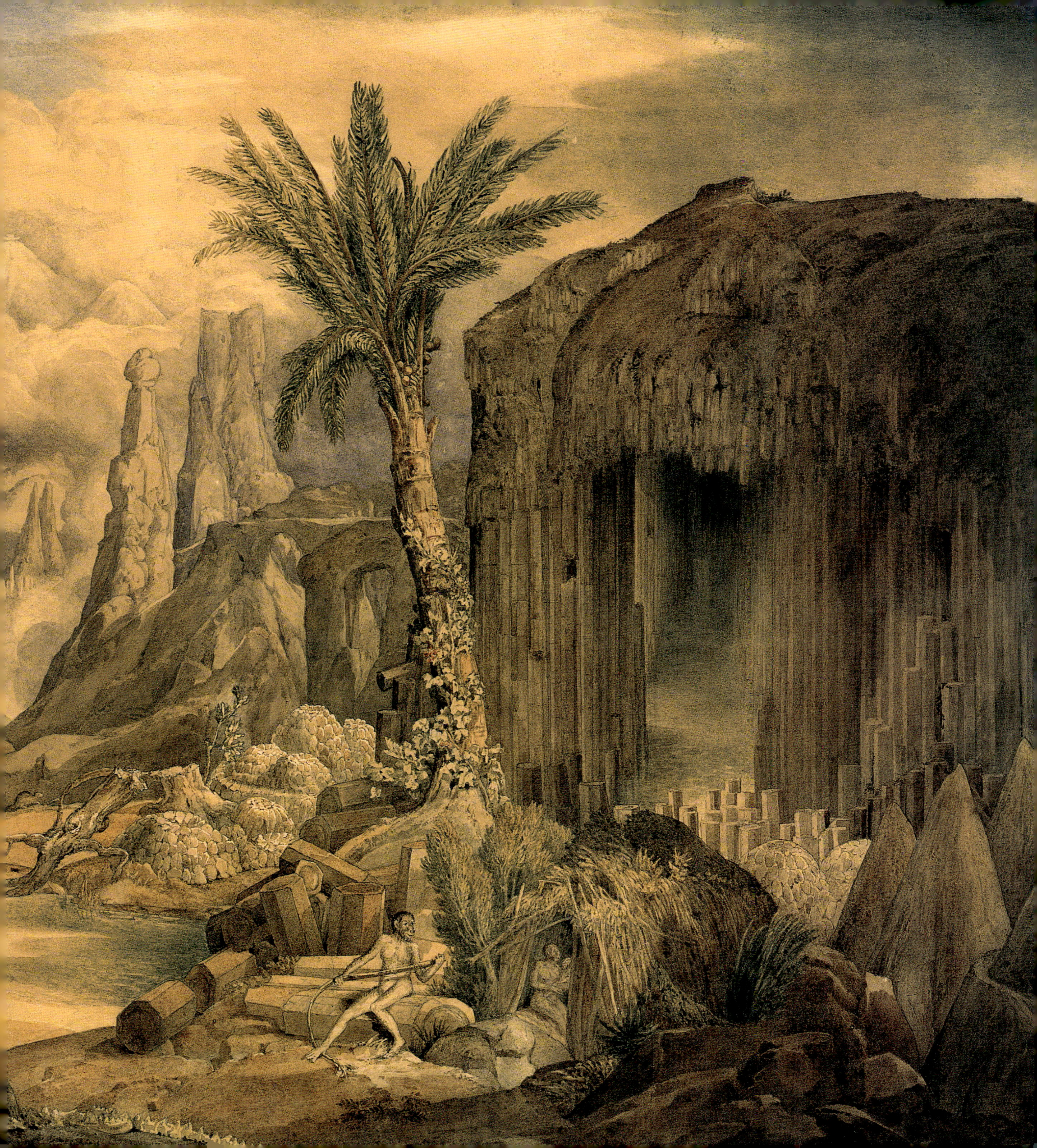

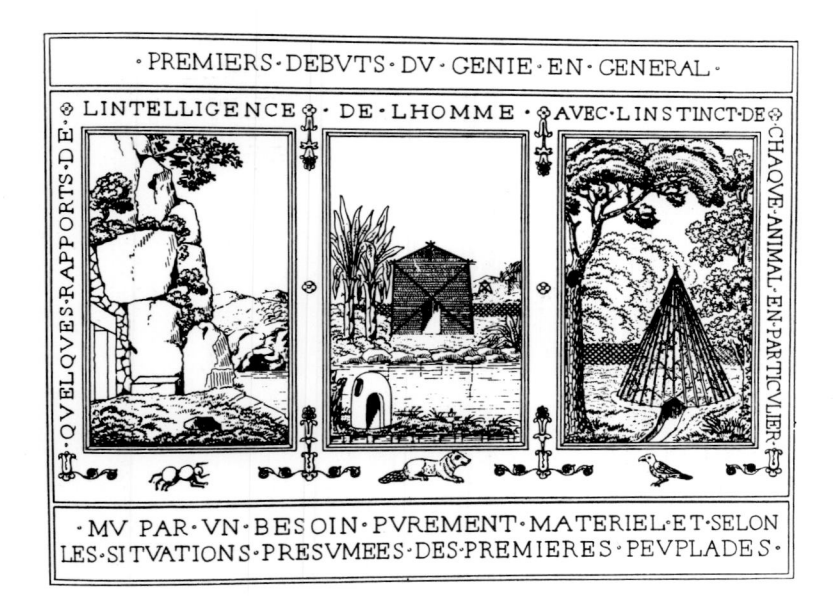

and the imposing nave of Fingal's Cave. Geographically remote landmarks, such as the natural arch of Mercury Bay, New Zealand, to the rock formations of Cappadocia in Anatolia, are brought into a single comprehensive view. The chromatic temperature of this highly atmospheric watercolor likewise ranges from the icy blue-greys of the arctic backdrop to the umber warmth of the tropical setting in the foreground, the entire picture acting, quite literally, as a *Weltlandschaft* of geographic and climatic extremes. Nature's artifacts appear in lithic singularity as well as in scenic ensembles, visually orchestrated through the succession of irregular outlines, projecting shapes, and penetrated spaces. Here the natural world is perpetually framing itself, suggestive once again of the self-generative power of design that animates every aspect of the landscape. The picturesque union of nature and architecture is posited not only as an esthetic principle but as a scientific imperative.

The imaginative variety of Gandy's natural historical picture drew upon both architectural and scientific illustrative prototypes. Jean Coussin's romantic architectural treatise, *Du Génie de l'architecture* (1822), a work cited by Gandy in his manuscript, presented a historical survey of architecture from its origins in material nature to its utopian destiny as "speaking signs."[46] In a tripartite line engraving for his treatise [197], Coussin illustrated cave entrances, bowers, and Phrygian huts alongside insect mounds and animal burrows to demonstrate the interplay between instinctive invention and human intelligence. These antecedents to architecture would be multiplied and monumentalized by Gandy for his later watercolor. Gandy's method of collecting, and decontextualizing, the geologic wonders of the world for *Architecture; Its Natural Model* has its most immediate source in popularizing science books like Simeon Shaw's *Nature Displayed in the Heavens and on the Earth* (1823), a multi-volume work illustrating nature's prodigies—towering termite cones, needle rocks, basaltic columns—of the kind seen in Gandy's picture. In one of the more spectacular illustrations from this natural historical encyclopedia, the most celebrated mountains of the world are gathered together to make up an imaginary landscape view [198]. This sublime and crowded congregation of natural monuments, epitomizing the sculpted scenery of the earth, anticipated Gandy's geological *vedute ideate*. The anthropological and entomological themes of *Architecture; Its Natural Model* were borrowed in part from James Rennie's scientific pocket guide entitled *Insect Architecture* (1830), whose frontispiece depicted an African native in a landscape of palms and clay termitaries [199]. Here again, the exotic landscape does not merely contain but rather is materially identified with an indigenous prehistoric form of architecture. Gandy's postdiluvian landscape illustrated what natural historians had for centuries referred to as "the plastick virtue of the earth."[47] In his treatise, Gandy held intriguing, though scientifically retrograde, notions about the creativity of nature: figured stones and *lusus naturae* were miraculous evidence of the earth's mimetic tendencies (5:1618–19). Similarly, primitive monuments,

197 *Natural Origins of Architecture Illustrated*,
from Jean Coussin's *Du Génie de l'architecture*, 1822
198 *Celebrated Mountain Ranges Around the World*,
from Simeon Shaw, *Nature Displayed in the Heavens and on the Earth*, 1823
199 *Termite Mounds in Africa*, from
James Rennie's *Insect Architecture*, 1830

from Druid megaliths to the carved deities of Easter Island, seemed, in Gandy's mind, to be as much the work of nature as that of man. Syncretism was not only the guiding principle behind ancient civilization and its mythopoeic reveries and architectural symbols: it also operated at the paleontological level of nature's recombinative properties, as when fragments of the earth are decomposed by deluges and cataracts, for as Gandy wrote, "They are carried away to reaugment future fossils, the separation of all particles again reunite in other forms and fossils" (6:1816). The earth itself was but an eclectic assemblage of historic traces and geologic styles. Fascinated by the legend of Atlantis and influenced by such fanciful cosmological theories as those proposed in Benoît de Maillet's *Telliamed, or Discourses on the Dimunition of the Sea, the Formation of the Earth, and the Origin of Men and Animals* (1750),

Gandy could even spin his own cosmic fables that would further dissolve the boundaries between nature and architecture:

> a new continent emerging in resurrection will again take its turn to reanimate the travels of genius, while nations with their records may be destroyed by armed men or natural causes, as in the deluge, without annihilating this globe—this ball we inhabit rolling in space, may disperse or unite with another planet and mingle with a non-descript race of beings.
>
> Countries may be submerged by the great agents of fire and water, shifting the solid matters of this earth in its rotatory motion, new continents thrown up and the old

GANDY'S LATER PERIOD: TOWARD A MYTHOGRAPHY OF ARCHITECTURE   193

undermined sink forever. Another parent of mankind like Noah will succeed, thus perpetually reproducing all things. The architecture of all nations points to a prior origin. (1:46)

Extrapolating from this passage, one is led to imagine the discovery of unknown civilizations entombed within the earth, its geology already bearing the imprint of long-vanished architectural antiquities belonging to the histories of other worlds. This may explain why *Architecture; Its Natural Model* appears almost extraterrestrial in its compilation of geological forms. Nature and culture are made truly indissoluble, human, natural, and cosmic histories so intertwined as to render meaningless the temporal significance of history itself. The trajectory of Gandy's *Comparative Architecture* series appears to illustrate Roland Barthes's insight about the naturalizing strain to mythic conceptions: "We reach here the very principle of myth: it transforms history into nature."[48]

By postulating an eternal return of origins for architecture, Gandy was in many respects circumventing any pretence of historical empiricism in the reconstitution of the past. His mythographic conception of world history simultaneously sought to stimulate and neutralize the stylistic polemics and colonizing debates over the relativity of divergent cultures and architectures. This mythography of architecture, with its surfeit of comparative styles and hermetic symbols, was primarily homological in its formulations, always searching for a principle of similitude across the spectrum of history, human and natural, that would sanction the recovery of a universalizing architectural symbolism, or that would finally obliterate the dichotomy of nature and culture within some speculative cosmology. The *Comparative Architecture* exhibits can be seen as visionary literalizations—admittedly a contradiction in terms—of the Enlightenment's theoretical inquiry into all forms of primitive origins. However, Enlightenment primitivism and its claim to a regressive rationality was accelerated by Gandy into a romantic panacea associated with the mystical and natural wellsprings of civilization.

Gandy's projected list of drawings for *Comparative Architecture* involved criteria that were both historical and esthetic: representing architectural history by epoch and by nation, as well as through "best of" surveys for building types and architects.[49] These criteria would become fairly commonplace in the museological construction of history. Not surprisingly, Gandy's treatise contains a prospectus for an ideal "pansophic" museum to be erected in London, "a very extensive collection fit to adorn the Metropolis of a great Kingdom" (6:2088). Consisting of six triangular buildings concentrically planned, each row of apartments and displays devoted to a separate realm of knowledge, this museum was meant to enclose all human learning, unifying art and science

200 A. B. Clayton, *Imaginary Museum and Art Academy*, 1842
201 *A Series of Pagan Temples, Fire Altars &c.*, from Richard Brown's *Sacred Architecture, Its Rise, Progress, and Present State*, 1845
202 *A Portal of Strangely Compounded Architecture*, from George Wightwick's *The Palace of Architecture, a Romance of Art and History*, 1840

within its architectural complex. The exhibits were to encompass the natural world, from mineral and fossil cabinets to exotic gardens and menageries, the museum housing everything from libraries, sculpture galleries, and art academies, to anatomical theaters, mechanical demonstrations, and global panoramas. Gandy's hypothetical museum might have stood somewhere between the mythographic sanctuary of Noah's ark and Francis Bacon's natural philosophical laboratories of Salomon's House in his *New Atlantis*. It would have also presaged the colonial and technological emporium of the Crystal Palace. As spectacles of knowledge, this imaginary museum and its pictorial equivalent—the *Comparative Architecture* illustrations—were both retrospective and anticipatory in scope: collecting and ordering the lexicons of nature and history from out of which were to evolve the syncretic compounds of future invention. The compendious visual format of Gandy's *Comparative Architecture* directly influenced other contemporaneous artists whose complex imagery likewise served as pictorial or graphic museums. The architect Alfred B. Clayton's 1842 watercolor [200] of an imaginary museum and academy of the arts emulated Gandy's synoptic presentation of different historical periods of art and architecture within a vertically expansive space. Even closer in style and conception was the antiquarian artist James Stephanoff's *Assemblage of Works of Art in Sculpture and Painting, from the Earliest Period to the Time of Phidias*, exhibited in 1845 at the Old Water Colour Society. Here the compact history of ancient art from around the world was presented as an impenetrable plane of wall paintings, relief sculptures, statues, totems, and ceramics [203]. The geographical and chronological distance between these artistic specimens is compressed within a fictive visual museum that both invites and defies historical systems of evolution and periodization. As in Gandy's *Comparative Architecture*, the order of history and its graduated progress from bottom to top teeters precariously toward hallucinatory disorder.

Although Gandy's conjectures on the mythography of architecture never reached an audience in early Victorian England, many strains of his architectural thought found further elaboration in several popularizing architectural books of the period. Two of them were written by architects and critics in the circle of Gandy and Soane. George Wightwick's *The Palace of Architecture: A Romance of Art and History* (1840) was a whimsical dream narrative centered around an architectural parkland adorned with worldwide building specimens, the imaginary gate lodge to this "palace of congress" incorporating the diverse styles of architecture within a single monument [202] in much the same manner as Gandy had done for the initial *Comparative Architecture* picture. The commentary for the illustration of this architectural confection explained: "It symbolizes MUSEUM. It is a prologue, spoken by Retrospection ... a Masonic riddle, teeming with multiplied significancy, and exhibiting a kind of monstrous combination."[50] Historical awareness, ritualistic mystery, and enriched meaning were all implicated in this accretive design, Wightwick later recalling that at the time he composed his book he was gaining "an apprehension of architecture as the many-languaged history of the great religions of the civilized quarters of the earth," an understanding that also closely approximated Gandy's treatise and *Comparative Architecture* series.[51] Similarly, Richard Brown's *Sacred Architecture, Its Rise, Progress, and Present State* (1845) [201] addressed the mythic and religious development of temple architecture throughout the world, illustrating comparative examples in comprehensive visual surveys much as Gandy had planned for *Comparative Architecture*. Like Gandy, Wightwick and Brown were putting all of architectural history at the disposal of the present, reacting against, while also advancing, the cultural fragmentation of manifold historic revival styles by freely intermingling antiquarian knowledge with mystical reverie. Their compilations of world architecture were meant to liberate the architectural mind and to infuse contemporary design with poetic significance and historical self-consciousness.

The architect C. R. Cockerell, who had succeeded Soane as Professor of Architecture at the RA in 1839, expressed alarm over this modern uncertainty of architectural principles. "The art of architecture," Cockerell argued, "has reached its ne plus ultra by the confusion of all ages." He also warned against those architects who would lose themselves in theoretical and antiquarian speculation about the origins and evolution of architecture, for it was futile, he cautioned, to quest after "the attainment of this visionary learning."[52] Gandy was very likely in the back of Cockerell's mind in issuing this admonition. Yet Cockerell would also illustrate the world history of architecture within one comprehensive picture in his decidedly Gandyesque watercolor entitled *The Professor's Dream* (1848) [204]. Cockerell's profound ambivalence toward the relativity of architectural styles and the proposed affiliation of world cultures throughout history stems in part from the assault on the

203 James Stephanoff, *An Assemblage of Works of Art in Sculpture and Painting*, 1845
204 C. R. Cockerell, *The Professor's Dream*, 1848

authority of the Greco-Roman tradition that was coming from outside the academy, and particularly from the socially incisive and sectarian architectural polemics of A. W. N. Pugin. In the second edition of his controversial treatise *Contrasts* (1841), Pugin railed against "that extraordinary conglomeration" of historic styles corrupting modern architecture, his illustrations mocking the architectural marketplace and academies of "mixed styles" (at least for this edition Pugin omitted his vitriolic attacks on Soane).[53] But in the most general terms, Pugin's objectives were not very different from those of Gandy, Soane, and even Cockerell: to open up theoretical discourse about the cultural and spiritual connotations of architectural idioms and to reestablish a greater sense of representative meaning in modern design. Quite obviously, though, Pugin's tersely dogmatic argument, his religious certitude and invective social criticism, were antithetical to the all-embracing mysticism and diffuse historicism of Gandy's syncretic ideals. Pugin spoke of the true principles and unerring wisdom of Catholic tradition, Gandy of pantheistic emanations and regenerative geologies. As close as Pugin ever came to responding directly to Gandy's *Comparative Architecture* was in a footnote to his *Apology for the Revival of Christian Architecture in England* (1843) in which he expressed confidence in the human instinct for design and promised "to produce a treatise on *Natural Architecture*."[54] He never did. William Blake, who was well versed in the Enlightenment mythographic scholarship that would later obsess Gandy, had famously proclaimed that "All religions are one."[55] Pugin steadfastly insisted on reducing architecture to one religion and to one style. Gandy's explorations into the mythography of architecture may best be encapsulated by modifying Blake's mystical epigram: "All architectures are one."

GANDY'S LATER PERIOD: TOWARD A MYTHOGRAPHY OF ARCHITECTURE

Conclusion: On the Madness of Architecture

Along with *Architecture; Its Natural Model* at the 1838 RA exhibition Gandy showed an elaborate drawing (unfortunately lost) entitled *Sketch of a Design for a Cast-Iron Necropolis*. It was to be the sepulchral coda of his career. To Gandy, the dead always took precedence over the living in their architectural needs. The catalogue entry for the design gave a succinct history of ancient burial practices and petitioned for the nation to create what Gandy called "a living sepulchre." This proposal was both archaic and futuristic. Its sanction came from the monumental tombs of Egypt and Assyria while utilizing the most technologically advanced building materials. Cast-iron towers and pyramids were to house catacombs into which metal cylinders containing the dead were to be sealed. Although Gandy's final sepulchral dream conformed to his longstanding passion for commemorative architecture, it was also informed by a wider sociological anxiety about the disposal of the dead in the modern metropolis. The radical reformer Flora Tristan mordantly observed in 1840 that London should be known not as "the metropolis of the world" but as "the necropolis of the world."[1] Other architectural proposals of the period broached this challenge, albeit in as similarly improbable vein as Gandy, of accommodating the high quotient of corpses spawned by the modern industrial city. Francis Godwin exhibited an aerial perspective of a Greco-Roman-style national cemetery on Primrose Hill in 1830 that resembled the cumbersome royal palace designs of Soane. Also in that year, Thomas Wilson published his treatise *The Pyramid*. The proposal for this massive sepulcher trumpeted that it would hold five million corpses and would occupy the space of Russell Square. Along with the "sepulchral magnificence of its presence," the structure was projected to alleviate the plight of the urban poor: the arduous and protracted construction of the pyramid would, as Wilson wrote, "award its labours among the famishing portion of the community."[2] Aspiring to a kind of deliriously Malthusian functionalism, these utopian monuments of death were of course horrifyingly dystopian in their grim calculations.

Gandy, as we have seen, responded to the social conditions of modernity with acute doubt and uncertainty. His treatise is particularly revealing in this respect. At times, he viewed industrial and technological progress as an agent of architectural innovation, as a means of overcoming impossibility and of attaining the marvelous. But his intuitive philosophy of history and progress yielded only paranoid nightmares, as in this remarkable and mysterious rumination:

> The age of science is an age of reason. The laws of nature and of conventional men ought not to be invaded by self willed individuals, when physical power gives them an easy dominion over life and death, and whose possession must be gratified by subjugating the multitude, the majority of whose occupations renders them unfit for deep researches. The terrors of the sword puts to flight the reason of science, where safety is darkness and the dominant power glitters

over automatons ... The quietude of science and reason is disturbed by excited agitation. The laws cannot protect the insidious attacks on the studious, whose minds become alienated, and all sink into a chaos instead of pursuing uninterruptedly art or science. (5:looseleaf)

The satanic patron who had persecuted Gandy in his youthful dream while en route to Italy had now become an omnipresent and oppressive force of history. As confusing and self-involved as this passage may be, it belongs to an aging and jaded romantic generation that had survived the Napoleonic Wars and that had witnessed the productive (and destructive) flourishing of the Industrial Revolution and the March of Intellect. Like-minded and far more literate jeremiads against modern England recur in the letters and journals of Wordsworth and Beckford during the 1830s. They believed that the widening struggle for political representation and the promised liberation of mind and body through science and machinery precipitated only social disorder; imagination, knowledge, and nature had ceded to the new generation of the automaton. Gandy's cast-iron necropolis was to have stood ready to receive the alienated and mechanically imprisoned souls of this lapsed age of reason.

Both in Gandy's treatise and in his last surviving letters to his son Thomas written in 1837 there are many references to the vexed interrelation between art and politics in modern society. While recognizing the decisive emergence of democracy and capitalism in his lifetime, Gandy held little hope for the future of art under these conditions. He felt that both "a republican system" and "a great commercial soul" were anathema to the cultivation of the fine arts. His son Thomas had settled in Plymouth to establish a studio as a portrait painter (Devon and Exeter had been the haunt of a branch of the Gandy family since the seventeenth century) and so his father offered advice about the direction of his son's intellectual and professional development. He encouraged Thomas to become more politically informed and to begin writing about art theory. "I do not suppose," Gandy wrote, "you enter much into the political state of the country, although every man ought to have some regard to the motions and motives of its complicated machinery, for on it depends the welfare of the country and the fate of every individual."[3] Elsewhere in this correspondence, he disparages the ideological factions of parliamentary democracy ("the Whigs and the Tories, the religious and the radicals are all at variance for place and self") and concludes, "the state of all civilized society is a mixture of many incongruities."[4] Even the mythographic syncretism of his thinking could not adequately modulate the cacophonous politics of contemporary Britain.

Gandy's esoteric mysticism did not make him entirely unreceptive to the democratic scientism of the new Victorian age. Writing to his son, he extolled the invention of "the universal telegraph." He had most likely seen newspaper reports of early experiments in this technology carried out by the London inventor and surgeon Edward Davy in 1836–37. His panegyric bears quoting: "You may imagine what a new beginning to intellect will be set afloat, and how men of different languages in different parts of the world may by reference to a book of signs discourse on any subject a thousand miles apart in any part of the world as quick as the electric matter will convey it." The natural philosophical and mystical sections of Gandy's treatise often spoke of the electric properties of souls and atoms flying through infinite space—these were the spectral physical traces of the divine emanation that had created the universe and that had inspired the higher consciousness of the human race. Now these emanations were encoded into electrical pulses forming a new semiotic system that would overcome the "incongruities" of the disparate creeds and cultures of the globe. The promise of the telegraph for Gandy also consolidated many of his own lifelong preoccupations: the dissolution of the boundaries between matter and spirit, the transformation of divine light into a signifying language of human advancement, and the reconciliation of primeval myth with modern science.

The overall tone of these last surviving letters by Gandy is without the unrelenting anomie normally found in his correspondence. Lively family gossip is interspersed with arcane digressions on the outlawed practice of ritual murder in India and the fate of the ten tribes of Israel. There are some gently melancholic asides about the ephemeral quality of a life's accomplishment, as when he muses, "we arise like sparks and perform a meteor course and are seen no more." Although the press coverage of Gandy's entries at the RA exhibitions diminished throughout the 1830s, he was not entirely ignored during this period. *The Times* reported of the *Comparative Architecture* series, "For imagination and powerful execution, the drawings are worthy of the highest praise."[5] By now, however, such praise was of little consequence. Gandy took greater solace in the emerging careers and marriages of his children than in the passing recognition of his RA exhibits in newspaper reviews. In recounting to his son news of the death of Soane, who had died on January 20, 1837, Gandy commented particularly on the insidious family strife that had so tortured Sir John while alive, and now also in death. Gandy somewhat sardonically referred to Soane as "Ivano," as though casting him as a pitiably cursed character from a Gothic family romance by Ann Radcliffe. He noted that George Soane, who traded miserably in Gothic theatricals, was contesting the will of his father on grounds of insanity. These legal entanglements and public accusations about Soane's mental infirmity delayed Gandy's receipt of the £100 per annum bequeathed to him by Ivano. The shadow of madness had long hovered around Soane. His remaining friends worried over the irrational compulsiveness of the elderly architect. This temperamental aspect of Soane, as mentioned earlier, was not overlooked in the public appraisal of his work. In 1832, a critic excoriated Soane's RA exhibits as "odd fancies in the most preposterous manner," concluding in a later article, "he has occasionally exhibited 'the madness of architecture.'"[6] Of course, Gandy had been instrumental in exhibiting this mental delirium of Soane's architectural fancies. Certainly Gandy's own last showing at the 1838 RA exhibition pressed dramatically forward into this madness of architecture independent of Soane: *Architecture; Its Natural Model* and *Design for a Cast-iron Necropolis* formed a harrowing alpha and omega of architectural beginnings and endings.

If Soane's particular madness had as its place of confinement the highly customized and self-memorializing asylum of his house-museum, Gandy would not be nearly so fortunate. The animated spirit of Gandy's letters to his son did not intimate the distressing turn of events about to ensue. Some time between 1839 and 1841, he was placed by his family in Plympton House, a privately administered lunatic asylum in the village of Plympton St. Maurice outside of Plymouth. A national census lists him as a resident of Plympton House Asylum on the night of June 6, 1841: "Joseph M. Gandy, 65, architect."[7] He was actually 69 years of age. Plympton House was representative of a growing trend in the managed care of the insane during the late eighteenth and early nineteenth centuries, in which Georgian manor houses were being converted into profitable lunatic asylums. A Victorian gazetteer explained: "Plympton House, a handsome mansion, was formerly the seat of the Treby family, but is now a well-conducted lunatic asylum established in 1835 and having accommodations for 90 patients. It was first opened by Dr. Duck but was taken by Mr. Richard Langworthy in 1842, and the reports of the inspecting magistrates are highly complementary to his skill and management."[8] Gandy's period of residency spanned the administration of Dr. Duck and that of the former naval surgeon Langworthy. The repute of Plympton House Asylum, moreover, was not one of official acclaim, for it had actually received harsh censure from regulating authorities during its early history. In 1844, the Metropolitan Commission on Lunacy issued a damning report after repeated inspections in 1842–43. The premises were found to be unhygienic and overcrowded with private patients sharing insalubrious quarters with pauper patients. After an inspection of Plympton House in October 1843—two months before Gandy's death—the commissioners in lunacy described these deplorable conditions with a near-Dickensian sense of outrage: "The whole of these cells were as dark and damp as an underground cellar, and were in such a foul and disgusting state, that it was scarcely possible to endure the offensive smell. We sent for a candle and a lantern to enable us to examine them."[9]

The tenebrous and subterranean spaces of Gandy's architectural imagination had come to this—a confined cellar of madness and disease, bereft of ever-burning sepulchers and numinous lamps. "It is not wonderful that men should take a disgust to the world," Gandy had written, "the tumults of society composed of numberless heterogeneous parts" (6: 1816). He had endured repeated incarceration in debtor's prison where the random heterogeneity of society had earlier distressed him. His anxious dreams of struggling to emerge out of darkness into light, from his shipboard nightmare of "the different views of mankind" entombed in an inferno to the lamp-lit perspectives of the antiquarian museum of Soane's psyche, seemed to have held a fateful germ of prophecy, as in the tragedies of Sophocles and Shakespeare that he knew so well. On Christmas Day, 1843, Gandy died of dysentery at Plympton House Asylum. His place of burial is not known—especially unfortunate for one who had been so consumed by the power of architectural remembrance. There are other ironic coincidences. If one were to throw a stone down the hill in front of Plympton House Asylum, it would land at the doorstep of the birthplace of Sir Joshua Reynolds, who had awarded Gandy his gold medal and student diploma at the RA to inaugurate his career. The adjacent grammar school, founded by Reynolds' father, had also seen the education of Benjamin Haydon and the then president of the Royal Academy Charles Eastlake. The ambiguity of Gandy's professional identity that had so complicated his career only deepened in the years surrounding his death. The 1841 census listed his occupation as "architect." His death certificate gave his profession as "lieutenant," in reference to his brief service in the Westminster volunteer guard during the Napoleonic invasion scares. In February 1844, Gandy's probated will identified him as "Artist."[10]

Gandy would have surely preferred "architect" above all, although the evidence of his accomplishments would suggest otherwise. He was an inspired draftsman and a speculative archaeologist; a topographic delineator and a conjecturer of myth and mysticism; an architectural reformer and a historical landscape painter. Gandy conceived of architecture as a primordial force of nature, as a religious hallucination of lost origins, and as the truest expression of the historical purpose of nations and civilizations throughout the unfolding ages. He had convinced himself and many of his contemporaries that he was a studious genius suffering through a dark and turbulent period of history. Writing about the ambitions of artistic genius, Gandy argued, "if [genius] proceeds farther and represents supernatural effects, revealed religion, or the poet's ideas of the representations of the attributes of Deity, he is working on the sublime" (5:1486). In becoming so dedicated a worker of the sublime (often impractically so), he removed architecture to the realms of thought and pictorial representation with results that were both liberating and disempowering. The spectrum of Gandy's ideas tended decidedly toward the transcendent: the eternal dialogue between architecture and nature, the utopian dream of architecture as a universal language, and the envisioning of monuments inscribed with and shaped by religious belief, scientific knowledge, and historical memory. These fundamental concerns in Gandy's work would resonate profoundly in the architectural imagination of subsequent generations. His attempts to formulate a mythography and natural philosophy of architecture are reflected in speculative architectural thinking long after him, from W. R. Lethaby's *Architecture, Mysticism, and Myth* (1891) to Bernard Rudofsky's *Architecture Without Architects* (1964).

Gandy's vision of architecture adjudicated between Enlightenment primitivism and Victorian historicism. An exhilarating purging of the past and an erudite accumulation of histories and cultures were paradoxically merged in his drawings and theories. Although primarily a classicist, Gandy acknowledged the belatedness and relativity of the classical tradition and even questioned its perpetuation; he wondered whether in the future history of British architecture the ancient models of Indian architecture would some day supplant the Greco-Roman heritage. In delving into the unsolvable problem of how architecture may become more meaningful, both through esthetic emotion and semiotic calculation, Gandy sought to transform the polemical arguments about historical style into a branch of architectural metaphysics. Despite the professional and personal crises that beset him, he never disavowed the significance of his own artistic and theoretical pursuits. "Architecture ascends and descends with the human mind," Gandy wrote, "it oscillates into the obscurity of time, filling up the perpetual succession or regeneration ordained by Eternity" (1:1). The poetical retrieval of a long-vanished architectural landscape and the imaginative projection of an improbable architectural future seemed to fulfill this mystic doctrine of perpetual succession. He remained confident that his atmospherically charged perspectives and his syncretic theories of human culture would eventually inhabit a future moment. Historical awareness became for Gandy synonymous with a futuristic state of mind. In an annotation to the opening chapter of his treatise, he inscribed this forceful message: "history explodes errors, dissolves prejudices, and directs our thoughts and actions for the future."

Notes

Introduction

1 Leon Battista Alberti, *Ten Books on Architecture*, trans. James Leoni (1726; London, 1955), x.
2 [John Summerson], "Sir John Soane, Architecture of the Mind," *The Times*, January 20, 1937, 17.
3 Manfredo Tafuri, *The Sphere and the Labyrinth: Avant-Gardes and Architecture from Piranesi to the 1970s*, trans. Pellegrino d'Acierno and Robert Connolly (Cambridge, MA, 1987), 29.
4 Gandy's correspondence to and from his father during his period of study in Italy survives as handwritten transcripts in a manuscript volume known as the *Gandy Green Book* (so called because of its green binding). I examined this volume when it was in the possession of Gandy's descendant the late Joan Rising. Its present whereabouts are not known. The volume also contained genealogical notes, diary entries, religious musings, and a few letters from family friends and colleagues of Joseph Gandy. There are typed transcripts of the *Gandy Green Book* in the libraries of Sir John Soane's Museum and the Drawings Collection of the Royal Institute of British Architects. The letter from Pether is dated September 28, 1796. *Gandy Green Book*, 121–22.
5 See *A Catalogue of a Choice and Select Collection of Paintings and Drawings of the Modern English and French Schools, the Property of Alaric A. Watts, Esq., Which Will Be Sold at Mr. Sotheby and Son* (London, 1832).
6 Joseph Gandy, "The Art, Philosophy, and Science of Architecture," MS., Library of the Royal Institute of British Architects, London, vol. I, i. Further discussion of this treatise, its content and organization, occurs below in Chapter VI.
7 Emil Kaufmann, *Architecture in the Age of Reason* (1955; New York, 1968), 235, n. 592.
8 George Wightwick, "The Life of an Architect," *Bentley's Miscellany* 33 (1853): 468.
9 See Robin Evans, *Translations from Drawing to Building* (Cambridge, MA, 1997).
10 Walter Benjamin, "Rigorous Study of Art," *October* 47 (Winter 1988): 89. Benjamin's comments occur in reviewing an important essay by Carl Linfert entitled "Die Grundlagen der Architekturzeichnung" ("The Foundations of Architectural Drawing"), *Kunstwissenschaftliche Forschungen* I (1931): 133–246. Linfert's ambitious monograph theorized a systematic classification for the pictorial, spatial, ornamental, and tectonic effects of eighteenth-century French and Italian architectural rendering. Benjamin admired the essay immensely and saw it as parallel to his own research into seemingly marginal and esoteric areas of imaginative production. See the essay by Thomas Levin, "Walter Benjamin and the Theory of Art History," that precedes his translation of Benjamin's review in the same issue of *October*, 77–83.

Chapter 1

1 Anthony Pasquin, *Memoirs of the Royal Academicians; Being an Attempt to Improve the National Taste* (London, 1796), 84. Also see Raymond Needham and Alexander Webster, *Somerset House—Past and Present* (New York, 1926), 228–30.
2 James Northcote, *Life of Sir Joshua Reynolds* (London, 1819), 2:263.
3 *Gandy Green Book*, 1. The previous year, 1789, Gandy had been awarded the Silver Medal for architecture. See Sidney C. Hutchinson, "The Royal Academy Schools 1768–1830," *The Walpole Society* 38 (1960–62): 150.
4 Burke's remark is from a letter, dated September 14, 1791, to the Duke of Dorset regarding the proposed remodelling of Knole, "not the sort of place which every Banker, contractor, or Nabob can create at his pleasure." *The Correspondence of Edmund Burke*, ed. A. Cobban and R.A. Smith (Cambridge, 1967), 6:395.
5 Joseph was baptized on September 29, 1771 at St. Botolph, Aldgate.
6 *The Diary of Joseph Farington*, ed. K. Garlick, A. Macintrye, and K. Cave (New Haven, 1978–84), 6:2158. The comment to Farington was made by Henry Thomson, a painter who was in Rome during the same time as Gandy and who would become Keeper of the RA. Further references to this source will be cited as *Farington Diary* with volume and page numbers.
7 See John Timbs, *Clubs and Club Life in London* (London, 1873), 1:96–103 and [A.B. Boulton], *The History of White's* (London, 1892), 1:135–51.
8 On the architectural history of White's, see *Survey of London: Parish of St. James's Westminster*, ed. F. H. W. Shepherd (London, 1960), 30:450–58.
9 *Gandy Green Book*, 145.
10 C. R. Leslie and Tom Taylor, eds., *The Life and Times of Sir Joshua Reynolds* (London, 1865), 1:32–33. William Gandy had followed in the footsteps of his father James Gandy, who was a student of Van Dyck. It is uncertain as to whether these Devonshire Gandys have a genealogical connection to Joseph, but he thought they did.
11 *Gandy Green Book*, 154.
12 Ibid., 64.
13 On architectural training at the RA during the late eighteenth century, see Pierre de la Ruffinière du Prey, *John Soane, The Making of an Architect* (Chicago, 1982), 59–67. On the role of drawing in architectural training during this period, see Giles Worsley, *Architectural Drawings of the Regency Period, 1790–1837* (London, 1991), 1–13.
14 *Farington Diary*, 3:931.
15 *Gandy Green Book*, 6–8 for this citation and the passages below.
16 See John Harris, "Precedents and Various Designs Collected by C. H. Tatham," in *In Search of Modern Architecture: A Tribute to Henry-Russell Hitchcock*, ed. Helen Searing (Cambridge, MA, 1982), 52–63.
17 *Gandy Green Book*, 17–18.
18 Ibid., 94.
19 Gandy's movements in Italy are also charted in Frank Salmon, "GANDY, Joseph Michael," the entry in *A Dictionary of British and Irish Travellers in Italy 1701–1800*, ed. John Ingamells (New Haven and London, 1997), 387–89. On the importance of study in Rome for the late eighteenth-century British architectural student, see Frank Salmon, *Building on Ruins: The Rediscovery of Rome and English Architecture* (Aldershot, 2000), 26–75.
20 *Gandy Green Book*, 56.
21 Ibid., 39.
22 On this mid- to late eighteenth-century trend among British architects studying in Italy, see Damie Stillman, "British Architects and Italian Architectural Competitions, 1758–1780," *Journal of Society of Architectural Historians* 32 (March 1973): 43–66. For the programs and entries of the architectural competitions at the Accademia di San Luca in Rome, see P. Marconi, A. Cipriani, and E. Valeriani, *I disegni di architettura dell'Archivio Storico dell'Accademia di San Luca*, 2 vols. (Rome, 1974). For a close study of Gandy's complicated participation in the 1795 concorso, see Frank Salmon, "An Unaccountable Enemy: Joseph Michael Gandy and the Accademia di San Luca in Rome," *The Georgian Group Journal* (1995): 25–36.
23 *Gandy Green Book*, 53.
24 This proposal, more a literary flight of fancy than an architectural scheme, appeared in the second edition of Chambers's *Dissertation on Oriental Gardening* (1773). On this sepulchral project and its debt to Piranesi, see Dora Wiebenson, *The Picturesque Garden in France* (Princeton, 1978), 55–56, 117–18.
25 From the dedication to *Prima parte di architettura e prospettive* (1743), cited in John Wilton-Ely, *The Mind and Art of Giovanni Battista Piranesi* (London, 1978), 12.
26 Gandy was most likely familiar with such plans from the published treatises of Patte and Neufforge from the 1760s and 1770s as well as with later Grand Prix funerary designs that excelled in monumental geometries. For a comprehensive account of French neo-classical sepulchral design and planning, see Richard A. Etlin, *The Architecture of Death* (Cambridge, MA, 1984).
27 See Damie Stillman, "The Pantheon Redecorated: Neoclassical Variations on an Antique Spatial and Decorative Theme," *VIA* 3 (1977): 83–97.
28 *Gandy Green Book*, 39.
29 Edmund Burke, *A Philosophical Enquiry into the Origin of Our Ideas of the Sublime and the Beautiful*, ed. J. T. Boulton (London, 1958), 81, 108–09, 140–42.
30 The influence of theories of the sublime on late eighteenth-century architectural theory are summarzied in Dora Wiebenson, "'L'Architecture Terrible' and the 'Jardin Anglo-Chinois,'" *Journal of Society of Architectural Historians* 27 (March 1968): 136–39. On the esthetics of terror in relation to Piranesi and the Enlightenment, see Manfredo Tafuri, *The Sphere and the Labyrinth* (Cambridge, MA, 1987), 29–33.
31 Burke, *Enquiry into the Sublime*, 76.
32 A comparative discussion of these two designs is also undertaken in Werner Oechslin, "Pyramide et Sphère, notes sur l'architecture révolutionnaire du XVIIIe siècle et ses sources italiennes," *Gazette des Beaux-Arts* 77 (April 1971): 201–05.
33 See Rudolf Berliner, "Zeichnungen des Romischen Architekten Giuseppe Barberi," *Münchner Jahrbuch der bildenen Kunst* 6 (1965): 165–216; 7 (1966): 201–13.
34 *Gandy Green Book*, 40.
35 Quoted in John Fleming, *Robert Adam and His Circle* (London, 1962), 315–16. On the Adams brothers' Italian landscape and architectural drawings, see A. A. Tait, *Robert Adam, Drawings and Imagination* (Cambridge, 1993), 5–70.
36 Uvedale Price, *On the Picturesque* (Edinburgh, 1842), 329.

37. Joshua Reynolds, *Discourses on Art*, ed. Robert Wark (New Haven, 1975), 241–44, for this passage and the citations that follow.
38. Gandy first mentions Wallis in a letter dated April 24, 1795, *Gandy Green Book*, 37. For background on Wallis, see Colin J. Bailey, "The English Poussin—an Introduction to the Life and Work of George Augustus Wallis," Walker Art Gallery, Liverpool, *Annual Report* 6 (1975–76): 35–54.
39. For a recent survey of neo-classical landscape and architectural painting around Rome during the late eighteenth century, see Anna Ottani Cavina, *I paesaggi della ragione: La città neoclassica da David a Humbert de Superville* (Rome, 1994).
40. Almost identical in style to these landscape drawings by Gandy is a 1795 Italian sketchbook by the history painter Guy Head, with whom Gandy was friendly during this Roman period. See Guy Head, "Noted Buildings and Landscapes in Italy," D676–719, 1899, Prints & Drawings Room, Victoria & Albert Museum, London.
41. *Gandy Green Book*, 31. A damaged fragment of the watercolor view of Vesuvius that Gandy sent to his father is in the collection of a family descendant, Ms. Virginia Novarro.
42. Gandy's interest in philosophy and the sciences would be sustained throughout his life. In correspondence with his father, there are references to a family friend, Thomas Edwards, whose death in October 1795 inspired Gandy to refer to him as "my mentor," while observing that he was "endowed with so much natural philosophy." *Gandy Green Book*, 61. I have been unable to elucidate the identity and intellectual background of Thomas Edwards.
43. Ibid., 48.
44. Ibid., 51.
45. Ibid., 93.
46. Ibid., 70.
47. E. P. Thompson, *The Making of the English Working Class* (1963; New York, 1966), 65.
48. *Gandy Green Book*, 104.
49. Ibid., 77.
50. Latrobe recalled his youthful enthusiasm for political radicalism and the promise of America from the dejected perspective of his later career as a frustrated and under-recognized architect in "the republican court of Washington." See Talbot Hamlin, *Benjamin Henry Latrobe* (New York, 1955), 52–53.
51. *Gandy Green Book*, 90.
52. C. H. Tatham to Henry Holland, July 8, 1796; MS. transcriptions in Sir John Soane's Museum, London.
53. *Gandy Green Book*, 81–82. This modern sacking of Rome was also reported by Gandy's acquaintance Richard Duppa in his *A Journal of the Most Remarkable Occurrences That Took Place in Rome* (London, 1799). For background on the Napoleonic sacking of Rome, see Paul Wescher, *Kunstraub unter Napoleon* (Berlin, 1976).
54. *The Farington Diary*, 8:2952–53.
55. *Gandy Green Book*, 81.
56. Ibid., 115–16.
57. Ibid., 133.
58. *Dictionary of British and Irish Travelers in Italy*, 728.
59. *Gandy Green Book*, 2.

Chapter 11

1. "Sketches by a Practicing Architect," *Arnold's Magazine of the Fine Arts*, n.s., May 1833, 72.
2. Summerson, *Heavenly Mansions*, 129. On the neo-classical preoccupation with sepulchral architectural projects in England and Europe, see Damie Stillman, "Death Defied and Honor Upheld: The Mausoleum in Neo-Classical England," *Art Quarterly*, n.s., 1 (Summer 1978): 175–213; and Howard Colvin, *Architecture and the After-Life* (London and New Haven, 1991), 327–63.
3. "Catalogue of Works of English Artists in the Collection of Thomas Hope," *Annals of the Fine Arts*, 4 (1819): 97. My discussion of Hope is indebted throughout to David Watkin, *Thomas Hope and the Neo-Classical Idea* (London, 1968).
4. *Household Furniture and Interior Decoration Executed from Designs by Thomas Hope*, (London, 1807), 28.
5. Ibid., 9.
6. Richard Brown, *The Rudiments of Drawing Cabinet & Upholstery Furniture*, (London, 1822), x–xi.
7. Edward Edwards, *A Practical Treatise on Perspective (On the Principles of Dr. Brook Taylor)* (London, 1803), 302–03.
8. For a discussion of this set design by Desprez, see Nils Wollin, *Desprez en Suède … 1784–1804* (Stockholm, 1939), 44–46; and Régis Michel et al., *La Chimère de Monsieur Desprez*, Réunion des Musées Nationaux (Paris, 1994), 40–41, 133–34.
9. *Diary of Farington*, 6:2155.
10. *Gandy Green Book*, 2.
11. On Soane's student sepulchral designs, including this example, see du Prey, *Soane: Making of an Architect*, 10, 94–98, and 172–76.
12. David Watkin, *Sir John Soane, Enlightenment Thought and the Royal Academy Lectures* (Cambridge, 1996), 576. This essential volume contains a thorough study of Soane's intellectual development and course of readings that he undertook in preparation for his Royal Academy lectures on architecture. There is also a corrected transcription of Soane's lectures prepared by Susan Palmer.
13. John Gregory, *An Account of the Sepulchers of the Antients and a Description of their Monuments from the Creation of the World to the Building of the Pyramids* (London, 1712), xxxv.
14. Watkin, *Soane Lectures*, 545. Watkin, however, does not correlate these passages between Gregory and Soane.
15. William Godwin, *Essay on Sepulchres: A Proposal for Erecting Some Memorial of the Illustrious Dead in All Ages* (London, 1809), 96.
16. See the indispensable account provided in Alison Yarrington, *The Commemoration of the Hero 1800–1864: Monuments to the British Victors of the Napoleonic Wars* (New York, 1988).
17. For background on Cartwright, see *The Life and Correspondence of Major Cartwright, Edited by His Niece*, F. D. Cartwright (London, 1826) and John Osborne, *John Cartwright* (Cambridge, 1972).
18. For assistance in my efforts to locate the "Hieronauticon" drawings, I would like to thank Clive Powell of the National Maritime Museum, Peter Cowling of the Royal Society for the Arts, and Stephen Howarth of The 1805 Club.
19. From the checklist of drawings in the appendix of *Life and Correspondence of Cartwright*, 2:355.
20. Anon. [John Cartwright], *The Trident; or the National Policy of Naval Celebration, Describing a Hieronauticon or Naval Temple* (London, 1802), 15, 27.
21. Gerald Newman, *The Rise of English Nationalism, A Cultural History 1740–1830* (New York, 1987), 231. Also see Linda Colley, *Britons, Forging the Nation 1701–1837* (New Haven and London, 1992), 283–320.
22. *Diary of Farington*, 7:2758
23. See Eric Shanes, "Dissent in Somerset House: Opposition to the Political Status-quo within the Royal Academy around 1800," *Turner Studies* 10 (Winter 1990): 40–46. For a study of the submerged political critique of culture, from both conservative and radical positions, within the academic art theory of Reynolds, Barry, Fuseli, and Opie, see John Barrell, *The Political Theory of Painting from Reynolds to Hazlitt* (New Haven and London, 1986). For a study of the shifting connotations of patriotism and radicalism in late eighteenth- and early nineteenth-century England, see Hugh Cunningham, "The Language of Patriotism," in *Patriotism: The Making and Unmaking of British National Identity*, ed. Raphael Samuel (London, 1989), 1:57–86.
24. *Life and Correspondence of Cartwright*, 1:339–40.
25. For Cartwright's account of the political machinations within the Royal Academy over the Riego drawing, see *Life and Correspondence of Cartwright*, 1:249. The minutes of the RA Council meetings from 1824 do not contain any references to this issue.
26. The primary and secondary material on these British pattern books is voluminous, but the essential bibliographic guide and critical commentary on this subject is John Archer, *The Literature of British Domestic Architecture 1715–1842* (Cambridge, MA, 1985), to which I have had constant recourse. Also see Georges Teyssot, "Cottages et pittoresque," *Architecture, mouvement, continuité* 34 (July 1974): 26–37; Johannes Dobai, *Die Kunstliteratur des Klassizismus und der Romantik in England* (Bern, 1977), 3:665–747; Dora Wiebenson, "Documents of Social Change: Publications about the Small House," in *Studies in Eighteenth-Century British Art and Aesthetics*, ed. Ralph Cohen (Berkeley, 1985), 82–127; Robin Middleton et al., *The Mark J. Millard Architectural Collection: British Books* (Washington, D.C., 1998), 98–102.
27. Price, *On the Picturesque*, 398–99.
28. Among the extensive scholarship on the political and social formation of the picturesque esthetic, see especially Malcolm Andrews, *The Search for the Picturesque* (Stanford, 1989), *The Politics of the Picturesque: Literature, Landscape, and Aesthetics since 1770*, ed. Stephen Copley and Peter Garside (Cambridge, 1994), and Nigel Everett, *The Tory View of Landscape* (London, 1994).
29. William Wordsworth, *The Prelude* (Harmondsworth, Middlesex, 1975), 489. Future references are from this edition, indicated parenthetically in the text by book and line numbers.
30. Robert Morris, *Rural Architecture* (London, 1750), iii. My discussion of architectural primitivism of the eighteenth century is indebted to Joseph Rykwert, *On Adam's House in Paradise: The Idea of the Primitive Hut in Architectural History* (New York 1972), 43–103; and Anthony Vidler,

"Rebuilding the Primitive Hut: The Return to Origins from Lafitau to Laugier," in *The Writing of the Walls* (Princeton, 1987), 7–21.
31. Thomas Wright, *Universal Architecture, Book I* (London, 1755), n.p.
32. On this subject, see John Martin Robinson, *Georgian Model Farms: A Study of Decorative and Model Farm Buildings in the Age of Improvement, 1700–1846* (Oxford, 1983).
33. John Wood, *A Series of Plans, for Cottages or Habitations of the Labourer* (1781; London, 1806), 3.
34. James Malton, *An Essay on British Cottage Architecture* (London, 1798), 5.
35. Richard Payne Knight, *An Analytical Inquiry into the Principles of Taste* (1805; London, 1808), 225.
36. Humphry Repton, *An Inquiry into the Changes in Taste in Landscape Gardening* (London, 1806), 65. On Repton's place within the picturesque controversy, see Stephen Daniels, *Humphry Repton, Landscape Gardening and the Geography Of Georgian England* (London and New Haven, 1999), 122–47.
37. See Everett, *Tory View of Landscape*, 136–45.
38. [Anon.], "On the Modern System of Agriculture," *Cobbett's Political Register* 10 (July–December 1806): 282.
39. On the subject of Spence and his ideas of rural reform, see Malcolm Chase, *"The People's Farm": English Radical Agrarianism 1775–1840* (Oxford, 1988). Also see David Worrall, "Agrarians against the Picturesque: Ultra-radicalism and the Revolutionary Politics of the Land," in Copley and Garside, eds., *Politics of the Picturesque*, 240–60.
40. Price, *On the Picturesque*, 401.
41. *The Early Poems of John Clare*, ed. Eric Robinson and David Powell (Oxford, 1989), 1:171.
42. *Gandy Green Book*, 56.
43. Watkin, *Thomas Hope and the Neo-classical Idea*, 140.
44. See F.-L. Seheult, *Recueil d'architecture dessine et mesure en Italie, dans les anées 1791, 1792, 1793...* (Paris: n.p., 1821). On Pistocchi's rural architecture, see the exhibition catalogue by Ezio Godoli, *Giuseppe Pistocchi (1744–1814), Architetto Giacobino* (Firenze: Commune di Faenziza, 1974), 122–23.
45. *New Monthly Review*, October 1805, 211.
46. *The Annual Review and History of Literature for 1805* 4 (1806): 891.
47. *New Monthly Review*, October 1805, 212.
48. As first recognized in Melanie Louise Simo, *Loudon and the Landscape* (New Haven, 1988), 98, 311 n. 21.

49. Emil Kaufmann, *Architecture in the Age of Reason* (1955; New York, 1968), 65–66. The bibliography on Ledoux is extensive, but I have relied primarily on Anthony Vidler, *Claude-Nicolas Ledoux: Architecture and Social Reform at the End of the Ancien Régime* (Cambridge, MA, 1990) and Daniel Rabreau, *Claude-Nicolas Ledoux, l'architecture et les fastes du temps* (Paris, 2000).
50. *Gandy Green Book*, 8.
51. Edmund Bartell, *Hints for Picturesque Improvements* (London, 1804), 102–03.
52. My thanks to Mr. William Garner of the Irish Architectural Archive for his assistance with my research inquiries about Ballon Town.
53. Gandy exhibited three drawings at the RA relating to his work at Lancaster: in 1817, 1822, and 1823, none of which I have been able to locate. A plan of the county court at Lancaster by Gandy is in the collection of Sir John Soane's Museum, London (Drawer 37. Set 3. 29). For further references to Gandy's employment at Lancaster Castle, see J. Mordaunt Crook, "A Reluctant Goth—The Architecture of Thomas Harrison," *Country Life* 149 (1971): 876–79; Robin Evans, *The Fabrication of Virtue: English Prison Architecture 1750–1840* (Cambridge, 1982), 228–32.
54. *The Exhibition of the Royal Academy* (London, 1822), 42.
55. Talbot Hamlin, *Architecture Through the Ages* (New York, 1940), 556. In a similar vein, see Dimitris Tselos, "Joseph Gandy: Prophet of Modern Architecture," *Magazine of Art* 34 (May 1941): 251–53; Edward R. De Zurko, *Origins of Functionalist Theory* (New York, 1957), 113–14.
56. Hans Sedlmayr, *Art in Crisis: The Lost Center* (Chicago, 1958), 25.
57. Jean Starobinski, *The Invention of Liberty* (Geneva, 1964), 206.

Chapter III

1. *Survey of London: The Parish of St. Anne Soho*, ed. F. H. Sheppard (London, 1966), 33:105.
2. Letter dated March 8, 1816, Correspondence Cupboard, Division III, Letter "G" (Sir John Soane's Museum Archive, London).
3. *The Portrait of Sir John Soane, R.A.*, ed. Arthur T. Bolton (London, 1927), 323.
4. Undated Letter, Correspondence Cupboard, Division III, Letter "G" (Soane Museum Archive).
5. Entry dated November 24, 1816, Soane Notebooks (Soane Museum Archive, London).
6. *Portrait of Soane*, 324.
7. Letter dated December 25, 1816, Correspondence Cupboard, Division III, Letter "G" (Soane Museum Archive).
8. Letter dated October 28, 1830, Correspondence Cupboard, Division III, Letter "G" (Soane Museum Archive).
9. The auction notice appeared in *The Times*, November 12, 1830, 4.
10. *Farington Diary*, 4:1141, 6:2155.
11. Ibid., 6:2164–65.
12. Royal Academy Council Meeting Minutes, 7 (1824–32): 396 (Royal Academy Library, London).
13. *John Constable's Correspondence*, ed. R. B. Beckett (Ipswich, 1965), 3:51.
14. *Farington Diary*, 6:2158.
15. *Constable's Correspondence*, 3:50.
16. *Morning Post*, May 20, 1808, 274; *The Examiner*, July 2, 1808, 426. On the development of English architectural criticism in the early nineteenth century, see Roger Kindler, "Periodical Criticism 1815–40: Originality in Architecture," *Architectural History* 17 (1974): 22–37.
17. *The Literary Gazette*, May 29, 1819, 346.
18. *The Guardian*, 27 May 1821, n.p., June 3, 1821, n.p. In response to these articles, Gandy wrote a series of letters to *The Guardian* defending his status as an architect, which will be discussed below.
19. *Arnold's Magazine of the Fine Arts*, n.s., June 1834, 150.
20. *Architectural Magazine* 4 (June 1837): 304.
21. *Morning Chronicle*, May 7, 1832, 4.
22. Anon., "The Phoenix Fire and Pelican Life Assurance Offices," *The Builder* 108 (February 12, 1915): 150.
23. The undated drawing is inscribed to the military painter Abraham Cooper and is adorned with the coat of arms of Sir John Swinburne of Northumberland, an important patron of British genre and history painting.
24. See Walter Ison, *The Georgian Buildings of Bath* (Bath, 1969), 182; Neil Jackson, *Nineteenth-Century Bath Architects and Architecture* (Bath, 1991), 37–41.
25. Watkin, *Thomas Hope*, 88.
26. *The Auto-biography of John Britton* (London, 1850), 1:177.
27. My brief account of Storrs Hall relies on the English National Heritage Report by Ian Goodall and Simon Taylor, *Storrs Hall, Windermere, Cumbria* NBR Index No. 30550, NGR: SD 3926 9413, 2002.

28. John Wilson, "Apology for the Little Naval Temple, on Storrs' Point, Windermere," in *The Isle of Palms and Other Poems* (Edinburgh, 1812), 312.
29. Gandy had already made Gothic alterations to Bolton's estate in Yorkshire in 1806. See Colvin, *Biographical Dictionary*, 329.
30. Ian Goodall and Margaret Richardson, "A Recently Discovered Gandy Sketchbook," *Architectural History* 44 (2001): 45–56. The authors also clarify the complicated building history at Storrs. The sketchbook is in the collection of Sir John Soane's Museum.
31. Christopher North [John Wilson], "A Day at Windermere," *Blackwood's Edinburgh Magazine* 28 (September 1830): 524.
32. See Harold Kalman, *A History of Canadian Architecture* (Oxford, 1995), 1:257–60.
33. Cited in Clive Wainwright, *George Bullock, Cabinet-Maker* (London, 1988), 14–15.
34. This design probably remained unexecuted. In his 1821 letters to *The Guardian* in which he defended his standing as a practicing architect, Gandy did not list any built works in Liverpool. In June 1815, five years after the design was first exhibited, Gandy threatened legal action against a group of Liverpool investors for never having paid him for the Ballroom design. See Gandy's letters to John Soane, dated June 12, 13, 14, 1815, Private Correspondence Packet, Division III, Letter "G" (Soane Museum Archive).
35. The documentation for the attribution of these furnishings to Gandy is presented in June Dean, "The Regency Furniture in Liverpool Town Hall," *Furniture History* 25 (1989): 127–34. Designs for the Liverpool Exchange, or Town Hall, were by James Wyatt and were carried out by John Foster. As Dean has documented, Gandy received payments in 1810 and 1811 for the design of interior furnishings. Other examples of Gandy's designs for Regency decor are in the Getty Research Institute Collection.
36. A surviving example of these modest commissions is Swerford House, Chipping Norton, Oxfordshire, built for Sir Robert Bolton from 1824–27. It is an understated and rather generic essay in late Georgian classicism, lacking the distinction and originality of Doric House and Storrs Hall.
37. In 1832, one of Gandy's RA exhibits was a design for an entrance hall for

Ince Blundell, even though the intended patron, Henry Blundell, died in 1810, soon after Gandy had quit Liverpool for London.
38. *Farington Diary*, 3:931. Ironically, it was Wyatt who extracted the confession from his own student.
39. Letter dated May 10, 1812, Correspondence Cupboard, Division III, Letter "G" (Sir John Soane's Museum Archive, London).
40. "Obituary—J. P. Deering," *Art Journal* 12 (March 1, 1850): 100.
41. "The Fine Arts," *The European Magazine* 85 (June 1824): 556.
42. Ralph Hyde, *Panoramania!* (London, 1988), 80–85; Stephan Oettermann, *The Panorama, History of a Mass Medium*, trans. D. L. Schneider (New York, 1997), 132–40.
43. Letter dated September 15, 1837, formerly in the collection of Ms. Rosalie Gandy, a family descendant.
44. Told to me in conversation with Ms. Rosalie Gandy in April 1982.
45. Anon., *The Anti-Jacobin Review* 29 (January–April 1808), 266. The British culture of antiquarianism during this period is addressed in Stuart Piggott, *Ruins in a Landscape: Essays on Antiquarianism* (Edinburgh, 1976) and M. Myrone and L. Peltz, eds., *Producing the Past: Aspects of Antiquarian Culture and Practice 1700–1850* (Aldershot, 1999).
46. See J. Mordaunt Crook, "John Britton and the Genesis of the Gothic Revival," in J. Summerson, ed., *Concerning Architecture: Essays in Architectural Writers and Writing Presented to Nikolaus Pevsner* (London, 1968), 98–119; and Brian Lukacher, "Britton's Conquest: Creating an Antiquarian Nation, 1790–1860," in the exhibition catalogue *Landscapes of Retrospection, The Magoon Collection of British Drawings and Prints 1739–1860* (Poughkeepsie, 1999), 1–39.
47. Letter from Gandy to Soane, November 3, 1825, Private Correspondence Packet, Division III, Letter "G" (Sir John Soane's Museum Archive).
48. Anon., Review of Britton's *Cathedral Antiquities*, *The Quarterly Review* 34 (June–September 1826): 309, 348.
49. See Angelo Maggi, "Poetic Stones: Roslin Chapel in Gandy's Sketchbook and Daguerre's Diorama," *Architectural History* 42 (1999): 263–83; Helen Rosslyn and Angelo Maggi, *Rosslyn, Country of Painter and Poet* (Edinburgh, 2002).
50. John Britton, *The Architectural Antiquities of Great Britain* (London, 1812), 3:47n.
51. Ibid., 3:59.
52. Ibid., 3:62n.
53. Letter from Joseph Gandy to John Britton, undated, 1998–A.666, Collection Frits Lugt, Fondation Custodia, Paris. Gandy's complaints were especially unwarranted as many of his topographic sketches of Rosslyn indicate that he modified or altered the architectural details under inspection. See Maggi's article, as in note 49 above.
54. *Portrait of Soane*, 107.
55. *The Collected Letters of A. W. N. Pugin*, ed. Margaret Belcher (Oxford, 2001), 1:36
56. John Britton, *The Fine Arts of the British School* (London, 1812), ii–iii.
57. These drawings at the Victoria and Albert Museum may be connected to designs for St. Michael's Church, Toxteth, and St. George's Church, Everton by John Cragg and Thomas Rickman and St. Luke's Church, Liverpool by John Foster, as suggested to me in correspondence by architectural historian Joseph Sharples. Mr. Sharples has found a number of references to Gandy's church designs in the Rickman diary. My thanks to him for sharing his research on Gandy's activity in Liverpool.
58. *Portrait of Soane*, 348.
59. Ibid., 230.
60. Letter to Britton, as in note 53; and Bolton, *Portrait of Soane*, 230.
61. These landscapes were assembled in two bound volumes that were passed down through the family of Richard Westmacott. One volume was acquired by Sir John Soane's Museum and the other was sold at auction and dispersed. They contain sheets that range in period from Gandy's Italian journey to the late 1820s. Many of the landscapes have highly colored and detailed still-life arrangements in coastal settings that may indicate the collaborative hands of Gandy's daughters, Hannah and Celia.
62. *Portrait of Soane*, 339–52; Gillian Darley, *John Soane, an Accidental Romantic* (London and New Haven, 1999), 264–65.
63. James Spiller to John Soane, September 3, 1821, Correspondence Cupboard, Division IV, Letter "S" (Soane Museum Archive, London).
64. Joseph Gandy, "On the Philosophy of Architecture," *Magazine of Fine Arts* 1 (1821): 290.
65. Joseph Gandy, "Letter to the Editor," *The Guardian* 2 (June 24, 1821): n.p.
66. Joseph Gandy, "On the Philosophy of Architecture—Letter II," *Magazine of the Fine Arts* 1 (1821): 371.
67. Knight, *Analytical Inquiry into Taste*, 216.
68. Joseph Gandy, "Letter to the Editor," *The Guardian* 2 (June 24, 1821): n.p.
69. *The Guardian* 2 (June 3, 1821): n.p.
70. John Soane, *Description of the House and Museum of John Soane* (London, 1830), 52.
71. On these questions, see Giles Worsley, *Architectural Drawings of the Regency*, 1–31; Nicholas Savage, "Exhibiting Architecture: Strategies of Representation in English Architectural Exhibition Drawings, 1760–1836," in *Art on the Line, The Royal Academy Exhibitions at Somerset House 1780–1836*, ed. David Solkin (New Haven and London, 2001), 201–16; and Greg Smith, *The Emergence of the Professional Watercolourist* (Aldershot, 2002), 80–90, 146–53.
72. "Royal Academy Exhibition," *The Repository of the Arts* 12 (July 1814): 75.
73. "A Slight Sketch of the Rise and Progress of Domestic Architecture in Great Britain," *Annals of the Fine Arts* 1 (1816): 23.
74. "Remarks on Contemporary Criticism," *Magazine of the Fine Arts* 1 (1821): 167–68.
75. Anon., "Royal Academy Exhibition," *Annals of the Fine Arts* 1 (1816): 72. For a summary of Turner's architectural interests, see James Hamilton, "Foundations: Consider the Pleasure of Being Your Own Architect," in *Turner and the Scientists* The Tate Gallery (London, 1998), 21–36.
76. Turner Lecture Notes, ADD, MS. 46151 S f.13v., J f.16r. (British Library, Manuscript Collection, London)
77. Watkin, *Soane Lectures*, 561.
78. Cockerell Family MSS., Box 1 COC 1/1–16, xvi–xvii (Royal Institute of British Architects Library, London).
79. *The Guardian* 2 (June 3, 1821), n.p.
80. Ibid.
81. *Farington Diary* 4:2276.
82. Watkin, *Soane Lectures*, 576.
83. Anon. [James Elmes], "On the Analogy Between Language and Architecture," *Annals of the Fine Arts* 5 (1820): 262
84. In the English column text of Piranesi's "An Apologetical Essay in Defence of the Egyptian and Tuscan Architecture" (1769), in *The Polemical Works of Piranesi*, ed. John Wilton-Ely (Westmead, 1977), 33. This connection between the architectural theory of Piranesi, Dance, and Soane is also discussed in Watkin, *Soane Lectures*, 60–62.

Chapter IV
1. Madame de Staël, *Corinne, or Italy*, trans. Sylvia Raphael (Oxford and New York, 1998), 200. In a chapter devoted to Corinne's art collection, de Staël includes a description of two historical landscapes by George Wallis, Gandy's companion and artistic mentor during his Italian travels. See 154, 407 n. 21.
2. Abbé de Saint-Non, *Voyage pittoresque, ou description des royaumes de Naples et de Sicile* (Paris, 1782), 2:118.
3. Ibid., 2:146.
4. P.-H. Valenciennes, *Élémens de perspective pratique* (Paris, An VII [1799]), 412, 414. For a recent summary of Valenciennes' career and work, see Luigi Gallo, "Pierre-Henri de Valenciennes et la tradition du paysage historique," in *Imaginaire et création artistique a Paris sous l'ancien régime*, ed. Daniel Rabreau (Paris, 1998), 185–207.
5. Edward Edwards, *A Practical Treatise on Perspective* (London, 1803), 296.
6. Turner Lecture Notes, ADD. MS. 46151 BB f.5v.
7. The existence of this drawing was generously brought to my attention by Linda Tompkins-Baldwin, a graduate student at the University of Texas, Austin in 1990. The attribution to Hadfield I owe to Mr. John Harris.
8. The badly faded and torn *Priam's Palace* is in the RIBA Drawings Collection, London. On this aspect of Wyatville's work, see Derek Linstrum, *Sir Jeffry Wyatville, Architect to the King* (Oxford, 1972), 15–17, 225–26.
9. *The Examiner*, June 18, 1809, 399; *Library of the Fine Arts*, June 1831, 435.
10. There were two editions of Taylor's translation of Pausanias, in 1794 and 1824, both containing the copious philosophical and mystical digressions of Taylor's notes.
11. On the historical context, rhetorical strategies, and critical heritage of Pausanias, see *Pausanias, Travel and Memory in Roman Greece*, ed. S. E. Alcock, J. F. Cherry, and J. Elsner (Oxford, 2001).
12. Richard Brown, *The Principles of Practical Perspective* (London, 1815), 62. Gandy also spoke of his adherence to spherical or curvilinear perspective while he was petitioning to become Professor of Perspective in 1807. See *Farington Diary*, 8:2971.
13. Pausanias, *The Description of Greece* (London, 1794), 1:156–57.
14. Ibid., 1:105.
15. William Hutchinson, *The Spirit of Masonry* (New York, 1982), 69n. This volume was the standard text on Freemasonry during the late

Georgian period and went through four reprintings between 1775 and 1815. The same passage about the Eleusinian Mysteries appears in *Bell's New Pantheon: or Historical Dictionary of the Gods* (London, 1790), 1:282, a standard reference book of the period. Both Hutchinson and Bell were paraphrasing from the work of the early seventeenth-century Dutch classicist-antiquary Johannes van Meurs (or Meursius).

16. The possibility should be entertained that the identifying label in Gandy's hand that accompanied the Getty drawing when it was acquired relates to a still missing drawing of the Persian porch. The Getty drawing may be identifiable with Gandy's *Temple of Neptune, Taenarius*, exhibited at the British Institution in 1821. This site is described in the chapter following the one with Pausanias' account of the Lacedaemonian forum. Because Gandy avoided overly literal illustrations of Pausanias, it is often difficult to match his extant classical re-constructions to the lengthy titles and citations for his Pausanian exhibits in the Royal Academy and British Institution catalogues.

17. Ibid., 2:206.
18. "Royal Academy Exhibition," *Library of the Fine Arts*, June 1832, 527.
19. *Farington Diary*, 12:4281.
20. S....Y, *Critical and Impartial Observations on the Principal Pictures and Drawings Exhibited at Somerset House* (London, 1819), 53.
21. Bolton, *Portrait of Soane*, 326.
22. *The Examiner*, July 11, 1819, 444.
23. *The Literary Gazette*, May 8, 1819, 295.
24. Ibid., May 29, 1819, 345.
25. These watercolors, formerly in the collection of the late Mr. John Gandy, are now split between the Victoria and Albert Museum and the Getty Research Institute. A list of stage-set designs marked "for Covent Garden" in Gandy's hand was formerly in the possession of the late Miss Rosalie Gandy.
26. *The Diaries of William Charles Macready, 1833–1851* (New York, 1912), 1:144.
27. For an excellent discussion of these British ideal restorations of the Forum Romanum during the post-Waterloo period, see Salmon, *Building on Ruins*, 89–112.
28. The collection was formed by the watercolorist George Robson for Mrs. Haldimand to exemplify the finest achievements in modern British watercolor painting. See Michael Clarke, *The Tempting Prospect: A Social History of English Watercolours* (London, 1981), 137–38. Gandy exhibited another version of this subject at the 1834 RA exhibition.
29. Pausanias, *Description*, 3:101.
30. Anon., "Greek and English Tragedy," *The Reflector* 2 (March–December 1811): 131.
31. In 1827, Thomas Gandy exhibited a design for a Temple of the Furies, after his father, at the RA.
32. The latter drawing at the Nelson-Atkins Museum of Fine Arts, Kansas City, has traditionally been attributed to Gandy. Maddox's works are often misidentified as being by Gandy, as indicated by auction-house photograph files.
33. Anon., "Pie-Crust; or Architectural Madness," *Fraser's Magazine* 4 (October 1831): 281.
34. William Hazlitt, "On Antiquity," *London Magazine*, May 1821, 527.
35. *The Examiner*, June 13, 1813, 379.
36. *Gandy Green Book*, 82.
37. See Marcia Pointon, *Milton and English Art* (Manchester, 1970).
38. The best account of the Eidophusikon is in Richard Altick, *The Shows of London* (Cambridge, MA, 1978), 117–27.
39. *Diderot Salons*, ed. Jean Seznec (Oxford, 1967), 4:205–06.
40. John Milton, *Paradise Lost*, ed. Alastair Fowler (London, 1971), 82–84. All future citations from *Paradise Lost* will be from this edition, with book and line numbers indicated parenthetically in the text.
41. Ledoux, *L'architecture considérée...*, 238.
42. The British Library catalogue contains twenty-one pamphlets published between 1793 and 1802 entitled "Pandemonium."
43. John Papworth, *Select Views of London* (London, 1816), 89.
44. Cited in Timothy Mowl, *William Beckford* (London, 1998), 255.
45. Burke, *Philosophical Enquiry into ... the Sublime and the Beautiful*, 63.
46. These entries are in the *Gandy Green Book*, 141–44. In introducing these 1805 diary entries, a caveat must be noted. The entries are in a different hand than the transcripts of Gandy's Italian letters that come before them. The pagination throughout is in Gandy's own hand, as are the philosophical and genealogical commentaries that follow them. One could justifiably question whether the entries are taken from a lost diary of Gandy. Could they be the entries of another member of the family, his wife Eleanor or his father Thomas? It is doubtful since everything else in the *Gandy Green Book* relates to or is authored by Joseph, but the ambiguity should be noted.
47. *Gandy Green Book*, 94. Richard Brother's religious utopian treatise was entitled *A Description of Jerusalem: Its Houses and Streets ... with the Garden of Eden in the Centre* (London, 1801). For background on Brothers, see J. F. C. Harrison, *The Second Coming, Popular Millenarianism 1780–1850* (New Brunswick, 1979), 57–85.
48. Erasmus Darwin, *Zoonomia, or the Laws of Organic Life* (London, 1796), 2:379. On the subject of "religious melancholy and madness" in late eighteenth-century Britain, see Roy Porter, *Mind-Forg'd Manacles: A History of Madness in England* (Cambridge, MA, 1987), 62–89.
49. Anon. [Leigh Hunt], "Remarks on the Past and Present State of the Arts in England," *The Reflector* 1 (October 1810–March 1811): 231.
50. *Noah, Attempted from the German of Mr. Bodmer*, in *Twelve Books by Joseph Collyer* (London, 1767), 1:183.
51. Emanuel Swedenborg, *Heaven and Its Wonder and Hell, from Things Heard and Seen* (London, 1966), 126.
52. *The Literary Gazette*, May 23, 1818, 329–30.
53. See David Brewster, *The Kaleidoscope: Its History, Theory and Construction* (London, 1819).
54. See Iwan Rhys Morus, *Frankenstein's Children, Electricity, Exhibition, and Experiment in Early Nineteenth-Century London* (Princeton, 1998).
55. Quoted in G. Wilson Knight, *The Starlit Dome* (1941; London, 1968), 309.
56. *The Exhibition of the Royal Academy* (London, 1815), 35.
57. Thomas Heywood, *The Life of Merlin, Surnamed Ambrosius, His Prophecies and Predictions Interpreted* (1626; London, 1813), 44. Soane owned a copy of this volume.
58. Gandy cited this edition of Josephus in the RA entry for his *A Temple and Portico, with the Drowning of Aristobulus* of 1808.
59. *Gandy Green Book*, 47–48.
60. *The Exhibition of the Royal Academy* (London, 1802), 18.
61. Pausanias, *Description of Greece*, 3:215–19.
62. See the artist George Cumberland's account of these lectures in G. E. Bentley, Jr. *The Stranger in Paradise: A Biography of William Blake* (New Haven and London, 2001), 82–83. Incidentally, the lamps exploded.
63. See Stuart Piggott *Ruins in a Landscape, Essays on Antiquarianism* (Edinburgh, 1976), 77–99.
64. Eusebius Pamphilus, *The History of the Church, Also the Life of Constantine* (Cambridge, 1683), 626.
65. John Ball, *A Description of the City of Constantinople* (London, 1729), 221.
66. Quoted in Count Ouvaroff [Uvarov], *Essay on the Mysteries of Eleusis, ... with Observations by James Christie* (London, 1817), 62. The first French edition of this work was published in 1812.
67. William Blake, *Complete Writings*, ed. G. Keynes (London, 1972), 429
68. S. T. Coleridge, *Poetical Works*, ed. E. H. Coleridge (London, 1974), 592.
69. *Tales of Edgar Allan Poe* (New York, 1944), 366.
70. See Altick, *Shows of London*, 211–21; also Terry Castle, "Phantasmagoria and the Metaphorics of Modern Reverie," in *The Female Thermometer* (New York, 1995), 140–67.
71. See John Summerson, *The Life and Work of John Nash, Architect* (Cambridge, MA, 1980), 97–99.
72. Summerson, *Heavenly Mansions*, 128.
73. *Fraser's Magazine*, July 1832, 712.
74. *Library of the Fine Arts*, June 1832, 532.
75. Thomas Cole's pictorial cycle is very much like a distended elaboration of Gandy's picture. Cole was in London during 1829–30 and visited with leading British landscape artists such as Turner, Constable, and Martin. There is no evidence that he came into contact with Gandy and Soane, though the possibility is not so remote. On Cole's *The Voyage of Life*, see Ellwood C. Parry III, *The Art of Thomas Cole, Ambition and Imagination* (Newark and London, 1988), 226–68.
76. Soane, *Lectures*, 19.
77. Burke, *Enquiry on the Beautiful and the Sublime*, 62.
78. *London Magazine* 4 (July 1821): 69.
79. *Westminster Review* 20 (April 1834): 458.
80. Wightwick, "Life of an Architect," 292.

Chapter v

1. Watkin, *Soane Lectures*, 629.
2. John Soane, *Description of the House and Museum of Sir John Soane* (London, 1830), 30. A similar lament appeared in Soane's eighth Royal Academy lecture. See Watkin, *Soane Lectures*, 594.
3. Letter dated November 1, 1802, Private Correspondence Packet, Division III, Letter "G" (Soane Museum Archive).
4. Bolton, *Portrait of Soane*, 124.
5. Darley, *Soane, Accidental Romantic*, 145
6. Bolton, *Portrait of Soane*, 351.
7. *Fraser's Magazine*, July 1832, 713.

8. C. R. Leslie and Tom Taylor, eds., *The Life and Times of Sir Joshua Reynolds* (London, 1865), 1:589 n.1.
9. Gandy told Flaxman in 1803 that Soane paid him £150 per year, though £100 was the sum typically recorded in Soane's account books. Gandy took in an extra £100 per year for the brief period that John Soane Jr. was articled to him. During the mid-1820s, Gandy's annual salary from Soane approached £300. During the 1830s, it was customary for Gandy to receive from £25 to £50 per drawing from Soane. Although these amounts may be considered generous for the time, they were meager when compared to the professional fees commanded by even a marginally successful architect. George Wightwick, briefly a student of Soane who settled in Plymouth in 1829, averaged £1000 per year. See Worsley, *Architectural Drawings of the Regency*, 27–29.
10. Watkin, *Soane Lectures*, 661.
11. Letter dated March 8, 1816, Correspondence Cupboard, Letter "G" (Soane Museum Archive).
12. Watkin, *Soane Lectures*, 592.
13. The first passage is from MS Extracts Hints etc. for Lectures on Architecture by J. Soane 1813 to 1818, fol. 200, Soane Case 170/1 (Soane Museum, London). The second is from Soane's annotations to Joseph Forsyth's *Remarks on Antiquities, Arts, and Letters* (1813), quoted in Watkin, *Soane's Lectures*, 254.
14. Soane, *Memoirs of Professional Life*, 70.
15. Watkin, *Soane Lectures*, 576.
16. John Summerson, *Sir John Soane* (London, 1952), 14.
17. "Royal Academy Exhibition," *Annals of the Fine Arts* 5 (1820): 402.
18. "Royal Academy," *The Englishman*, June 11, 1820, n.p.
19. Anon. [George Stonestreet], *Domestic Union, or London As It Should Be!!* (London, 1800), 26–27.
20. Anon., "Publius on the Proposed Waterloo Monuments," *Annals of the Fine Arts* 2 (1817): 156.
21. Archibald Alison, "National Monuments" in *Miscellaneous Essays* (New York, 1865), 74–75.
22. See Celina Fox et al., *London, World City 1800–1840* (New Haven and London, 1992); Dana Arnold, *Representing the Metropolis, Architecture, Urban Experience and Social Life in London 1800–1840* (Aldershot, 2000).
23. Anon., "On the Cultivation of Popular Taste in the Arts," *Arnold's Library of the Fine Arts*, March, 1833, 358.
24. *The Athenaeum*, August 21, 1830, 522.
25. These schemes have been explicated by Sean Sawyer, "Sir John Soane's Symbolic Westminster: The Apotheosis of George IV," *Architectural History* 39 (1996): 54–76. The complicated publishing history of Soane's volumes on these "public improvements" and the political and personal vicissitudes associated with them are documented and clarified by Robin Middleton, "The History of John Soane's 'Designs for Public and Private Buildings,'" *Burlington Magazine* 138 (August 1996): 506–16.
26. The publication by Rudolph Ackermann was entitled *A Graphic Illustration of the Colosseum, Regent's Park, in Five Plates from Drawings by Gandy, Mackenzie, & Other Eminent Artists* (London, 1829). It should be noted that Gandy used bird's-eye perspective for Soane's imaginary design for a triumphal bridge soon after entering the office in 1799.
27. "Architectural Portraiture," *Magazine of Fine Arts* 1 (1821): 459–64.
28. John Soane, *Designs for Public and Private Buildings* (London, 1832), 37. Soane's discussion of these palace designs was also added to his RA lectures. See Watkin, *Soane Lectures*, 694–95.
29. Soane, *Public and Private Buildings*, 4.
30. Royal Academy Council Meeting Minutes, 5 (1813–18): 242 (Royal Academy Library, London). The text of the letter from the Committee on Taste was recorded as being read at the RA Council Meeting on December 14, 1815, with Benjamin West ordering that a copy be printed and distributed to Academicians and Associates in the new year.
31. For an overview of these various Wellington monuments and palaces, see Yarrington, *Commemoration of the Hero*, 167–216.
32. "Remarks on Mr. White's Plan for the Improvement of Mary-le-bone," *The European Magazine*, September 1815, 232. On the sparring between White and Nash, see Summerson, *Life and Work of Nash*, 70–72.
33. *Annals of the Fine Arts*, 1 (June 1816): 83.
34. Ibid., 5 (June 1820): 122.
35. *The Guardian*, June 17, 1821, n.p.
36. Ibid., n.p.
37. I am grateful to my colleague Margaret Kitzinger in the Classics Department of Vassar College for identifying this inscription.
38. Bolton, *Portrait of Soane*, 521.
39. "Fine Arts," *European Magazine*, June 1824, 557–58.
40. *The Exhibition of the Royal Academy* (London, 1826), 39.
41. *The Literary Gazette*, June 24, 1826, 395.
42. *The Exhibition of the Royal Academy* (London, 1826), 39.
43. Watkin, *Soane Lectures*, 518.
44. "Royal Academy Exhibition," *The Literary Gazette*, June 18, 1825, 395.
45. *The Exhibition of the Royal Academy* (London, 1825), 36–37. If Gandy cribbed these verses from another source, I have not been able to locate the original, though they certainly imitate James Thomson's poetic style of prospect description.
46. *The Exhibition of Royal Academy* (London, 1830), 40. The entry was number 1018 entitled *Bird's eye view of a design for a metropolitan palace*.
47. "Exhibitions," *The Architectural Magazine* 2 (July 1835): 314.
48. Anon. [Robert Mudie], *Babylon the Great: A Dissection and Demonstration of Men and Things in the British Capital* (London, 1825), 1:16.
49. Anon. [Robert Mudie], *A Second Judgement of Babylon the Great* (London, 1829), 1:143.
50. Anon., "The British School of Architecture," *Blackwood's Magazine* 40 (August 1836): 234.
51. Reinhart Koselleck, *Futures Past, on the Semantics of Historical Time*, trans. K. Tribe (1979; Cambridge, MA, 1985), 142–43.
52. The bibiliography on Soane's house-museum is extensive. Begin with Soane's own account, *Description of the House and Museum of John Soane* (London, 1830) and the museum guide by John Summerson, *A New Description of Sir John Soane's Museum*, 9th ed. (London, 1991). Also see Susan Feinberg Millenson, *Sir John Soane's Museum* (1979; Ann Arbor, 1987); Darley, *Soane, Accidental Romantic*, 209–15, 266–86; Helen Dorey, "12–14 Lincoln's Inn Fields," in the exhibition catalogue *John Soane Architect, Master of Space and Light*, Royal Academy (London, 1999), 150–73. For more focused studies on distinctive aspects of the Soane Museum (its collection of models and the use of reflection in interior space), see John Elsner, "A Collector's Model of Desire: The House and Museum of Sir John Soane," in *The Cultures of Collecting*, ed. J. Elsner and R. Cardinal (Cambridge, MA, 1994), 155–76; and Helene Furján, "The Specular Spectacle of the House of the Collector," *Assemblage* 34 (1998): 56–91.
53. John Britton, *The Union of Architecture, Sculpture, and Painting* (London, 1828), 6.
54. *The Athenaeum*, October 8, 1831, 650.
55. G. F. Waagen, *Works of Art and Artists in England* (London, 1838), 2:181.
56. The manuscript "Crude Hints Towards a History of My House" has been published with valuable commentary and notes by Helen Dorey in the exhibition catalogue *Visions of Ruin, Sir John Soane's Museum* (London, 1999), 53–78.
57. Ibid., 63.
58. Ibid., 73. Soane had begun this failed project of instilling in his sons an affection for architectural invention in their domestic environment with the design of his former estate Pitzhanger Manor, which he sold in 1810. At Pitzhanger, Soane constructed a courtyard of fake Roman ruins, anticipating the antiquarian playfulness and temporal slippage of his house-museum at Lincoln's Inn Fields.
59. Soane Notebooks, "The Genius of Architecture, or the Analogy of This Art with Our Sensations," fol. 9–10, Soane Case 160, Architectural Library, Sir John Soane's Museum, London.
60. Summerson, *Unromantic Castle*, 142.
61. Peter Conrad, *Shandyism: The Character of Romantic Irony* (Oxford, 1978), 38.
62. *The Literary Gazette*, June 29, 1822, 410; [Mudie], *Second Judgement of Babylon*, 2:144; *Fraser's Magazine* 15 (March 1837), 338–39; Waagen, *Works of Art*, 2:181; *Diaries of Macready*, 2:393.
63. Bolton, *Portrait of Soane*, 529.
64. Benjamin Robert Haydon, *Correspondence and Table Talk* (London, 1876), 2:93. Haydon's account of this nocturnal reception at the Soane Museum quickly takes a satirical turn, as he comments on the bizarre intersection of Soane's imaginatively morbid antiquarianism and the fashionable society and contemporary intellectuals in attendance. For a thorough account of this event, see Helen Dorey, "Sir John Soane's Acquisition of the Sarcophagus of Seti I," *Georgian Group Journal* (1991), 25–35.
65. John Britton, *The Union of Architecture, Sculpture, and Painting* (London, 1827), 6.
66. John Soane, *Description of the House and Museum of Sir John Soane* (London, 1830), 2. Another expanded version of this book, with sentimental glosses by Soane's friend, the writer Barbara Hofland, was published in a very limited private edition in 1835.
67. Letter from Gandy to Soane, inscribed "Prince Eugene's Dressing Room, Paris 1814," with a small interior elevation drawing, Brettingham Volume, fol. 7, Soane Library (Soane Museum, London). Prince Eugène de Beauharnais was Napcleon's stepson. He and his

sister Queen Hortense of the Netherlands commissioned the notoriously extravagant rehabilitation of this hotel on the rue de Lille. The expense was so great that Napoleon reprimanded Eugène about the project in 1807. The architects responsible for the interiors are not known, though the comparison with Percier and Fontaine is plain enough. In their commentary on the use of reflection in interior space, Percier and Fontaine wrote in a manner that predicted Gandy's letter: "The mirror of the gallery repeats to infinity the decoration of the design, and multiplies the richness of its ornament." C. Percier and P. F. L. Fontaine, *Recueil de décorations intérieures* (Paris, 1812), 30. Gandy's account of this room raises the possibility that he had joined Soane in the autumn of 1814 during the architect's two-week journey to Paris, about which little is known. There is, however, no other evidence that Gandy visited Paris, excepting his father's earlier encouragement to his son to travel to France on his way home from Italy in 1797. Assuming that Gandy's description of this room is taken from another source, I have been unable to locate the original description. The possibility of Gandy and Soane traveling together to Paris and inspecting its architectural achievements under Napoleon remains an intriguing question. My thanks to Professor Alden Gordon of Trinity College for sharing information about the Hôtel de Beauharnais.

68. Letter dated August 12, 1836, Architectural Library, Soane Case 11 (Soane Museum, London)

69. On this aspect of Soane and Gandy's work, see Werner Oechslin, "Die Bank of England und ihre Darstellung als Ruine," *Archithese* 2 (March/April 1981): 19–25; and the exhibition catalogue *Visions of Ruin* as cited above in note 58. For analyses of this theme in eighteenth-century French art and art criticism, especially in ruin painting and architectural topographic views of Paris, see André Corboz, *Peinture militante et architecture révolutionnaire à propos du thème du tunnel chez Hubert Robert* (Basel, 1978), 45–51; Philippe Junod, "Futures in the Past," *Oppositions* 26 (Spring 1984): 43–63; Jutta Held, *Monument und Volk, Vorrevolutionäre Wahrnehmung in Bildern des ausgehenden Ancien Régime* (Wien, 1990), 277–326.

70. *The Diaries of George Price Boyce*, ed. Virginia Surtees (Norfolk, 1980), 6.

71. *The Exhibition of the Royal Academy* (London, 1830), 42. The original text by Le Sage reads: "Je vais par mon pouvoir diabolique enlever les toits des maisons, et malgré les ténèbres de la nuit, le dedans va se découvrir à vos yeux ... qu'on voit le dedans d'un pâté dont on vient d'ôter la croute." Le Sage, *Le Diable Boiteux, or the Crippled Devil* (London, 1796), 1:14.

72. Burke, *Enquiry ... Sublime*, 48.

73. *The Examiner*, April 17, 1808, 255.

74. James Elmes, *Lectures on Architecture* (London, 1823), 401–02.

75. Margaret Richardson, "The Image of Construction," in the exhibition catalogue *Buildings in Progress: Soane's Views of Construction*, The Soane Gallery (London, 1995), 3.

76. *The Exhibition of the Royal Academy* (London, 1832), 42.

77. Watkin, *Soane Lectures*, 496, 593. Soane also cited these lines in one of his last writings, *Description of Three Designs for the Two Houses of Parliament* (1835). See Sean Sawyer, "'The Baseless Fabric of a Vision': Civic Architecture and Pictorial Representation at Sir John Soane's Museum," *The Built Surface, Architecture and the Pictorial Arts from Antiquity to the Enlightenment*, ed. C. Anderson (Aldershot, 2002), 260–77. This Shakespearean passage was also popular in antiquarian publications; Saint-Non and Britton both cited it in frontispieces to their volumes.

78. *The Sun*, May 20, 1820, 14. This editorial was among those clipped by Soane.

79. On the subject of Soane and Freemasonry, see David Watkin, "Freemasonry and John Soane," *Journal of the Society of Architectural Historians* 54 (December 1995): 402–17; Terrance Galvin, "The Architecture of Sir John Soane and Joseph Michael Gandy: An Exploration into the Masonic and Occult Imagination of the Late Enlightenment," Ph.D. Dissertation, University of Pennsylvania, 2003.

80. "On the Sixth, or the Bœotian Order of Architecture," *Knight's Quarterly Magazine* 2 (1824), 457. Soane unsuccessfully brought legal action against the publisher.

81. John Summerson, *Architecture in Britain, 1530 to 1830* (1953; Hammondsworth, 1963), 287.

82. Thomas de Quincey, "Historico-Critical Inquiry into the Origins of the Rosicrucians and the Free-Masons," *De Quincey's Works* (Edinburgh, 1871), 16:21. This essay, a purported translation from the German, first appeared in 1824 in *London Magazine*.

83. *Jachim and Boaz; or the Authentic Key to the Door of Freemasonry, Both Ancient and Modern* (London, 1812), 42–44.

84. "The Election of Editor for Fraser's Magazine," *Fraser's Magazine* 1 (May 1830), 497–98.

85. John Soane, *Memoirs of the Professional Life of an Architect* (London, 1835), 70.

Chapter VI

1. These have been destroyed, though the façade of nearby No. 363 Kennington Lane, an ingenious Greek Revival treatment of a narrow urban residence, has been attributed to Gandy by Summerson. I have not been able to document and confirm this attribution.

2. Gandy, "Philosophy of Architecture," 371.

3. Ibid., 373.

4. Thomas Maurice, *Indian Antiquities* (London, 1793–1800), 3:521.

5. I examined the fragments of this manuscript when it was in the possession of Joseph Gandy's great-great-granddaughter, the late Miss Joan Rising, who discovered the three surviving volumes of the seven-volume treatise in her attic after receiving research inquiries from me. She also found an unmarked volume that contains drafts of a text on "Defenses and Military Architecture," however most of the pages are either torn out or scratched over with pen marks. In 1986, Miss Rising donated the volumes of the manuscript to the Architectural Library of the Royal Institute of British Architects, London. The watermarks of the manuscript are quite various in date: 1821, 1826, 1833, 1837. But most importantly, the first ten pages of the first volume have an 1833 watermark; the first volume also contains a complete table of contents for the entire seven-volume set. Gandy also indicates that there was to have been an eighth volume, which was to have been an index. Further references to this source will be given in the text, indicated parenthetically with volume and page number.

6. John Livingston Lowes, *The Road to Xanadu, a Study in the Ways of the Imagination* (1927; Princeton, 1986), 213.

7. Letter dated March 15, 1837. Formerly in the collection of the late Miss Rosalie Gandy. Present whereabouts unknown.

8. For a historical and intellectual survey of pansophic utopian ideals, see Frank E. Manuel and Fritzie P. Manuel, *Utopian Thought in the Western World* (Cambridge, MA, 1979), 205–331.

9. *The Exhibition of the Royal Academy* (London, 1836), 41.

10. Watkin, *Soane Lectures*, 666.

11. On this topic, see Adrian Desmond, *The Politics of Evolution, Morphology, Medicine, and Reform in Radical London* (Chicago, 1989).

12. John Britton, *Appendix to Britton's Auto-Biography: Containing Biographical, Archaeological, and Critical Essays* (London, 1850), n.p. [37].

13. Thomas Hope, *Essay on the Origins and Prospects of Man* (London, 1831), 1:29.

14. Thomas Hope, *Historical Essay on Architecture* (London, 1835), 24.

15. *Library of the Fine Arts* (October 1832), 218. This critic's proposal for a gallery of architectural models had its prototype in the model collection and gallery of the antiquarian and collector F.-L. Cassas, which was on display in Paris from 1806 until 1813. Soane's own collection of models was installed in the Model Room of his museum in 1835. On these topics, see Werner Szambien, *Le Musée d'Architecture* (Paris, 1988), 59–76, 151–73; Margaret Richardson, "Model Architecture," *Country Life*, September 21, 1989, 224–27.

16. The essential study of eighteenth-century mythography remains Frank Manuel, *The Eighteenth-Century Confronts the Gods* (Cambridge, 1959). Equally valuable is the anthology by Burton Feldman and Robert Richardson, *The Rise of Modern Mythology, 1660–1860* (Bloomington, 1972). On the mythographic influences on French and English romantic literature see Brian Juden, *Traditions orphiques et tendances mystiques dans le romantisme français, 1800–1855* (Paris, 1971); and E. S. Shaffer, *Kubla Khan and the Fall of Jerusalem: The Mythological School in Biblical Criticism and Secular Literature, 1780–1880* (Cambridge, 1975). For discussions of the mythographic and antiquarian study of Egyptian and Indian art and culture during the eighteenth and nineteenth centuries, see Jurgis Baltrusaitis, *La Quête d'Isis* (Paris, 1967) and Partha Mitter, *Much Maligned Monsters* (Oxford, 1977).

17. George Eliot, *Middlemarch*, ed. Gordon Haight (Boston, 1956), 147

18. Jacob Bryant, *A New System, or an Analysis of Ancient Mythology* (London, 1774), 2:364.

19. G. S. Faber, *The Origin of Pagan Idolatry* (London, 1816), 3: 195. Although Gandy does not cite Faber, Drummond, and Higgins (he does cite Picart, Jones, and Maurice), his dependence on this contemporary generation of mythographic scholarship is extremely apparent in his preoccupation with the universality of arkite symbolism and the primacy of zodiacal signs as the origin of the language of myth and allegory.

20. On the political and religious reverberations of Volney's *Les ruines*, see James Epstein, *Radical Expression, Political Language, Ritual, and Symbol in England, 1790–1850* (Oxford, 1994), 100–06, 161–62; Martin Thom, *Republics, Nations, and Tribes* (London, 1995), 121–26, 142–49.

21. Comte de Volney, *A New Translation of Volney's Ruins; or Meditations on the Revolutions of Empires* (Paris, 1802), 1:168–78.

22. Ibid., 1:172n.

23. Ibid., 2:97–98.

24. Charles Dupuis, *Origine de tous les cultes, ou religion universelle* (Paris, 1795), 1:223, 257.

25. Ibid., 1:240.

26. Godfrey Higgens, *Anacalypsis … or an Inquiry into the Origin of Language, Nations, and Religion* (London, 1836), 1:35.

27. On Viel de Saint-Maux, see Jean-Marie Pérouse de Montclos, *Étienne-Louis Boullée, de l'architecture classique à l'architecture révolutionnaire* (Paris, 1969), 202–07; and Anthony Vidler, "Symbolic Architecture: Viel de Saint-Maux and the Decipherment of Antiquity," in *The Writing of the Walls* (Princeton, 1987), 139–46.

28. Richard Payne Knight, *The Symbolical Language of Ancient Art and Mythology* (1818; New York, 1876), 3. Much of this book was culled from Knight's earlier, and more scandalous, antiquarian study, *A Discourse on the Worship of Priapus* (1786). For a discussion of these works and of Knight's relation to d'Hancarville and the collectors Hamilton and Townley, see Peter Funnell, "The Symbolical Language of Antiquity," in *The Arrogant Connoisseur: Richard Payne Knight 1751–1824*, ed. M. Clarke and N. Penny (Manchester, 1982), 51–64; Alessandra Ponte, "Architecture and Phallocentrism in Richard Payne Knight's Theory," in *Sexuality and Space*, ed. Beatriz Colomina (Princeton, 1992), 273–305; Andrew Ballantyne, *Architecture, Landscape and Liberty: Richard Payne Knight and the Picturesque* (Cambridge, 1997), 86–109.

29. Knight, *Symbolical Language*, 41.

30. Erasmus Darwin, *The Temple of Nature, or the Origin of Society* (London, 1803), 21. For a history of these universal language theories, see James Knowlson, *Universal Language Schemes in England and France 1600–1800* (Toronto, 1975); Paolo Rossi, *Logic and the Art of Memory, the Quest for a Universal Language* (Chicago, 2000).

31. Quatremère de Quincy, *De l'architecture égyptienne* (Paris, 1803), 59. On this linguistic analogy for architectural decoration in Quatremère's writings, see Anthony Vidler, "From the Hut to the Temple: Quatremère de Quincy and the Idea of Type," in *Writing of the Walls*, 160–63; Sylvia Lavin, *Quatremère de Quincy and the Invention of a Modern Language of Architecture* (Cambridge, MA, 1992), 76–85, 114–25.

32. Watkin, *Soane Lectures*, 638.

33. "On the Use of Allegory in Architecture, Translated from the French of Quatremère de Quincy by P," *The Architectural Magazine* 4 (January 1837): 2.

34. George Williamson, *The Life and Work of Ozias Humphry* (London, 1918), 8–10.

35. E. H. Gombrich, *The Sense of Order* (Oxford, 1979), 233.

36. James Elmes, *Lectures on Architecture* (London, 1823), 121.

37. Following is the text of the RA catalogue entry: "1165. Architecture; its natural model—Vide Catalogue of Royal Academy Exhibition. 1836, for a textile notice. The natural models for building, most authors agree are derived from stony caverns, alluvial soils for bricks, and forests for timbers, with these men raised their huts, carved their lares, and formed their furniture; they first clothed themselves with the leaves of trees, and twisted the branches of shrubs into shady bowers, and by observing the instincts of other animals, they applied their hints for making tools, &c. Supposing there were antediluvian irons for marine fabrics like Noah's ark, and accidental caves or pre-adamite dwellings, we have exemplars remote as Chinese chronology. One writer says 'the earth is a dwelling, the skies a canopy, the grass a carpet, the heavenly bodies constitute a nychthemeron, and clouds are screens.'

"Detached masses of granite, the sketch endeavours to portray became objects of veneration, natural bridges over chasms and rivers. The Giant's Causeway, or basaltic formations in Ireland, Scotland, Hebrides, and Caserides mountain of Wales, also the Dresden caves, those of the Thoas and Mexico, natural Clier's or staircases to caverns, within and over caverns, and various entrances and passages extending many miles under limestone hills, the seven hundred semi-angular pillars over a waterfall in Thibet, many were models for good masonry in horizontal beds and articulations, or joints of pillars imitated by the earliest Nephalims, Titans, and Cyclopians in their works, called the giant race and companion builders of antiquity, who afterwards studies spontaneous cements, mortars, and plaster for adoption.

"The icebergs of the arctic circles suggest the form of icicled palaces, the spires of the glaciers exhibit scenic and ever various pictured models to an intuitive genius. The aiguille of the Dom river, the pyramidal and pinnacle-pointed Alpine mountains, piles sustained by subterranean vaults and piers, the ascents being left by subsiding waters, are now seen in steppes, prairies, and interminate terraces. The Banian tree, a prototype of a beamed ceiling, the palm and the oak, the vine and the water-lily, creepers entwined in rich foliages, have all been copied by mankind, the musk-rat and beaver associated lumberers, raise dams in lakes to sustain their lodges, and the white ants build conical huts twelve feet high, arranged like camps and villages; also the cayenne fly, and the bees' hexagonal honey-combs economizing space, who gather in colonies and repair their citadelled labyrinth and rafter covered ways, with many other winged tribes that forms nests, webs, and mechanism, the razor shell animal that bores holes in porphyry, the cochlea piercing chalky hills, and shell fish that penetrates our navies' planks, the serpent's jaw suggesting to Talus, nephew of Daedalus, the first idea of a saw, even the ouran-outan of Sierra Leone erects a dwelling to protect his female and young, commodious as the natives, help to form an ichonographic scenography, a protocol of architecture composed in the sketch before us."

38. Robert Morris, *Lectures on Architecture* (London, 1759), 100.

39. Turner Royal Academy Lecture Notes, ADD. MS 46151 S, 9v–10 (Manuscript Room, British Library). See Erasmus Darwin, *Zoonomia; or the Laws of Organic Life* (London, 1796), 1:181.

40. "Synopsis of Humbert's New System," *The Literary Gazette* 19 March 1825, 188. The unknown author of this brief précis of Humbert's theories probably meant "the physiognomy of architecture." This article interestingly precedes the publication of Humbert's *Essai sur les signes inconditionnels dans l'art* (1827–29). Gandy does not cite Humbert's publication, but their range of intellectual concerns certainly overlap. For a comprehensive study of Humbert's complex aesthetic theory and its sources, see Barbara Maria Stafford, *Symbol and Myth, Humbert de Superville's Essay on the Absolute Signs in Art* (Cranbury, NJ, 1979).

41. On the pictorial treatment and architectural theories of the primitive hut, see Joachim Gauss, "Die Urhutte über ein Modell in der Baukunst und ein Motiv in der bildenen Kunst," *Wallraf-Richartz Jahrbuch* 33 (1971): 2–48, Joseph Rykwert, *On Adam's House in Paradise, The Idea of the Primitive Hut in Architectural History* (New York: Museum of Modern Art, 1972), and Stephanie Moser, *Ancestral Images, The Iconography of Human Origins* (Ithaca, 1998).

42. James Burnet, Lord Monboddo, *Of the Origin and Progress of Language* (Edinburgh: Balfour, 1774), 1:298.

43. On natural historical and geological illustration in Europe and England during this period, see Barbara Maria Stafford, *Voyages into Substance* (Cambridge, MA, 1984), M. J. S. Rudwick, *Scenes from Deep Time* (Chicago, 1992), and Charlotte Klonk, *Science and the Perception of Nature* (New Haven, 1996).

44. For excellent studies of the controversies surrounding scriptural geology and natural history in eighteenth- and early nineteenth-century England and France, see Roy Porter, *The Making of Geology, Earth Science in Britain* (Cambridge, 1970), Nicolaas A. Rupke, *The Great Chain of History, William Buckland and the English School of Geology (1814–1849)* (Oxford, 1983), and Rhoda Rappaport, *When Geologists Were Historians, 1665–1750* (Ithaca, 1997).

45. Faber, *Origins of Idolatry*, 3:201.

46. Jean Coussin, *De le génie de l'architecture* (Paris, 1822), 282.

47. On this speculative tradition in the interpretation of fossil matter, see Paolo Rossi, *The Dark Abyss of Time, the History of the Earth and the History of*

Nations from Hooke to Vico, trans. Lydia Cochrane (Chicago, 1984), 3–32. On the esthetic and scientific curiosity about figured stones, from the Renaissance to the Enlightenment, see Jurgis Baltrusaitis, *Aberrations: An Essay on the Legend of Forms*, trans. Richard Miller (1983; Cambridge, MA, 1989), 59–106.

48. Roland Barthes, *Mythologies*, trans. Annette Lavers (1957; New York, 1972), 129.

49. On the inside cover of volume five of the bound manuscript of Gandy's architectural treatise there is a list of "Drawings to be made" relating to the Comparative Architecture series. Included in this list were works that Gandy had exhibited from throughout his career; the names of the patrons who had purchased those pictures are also noted (e.g. the collector/designer Thomas Hope, the Liverpool architect John Foster, the Royal Academy professor and sculptor Richard Westmacott). A transcript of this list follows:

"N1. Noah's ark resting on Ararat surrounded by primitive huts and excavations one side of the ark in ruins to show the interior construction, the huts and excavations imitations of the ark, with a camp of Tents at bottom.

N2. Tower and Walls of Babylon a kind of Pyramid in 7 stories or Towers an imitation of the ark at top as an observatory &c.

N3. Hindoo excavations with the Avatar of Vishnu bursting forth from a Column and from whence a glory of light issues illumines the Cave with lightnings and bolts.

N4. Hindoo excavations exterior of rock cut in the forms of Palaces, Lions, Elephants and Giants.

N5. Chinese exterior gaudy colours, rich composition, gigantic figures on mountains, pagodas, bridges, gates, Palaces, pavilions, &c.

N6. Chinese interior, rich with draperies & other works of porceline and a tomb of a Lama of Thibet.

N7. Egyptian. The Sun & Constellations with all the columnal figures, animals of the Zodiac &c.

N8. Exterior Egyptian. All the grandeur of Pyramids, Obelisks, Gates, Towers, Temples, &c. with Processions.

N9. Persepolis Temple the mountains at the back the Sun rising behind the morning mists, the multitude in front awaiting the moment.

N10. Druids. Exterior of a Temple the distance with hill forts and British huts and fortifications, a human sacrifice in the wicker man, a colossal basket work and all the objects or stones of Druid superstition.

N11. Roman exterior their variety of Temples, arches, &c. Palatine Palace Tomb of Hephestion.

N12. Interior Subterranean Temple done sold to Allnutt

N13. Roman & Saxon 6thc. Merlin's Tomb done sold to Westmacott Melrose Abbey sold to Foster 16.

N14. Gothic Exterior Castle of Otranto done sold to Foster

Roslin Chapel sold to Watt 15.

N17. Saxon Town, Towers, & Churches, houses & groups.

N18. Turkish Interior style Alhambra

N19. Exterior Sultans tents &c.

N19. One picture of a vision to give a group of the best examples of all styles. Various known masters groups of buildings they have erected to give their peculiar taste and excellences. such as Wren, Jones, Chambers, Wyatt &c.

Groups of Tombs of Kings in all Countries

1st Rate Buildings in Groups selected by Centuries

Exterior of best Cathedrals

Cottages of all Countries

National styles by groups of buildings

Ornaments—the best kind on first principles on fragments in groups &c.

Greek—done sold—Market Place Pharae, Westmacott. Temple of Venus, Snow. Temple of Juno, Bullock. Greek Port, Beckford. Pandemonium, Hope. Sepulchral Chamber, Allnutt. another, Hope."

50. George Wightwick, *The Palace of Architecture: A Romance of Art and History* (London, 1840), 2. For remarks on Wightwick's book, see Hersey, *High Victorian Gothic*, 34–37; and John Archer, *The Literature of British Domestic Architecture, 1715–1842* (Cambridge, MA, 1985), 833–35.

51. George Wightwick, "The Life of an Architect," *Bentley's Miscellany* 32 (1852): 34.

52. Citations from Cockerell's lecture notes are taken from Cockerell Family MSS, Box 1 COC 1/1–16, xv. 37; xvi. 39; xi. 3 (Architectural Library, Royal Institute of British Architects, London). For background on Cockerell's Royal Academy lectures, see David Watkin, *The Life and Work of C. R. Cockerell* (London, 1974), 105–31.

53. A. Welby Pugin, *Contrasts*, 2nd ed. (London, 1841), v.

54. A. Welby Pugin, *An Apology for the Revival of Christian Architecture in England* (London, 1843), 15.

55. In his etching of the same name from ca. 1788. See William Blake, *Complete Writings*, ed. G. Keynes (Oxford, 1966), 98. Blake's mythographic knowledge also informed his commentary about his own work in "A Descriptive Catalogue of Pictures" (1809), 578–79.

Conclusion

1. Flora Tristan, *London Journal* (1840; Charlestown, 1980), 8.
2. Thomas Wilson, *The Pyramid, a General Metropolitan Cemetery* (London, 1830), 3–4.
3. Letter dated September 15, 1837, formerly in the collection of Miss Rosalie Gandy (present whereabouts unknown).
4. Letter dated July 11, 1837, as above.
5. "The Exhibition of the Royal Academy," *The Times*, May 13, 1836, 6.
6. *Library of the Fine Arts*, June 1832, 516 & September 1832, 137.
7. National Census, County Devon, Plympton Maurice, 3. Public Record Office Ref. HO 107/238/5.
8. William White, *History, Gazetteer, and Directory of Devonshire* (Broom Battle, 1850), 553. On the private care of the insane during this period, see William Ll. Parry-Jones, *The Trade in Lunacy, a Study of Private Madhouses in England* (London, 1972). I am grateful for the assistance of Ms. Audrey Mills, a local historian in Plympton St. Maurice, during my visits to the village and with research inquiries afterwards.
9. *The Sessional Papers by Order of the House of Lords. Report of the Metropolitan Commissioners in Lunacy to the Lord High Chancellor* (London, 1844), 26:63.
10. Entry of Death No. 76, registered December 28, 1843. West Devon Record Office, Unit 3, Plymouth. Gandy's will was administered in February 1844, his estate valued at £200 and granted to his widow.

Bibliography

i. Unpublished Sources

Cockerell, C. R., Cockerell Family MS. (Royal Institute of British Architects Library, London).

Gandy, Joseph Michael, "The Art, Philosophy, and Science of Architecture," MS., formerly in the collection of the late Joan Rising, Fishguard, Wales (Royal Institute of British Architects Library, London).

–, letters to his son from 1836–37, formerly in the possession of the late Miss Rosalie Gandy, Heathfield, Sussex (present whereabouts unknown).

–, correspondence to John Britton, undated, 1998–A.666, Collection Frits Lugt, Fondation Custodia, Paris.

–, Gandy Green Book (correspondence, diary entries), formerly in the possession of the late Miss Joan Rising, Fishguard, Wales (present whereabouts unknown).

–, Private Correspondence Cupboard, Division III, Letter "G" (Sir John Soane's Museum Archive, London).

Royal Academy Council Meeting Minutes, 5–7 (1813–1832) (Royal Academy Library, London).

Soane, John, "Extracts and Hints for Lectures on Architecture by John Soane, 1813 to 1818" (Architectural Library, Sir John Soane's Museum, London).

Tatham, C. H., correspondence with Henry Holland (Transcriptions) (Architectural Library, Sir John Soane's Museum, London).

Turner, J. M. W., Royal Academy Lecture Notes (Manuscript Room, British Library, London).

ii. Unpublished Theses and Dissertations

Braly, David Keith, "The Use of Drawing in Joseph Michael Gandy (1771–1843)," M.Phil. Thesis, Cambridge University, 1987.

Galvin, Terrance, "The Architecture of Sir John Soane and Joseph Michael Gandy: An Exploration into the Masonic and Occult Imagination of the Late Enlightenment," Ph.D. Dissertation, University of Pennsylvania, 2003.

Lukacher, Brian, "Joseph Michael Gandy: The Poetical Representation and Mythography of Architecture," Ph.D. Dissertation, University of Delaware, 1987.

Nachmani, Cynthia Wolk, "'Enrapt in a Cloud of Darkness...': Joseph Michael Gandy, Architecture, and the Romantic Imagination," Ph.D. Dissertation, New York University, 1984.

iii. Published Sources before 1900

Ackermann, Rudolph, A Graphic Illustration of the Colosseum, Regent's Park, in Five Plates from Drawings by Gandy, Mackenzie & Other Eminent Artists (London, 1829).

Alison, Archibald, "National Monuments," Miscellaneous Essays (New York, 1865).

Alberti, Leon Battista, Ten Books on Architecture, trans. James Leoni (1726; London, 1955).

"Architectural Portraiture," Magazine of Fine Arts, 1 (1821), 459–64.

Ball, John, A Description of the City of Constantinople (London, 1729).

Bartell, Edmund, Hints for Picturesque Improvements (London, 1804).

Basoli, Antonio, Collezione di varie scene teatrali (Bologna, 1821).

Bell's New Pantheon: or Historical Dictionary of the Gods (London, 1790).

Bodmer, J. J., Noah, Attempted from the German of Mr. Bodmer, in Twelve Books by Joseph Collyer (London, 1767).

[Boulton, A.B.], The History of White's (London, 1892).

Brewster, David, The Kaleidoscope, Its History, Theory and Construction (London, 1819).

"The British School of Architecture," Blackwood's Magazine, 40 (August 1836), 225–38.

Britton, John, Appendix to Britton's Auto-Biography: Containing Biographical, Archaeological, and Critical Essays (London, 1850).

–, The Auto-biography of John Britton, (London, 1850).

–, The Architectural Antiquities of Great Britain (London, 1807–26).

–, The Cathedral Antiquities of Great Britain (London, 1814–35).

–, The Fine Arts of the British School (London, 1812).

–, The Union of Architecture, Sculpture, and Painting (London, 1828).

Brothers, Richard, A Description of Jerusalem: Its Houses and Streets, ... Royal and Private Palaces with the Garden of Eden (London, 1801).

Brown, Richard, Domestic Architecture (London, 1842).

–, The Principles of Practical Perspective, or Scenographic Projection (London, 1815).

–, Sacred Architecture, Its Rise, Progress, and Present State (London, 1845).

–, The Rudiments of Drawing Cabinet and Upholstery Furniture (London, 1822).

Bryant, Jacob, A New System, or an Analysis of Ancient Mythology (London, 1774).

Burke, Edmund, A Philosophical Enquiry into the Origin of Our Ideas of the Sublime and the Beautiful (1757), ed. J. T. Boulton (London, 1958).

Burnet, James, Lord Monboddo, Of the Origin and Progress of Language (Edinburgh, 1774).

Burnet, Thomas, The Sacred Theory of the Earth (1684; Carbondale, 1965).

[Cartwright, John], The Trident; or the National Policy of Naval Celebration, Describing a Hieronauticon or Naval Temple (London, 1802).

A Catalogue of a Choice and Select Collection of Paintings and Drawings of the Modern English and French Schools, the Property of Alaric A. Watts, Esq., Which Will Be Sold at Mr. Sotheby and Son (London, 1832).

"Catalogue of Works of English Artists in the Collection of Thomas Hope," Annals of the Fine Arts, 4 (1819), 96–99.

Chambers, William, Dissertation on Oriental Gardening (London, 1773).

Christie, James, An Essay on That Earliest Species of Idolatry, the Worship of the Elements (London, 1814).

Coussin, Jean, De le genie de l'architecture (Paris, 1822).

Darwin, Erasmus, The Temple of Nature, or the Origin of Society (London, 1803).

–, Zoonomia, or the Laws of Organic Life (London, 1796).

Delafosse, Jean-Charles, Nouvelle iconologie historique (Paris, 1768).

De Quincey, Thomas, "Historico-Critical Inquiry into the Origins of the Rosicrucians and the Free-Masons" (1824), De Quincey's Works (Edinburgh, 1871).

Drummond, William, The Oedipus Judaicus (London, 1811).

–, Origines; or Remarks on the Origin of Several Empires, States, and Cities (London, 1824).

Dubut, L.-A., Architecture civile maisons de ville et de campagne, de tous formes et de tous genres (Paris, 1803).

Duppa, Richard, A Journal of the Most Remarkable Occurrences That Took Place in Rome (London, 1799).

Dupuis, Charles, Origine de tous les cultes, ou religion universelle (Paris, 1795).

Durand, J.-N.-L., Recueil et parallèle des édifices de tout genre, anciens et modernes (Paris, 1801).

Edwards, Edward, A Practical Treatise on Perspective (On the Principles of Dr. Brook Taylor) (London, 1803).

Elmes, James, Lectures on Architecture (London, 1823).

Faber, G. S., The Origin of Pagan Idolatry (London, 1816).

Fischer, von Erlach, Johann Bernhard, A Plan of Civil and Historical Architecture in the Representation of the Most Noted Buildings of Foreign Nations (London, 1738).

Gandy, Joseph, Designs for Cottages, Cottage Farms, and Other Rural Buildings (London, 1805).

–, "Letter to the Editor," The Guardian, 2 (May 27, 1821, June 3, 1821, June 10, 1821, June 17, 1821, June 24, 1821).

–, "On the Philosophy of Architecture," Magazine of Fine Arts, 1 (1821), 289–93 and 370–79.

–, The Rural Architect (London, 1805).

Gilpin, William, Three Essays on the Picturesque (London, 1792).

Godwin, William, Essay on Sepulchres, A Proposal for Erecting Some Memorial of the Illustrious Dead in All Ages (London, 1809).

Gough, Richard, Sepulchral Monuments in Great Britain (London, 1786).

Gregory, John, An Account of the Sepulchers of the Antients and a description of their monuments from the Creation of the World to the Building of the Pyramids (London, 1712).

Grohmann, J. G., Ideenmagazin für Liebhaber von Gärten, Englischen Anlagen und für Besitzer von Landgütern (Berlin, 1797–1802).

Haydon, Benjamin Robert, Correspondence and Table Talk (London, 1876).

Hazlitt, William, "On Antiquity," London Magazine (May 1821), 527–30.

Herbert, Algernon, Nimrod, a Discourse Upon Certain Passages of History and Fable (London, 1826).

Heywood, Thomas, The Life of Merlin, surnamed Ambrosius, His Prophecies and Predictions Interpreted (1626; London, 1813).

Higgens, Godfrey, Anacalypsis ... or an Inquiry into the Origin of Language, Nations, and Religion (London, 1836).

Hope, Thomas, Essay on the Origins and Prospects of Man (London, 1831).

–, An Historical Essay on Architecture (London, 1835).

–, Household Furniture and Interior Decoration Executed from Designs by Thomas Hope (London, 1807).

Hutchinson, William, The Spirit of Masonry (1775; New York, 1982).

Jachim and Boaz; or the Authentic Key to the Door of Freemasonry, Both Ancient and Modern (London, 1812).

Knight, Richard Payne, An Analytical Inquiry into the Principles of Taste (1805; London, 1808).

–, The Progress of Civil Society: A Didactic Poem (London, 1796).

–, The Symbolical Language of Ancient Art and Mythology (1818; New York, 1876).

Lamy, Bernard, Apparatus Biblicus, trans. Richard Bundy (London, 1723).

Landseer, John, Sabaean Researches (London, 1823).

Laugier, Marc-Antoine, Essai sur l'architecture (Paris, 1755).

Le Camus de Mézières, Nicolas, Le Génie de l'architecture, ou l'analogie de cet art avec nos sensations (Paris, 1780).

Ledoux, Claude-Nicolas, L'Architecture considérée sous le rapport de l'art, des moeurs et la législation (Paris, 1804).

Le Sage, Le Diable boiteux, or the Crippled Devil (London, 1796).

Leslie, C.R., and Tom Taylor, eds., The Life and Times of Sir Joshua Reynolds (London, 1865).

Lethaby, W. R., Architecture, Mysticism and Myth (1891; New York, 1975).

The Life and Correspondence of Major Cartwright, Edited by his Niece, F.D. Cartwright (London, 1826).

Loudon, J. C., Encyclopedia of Cottage, Farm, and Villa Architecture (London, 1833).

Maillet, Benoit de, Telliamed, … sur la diminution de la mer, la formation de la terre, l'origine de l'homme (Amsterdam, 1748).

Malton, James, An Essay on British Cottage Architecture (London, 1798).

Maurice, Thomas, Indian Antiquities: or … the History of Hindostan (London, 1793–1800).

–, Observations Connected with Astronomy and Ancient History, Sacred and Profane, on the Ruins of Babylon (London, 1816).

–, Observations on the Remains of Ancient Egyptian Grandeur and Superstition (London, 1818).

Middleton, Charles, Picturesque and Architectural Views (London, 1793).

Montfaucon, Bernard de, Antiquity Explained, as Represented in Sculptures by Their Learned Father Monfaucon, trans. David Humphreys (London, 1721).

Morris, Robert, Lectures on Architecture (London, 1759).

–, Rural Architecture (London, 1750).

[Mudie, Robert], Babylon the Great: A Dissection and Demonstration of Men and Things in the British Capital (London, 1825).

[–], A Second Judgment of Babylon the Great (London, 1829).

North, Christopher [John Wilson], "A Day at Windermere," Blackwood's Edinburgh Magazine, 28 (September 1830), 524–26.

Northcote, James, Life of Sir Joshua Reynolds (London, 1819).

"Obituary—J. P. Deering," Art Journal, 12 (March 1, 1850), 100.

"On the Use of Allegory in Architecture, Translated from the French of Quatremère de Quincy by P," The Architectural Magazine, 4 (January 1837), 2–21.

Ouvaroff [Uvarov] Count M., Essay on the Mysteries of Eleusis … with Observations by James Christie (London, 1817).

Pamphilus, Eusebius, The History of the Church, Also the Life of Constantine (Cambridge, 1683).

Papworth, John, Select Views of London (London, 1816).

Pasquin, Anthony [John Williams], Memoirs of the Royal Academicians; Being an Attempt to Improve the National Taste (London, 1824).

Pausanias, The Description of Greece, trans. and ed. Thomas Taylor (London, 1794).

Peacock, James, Oikidia, or Nutshells (London, 1785).

Percier, C., and P. F. L. Fontaine, Recueil de décorations intérieures (Paris, 1812).

"Pie-Crust; or Architectural Madness," Fraser's Magazine, 4 (October 1831), 277–92.

Piranesi, Giovanni Battista, "An Apologetical Essay in Defense of the Egyptian and Tuscan Architecture" (1769), The Polemical Works of Piranesi, ed. John Wilton-Ely (Westmead, 1977).

Price, Uvedale, On the Picturesque (1794; Edinburgh, 1842).

Priestley, Joseph, The History and Present State of Discoveries Relating to Vision, Light, and Colours (London, 1772).

–, Disquisition Relating to Matter and Spirit (Birmingham, 1782).

"Publius on the Proposed Waterloo Monuments," Annals of the Fine Arts, 2 (1817), 156–60.

Pugin, A. Welby, An Apology for the Revival of Christian Architecture in England (London, 1843).

–, Contrasts, 2nd ed. (London, 1841).

de Quincy, Quatremère, De l'architecture Egyptienne (Paris, 1803).

–, The Destination of Works of Art, trans. Henry Thomson (London, 1821).

–, An Essay on the Nature, the End, and the Means of Imitation in the Fine Arts, trans. J. C. Kent (London, 1837).

Ramée, Daniel, Manuel de l'histoire générale de l'architecture chez tous les peuples (Paris, 1843).

"Remarks on Mr. White's Plan for the Improvement of Mary-le-bone," The European Magazine, September 1815, 231–35.

Rennie, James, Insect Architecture (London, 1830).

Repton, Humphry, An Inquiry into the Changes in Taste in Landscape Gardening (London, 1806).

Reynolds, Joshua, Discourses on Art, ed. Robert Wark (New Haven, 1975).

S….Y, Critical and Impartial Observations on the Principal Pictures and Drawings Exhibited at Somerset House (London, 1819).

Saint-Non, Abbé de, Voyage pittoresque, ou description des royaumes de Naples et de Sicile (Paris, 1781–86).

Saint-Valéry-Seheult, A., Le génie et les grands secrets de l'architecture (Paris, 1813).

Seheult, F.-L., Recueil d'architecture dessiné et mesuré en Italie, dans les années 1791, 1792, 1793… (Paris, 1821).

Seroux d'Agincourt, J. B. L. G., Histoire de l'art par les monumens (Paris, 1823).

The Sessional Papers by Order of the House of Lords. Report of the Metropolitan Commissioners in Lunacy to the Lord High Chancellor (London, 1844).

Shaw, Simeon, Nature Displayed in the Heavens and on the Earth (London, 1823).

Shepherd, Thomas, and James Elmes, Metropolitan Improvements; or London in the Nineteenth Century (London, 1824).

Soane, John, Description of the House and Museum of John Soane (London, 1830).

–, Description of Three Designs for the Two Houses of Parliament (1835).

–, Designs for Public and Private Buildings (London, 1832).

–, Lectures on Architecture, ed. Arthur Bolton (London, 1929).

–, Memoirs of the Professional Life of an Architect (London, 1835).

[Stonestreet, George], Domestic Union, or London as it Should Be!! (London, 1800).

Taylor, Thomas, Concerning the Beautiful, or a Paraphrased Translation from the Greek of Plotinus (London, 1793).

Timbs, John, Clubs and Club Life in London (London, 1873).

Tristan, Flora, London Journal (1840; Charlestown, 1980).

Valenciennes, P.-H., Élémens de perspective pratique (Paris, An VII [1799]).

Viel de Saint-Maux, J.-L., Lettres sur l'architecture des anciens et celle des modernes (Paris, 1787).

Volney, Comte de, A New Translation of Volney's Ruins; or Meditations on the Revolutions of Empires (Paris, 1802).

Waagen, G. F., Works of Art and Artists in England (London, 1838).

Walpole, Horace, Anecdotes of Painting in England (1771; London, 1862).

White, William, History, Gazetteer, and Directory of Devonshire (Broom Battle, 1850).

Wightwick, George, "The Life of an Architect," Bentley's Miscellany, 32 (1852), 28–44.

–, "The Life of an Architect," Bentley's Miscellany, 33 (1853), 441–59.

–, The Palace of Architecture: A Romance of Art and History (London, 1840).

Wilson, John, The Isle of Palms and Other Poems (Edinburgh, 1812).

Wilson, Thomas, The Pyramid, a General Metropolitan Cemetery (London, 1830).

Wood, John, A Series of Plans, for Cottages or Habitations of the Labourer (1781; London, 1808).

Wright, Thomas, Universal Architecture, Book I (London, 1755).

–, Universal Architecture, Book II (London, 1758).

iv. Published Sources after 1900

Alcock, S. E., J. F. Cherry, and J. Elsner, eds., Pausanias, Travel and Memory in Roman Greece (Oxford, 2001).

Altick, Richard, The Shows of London (Cambridge, MA, 1978).

Andrews, Malcolm, The Search for the Picturesque (Stanford, 1989).

Archer, John, "The Beginnings of Association in British Architectural Esthetics," Eighteenth-Century Studies, 16 (Spring 1983), 241–264.

–, The Literature of British Domestic Architecture 1715–1842 (Cambridge, MA, 1985).

Arnold, Dana, Re-presenting the Metropolis: Architecture, Urban Experience and Social Life in London 1800–1840 (Aldershot, 2000).

Bailey, Colin J., "The English Poussin— an Introduction to the Life and Work of George Augustus Wallis," Walker Art Gallery, Liverpool, Annual Report, 6 (1975–76), 35–54.

Ballantyne, Andrew, Architecture, Landscape and Liberty: Richard Payne Knight and the Picturesque (Cambridge, 1997).

–, "Joseph Gandy and the Politics of Rustic Charm," Articulating British Classicism, ed. B. Arciszewska and E. McKellar (Aldershot, 2004).

Baltrusaitis, Jurgis, Aberrations, An Essay on the Legend of Forms, trans. Richard Miller (1983; Cambridge, MA, 1989).

–, La Quête d'Isis (Paris, 1967).

Bann, Stephen, The Clothing of Clio: A Study of the Representation of History in Nineteenth-Century Britain and France (Cambridge, 1984).

–, *The Invention of History* (Manchester, 1990).

Barrell, John, *The Political Theory of Painting from Reynolds to Hazlitt* (London and New Haven, 1986).

Barthes, Roland, *Mythologies*, trans. Annette Lavers (1957; New York, 1972).

Bayard, Jane, *Works of Splendor and Imagination: The Exhibition Watercolor, 1770–1870*, Yale Center for British Art (New Haven, 1981).

Beckett, R.B., ed., *John Constable's Correspondence* (Ipswich, 1965).

Belcher, Margaret, ed., *The Collected Letters of A. W. N. Pugin* (Oxford, 2001).

Benjamin, Walter, "Rigorous Study of Art," *October*, 47 (Winter 1988), 84–90.

Bentley Jr., G.E., *The Stranger in Paradise, A Biography of William Blake* (New Haven and London, 2001).

Berliner, Rudolf, "Zeichnungen des Romischen Architekten Giuseppe Barberi," *Münchner Jahrbuch der bildenen Kusnt*, 6 (1965), 165–216; 7 (1966), 201–13.

Bermingham, Ann, *Learning to Draw* (London and New Haven, 2000).

Bingham, Neil, "Architecture at the Royal Academy Schools, 1768–1836," *The Education of the Architect*, proceedings of the 22nd Annual Symposium of the Society of Architectural Historians of Great Britain (1993).

Bolton, Arthur T., ed., *The Portrait of Sir John Soane, R.A.* (London, 1927).

Braegger, Carlpetter, ed., *Architektur und Sprache* (Munich, 1982).

Castle, Terry, *The Female Thermometer* (New York, 1995).

Cavina, Anna Ottani, *I paesaggi della ragione: La città neoclassica da David a Humbert de Superville* (Rome, 1994).

Chase, Malcolm, *"The People's Farm": English Radical Agrarianism 1775–1840* (Oxford, 1988).

Cipriani, A., P. Marconi and E. Valeriani, *I disegni di architettura dell'Archivio Storico dell'Accademia di San Luca* (Rome, 1974).

Clarke, Michael, *The Tempting Prospect: A Social History of English Watercolours* (London, 1981).

–, and Nicholas Penny, eds., *The Arrogant Connoisseur: Richard Payne Knight* (Manchester, 1982).

Cobban, A., and R.A. Smith, eds., *The Correspondence of Edmund Burke* (Cambridge, 1967).

Colley, Linda, *Britons, Forging the Nation 1701–1837* (London and New Haven, 1992).

Collins, Peter, *Changing Ideals in Modern Architecture, 1750–1950* (Montreal, 1965).

Colvin, Howard, *Architecture and the After-Life* (London and New Haven, 1991).

–, *A Biographical Dictionary of British Architects 1600–1840* (London, 1978).

–, and John Harris, eds., *The Country Seat: Essays in Honour of Sir John Summerson* (London, 1970).

Copley, Stephen, and Peter Garside, eds., *The Politics of the Picturesque: Literature, Landscape, and Aesthetics since 1770* (Cambridge, 1994).

Conrad, Peter, *Shandyism, The Character of Romantic Irony* (Oxford, 1978).

Corboz, André, *Peinture militante et architecture révolutionnaire à propos du thème du tunnel chez Hubert Robert* (Basel, 1978).

Crook, J. Mordaunt, *The Greek Revival* (London, 1972).

–, "John Britton and the Genesis of the Gothic Revival," *Concerning Architecture: Essays in Architectural Writers and Writing Presented to Nikolaus Pevsner*, ed. J. Summerson (London, 1968).

–, "A Neo-classical Visionary—The Architecture of Thomas Harrison," *Country Life*, 149 (1971), 1088–91.

–, "A Reluctant Goth—The Architecture of Thomas Harrison," *Country Life*, 149 (1971), 876–79.

–, *The Dilemma of Style, Architectural Ideas from the Picturesque to the Post-Modern* (London, 1987).

Daniels, Stephen, *Humphry Repton, Landscape Gardening and the Geography of Georgian England* (London and New Haven, 1999).

Darley, Gillian, *John Soane, an Accidental Romantic* (London and New Haven, 1999).

–, *Villages of Vision* (London, 1975).

Dean, June, "The Regency Furniture in Liverpool Town Hall," *Furniture History*, 25 (1989), 127–34.

De Bolla, Peter, *The Discourse of the Sublime* (Oxford, 1989).

De Zurko, Edward R., *The Origins of Functionalist Theory* (New York, 1957).

Desmond, Adrian, *The Politics of Evolution: Morphology, Medicine, and Reform in Radical London* (Chicago, 1989).

The Diaries of William Charles Macready, 1833–1851 (New York, 1912).

Dobai, Johannes, *Die Kunstliteratur des Klassizismus und der Romantik in England* (Berne, 1977).

Dorey, Helen, "Sir John Soane's Acquisition of the Sarcophagus of Seti I," *Georgian Group Journal* (1991), 25–35.

– et al., *Visions of Ruin, Architectural Fantasies and Designs for Garden Follies, with "Crude Hints Towards a History of My House" by John Soane*, The Soane Gallery (London, 1999).

Elsner, John, "A Collector's Model of Desire: The House and Museum of Sir John Soane," *The Cultures of Collecting*, ed. J. Elsner and R. Cardinal, (Cambridge, MA, 1994).

Engell, James, *The Creative Imagination: Enlightenment to Romanticism* (Cambridge, MA, 1981).

Epstein, James, *Radical Expression, Political Language, Ritual, and Symbol in England, 1790–1850* (Oxford, 1994).

Ernst, Wolfgang, *Historismus im Verzug* (Hagen, 1992).

Etlin, Richard A., *The Architecture of Death: The Transformation of the Cemetery in Eighteenth-Century Paris* (Cambridge, MA, 1984).

Evans, Robin, *The Fabrication of Virtue: English Prison Architecture 1750–1840* (Cambridge, 1982).

–, *Translations from Drawing to Building* (Cambridge, MA, 1997).

Everett, Nigel, *The Tory View of Landscape* (London, 1994).

Feaver, William, *The Art of John Martin* (Oxford, 1975).

Feinberg, Susan G., "The Genesis of Sir John Soane's Museum Idea: 1801–1810," *Journal of the Society of Architectural Historians*, 43 (October 1984), 225–37.

–, *Sir John Soane's Museum* (Ann Arbor, 1987).

Feldman, Burton, and Robert Richardson, *The Rise of Modern Mythology, 1660–1860* (Bloomington, 1972).

Fleming, John, *Robert Adam and His Circle* (London, 1962).

Fox, Celina, et al., *London, World City 1800–1840* (New Haven and London, 1992).

Furján, Helene, "The Specular Spectacle of the House of the Collector," *Assemblage*, 34 (1998), 56–91.

–, "Sir John Soane's Spectacular Theatre," *AA Files: Annals of the Architectural Association*, 47 (2002), 12–22.

Gage, John, ed., *Collected Correspondence of J. M. W. Turner* (Oxford, 1980).

Gallo, Luigi, "Pierre-Henri de Valenciennes et la tradition du paysage historique," *Imaginaire et création artistique à Paris sous l'ancien régime*, ed. Daniel Rabreau (Paris, 1998).

Garlick, K., A. Macintrye, and K. Cave, eds., *The Diary of Joseph Farington* (New Haven, 1978–84).

Gauss, Joachim, "Die Urhütte; uber ein Modell in der Baukunst und ein Motiv in der bildenen Kunst," *Wallraf-Richartz Jahrbuch*, 33 (1971), 2–48.

Godoli, Ezio, *Giuseppe Pistocchi (1744–1814), Architetto Giacobino* (Firenze, 1974).

Gombrich, E. H., *The Sense of Order* (Oxford, 1979).

Goodall, Ian, and Margaret Richardson, "A Recently Discovered Gandy Sketchbook," *Architectural History*, 44 (2001), 45–56.

–, and Simon Taylor, *Storrs Hall, Windermere, Cambria*, NBR Index No. 30550, NGR: SD 3926 9413, 2002.

Hamilton, James, *Turner and the Scientists*, The Clore Gallery (London, 1998).

Hamlin, Talbot, *Architecture Through the Ages* (New York, 1940).

–, *Benjamin Henry Latrobe* (New York, 1955).

Harbison, Robert, *The Built, the Unbuilt, and the Unbuildable* (Cambridge, MA, 1991).

Harding, Anthony John, *The Reception of Myth in English Romanticism* (Columbia, 1995).

Harris, John, "Le Geay, Piranesi and International Neo-Classicism in Rome, 1740–1750," *Essays in the History of Architecture Presented to Rudolf Wittkower*, ed. D. Fraser, H. Hibbard, and M. J. Lewine (London, 1967).

–, "Precedents and Various Designs Collected by C. H. Tatham," *In Search of Modern Architecture: A Tribute to Henry-Russell Hitchcock*, ed. Helen Searing (Cambridge, MA, 1982).

–, *Sir William Chambers* (London, 1970).

–, "Wizard Genius," *AA Files: Annals of the Architectural Association*, 4 (1983), 91.

Harrison, J. F. C., *The Second Coming, Popular Millenarianism 1780–1850* (New Brunswick, 1979).

Held, Jutta, *Monument und Volk, Vorrevolutionäre Wahrnehmung in Bildern des ausgehenden Ancien Régime* (Wien, 1990).

Hersey, George, *High Victorian Gothic: A Study in Associationism* (Baltimore, 1972).

–, *The Monumental Impulse: Architecture's Biological Roots* (Cambridge, MA, 1999).

Hitchcock, Henry-Russell, *Early Victorian Architecture in Britain* (New Haven, 1954).

Hussey, Christopher, "Ince Blundell Hall, Lancashire," *Country Life*, 123 (April 1958), 816–19.

–, *The Picturesque: Studies in a Point of View* (1927; London, 1967).

Hutchinson, Sidney C., "The Royal Academy Schools 1768–1830," *The Walpole Society*, 38 (1960–62), 132–91.

Hyde, Ralph, *Panoramania!* (London, 1988).

Images et imaginaires d'architecture, Centre Georges Pompidou (Paris, 1984).

Ison, Walter, *The Georgian Buildings of Bath* (Bath, 1969).

Jackson, Neil, *Nineteenth-Century Bath Architects and Architecture* (Bath, 1991).

Jacobs, Margaret C., *The Radical Enlightenment: Pantheists, Freemasons, and Republicans* (London, 1981).

Jenkins, Ian, "James Stephanoff and the British Museum," *Apollo*, 121 (March 1985), 174–81.

Jennings, Humphrey, *Pandaemonium, 1660–1886: The Coming of the Machine as Seen by Contemporary Observers* (New York, 1985).

Joseph Michael Gandy (1771–1843), Architectural Association (London, 1982).

Juden, Brian, *Traditions orphiques et tendances mystiques dans le romantisme français, 1800–1855* (Paris, 1971).

Junod, Philippe, "Future in the Past," *Oppositions*, 26 (Spring 1984), 43–63.

Kalman, Harold, *A History of Canadian Architecture* (Oxford, 1995).

Kaufmann, Emil, *Architecture in the Age of Reason* (1955; New York, 1968).

Kindler, Roger, "Periodical Criticism 1815–40: Originality in Architecture," *Architectural History*, 17 (1974).

Klonk, Charlotte, *Science and the Perception of Nature* (London and New Haven, 1996).

Knight, G. Wilson, *The Starlit Dome: Studies in the Poetry of Vision* (1941; London, 1968).

Knowlson, James, *Universal Language Schemes in England and France 1600–1800* (Toronto, 1975).

Koselleck, Reinhart, *Futures Past, on the Semantics of Historical Time*, trans. K. Tribe (1979; Cambridge, MA, 1985).

Lavin, Sylvia, *Quatremère de Quincy and the Invention of a Modern Language of Architecture* (Cambridge, MA, 1992).

Lever, Jill, and Margaret Richardson, *The Architect as Artist* (New York, 1984).

Levin, Thomas, "Walter Benjamin and the Theory of Art History," *October*, 47 (Winter 1988), 77–83.

Linfert, Carl, "Die Grundlagen der Architekturzeichnung," *Kunstwissenschaftliche Forschungen*, 1 (1931), 133–246.

Linstrum, Derek, *Sir Jeffry Wyatville, Architect to the King* (Oxford, 1972).

Lowenthal, David, *The Past Is a Foreign Country* (Cambridge, 1985).

Lowes, John Livingston, *The Road to Xanadu, a Study in the Ways of the Imagination* (1927; Princeton, 1986).

Lukacher, Brian, "Britton's Conquest: Creating an Antiquarian Nation, 1790–1860," *Landscapes of Retrospection. The Magoon Collection of British Drawings and Prints 1739–1860*, Lehman Loeb Art Center at Vassar College (Poughkeepsie, 1999).

–, "John Soane and his Draughtsman Joseph Michael Gandy," *Daidalos: Berlin Architectural Journal*, 25 (1987), 51–64.

–, "Joseph Gandy and the Mythography of Architecture," *Journal of Architectural Historians*, 53 (September 1994), 280–99.

–, "Joseph Michael Gandy and the Natural History of Architecture," *Daidalos: Berlin Architectural Journal*, 12 (June 1984), 79–89.

–, *Joseph Gandy in the Shadow of the Enlightenment* (The Annual Soane Lecture), Sir John Soane's Museum (London, 2002).

–, "Phantasmagoria and Emanations: Lighting Effects in the Architectural Fantasies of Joseph Michael Gandy," *AA Files: Annals of the Architectural Association*, 4 (1983), 40–48.

Maggi, Angelo, "Poetic Stones: Roslin Chapel in Gandy's Sketchbook and Daguerre's Diorama," *Architectural History*, 42 (1999), 263–83.

Manuel, Frank, *The Eighteenth Century Confronts the Gods* (Cambridge, MA 1959).

–, and Fritzie P. Manuel, *Utopian Thought in the Western World* (Cambridge, MA, 1979).

McCormick, Thomas J., *Charles-Louis Clérisseau and the Genesis of Neo-classicism* (Cambridge, MA, 1990).

Michel, Régis, et al., *La Chimère de Monsieur Desprez*, Réunion des Musées Nationaux (Paris, 1994).

Middleton, Robin, "The History of John Soane's 'Designs for Public and Private Buildings,'" *Burlington Magazine*, 138 (August 1996), 506–16.

–, et al., *The Mark J. Millard Architectural Collection: British Books* (Washington D.C., 1998).

–, and David Watkin, *Neoclassical and Nineteenth-Century Architecture* (New York, 1980).

Mitter, Partha, *Much Maligned Monsters: History of European Reactions to Indian Art* (Oxford, 1977).

Monckton, Norah, "Architectural Backgrounds in the Pictures of John Martin," *Architectural Review*, 104 (August 1948), 81–84.

Morus, Iwan Rhys, *Frankenstein's Children, Electricity, Exhibition, and Experiment in Early Nineteenth-Century London* (Princeton, 1998).

Moser, Stephanie, *Ancestral Images, The Iconography of Human Origins* (Ithaca, 1998).

Mowl, Timothy, *William Beckford* (London, 1998).

Myrone, M., and L. Peltz, eds., *Producing the Past: Aspects of Antiquarian Culture and Practice 1700–1850* (Aldershot, 1999).

Needham, Raymond, and Alexander Webster, *Somerset House—Past and Present* (New York, 1926).

Newman, Gerald, *The Rise of English Nationalism, A Cultural History 1740–1830* (New York, 1987).

Nicolson, Marjorie Hope, *Mountain Gloom and Mountain Glory: The Development of the Aesthetics of the Infinite* (Ithaca, 1959).

Oechslin, Werner, "Architecture and Nature: On the Origin and Convertibility of architecture," *Lotus International*, 31 (1981), 5–20.

–, "Die Bank of England und ihre Darstellung als Ruine," *Archithese*, 2 (March/April 1981), 19–25.

–, "Pyramide et Sphère, notes sur l'architecture révolutionnaire du XVIIIe siècle et ses sources italiennes," *Gazette des Beaux-Arts*, 77 (April 1971), 201–38.

Oettermann, Stephan, *The Panorama, History of a Mass Medium*, trans. D. L. Schneider (New York, 1997).

Omer, Mordechai, "Turner and the 'The Building of the Ark' from Raphael's Third Vault of the Loggia," *Burlington Magazine*, 117 (November 1975), 699–702.

Osborne, John, *John Cartwright* (Cambridge, 1972).

Parry III, Ellwood C., *The Art of Thomas Cole, Ambition and Imagination* (Newark and London, 1988).

Parry-Jones, William L., *The Trade in Lunacy, a Study of Private Madhouses in England* (London, 1972).

Pérez-Gómez, Alberto, and Louise Pelletier, *Architectural Representation and the Perspective Hinge* (Cambridge, MA, 1997).

Pérousse de Montclos, Jean-Marie, *Étienne-Louis Boullée (1728–1799), de l'architecture classique à l'architecture révolutionnaire* (Paris, 1969).

"The Phoenix Fire and Pelican Life Assurance Offices," *The Builder*, 108 (February 12, 1915), 150.

Piranesi et les français, 1740–1790, Académie de France, Rome (Rome, 1976).

Pointon, Marcia, *Milton and English Art* (Manchester, 1970).

Ponte, Alessandra, "Architecture and Phallocentrism in Richard Payne Knight's Theory," *Sexuality and Space*, ed. Beatriz Colomina (Princeton, 1992).

Porter, Roy, *The Making of Geology: Earth Science in Britain* (Cambridge, 1970).

–, *Mind-Forg'd Manacles: A History of Madness in England* (Cambridge MA, 1987).

du Prey, Pierre de la Ruffinière, *John Soane, The Making of an Architect* (Chicago, 1982).

–, *Sir John Soane*, Victoria and Albert Museum (London, 1985).

Priestman, Martin, *Romantic Atheism* (Cambridge, 1999).

Rabreau, Daniel, *Claude-Nicolas Ledoux, l'architecture et les fastes du temps* (Paris, 2000).

Radisich, Paula Rea, *Hubert Robert: Painted Spaces of the Enlightenment* (Cambridge, 1998).

Rappaport, Rhoda, *When Geologists Were Historians, 1665–1750* (Ithaca, 1997).

Reudenbach, Bruno, *G. B. Piranesi, Architektur als Bild* (Munich, 1979).

Richardson, Margaret, "The Image of Construction," *Buildings in Progress: Soane's Views of Construction*, The Soane Gallery (London, 1995).

–, "Model Architecture," *Country Life* (September 21, 1989), 224–27.

–, and MaryAnne Stevens, eds., *John Soane, Architect*, Royal Academy of Arts (London, 1999).

Robinson, John Martin, *Georgian Model Farms: A Study of Decorative and Model Farm Buildings in the Age of Improvement, 1700–1846* (Oxford, 1983).

–, *The Wyatts: An Architectural Dynasty* (Oxford, 1979).

Rosenau, Helen, *Social Purpose in Architecture: Paris and London Compared, 1760–1800* (London, 1975).

Rosenfeld, Sybil, *Georgian Scene Painters and Scene Painting* (Cambridge, 1981).

Rosenblum, Robert, *Transformations in Late Eighteenth-Century Art* (Princeton, 1967).

Rossi, Paolo, *The Dark Abyss of Time, the History of the Earth and the History of Nations from Hooke to Vico* (Chicago, 1984).

–, *Logic and the Art of Memory, the Quest for a Universal Language* (Chicago, 2000).

Rosslyn, Helen, and Angelo Maggi, *Rosslyn, Country of Painter and Poet*, National Gallery of Scotland (Edinburgh, 2002).

Rowe, Colin, "Character and Composition; or Some Vicissitudes of Architectural Vocabulary in the Nineteenth Century," *The Mathematics* of the Ideal Villa & Other Essays (Cambridge, MA, 1976).

Rudwick, M. J. S., *Scenes from Deep Time* (Chicago, 1992).

Rupke, Nicolaas A., *The Great Chain of History, William Buckland and the English School of Geology (1814–1849)* (Oxford, 1983).

Rykwert, Joseph, *On Adam's House in Paradise: The Idea of the Primitive Hut in Architectural History* (New York, 1972).

–, *The First Moderns: Architects of the Eighteenth Century* (Cambridge, MA, 1980).

Salmon, Frank, *Building on Ruins: The Rediscovery of Rome and English Architecture* (Aldershot, 2000).

–, "GANDY, Joseph Michael," *A Dictionary of British and Irish Travelers in Italy 1701–1800*, ed. John Ingamells (London and New Haven, 1997), 387–89.

–, "Perspectival Restoration Drawings in Roman Archaeology and Architectural History," *The Antiquaries Journal*, 83 (2003), 397–424.

–, "An Unaccountable Enemy: Joseph Michael Gandy and the Accademia di San Luca in Rome," *The Georgian Group Journal*, 11 (1995), 25–36.

Samuel, Raphael, ed., *Patriotism: The Making and Unmaking of British National Identity* (London, 1989).

Savage, Nicholas, "Exhibiting Architecture: Strategies of Representation in English Architectural Exhibition Drawings, 1760–1836," *Art on the Line. The Royal Academy Exhibitions at Somerset House 1780–1836*, ed. David Solkin (London and New Haven, 2001).

Sawyer, Sean, "'The Baseless Fabric of a Vision': Civic Architecture and Pictorial Representation at Sir John Soane's Museum," *The Built Surface, Architecture and the Pictorial Arts from Antiquity to the Enlightenment*, ed. C. Anderson (Aldershot, 2002).

–, "Sir John Soane's Symbolic Westminster: The Apotheosis of George IV," *Architectural History*, 39 (1996), 54–76.

Schapiro, Meyer, "Architect's Utopia," *Partisan Review*, 4 (March 1938), 42–49.

Shaffer, E. S., *Kubla Khan and the Fall of Jerusalem: The Mythological School in Biblical Criticism and Secular Literature, 1780–1880* (Cambridge, 1975).

Sidlauskas, Susan, "Creating Immortality: Turner, Soane and the Great Chain of Being," *Art Journal*, 52 (Summer 1993), 59–65.

Sedlmayr, Hans, *Art in Crisis, the Lost Center* (1948; London and Chicago, 1958).

Seznec, Jean, ed., *Diderot Salons* (Oxford, 1967).

Shanes, Eric, "Dissent in Somerset House: Opposition to the Political Status-quo within the Royal Academy around 1800," *Turner Studies*, 10 (Winter 1990), 40–46.

Sheppard, F. H. W., ed., *Survey of London: Parish of St. Anne Soho* (London, 1966).

–, *Survey of London: Parish of St. James's Westminster* (London, 1960).

Simo, Melanie Louise, *Loudon and the Landscape* (London and New Haven, 1988).

Smiles, Sam, *The Image of Antiquity* (London and New Haven, 1994)

Smith, Greg, *The Emergence of the Professional Watercolourist* (Aldershot, 2002).

Stafford, Barbara Maria, *Symbol and Myth: Humbert de Superville's Essay on Absolute Signs in Art* (Cranbury, NJ, 1979).

–, *Voyage into Substance: Art, Science, Nature, and the Illustrated Travel Account, 1760–1840* (Cambridge, MA, 1984).

Starobinski, Jean, *The Invention of Liberty* (Geneva, 1964).

Stillman, Damie, "British Architects and Italian Architectural Competitions, 1758–1780," *Journal of Society of Architectural Historians*, 32 (March 1973), 43–66.

–, "Death Defied and Honor Upheld: The Mausoleum in Neo-Classical England," *Art Quarterly*, n.s., 1 (Summer 1978), 175–213.

–, "The Pantheon Redecorated: Neoclassical Variations on an Antique Spatial and Decorative Theme," *VIA*, 3 (1977), 83–97.

–, *English Neo-classical Architecture* (London, 1988).

Summerson, John, *Architecture in Britain, 1530 to 1830* (1953; Harmondsworth, Middlesex, 1963).

–, "Gandy and the Tomb of Merlin," *Architectural Review*, 89 (April 1941), 89–90.

–, *Georgian London* (Harmondsworth, Middlesex, 1962).

–, "J. M. Gandy: Architectural Draughtsman," *Image*, 1 (Summer 1949), 40–50.

–, "John Soane and the Furniture of Death," *Architectural Review*, 163 (March 1978), 147–55.

–, *The Life and Work of John Nash, Architect* (Cambridge, MA, 1980).

–, *A New Description of Sir John Soane's Museum*, 9th ed. (London, 1991).

–, *Sir John Soane* (London, 1952).

–, "Sir John Soane, Architecture of the Mind," *The Times*, January 20, 1937, 17.

–, "The Strange Case of J. M. Gandy," *Architect and Building News*, 145 (January 1936), 38–44.

–, *The Unromantic Castle and Other Essays* (London, 1990).

–, "The Vision of J. M. Gandy," *Heavenly Mansions and Other Essays in Architecture* (1949; New York, 1963).

Surtees, Virginia, ed., *The Diaries of George Price Boyce* (Norfolk, 1980).

Szambien, Werner, *Le Musée d'architecture* (Paris, 1988),

Tafuri, Manfredo, *Architecture and Utopia* (Cambridge, MA, 1976).

–, *The Sphere and the Labyrinth: Avant-Gardes and Architecture from Piranesi to the 1970s*, trans. Pellegrino d'Acierno and Rovert Connoly (Cambridge, MA, 1987).

Tait, A. A., *Robert Adam, Drawings and Imagination* (Cambridge, 1993).

Teyssot, Georges, "Cottages et pittoresque," *Architecture, mouvement, continuité*, 34 (July 1974), 26–37.

–, "John Soane and the Birth of Style," *Oppositions*, 14 (Fall 1978), 61–83.

Thom, Martin, *Republics, Nations, and Tribes* (London, 1995).

Thompson, E. P., *The Making of the English Working Class* (1963; New York, 1966).

Todd, Ruthven, *Tracks in the Snow: Studies in English Art and Science* (London, 1946).

Tselos, Dimitris, "Joseph Gandy: Prophet of Modern Architecture," *Magazine of Art*, 34 (May 1941), 251–53, 280–81.

Vesely, Dalibor, "Architecture and the Conflict of Representation," *AA Files: Annals of the Architectural Association*, 8 (1985), 21–38.

Vidler, Anthony, *Claude-Nicolas Ledoux: Architecture and Social Reform at the End of the Ancien Régime* (Cambridge, MA, 1990).

–, "Style and Type in Romantic Historiography," *Perspecta*, 22 (1986), 136–41.

–, *The Writing of the Walls* (Princeton, 1987).

Wainwright, Clive, *George Bullock, Cabinet-Maker* (London, 1988).

Waterfield, Giles, ed., *Soane and Death, Dulwich Picture Gallery* (Dulwich, 1996).

Watkin, David, "Freemasonry and John Soane," *Journal of the Society of Architectural Historians*, 54 (December 1995), 402–17.

–, *The Life and Work of C. R. Cockerell* (London, 1974).

–, *Sir John Soane, Enlightenment Thought and the Royal Academy Lectures* (Cambridge, 1996).

–, *The Rise of Architectural History* (Chicago, 1980).

–, *Thomas Hope and the Neo-Classical Idea* (London, 1968).

Wescher, Paul, *Kunstraub unter Napoleon* (Berlin, 1976).

Wiebenson, Dora, "Documents of Social Change: Publications about the Small House," *Studies in Eighteenth-Century British Art and Aesthetics*, ed. Ralph Cohen (Berkeley, 1985).

–, "'L'Architecture Terrible'" and the 'Jardin Anglo-Chinois,'" *Journal of Society of Architectural Historians*, 27 (March 1968), 136–39.

Williamson, George, *The Life and Work of Ozics Humphry* (London, 1918).

Wilton-Ely, John, *The Mind and Art of Giovanni Battista Piranesi* (London, 1978).

–, ed., *Piranesi: The Polemical Works* (Farnborough, 1972).

Wollin, Nils G., *Desprez en Italie* (Malmö, 1935).

–, *Desprez en Suède* (Stockholm, 1939).

Woodward, Christopher, *In Ruins* (London and New York, 2001).

Worsley, Giles, *Architectural Drawings of the Regency Period, 1790–1837* (London, 1991).

Yarrington, Alison, *The Commemoration of the Hero 1800–1864, Monuments to the British Victors of the Napoleonic Wars* (New York, 1988).

List of Illustrations

Frontispiece: Joseph Gandy, *Bridge over Chaos*, 1833 (detail). Pencil, pen, ink, and watercolor on paper. Private Collection

1. Joseph Gandy, *A Trophy and Temple, Leading to a Sepulchral Cavern*, 1821. Pen, ink, and watercolor on paper, 47.5 x 37.5 (18 3/4 x 14 3/4). Royal Institute of British Architects, London

2. Henry William Pickersgill, *Portrait of Joseph Gandy*, 1822. Pencil on paper, 21.3 x 17.8 (8 3/8 x 7). National Portrait Gallery, London

3. Joseph Gandy, *Design in Perspective of Part of the Inside of a Museum*, 1793. Pen, ink, watercolor and body color on paper, 38.5 x 50.5 (15 1/4 x 19 1/2). British Museum, London

4. Joseph Gandy, *Design in perspective of part of the inside of a museum*, 1793 (detail). Pen, ink, watercolor and body color on paper, 38.5 x 50.5 (15 1/4 x 19 1/2). British Museum, London

5. George Dance II, *Portrait of James Wyatt*, 1795. Pencil on paper. The Royal Academy of Arts, London

6. Joseph Gandy, *Roman Capriccio*, ca. 1794–95. Pencil, pen, ink, and sepia on paper, 45.7 x 59.7 (18 x 23 1/2). Collection of Walter Chatham, New York. Photo Brian Lukacher

7. Joseph Gandy, *Design for a Church*. Pen, ink, and sepia on paper, 69.5 x 55 (27 3/8 x 21 5/8). Collezione Marsilio Papafava dei Carraresi, Padua

8. Joseph Gandy, *Ceiling of the Arch of the Silversmiths*, 1796. Pen, ink, and brown wash on paper, 39 x 55 (15 3/8 x 21 5/8). Royal Institute of British Architects, London

9. Joseph Gandy, *Entablature of the Temple of Jupiter Tonans*, 1796. Pencil, pen, ink, brown and gray wash on paper, 59 x 45.5 (23 1/4 x 17 7/8). Royal Institute of British Architects, London

10. Joseph Gandy, *Elevation of Sepulchral Chapel*, 1794–95. Pen, ink, and wash on paper, 55 x 90 (21 5/8 x 35 3/8). Accademia di San Luca, Rome

11. Joseph Gandy, *Section of Sepulchral Chapel*, 1794–95. Pen, ink, and wash on paper, 55 x 90 (21 5/8 x 35 3/8). Accademia di San Luca, Rome

12. Joseph Gandy, *Plan of Sepulchral Chapel*, 1794–95. Pen, ink, and wash on paper, 63 x 100 (24 3/4 x 39 3/8). Accademia di San Luca, Rome

13. Giovanni Battista Piranesi, Frontispiece etching of the Appian Way from Vol. II of *Antichità Romane* (1756)

14. Joseph Gandy, *Perspective of Sepulchral Chapel and Courtyard*, 1794–95. Oil and wash on paper, 60 x 100 (23 5/8 x 39 3/8). Accademia di San Luca, Rome

15. Brocklesby Mausoleum, Lincolnshire. © Country Life. Photo John Harris

16. Giorgio Duran, *Elevation and Section of Sepulchral Chapel*, 1793–95. Pen, ink, and wash on paper, 60 x 100 (23 5/8 x 39 3/8). Accademia di San Luca, Rome

17. Giovanni Campana, *Perspective of Sepulchral Chapel*, 1793–95. Pen, ink and wash on paper, 60 x 100 (23 5/8 x 39 3/8). Accademia di San Luca, Rome

18. Joseph Gandy, *Two Plans and Elevations for a Neoclassical Triumphal Arch* (Project submitted for entry to Academia di San Luca, Rome), May 27, 1795. Graphite, pen, ink, brush, and gray wash on paper, 47.5 x 31.8 (18 3/4 x 12 1/2). Cooper-Hewitt, National Design Museum, Smithsonian Institution, Washington, D.C. Museum purchase through gift of various donors, 1901-39-271. Photo Matt Flynn

19. George Augustus Wallis, *Landscape near Rome*, 1794. Oil on canvas, 115.5 x 176.8 (45 1/2 x 69 5/8). National Museums Liverpool (The Walker)

20. Joseph Gandy, *View of San Fiorenza, Corsica*, #92 in Westmacott Volume, 1794. Pencil and watercolor on paper, 11 x 18.2 (4 3/8 x 7 1/8). By courtesy of the Trustees of Sir John Soane's Museum, London

21. Joseph Gandy, *Abruzzi Landscape*, 1795. Pencil, pen, ink, and wash on paper, 22.1 x 30.8 (8 3/4 x 12 1/8). Private Collection

22. Joseph Gandy, *Abruzzi Landscape*, 1795. Pencil, pen, ink, and wash on paper, 22.3 x 33 (8 3/4 x 13). Private Collection

23. Joseph Gandy, *Italianate Landscape with Castel di Sangro*, 1795–96. Pen, ink, and watercolor on paper, 34.8 x 60.7 (13 3/4 x 23 7/8). Private Collection

24. Francesco Panini, *Il Prospetto Del St. Angiolo*, ca. 1780. Color etching, 19.5 x 81 (7 5/8 x 31 7/8). Research Library, The Getty Research Institute, Los Angeles

25. Louis Gauffier, *Sir Godfrey Webster Bt.*, 1794. Oil on canvas, 69 x 52 (27 x 20). Battle Abbey, Hastings. © English Heritage Photo Library

26. Joseph Gandy, *Gothic Monument for Battle Abbey*, 1796. Pencil, pen, ink, and wash on paper, 61.5 x 36 (24 1/4 x 14 1/8). Private Collection, New York

27. Joseph Gandy, *Sepulchral Chamber*, 1800. Pen, ink, and watercolor on paper, 70.6 x 106.7 (27 3/4 x 42). Canadian Centre for Architecture, Montreal

28. Joseph Gandy, *Sepulchral Chamber*, 1800 (detail). Pen, ink, and watercolor on paper, 70.6 x 106.7 (27 3/4 x 42). Canadian Centre for Architecture, Montreal

29. Joseph Gandy, *Design for a Cenotaph*, 1804. Pen, ink and watercolor on paper, 75 x 130 (29 1/2 x 51 1/8). Private Collection, London

30. E. Aiken and G. Dawe after Thomas Hope, *Doric Picture Gallery*, outline engraving in Thomas Hope, *Household Furniture and Interior Decoration* (1807)

31. John Porter after Joseph Gandy, *Design for a Temple and Bridge in a Nobleman's Park*, 1807. Engraving, 25.4 x 20.3 (10 x 8). Yale Center for British Art, Paul Mellon Collection

32. John Baber, *Design for Interior of Cemetery*, 1809. Pen, ink, and wash on paper, 90.8 x 58.4 (35 3/4 x 23). Harry Ransom Humanities Research Center Art Collection, University of Texas at Austin

33. Louis-Jean Desprez, *The Tomb of Agamemnon* (set design for the opera *Electre* by François Guillard, 1787). Engraving, 25.4 x 32.5 (10 x 12 3/4). Institut Tessin, Paris. © Photo RMN/Hervé Lewandowski

34. John Soane (rendered by Gandy), *Design for a Mausoleum*, 1800. Pencil, pen, ink, and watercolor on paper, 63.6 x 97.3 (25 x 38 1/4). By courtesy of the Trustees of Sir John Soane's Museum, London

35. John Soane (rendered by Gandy), *Tyringham Gate Lodge in a Storm*, 1798–1800. Pen, ink, and watercolor on paper, 52 x 87 (20 1/2 x 34 1/4). V&A Picture Library

36. John Soane (rendered by Gandy), *Design for Sepulchral Church at Tyringham*, 1796 (detail). Pen, ink, and watercolor on paper, 88.4 x 122 (34 3/4 x 48). By courtesy of the Trustees of Sir John Soane's Museum, London

37. John Soane (rendered by Gandy), *Design for Sepulchral Church at Tyringham*, 1796. Pen, ink, and watercolor on paper, 88.4 x 122 (34 3/4 x 48). By courtesy of the Trustees of Sir John Soane's Museum, London

38. Joseph Gandy, *Design for a Temple (Preliminary Sketch for the Hieronauticon)*, ca. 1800–05. Pencil, pen, and wash on paper, 15 x 24 (5 7/8 x 9 1/2). Canadian Centre for Architecture, Montreal

39. James Gillray, *Design for the Naval Pillar*, 1800. Hand-colored etching, engraving, and aquatint, 54.6 x 30.6 (21 1/2 x 12). British Museum, London

40. Joseph Gandy, *Sepulchral Monument*, ca. 1820–25. Pencil, pen, ink and sepia on paper, 16.5 x 23.5 (6 1/2 x 9 1/4). Brian Lukacher's Collection

41. James Malton, *An Essay on British Cottage Architecture, Being an Attempt to Perpetuate, on Principle...* (1798), Plate No. 4. Aquatint, 14.4 x 22.2 (5 5/8 x 8 3/4). Yale Center for British Art, Paul Mellon Collection, New Haven

42. C. Rosenberg after Joseph Gandy, *A Double Cottage with Places for Poultry or Pigs Behind...*, Plate No. XXIX from *Designs for Cottages, Cottage Farms, and Other Rural Buildings...* (1805). Aquatint, 12.8 x 13.1 (5 x 5 1/8). Yale Center for British Art, Paul Mellon Collection, New Haven

43. C. Rosenberg after Joseph Gandy, *A Shepherd's Cottage, and Conveniences...*, Plate No. XV from *Designs for Cottages, Cottage Farms, and Other Rural Buildings...* (1805). Aquatint, 15.4 x 19.7 (6 1/8 x 7 3/4). Yale Center for British Art, Paul Mellon Collection, New Haven

44. C. Rosenberg after Joseph Gandy, *Plan for a Bath*, Plate No. VII from *The Rural Architect: Consisting of Various Designs of Country Buildings...* (1805). Aquatint, 17.4 x 20.5 (6 7/8 x 8 1/8). Yale Center for British Art, Paul Mellon Collection, New Haven

45. C. Rosenberg after Joseph Gandy, *A Labourer's Cottage, Who Keeps Poultry and Pigs for Sale*, Plate No. III from *Designs for Cottages, Cottage Farms, and Other Rural Buildings...* (1805). Aquatint, 10 x 19.1 (3 7/8 x 7 1/2). Yale Center for British Art, Paul Mellon Collection, New Haven

46. S. Alken after Joseph Gandy, *Entrance Gate and Double Lodge*, Plate No. XXXIX from *The Rural Architect: Consisting of Various Designs of Country Buildings...* (1805). Aquatint, 16 x 21.2 (6 2/8 x 8 3/8). Yale Center for British Art, Paul Mellon Collection, New Haven

47. J. W. Harding after Joseph Gandy, *A Dairy Farm*, Plate No. XXVII from *The Rural Architect: Consisting of Various Designs of Country Buildings...* (1805). Aquatint, 18.8 x 20.6 (7 3/8 x 8 1/8). Yale Center for British Art, Paul Mellon Collection, New Haven

48. C. Rosenberg after Joseph Gandy, *A Cottage with Conveniences for Keeping Poultry, Pigs, and Pigeons: The Pigeon-house Has Access to It from the Bedroom*, Plate No. XIX from *Designs for Cottages, Cottage Farms, and Other Rural Buildings...* (1805). Aquatint, 14.4 x 19.7 (5 5/8 x 7 3/4). Yale Center for British Art, Paul Mellon Collection, New Haven

49. Joseph Gandy, *Elevation of Farm Buildings*, ca. 1795–97. Pencil, pen, ink, and sepia on paper, 20.4 x 39.3 (8 x 15 1/2). Yale Center for British Art, Paul Mellon Collection, New Haven

50. Joseph Gandy, *Italian Landscape*, ca. 1795–97 (detail). Pen, ink, and watercolor on paper, 32.2 x 48.8 (12 5/8 x 19 1/4). Private Collection

51. C. Rosenberg after Joseph Gandy, *A Rural Institute*, Plate No. XXXVI from *The Rural Architect: Consisting of Various Designs of Country Buildings...* (1805). Aquatint, 23.7 x 15.4 (9 3/8 x 6 1/8). Yale Center for British Art, Paul Mellon Collection, New Haven

52. C. Rosenberg after Joseph Gandy, *These Cottages Are Supposed to Be Situated near a Wood...*, Plate No. XXXV from *Designs for Cottages, Cottage Farms, and Other Rural Buildings...* (1805). Aquatint, 20.9 x 19.6 (8 1/4 x 7 3/4). Yale Centre for British Art, Paul Mellon Collection, New Haven

53. C.-N. Ledoux, Elevation from Plate 30 of *L'Architecture considérée sous le rapport de l'art, des moeurs et de la législation* (1804). Engraving, 9.7 x 8 (3 7/8 x 3 1/8). By courtesy of the Trustees of Sir John Soane's Museum, London

54. Joseph Gandy, *A Sketch of the Arms of Sir John Swinburne Bart. and Part of the Phoenix Office, Charing Cross*, ca. 1805. Pencil, pen, ink, and watercolor on paper, 31.1 x 18.4 (12 1/4 x 7 1/4). Private Collection

55. Charing Cross elevation of the Phoenix Fire and Life Insurance Co., London. Built 1805, demolished 1924

56. Spring Gardens elevation of the Phoenix Fire and Life Insurance Co., London. Built 1805, demolished 1924

57. Cavendish Place elevation of Doric House, Bath, 1803–06. Architectural Association, London. Photo Des Hill

58. Egyptian Revival Mantle in the Picture Gallery at Doric House, Bath. Architectural Association, London. Photo Des Hill

59. Side and rear elevations of Doric House, Bath, 1803–06. Architectural Association, London. Photo Des Hill

60. Joseph Gandy, *A Boat-House for Sir J. Legard, Bart., on the Lake Windermere*, 1804. Pen, ink, and watercolor on paper, 68 x 106 (26 3/4 x 41 3/4). Private Collection

61. T. Harwood after J. Tombleson, *View of Storrs, Windermere Lake*, from W. H. Pyne, *Lancashire Illustrated* (1831). Engraving, 10.2 x 15.9 (4 x 6 1/4)

62. John Buckler, *Northwest View of Storrs*, 1814. Pen, ink, and watercolor on paper. Private Collection

63. Garden elevation of Storrs. Architectural Association, London. Photo Des Hill

64. Interior rotunda of Storrs. © Crown copyright. NMR, Swindon

65. Joseph Gandy, *Storrs Sketchbook*, sheets of proposed summerhouse and Druid temple, 1806. Pencil, pen, and ink, 10.4 x 22.6 (4 1/8 x 8 7/8). By courtesy of the Trustees of Sir John Soane's Museum, London

66. Joseph Gandy, *Storrs Sketchbook*, sheets of proposed summerhouse and Druid temple, 1806. Pencil, pen and ink, 10.4 x 2.26 (4 1/8 x 8 7/8). By courtesy of the Trustees of Sir John Soane's Museum, London

67. Joseph Gandy, *Design for a New Senate House at Quebec*, 1811. Pen, ink, and watercolor on paper, 30.1 x 72.7 (11 7/8 x 28 5/8). Library and Archives Canada/NMC-4924, Ottawa

68. Joseph Gandy, *Imaginary Architectural Design Based on Storrs Hall*, ca. 1810–15. Watercolor, pencil, and ink on paper, 26.7 x 36.8 (10 1/2 x 14 1/2). Private Collection

69. John Soane Junior, *Design for a Public Bath*, 1811. Pen, ink and watercolor on paper, 58.3 x 80 (23 x 31 1/2). By courtesy of the Trustees of Sir John Soane's Museum, London

70. Joseph Gandy, *Interior of a New Ball and Assembly-room Surrounded by a Promenade, Designed for the Town of Liverpool*, 1810. Pencil, pen, ink, and watercolor on paper, 59 x 78 (23 1/4 x 30 3/4). By courtesy of the Trustees of Sir John Soane's Museum, London

71. Oblique view of the Screen designed by Joseph Gandy, viewed from the south west, Interior Shire Hall, Lancaster Crown Court and Shire Hall, Castle Park, Lancaster. © English Heritage. NMR, Swindon. Photo Roger Thomas

72. J. Burnett after Joseph Gandy, *Rosslyn Chapel, Interior View*, Plate VII from Britton's *Architectural Antiquities* (1812). Engraving, 15 x 21.2 (5 7/8 x 8 3/8). Vassar College Library, Poughkeepsie

73. W. Woolnoth after Joseph Gandy, *Rosslyn Chapel, View of Buttresses and Pinnacles*, Plate VIII from Britton's *Architectural Antiquities* (1812). Engraving, 20 x 14.9 (7 7/8 x 5 7/8). Vassar College Library, Poughkeepsie

74. J. Burnett after Joseph Gandy, *Rosslyn Chapel, Elevation of Part of the South side*, Plate VI from Britton's *Architectural Antiquities* (1812). Engraving, 20.2 x 14.7 (8 x 5 3/4). Vassar College Library, Poughkeepsie

75. Joseph Gandy, *View of Bishop Bronscombe's Monument, Exeter Cathedral*, 1825, for John Britton's *Cathedral Antiquities of Great Britain, Exeter* (1826). Watercolor and pencil on paper, 15.2 x 21.6 (6 x 8 1/2). Special Collections, Vassar College Library, Poughkeepsie

76. Joseph Gandy, *East End of South Aisle of Choir at Exeter Cathedral*, 1825, for John Britton's *Cathedral Antiquities* (1826). Watercolor and pencil on paper, 21.6 x 15.2 (8 x 6). Special Collections, Vassar College Library, Poughkeepsie

77. J. Le Keux after F. Mackenzie, *Lullington Church, North Doorway*, frontispiece to John Britton's *Architectural Antiquities* (1812). Engraving, 15 x 20 (5 7/8 x 7 7/8). Vassar College Library, Poughkeepsie

78. Joseph Gandy, *Calling Card*, ca. 1815. Engraving, 3.8 x 7.6 (1 1/2 x 3). Brian Lukacher's Collection

79. J. Le Keux after Joseph Gandy, *Design for a National Institution of the Fine Arts*, frontispiece to John Britton's *The Fine Arts of the British School* (1812). Engraving, 22.9 x 24.8 (9 x 9 3/4). Vassar College Library, Poughkeepsie

80. Entrance façade of Bolton Hall, Bolton by Bowland, Lancashire. Photo James Darwin

81. Joseph Gandy, *Pevensey Castle, entrance*, 1816. Pencil, pen, ink, and watercolor on paper, 15.4 x 21.3 (6 1/16 x 8 3/8). Frances Lehman Loeb Art Center at Vassar College, Poughkeepsie

82. Joseph Gandy, *Pevensey Castle, Gateway Tower*, 1816. Pencil, pen, ink, and watercolor on paper, 14.9 x 20.2 (5 7/8 x 7 1/8). Frances Lehman Loeb Art Center at Vassar College, Poughkeepsie

83. Joseph Gandy, *Richborough Castle*, 1825. Pencil, pen, ink, and watercolor on paper, 15.2 x 21.9 (6 x 8 5/8). Frances Lehman Loeb Art Center at Vassar College, Poughkeepsie

84. T. H. Fielding after Joseph Gandy, *Conway Castle*, Plate No. 29 from Thomas Compton, *Northern Cambrian Mountains; or a Tour Through North Wales...* (1820). Colored aquatint, 15.3 x 23.9 (6 x 9 3/8). Yale Center for British Art, Paul Mellon Collection, New Haven

85. Joseph Gandy, *Epsom*, 1822. Watercolor, gouache, and pencil on paper, 13.7 x 19.7 (5 3/8 x 7 3/4). Richard Feigen Ltd.

86. Joseph Gandy, *Leith Hill, Dorking*, 1822. Watercolor, gouache, and pencil on paper, 14.3 x 19.4 (5 5/8 x 7 5/8). Richard Feigen Ltd.

87. Joseph Gandy, *Brighton*, 1822. Watercolor and pencil on paper, 11.4 x 17.8 (4 1/2 x 7). Richard Feigen Ltd.

88. Joseph Gandy, *View of London from Peckham Rye*, 1822. Watercolor and pencil on paper, 11.4 x 18.4 (4 1/2 x 7 1/4). Richard Feigen Ltd.

89. Joseph Gandy, *Purfleet*, from Westmacott Volume in Soane Museum, 163, no. 29, 1821. Pencil and watercolor on paper, 11 x 18.2 (4 3/8 x 7 1/8). By courtesy of the Trustees of Sir John Soane's Museum, London

90. Joseph Gandy, *Coalbrookedale*, from Westmacott Volume in Soane Museum, 163, no. 54, 1821. Pencil and watercolor on paper, 11 x 18.2 (4 3/8 x 7 1/8). By courtesy of the Trustees of Sir John Soane's Museum, London

91. Joseph Gandy, *Moon with Nimbus*, from Westmacott Volume in Soane Museum, 163, no. 68, 1821. Pencil and watercolor on paper, 10.7 x 17.2 (4 1/4 x 6 3/4). By courtesy of the Trustees of Sir John Soane's Museum, London

92. Joseph Gandy, *Enclosed Commons at Milton*, from Westmacott Volume in Soane Museum, 163, no. 39, 1821. Pencil and watercolor on paper, 10 x 21.5 (3 7/8 x 8 1/2). By courtesy of the Trustees of Sir John Soane's Museum, London

93. J. M. W. Turner, *Interior of Brocklesby Mausoleum*, Lecture Diagram 76, ca. 1810 (detail). Pencil and watercolor on paper, support: 64 x 49 (25 1/4 x 19 1/4), TB CXCV 130, D17101. Photo Tate, London 2005

94. J. M. W. Turner, *Interior of a Prison*, Lecture Diagram 65, ca. 1810. Gouache, watercolor, pencil, and pen on paper, 19 x 27 (7 1/2 x 10 5/8), TB CXCV 120, D17090. Tate Britain, London

95. Joseph Gandy, *The Oracle of Mercury, a Hermes in the Market-place of Patrae*, 1815. Pen, ink, and watercolor on paper. Private Collection

96. Joseph Gandy, *The Oracle of Mercury, a Hermes in the Market-place of Patrae*, 1815 (detail). Pen, ink, and watercolor on paper. Private Collection

97. George Hadfield, *Imaginary Reconstruction of the Flavion Amphitheatre*, ca. 1790–94. Pen, ink, and watercolor on paper, 46.4 x 63.5 (18 1/4 x 25). Harry Ransom Humanities Research Center Art Collection, University of Texas, Austin

98. Jeffry Wyatville, *Imaginary Architectural Composition (sketch for The Palace of Alcinous)*, in Wyatville Scrapbook (198/C15), ca. 1797–99. Pen, ink, and watercolor on paper, 14.6 x 24.1 (5 3/4 x 9 1/2). British Museum, London

99. After Louis-Jean Desprez, *Temple of Isis, Pompeii*, 1785, from J.-C. de Saint Non, *Voyage pittoresque ... des royaumes de Naples et Sicile*, 1781–86. Etching and aquatint, 21.6 x 35.6 (8 1/2 x 14)

100. Joseph Gandy, *Architectural Composition, Agno*. 1813. Pen, ink, and watercolor on paper, 64.1 x 95.3 (25 1/4 x 37 1/2). Private Collection

101. Pierre Henri de Valenciennes, *Ancient City of Agrigentum*, exhibited 1787 (detail). Oil on canvas, 110 x 164 (43 1/4 x 64 5/8). Musée du Louvre, Paris. © Photo RMN/Jean Schormans

102. Joseph Gandy, *Temple of Minerva Chalinitis, Corinth*, ca. 1815–20. Pen, ink, and watercolor on paper, 42.3 x 63.1 (16 5/8 x 24 7/8). Private Collection

103. Joseph Gandy, *Landing Place to a Temple*, 1820. Ink, pen, and watercolor on paper, 73.5 x 129.5 (20 x 51). Canadian Centre for Architecture, Montreal

104. Joseph Gandy, *Idea of Titana from the Pira Grove*, 1820. Watercolor and pen on paper, 48.3 x 68.6 (19 x 27). Private Collection

LIST OF ILLUSTRATIONS 217

105. Joseph Gandy, *The Open Temple and Temple Tower of the Greeks, Designed from Various Remarks in Pausanias*, 1808. Pen, ink, and watercolor on paper, 73.5 x 129.5 (20 x 51). Canadian Centre for Architecture, Montreal

106. Joseph Gandy, *Idea of a Bridge and Palace amongst the Platxenses*, 1817. Pen, ink, and watercolor on paper, 59.5 x 93.5 (23 3/8 x 36 3/4). By courtesy of the Trustees of Sir John Soane's Museum, London

107. Joseph Gandy, *The Great Temple of Ceres, Eleusis*, 1818. Watercolor on paper, 74 x 129 (29 1/8 x 50 3/4). By courtesy of the Trustees of Sir John Soane's Museum

108. John Peter Gandy, *Mystic Temple of Ceres at Eleusis, in Attica*, 1817. Watercolor on paper, 11 x 16.5 (4 3/8 x 6 1/2). Research Library, The Getty Research Institute, Los Angeles

109. Joseph Gandy, *The Persian Porch and the Place of Consultation of the Lacedemonians*, 1816. Pen, ink, gouache, and watercolor on paper, 43.2 x 64.1 (17 x 25 1/4). Research Library, The Getty Research Institute, Los Angeles

110. Joseph Gandy, *Jupiter Pluvius*, 1819. Oil on canvas, 188 x 190.5 (74 x 75). Private Collection. Courtesy Ray Harryhausen

111. Joseph Gandy, *Landing-place to a Temple of Victory Through the Gate of Minerva*, 1821. Oil on canvas, 102 x 127 (40 x 50). Private Collection

112. Engraved illustration of Jupiter Pluvius from Bernard de Montfaucon's *Antiquity Explained, and Represented in Sculptures* (1721). British Library, London

113. T. Piroli after John Flaxman, Outline engraving of the Saturnian King of Crete from Dante's *The Divine Comedy* (designed 1793, published 1802)

114. Joseph Gandy, *Electra before the Palace of Aegisthus, Drawing of Stage set for Sophocles*, ca. 1820–30. Watercolor and ink on paper, 19.5 x 31.5 (7 5/8 x 12 3/8). Research Library, The Getty Research Institute, Los Angeles

115. Joseph Gandy, *Tomb in Ruins, Drawing for Stage set for Euripides*, ca. 1820–30. Watercolor and ink on paper, 19 x 31 (7 1/2 x 12 1/4). Research Library, The Getty Research Institute, Los Angeles

116. Joseph Gandy, *A Scene in Ancient Rome: A Setting for Titus Andronicus, I, ii*, ca. 1825–30. Watercolor and bodycolor with pen and brown ink over graphite on paper, 18.4 x 29.2 (7 1/4 x 11 1/2). Yale Center for British Art, Paul Mellon Collection, New Haven

117. Joseph Gandy, *Temple of Apollo, Delphi*, 1827. Pen, ink, and watercolor on paper. Private Collection

118. A. B. Clayton, *Design for a Temple Dedicated to Pericles*, 1825. Pen, ink, and watercolor on paper, 61 x 96 (24 x 37 3/4). Private Collection

119. A. B. Clayton, *Design for a Water Entrance to an Ancient City*, 1823. Pencil, pen, ink, and watercolor on paper, 36.8 x 53.3 (14 1/2 x 21). Private Collection

120. Joseph Gandy, *Temple of Furies, Oedipus at Colonus*, ca. 1825–27. Pen, ink, and watercolor on paper, 48.3 x 62.2 (19 x 24 1/2). Private Collection

121. George Maddox (formerly attributed to Joseph Gandy), *Part of Orchomenus, from Pausanias*, 1832. Pen, ink, watercolor, and gouache on paper, 31 x 45.6 (12 1/4 x 18). Nelson Atkins Museum, Kansas City

122. George Maddox, *Ruins of a Greek City in the Time of Pausanias*, 1827. Pen, ink, watercolor, and gouache, dimensions not known. Private Collection

123. Edward Burney, *A View of Philip James de Loutherbourg's "Eidophusikon,"* ca. 1782. Pen, ink, gray wash, and watercolor on paper, 21.2 x 29.2 (8 3/8 x 11 1/2). British Museum, London

124. L.-J. Desprez after Charles De Wailly, *Miltonic Theatre Design*, ca. 1775. Etching, 23.5 x 30 (9 1/4 x 11 3/4). Institut Tessin, Paris

125. Joseph Gandy, *Pandemonium, or Part of the High Capital of Satan and His Peers*. 1805. Pen, ink, and watercolor on paper, 71.4 x 123.4 (28 1/8 x 48 5/8). Private Collection

126. C.-N. Ledoux, *Cannon Foundry at Chaux*, Plate 125 from *L'Architecture* (1804). Engraving, 32.2 x 46.1 (12 5/8 x 18 1/8). By courtesy of the Trustees of Sir John Soane's Museum, London

127. Joseph Gandy, *Sketch for Pandemonium*, ca. 1804–05. Pencil, watercolor, and gouache on paper, 24 x 34.1 (9 1/2 x 13 1/2). Private Collection

128. Joseph Gandy, *The Mount of Congregation*, ca. 1818–30 (detail). Oil on canvas, 148.6 x 178.8 (58 1/2 x 70 3/8). By courtesy of the Trustees of Sir John Soane's Museum, London

129. Joseph Gandy, *The Mount of Congregation*, 1818. Pen, ink, and watercolor on paper, 71.1 x 129.5 (28 x 51). Private Collection

130. Joseph Gandy, landscape study for *The Mount of Congregation*, 1817–18. Watercolor and pencil on paper, 29 x 40.6 (11 3/8 x 16). Research Library, The Getty Research Institute, Los Angeles

131. L.-J. Desprez, *The Temple of Fortuna*, ca. 1785. Pencil, pen and ink, brown wash. 22.5 x 37.7 (8 7/8 x 14 7/8). National Museum, Stockholm. © Photo Rickard Karlsson

132. J. Grainger after T. West, *Breaking Open the Royal Sepulcher of King David*, from George Henry Maynard, *The Complete Works of Flavius Josephus* (1800). Engraving, 12 x 7 (4 3/4 x 2 3/4). Vassar College Library, Poughkeepsie

133. L.-J. Desprez, *Illumination of Cross at St. Peter's*, 1784. Etching with aquatint, 34.5 x 21.5 (13 5/8 x 8 1/2). British Museum, London

134. Joseph Gandy, *The Tomb of Merlin*, 1815. Pen, ink, and watercolor on paper, 76 x 132 (29 1/8 x 52). Royal Institute of British Architects, London

135. Joseph Gandy, *Sketch for "The Tomb of Merlin,"* ca. 1814–15. Pencil, pen, ink, and gray and brown wash on paper, 36 x 75 (14 1/8 x 29 1/2). Canadian Centre for Architecture, Montreal

136. Joseph Gandy, *Lamp Design*, ca. 1805–10. Pen, ink, and watercolor on paper. Private Collection

137. Girolamo Porro, engraved illustration of Merlin's Tomb from Harrington's *Orlando Furioso* (1591). Vassar College Library, Poughkeepsie

138. Joseph Gandy, *Nocturnal View of Temple of Concord in Green Park*, 1814. Plate 94 in Westmacott Volume. Pencil and watercolor on paper, 14.7 x 23.1 (5 6/8 x 9 1/8). By courtesy of the Trustees of Sir John Soane's Museum, London

139. Joseph Gandy, *Grave of Caithbat*, from *The tales of Ossian*, 1828. Pencil and watercolor on paper, 8 x 11.3 (3 1/8 x 4 1/2). Victoria and Albert Museum, London

140. Joseph Gandy, *Ghosts in Moonlight*, from *the tales of Ossian*, 1828. Pencil and watercolor on paper, 7.8 x 11.2 (3 1/8 x 4 3/8). Victoria and Albert Museum, London

141. Thomas Cole, *The Voyage of Life: Youth*, 1842. Oil on canvas, 134.3 x 194.9 (52 7/8 x 76 3/4). National Gallery of Art, Washington

142. Joseph Gandy, *The Staircase Leading to the Gates of Heaven*, 1832. Pen, ink, and watercolor on paper, 104.1 x 68.6 (41 x 27). Private Collection

143. W. Humphrys after J. M. W. Turner, title vignette for John Bunyan's *Pilgrim's Progress* (1836). Engraving, 16.5 x 10.2 (6 1/2 x 4). Brian Lukacher's Collection

144. Joseph Gandy, *Bridge over Chaos*, 1833. Pencil, pen, ink and watercolor on paper, 102.9 x 67.3 (40 1/2 x 26 1/2). Private Collection

145. T. Bensley after Thomas and William Daniell, *Part of the Interior of the Elephanta*, from *Antiquities of India* (1793–99). Aquatint. Photo Pauline Baines

146. Joseph Gandy, *Bridge over Chaos*, 1833 (detail). Pencil, pen, ink, and watercolor on paper, 102.9 x 67.3 (40 1/2 x 26 1/2). Private Collection

147. John Martin, *Courts of Heaven*, from *Paradise Lost*, 1826. Mezzotint, 19 x 26.9 (7 1/2 x 10 5/8). V&A Picture Library, London

148. John Martin, *Bridge over Chaos*, from *Paradise Lost*, 1826. Mezzotint, 19 x 26.9 (7 1/2 x 10 5/8). Victoria and Albert Museum, London

149. Joseph Gandy, *Tomb of Nitrocris*, ca. 1830. Pencil, pen, ink, and brown and gray wash on paper, 36.8 x 56.5 (14 1/2 x 22 1/4). Victoria and Albert Museum, London

150. John Soane (rendered by Gandy), *View of the Dome at Night*, 1811. Pen, ink, and watercolor on paper, 105.5 x 74.4 (41 1/2 x 29 1/4). By courtesy of the Trustees of Sir John Soane's Museum, London

151. John Soane (rendered by Gandy), *Library of Pitzhanger*, 1802. Pen and watercolor on paper, 69 x 129.5 (27 1/8 x 51). By courtesy of the Trustees of Sir John Soane's Museum, London

152. John Soane (rendered by Gandy), *Interior of Cricket Lodge*, 1803. Pencil, pen, ink and watercolor on paper, 67 x 110.7 (26 3/8 x 43 5/8). By courtesy of the Trustees of Sir John Soane's Museum, London

153. Daniel Maclise, *Portrait Caricature of John Soane*, 1834. Etching, 23.1 x 18 (9 1/8 x 7 1/8). By courtesy of the Trustees of Sir John Soane's Museum, London

154. Joseph Gandy, *A Preliminary Sketch of A Selection of ... Designs of John Soane*, vol. 60, folio V, p.103, 1818. Pencil, pen, and ink on paper, 23.8 x 36.7 (9 3/8 x 14 1/2). By courtesy of the Trustees of Sir John Soane's Museum, London

155. Joseph Gandy, *A Selection of Parts of Buildings, Public and Private, Erected from the Designs of John Soane*, 1818. Pencil, pen, ink, watercolor, and bodycolor on paper, 72.5 x 129.3 (28 1/2 x 50 7/8). By courtesy of the Trustees of Sir John Soane's Museum, London

156. John Soane (rendered by Gandy), *Architectural Visions of Early Fancy...*, 1820. Pencil, pen, ink, watercolor, and bodycolor on paper, 73.5 x 130.5 (28 7/8 x 51 3/8). By courtesy of the Trustees of Sir John Soane's Museum, London

157. John Soane (rendered by Gandy), *Bird's-Eye View of a Design for a Royal Residence*, 1821. Pen, ink, watercolor, and bodycolor on paper, 7.44 x 132 (29 1/4 x 52). By courtesy of the Trustees of Sir John Soane's Museum, London

158. After J. Gandy and F. Mackenzie, *Bird's-Eye View from the Staircase and the Upper Part of*

the Pavillion, in the Colosseum, Regents Park..., Plate No. 5 from *Graphic Illustrations of the Colosseum, Regents Park* (1829). Aquatint, 29.3 x 21.8 (11 1/2 x 8 5/8). Yale Center for British Art, Paul Mellon Collection, New Haven

159. John Soane (rendered by Gandy), *View in the Portico for a Royal Residence*, 1827. Pencil, pen, ink, and watercolor on paper, 74.8 x 131.3 (29 1/2 x 51 3/4). By courtesy of the Trustees of Sir John Soane's Museum, London

160. John Soane (rendered by Gandy), *Bird's-Eye View of a Design for a Royal Palace*, 1828. Pen, ink, and watercolor on paper, 72.5 x 129.5 (28 1/2 x 51). By courtesy of the Trustees of Sir John Soane's Museum, London

161. W. Wallis after A. C. Pugin, *The Entrance Front of Buckingham Palace, Designed by John Nash*, 1829. Engraving

162. Joseph Gandy, *A Proposed Town Residence for the Duke of Wellington to Commemorate the Battle of Waterloo*, 1816. Pen, ink, and watercolor on paper, 74 x 128.5 (29 1/8 x 50 5/8). Private Collection

163. Joseph Gandy, *Commemorative Monument*, ca. 1816–20. Pencil, pen, ink, and watercolor on paper, 49.5 x 33 (19 1/2 x 13). Harry Ransom Humanities Research Center Art Collection, University of Texas at Austin

164. Joseph Gandy, *A Geometrical Elevation of Part of One of the Fronts of an Idea for an Imperial Palace for the Sovereigns of the British Empire*, 1824. Pen, ink, and watercolor on paper, 76 x 132 (29 7/8 x 52). Royal Institute of British Architects, London

165. Joseph Gandy, *Perspective Sketch of a Trophal Entrance to Part of the Front of a Design for a Palace*, 1826. Pen, ink, and watercolor on paper, 76 x 134.5 (29 7/8 x 52). Royal Institute of British Architects, London

166. Joseph Gandy, *One of the Interior Courts of a Design for a Palace, Exhibited in 1824*, 1825. Pen, ink, and watercolor on paper, 76 x 134.5 (29 7/8 x 53). Royal Institute of British Architects, London

167. Joseph Gandy, *Perspective Sketch of a Chapel Viewed from the Basement Court, Part of a Design for a Palace*, 1827. Pen, ink, and watercolor on paper, 76 x 134.5 (29 7/8 x 53). Royal Institute of British Architects, London

168. John Soane (rendered by Gandy), *Design for a National Entrance into the Metropolis*, 1826. Pen, ink, and watercolor on paper, 93 x 150 (36 5/8 x 59). By courtesy of the Trustees of Sir John Soane's Museum, London

169. Joseph Gandy, *Sketch for New Senate Houses*, 1835. Pen, ink, watercolor, and bodycolor on paper, 67.5 x 101.5 (26 1/2 x 40). Royal Institute of British Architects, London

170. John Soane (rendered by Joseph Gandy), *View of the Dome of the Soane Museum*, 1811. Pen, ink, and watercolor on paper, 137 x 80 (53 7/8 x 31 1/2). By courtesy of the Trustees of Sir John Soane's Museum, London

171. John Soane (rendered by Gandy), *Interior of a Town House*, 1822. Watercolor on paper, 93 x 150 (36 5/8 x 59). By courtesy of the Trustees of Sir John Soane's Museum, London

172. John Soane (rendered by Gandy), *Multiple Views of the Soane Museum*, 1822 (detail). Pen, ink, and watercolor on paper, 75 x 132 (29 1/2 x 52). By courtesy of the Trustees of Sir John Soane's Museum, London

173. John Soane (rendered by Gandy), *Multiple Views of Soane Museum*, 1822 (detail). Pen, ink, and watercolor on paper, 75 x 132 (29 1/2 x 52). By courtesy of the Trustees of Sir John Soane's Museum, London

174. John Soane (rendered by Gandy), *View from Monk's Parlor*, vol. 82, Plate 67, 1825. Pencil and watercolor on paper, 33.2 x 20.7 (13 1/8 x 8 1/8). By courtesy of the Trustees of Sir John Soane's Museum, London

175. John Soane (rendered by Gandy), *A Bird's-Eye View of the Bank of England*, 1830. Pen and watercolor on paper, 84.5 x 140 (33 1/4 x 55 1/8). By courtesy of the Trustees of Sir John Soane's Museum, London

176. John Soane (rendered by Gandy), *Architectural Ruins—a Vision (Bank of England in Ruins)*, 1798–1832. Pen and watercolor on paper, 66 x 102 (26 x 40 1/8). By courtesy of the Trustees of Sir John Soane's Museum, London

177. John Soane (rendered by Gandy), *View of the Bank of England Rotunda as Built*, 1798 (detail). Pen and watercolor on paper, 63 x 69 (24 3/4 x 27 1/8). By courtesy of the Trustees of Sir John Soane's Museum, London

178. John Soane (rendered by Gandy), *Interior of the Edifice Devoted Exclusively to Freemasonry ... an Evening View*, 1832. Pen and watercolor on paper, 84 x 140 (33 1/8 x 55 1/8). By courtesy of the Trustees of Sir John Soane's Museum, London

179. Joseph Gandy, *Architectural Assemblage*, 69/4/18, 1821 (detail). Pen, ink, and gray washes on paper, 22.2 x 16.6 (8 3/4 x 6 1/2). By courtesy of the Trustees of Sir John Soane's Museum

180. Joseph Gandy, *Comparative Characteristics of Thirteen Selected Styles of architecture*, 1836. Pencil, pen, ink, and watercolor on paper, 120 x 83.4 (47 1/4 x 32 7/8). By courtesy of the Trustees of Sir John Soane's Museum, London

181. John Soane (rendered by E. Foxhall), *Architectural Pasticcio*, 1819. Pencil, pen, and ink on paper, 72 x 41 (28 3/8 x 16 1/8). By courtesy of the Trustees of Sir John Soane's Museum

182. Joseph Gandy, *Designs ... Illustrating Various Styles of Architecture Upon One Elevation (Greek Doric Elevation)*, 1825. Pencil, pen, ink, and watercolor on paper, 14 x 18.4 (5 1/2 x 7 1/4). Victoria and Albert Museum, London

183. Joseph Gandy, *Designs ... Illustrating Various Styles of Architecture Upon One Elevation (Persian Elevation)*, 1825. Pencil, pen, ink, and watercolor on paper, 14 x 18.4 (5 1/2 x 7 1/4). Victoria and Albert Museum, London

184. Joseph Gandy, *Architectural Assemblage*, 69/4/1, 1821. Pen, ink, and gray washes on paper, 15.1 x 20.8 (6 x 8 1/4). By courtesy of the Trustees of Sir John Soane's Museum, London

185. Joseph Gandy, *Architectural Assemblage*, 69/4/11, 1821. Pen, ink, and gray washes on paper, 22.2 x 16.4 (8 3/4 x 6 1/2). By courtesy of the Trustees of Sir John Soane's Museum, London

186. Joseph Gandy, *Comparative Architecture Continued, an Emblematic Sketch*, 1837. Pencil, pen, ink, and watercolor on paper, 46 x 62.6 (18 1/8 x 24 5/8). By courtesy of the Trustees of Sir John Soane's Museum, London

187. Joseph Gandy, *Still Life with Urns and Goblets*, 69/9/4, ca. 1837–37. Pencil, pen, ink, and watercolor on paper, 19 x 33.5 (7 1/2 x 13 3/4). By courtesy of the Trustees of Sir John Soane's Museum, London

188. *The Rise and Progress of Temple Architecture*, engraved illustration from G. S. Faber, *The Origin of Pagan Idolatry* (1816)

189. Joseph Gandy, *Landscape with Parhelion*, Westmacott Volume, pl. 70, upper watercolor, 11.7 x 18.4 (4 5/8 x 7 1/4). By courtesy of the Trustees of Sir John Soane's Museum, London

190. Plate VIII from Pierre d'Hancarville, *Recherches sur l'origine, l'espirit et les progrès des arts de la Grèce*, Volume III (1785)

191. Joseph Gandy, *Elevation of stepped pyramidal temple*. Pen and ink on paper, from *The Art, Philosophy, and Science of Architecture*. Royal Institute of British Architects, London

192. Joseph Gandy, *Diagram of self-consuming serpent*, inscribed *I am alpha and omega....* Pen and ink on paper, from *The Art, Philosophy, and Science of Architecture*. Royal Institute of British Architects, London

193. Joseph Gandy, *Heraldry Diagram*, from *The Art, Philosophy, and Science of Architecture*. Pen and ink on paper. Royal Institute of British Architects, London

194. Joseph Gandy, *Comparative Chart of Alphabets and Letters*. Pen and ink on paper, from *The Art, Philosophy, and Science of Architecture*. Royal Institute of British Architects, London

195. Joseph Gandy, *Signs of Human Knowledge*, inscribed *The moderns may use abbreviated marks as follows*. Pen and ink on paper, from *The Art, Philosophy, and Science of Architecture*. Royal Institute of British Architects, London

196. Joseph Gandy, *Architecture; Its Natural Model*, 1838. Pencil, pen, ink, and watercolor on paper, 105 x 142 (41 3/8 x 55 7/8). By courtesy of the Trustees of Sir John Soane's Museum, London

197. *Premiers débuts du génie en géneral*, outline engraving from Jean Coussin, *Du Génie de l'architecture* (1822). Brian Lukacher's Collection

198. *Celebrated Mountain ranges around the World*, engraving with mezzotint from Simeon Shaw, *Nature Displayed in the Heavens and on the Earth* (1823). Brian Lukacher's Collection

199. Engraved frontispiece depicting termite mounds in Africa, from James Rennie, *Insect Architecture* (1830). Brian Lukacher's Collection

200. A. B. Clayton, *Imaginary Museum and Art Academy*, 1842. Pencil, pen, ink, and watercolor on paper, 119.4 x 86.4 (47 x 34). Private Collection

201. *A Series of Pagan Temples, Fire Altars &c.*, Plate LVI from Richard Brown, *Sacred Architecture, Its Rise, Progress, and Present State* (1845). Vassar College Library, Poughkeepsie

202. *A Portal of Strangely Compounded Architecture*, engraved vignette from George Wightwick, *The Palace of Architecture, a Romance of Art and History* (1840). Vassar College Library, Poughkeepsie

203. James Stephanoff, *An Assemblage of Works of Art and Sculpture and Painting*, 1845 (detail). Pen, ink, and watercolor on paper, 77 x 64.6 (31 x 26). British Museum, London

204. C. R. Cockerell, *The Professor's Dream*, 1848. Pencil, pen, ink, and watercolor on paper, 112.2 x 171.1 (44 1/8 x 67 3/8). The Royal Academy of Arts, London

Index

Numbers in italics refer to illustration numbers

Accademia di San Luca, Rome 18–19, 22–23
Adam, James 23
Addison, Joseph 119
Aiken, Edmund 54
Alison, Archibald 42, 138
Allan, William 70
architectural history and natural history 171–73, 188–94
architectural language 184–88
architectural models 136–38, 162, 173
architectural primitivism 38–41, 45–46
architectural reconstructions 16, 19, 88–110
architectural representation (see also "perspective rendering") 8–11, 16, 84–87
Ariosto, *Orlando Furioso* 119–20
Artaud, William 44
Asprucci, Antonio 23
Atlantis 170, 193

Baber, John, *Design for Interior of a Cemetery* 36, *32*
Bacon, Francis 171, 195
Ball, John, *Description of the City of Constantinople* 123, *149*
Barberi, Giuseppe 22–23
Barker, Thomas 62
Barry, James 43, 111
Bartell, Edmund 54
Barthes, Roland 194
Bartlett, William 73
Beaumont, George 103, 144
Beckford, William 114, 156, 199
Belzoni Sarcophagus of Seti I 160, *185*
Benjamin, Walter 11
Bentham, Jeremy 55
Bernard, Thomas 48
Blake, William 10, 42, 118, 124, 197
Blondel, Jacques François 168
Blundell, Henry 70
Bodmer, J. J. 118
Boffrand, Germain 168
Bolton, John 10, 64–65, 68
Bonaparte, Napoleon 10, 29–30, 201
Bonomi, Joseph 58
Boullée, Étienne 22, 184
Boyce, George 162
Brewster, David 199
Brown, Richard 35–36, 94–95, 119; *Sacred Architecture* 196, *201*
British Institution 88, 103
Britton, John 10, 64, 73–78, 82, 84, 122, 135, 143, 156, 160, 167, 173

Brothers, Richard 114
Bryant, Jacob, *New System, Analysis of Ancient Mythology* 180–81
Buckland, William 189
Buckler, John C. 67
Bullock, George 68–70, 72
Bunyan, John 127
Burke, Edmund 10, 21–22, 111, 113, 114, 130, 160, 163
Burnet, Thomas 189
Burney, Edward *View of de Loutherbourg's Eidophusikon* 111, *123*
Burton, Decimus 73, 109
Byron, Lord 41

Campana, Giovanni 22, *Concorso Clementino entry* 17, *22*
Canning, George 68
Carlisle, Anthony 173
Cartwright, Major John 10; 41–44; the Hieronauticon 41–42; Riego monument 43–44; 48, 67. 73, 138
Chalmers, George 48
Chambers, William 19, 21, 22, 86
Christie, James 41
Clare, John 50
Clayton, A. B., 108–09; *Design for a Temple Dedicated to the Memory of Pericles* 118; *Design for a Water Entrance to an Ancient City* 119; *Imaginary Museum and Art Academy* 195, 200; *Imaginary Museum* 195, 200
Clérisseau, C.-L. 86, 95
Cobbett, William 48, 167
Cockerell, C. R. 87, 105, 196–97; *Professor's Dream* 204
Cockerell, S. P. 16, 109
Cole, Thomas, *Voyage of Life: Youth* 127, *141*
Coleridge, S. T. 124, 167, 171, 181
Collins, William 125
Campanella, Tommaso 171
Concorso Clementino of 1795 18–23
Congreve, William 124–25
Conrad, Peter 160
Constable, John 59
Coussin, Jean, *Du génie de l'architecture* 192, 197
Crystal Palace 195
Cuvier, Georges 173

Dance, George, the Younger 19, 36, 46, 58, 87
Daniell, Thomas & William, *Antiquities of India* 128, *145*
Dante Alighieri 104
Darley, Gillian 134
Darwin, Erasmus 114, 186, 188

Davy, Edward 199
Davy, Humphry 119
Deare, John 18
Delafosse, J.-C. 20
Delphi 107, *177*
Deluge, biblical and mythical 185–86, 189
Denon, Vivant 88
De Maillet, Benoit 192
De Quincey, Thomas 56, 166
Desprez, L.-J. 27, 36; *Temple of Isis, Pompeii* 88–90, *99*; *de Wailly's Miltonic Theatre Design* 111, *124*; *The Temple of Fortuna* 117, *131*; *Illumination of Cross at St. Peter's* 121, *133*
Diderot, Denis 111
D'Hancarville, Pierre 184–185
D'Israeli, Isaac 160
Dixon, John 14
Drummond, William, 180
Ducros, Louis 25
Duke of Sussex, Prince Augustus 43, 167
Dupuis, Charles 182
Duran, Giorgio 22; *Concorso Clementino entry* 22, 112, *16*
Durno, James 18
Durand, J.-N.-L. 174

Eagles, John 156
Easter Island 192
Eastlake, Charles 200
Edwards, Edward 14, 36, 90–91
Eidophusikon 11, 111, *125*
Eliot, George, *Middlemarch* 180–81
Elmes, James 87, 163, 188
Elland, Richard 70
Ellicott, Andrew 29
Emanations, doctrine of 182–84
Euripides 107
Eusebius 120, 123–24

Faber, G. S., *Origins of Pagan Idolatry* 180–81, 189
Farington, Joseph 30, 44, 58, 102
Faraday, Michael 119
Flaxman, John 42, 58, 104, 118
Fleet Prison 56–58
Foster, John 70, 78
Fox, Charles James 30
Freemasonry 75, 122, 166–67
Fuseli, Henry 44, 111, 118
Future ruin 105, 157, 161–66

Gandy, Celia 73
Gandy, Hannah 73
Gandy (Deering), John Peter 72–73, 98; *Mystic Temple of Ceres at Eleusis* 98, *108*

Gandy, Joseph Michael
– as antiquarian topographic illustrator 72–79
– as landscape painter 24–27, 79–82
– education and relations with the Royal Academy of Arts 12–15, 58–59, 104
– employment with Major John Cartwright 41–44
– employment with John Soane 36–38, 132–44, 156–67
– financial difficulties of 56–59
– insanity and death of 200–01
– interest in the natural sciences 27–28, 182–84, 198–99
– political opinions of 10, 31, 147–48, 198–99
– practice in Liverpool 68–72
– religious attitudes of 10, 114–15, 182, 199
– reputation in the contemporary press 59–61, 84, 104–05, 199
– travel in Italy, 15–18, 24–31

– Buildings by:
  Lancashire, Bolton Abbey 78
  Lancaster Castle, Civil Court and Female Penitentiary 55, 78
  London, Phoenix Fire and Pelican Life Insurance Offices 61–62
  Bath, Doric House 61–64
  Lake Windermere, Storrs Hall 64–68

– Publications and writings by:
  Designs for Cottages, Cottage Farms, and Other Rural Buildings 44–55
  "On the Philosophy of Architecture" (*Magazine of Fine Arts*) 82–84, 168–70
  The Art, Philosophy, and Science of Architecture 84, 170–71, 180–89, 192–95, 198–201, *191–95*
  The Guardian letters 82–84, 148–49
  The Rural Architect 44–55

– Pictures and designs by:
  Ancient Rome, Stage Set for Titus Andronicus 105–07, *116*
  Architecture; Its Natural Model 188–94, 200, *196*
  Architectural Assemblage 176, *179*, 184–85),
  Architectural Composition, the Fountain of Agno 92–94, *100*
  Boat-House for Sir J. Legard 65, *60*
  Bridge over Chaos 128–31, 144, *146*
  Brighton 80, *87*

Chapel, Part of a Design for a Palace 152, 166
Coalbrookedale 80, 90
Concorso Clementino entry (Designs for a sepulchral chapel) 19–22, 10–12, 14
Commemorative Monument 147, 163
Comparative Architecture, Comparative Characteristics of Thirteen Selected Styles of Architecture 171–74, 180
Comparative Architecture, an Emblematic Sketch 176–84, 186
Conway Castle (after Gandy) 79, 84
Design for a Cenotaph 34–36, 29
Design for a Church 17, 7
Design for a New Senate House at Quebec 68, 67
Design for a Temple and a Bridge in a Nobleman's Park 36, 31
Design for a National Institution of the Fine Arts (after Gandy) 78, 79
Design for the Rebuilding of Ballon Town, County Carlow, Ireland, 54
Design ... of the Inside of a Museum 14–15, 3, 4
Enclosed Commons at Milton 80, 92
Epsom 80, 85
Exeter Cathedral 77, 75–76
Gothic Monument for Battle Abbey 29, 26
Great Temple of Ceres at Eleusis 98–99, 107
Idea of a Bridge and Palace 95–97, 106
Idea of Jupiter Pluvius 103–05, 110
Idea of Titana from the Pira Grove 97–98, 104
Imperial Palace for Sovereigns of the British Empire 148–49, 164
Interior Court of a Design for a Palace 152–54, 167
Interior of a New Ball and Assembly-Room for the Town of Liverpool 71–72, 70
Italianate Landscape 27, 23
Landing Place to a Temple 95, 103
Landing-place to a Temple of Victory 103, 111
Lamp Design 122, 136
Landscape sketch for Mount of Congregation 117, 130
Landscape with Parhelion 183–84, 189
Leith Hill, Dorking 80, 86
Moon with Nimbus 80, 91
Mount of Congregation 116–19, 129
Nocturnal View of Temple of Concord 125, 138
Open Temple and Temple Tower of the Greeks 95–97, 105
Oracle of Mercury 99–102, 95–96
Ossian 127, 139–40
Pandemonium 112–15, 125
Persian Porch and the Place of Consultation 99–102, 109
Proposed Town Residence for the Duke of Wellington 146–47, 162
Purfleet 80, 89
Richborough Castle 79, 83
Roman Capriccio 17, 6
Rosslyn Chapel (after Gandy) 74–76, 72–74
Selection of Buildings from the Designs of John Soane 136–38, 155
Sepulchral Chamber 32–34, 122, 27–28
Sketch of a Design for a Cast-iron Necropolis 198, 200
Sketch for Pandemonium 114, 127
Sketch for Tomb of Merlin 122, 135
Sketch for a New Senate House 155–56, 169
Stairway Leading to the Gates of Heaven 127–28, 142
Tomb of Merlin 119–25, 134
Temple of Apollo at Delphi 107, 117
Temple of Furies, Oedipus at Colonus 107–08, 120
Temple of Minerva Chalinitis, Corinth 95, 102
Tomb of Nitocris 131, 149
Trophal Entrance to Part of a Palace 149–52, 165
Trophy and Temple 11, 1
View of London from Peckham Rye 80, 88
View of San Fiorenza 25, 20
View of Pevensey Castle 78–79, 81–82

Gandy, Michael 20, 72
Gandy, Thomas (Joseph's father) 14, 28, 31
Gandy, Thomas (Joseph's son) 73, 199–200
Gandy, William 14
Gell, William 72
George IV 142, 154
Gillray, James, *Design for the Naval Pillar* 42–43, 39
Godwin, Francis 198
Godwin, William 41
Gombrich, E. H. 186
Grieve, John 105
Gregory, John 39–41

Hackert, Philipp 25
Hadfield, George, *Imaginary Reconstruction of the Flavian Amphitheater* 91, 97
Haldiman, Mrs. George 107
Hamilton, Sir William 24
Hamilton, William 41
Hamlin, Talbot 55
Harding, John 44
Harrison, Thomas 19, 54–55, 78, 146
Harwood, Thomas 67
Haydon, Benjamin R. 160, 200
Hazlitt, William 41, 110, 131
Head, Guy 18, 23
Herschel, John 184
Herschel, William 184
Heywood, Thomas 120
Higgens, Godfrey, *Anacalypsis* 180–82
Hitchcock, Henry-Russell 6
Holland, Henry 16, 47, 159
Hope, Thomas 10, 24; Duchess Street Mansion 35; 36, 51, 54, 64, 71, 115, 122, 156; *Essay on the Origins and Prospects of Man* 173; *Historical Essay on Architecture* 173
Hornor, Thomas, 73
Hotel de Beauharnais, Paris, Gandy's account of 161
Humbert de Superville, D. P. G. 188
Humphry, Ozias 186
Hunt, Leigh 115–16
Hunt, Robert 104
Hutchinson, William, *Spirit of Masonry* 98–99

Johnson, Joseph 42
Johnson, Samuel 149
Jones, William 71
Josephus 121

Kames, Henry Homes, Lord 48
Kaufmann, Emil 11, 53
King, Edward 171
Knight, Richard Payne 46, 83, 144, 174; *Symbolical Language of Ancient Art* 184

Landi, Gaetano 71
Langworthy, Richard 200
Laugier, Marc-Antoine 46, 188
Latrobe, Benjamin Henry 29
Le Camus de Mézières, Nicolas 22, 158
Ledoux, C.-N. 22, 53–54, 112–13, 53, 126
Legard, Sir John 64–65
L'Enfant, Major P. C. 29

Le Sage, Alain René 162
Leslie, C. R. 59, 135
Lethaby, W. R. 201
Locke, John 48
London Corresponding Society 43, 73
Loudon, J. C. 60, 155, 174, 186
Loutherbourg, Philippe Jacques de 111, 124
Lowes, J. L. 171
Lukacher, Julia & Katherine 220

Mackenzie, Frederick 73, 143
Macready, William Charles 105
MacPherson, James 125
Maddox, George 109–10; Part of Orchomenus 121; Greek City in the Time of Pausanias 122
Malton, James, *Essay on British Cottage Architecture* 46
Martin, John 142, 156, 189; Illustrations to *Paradise Lost* 130–31, 147–48
Martindale, John 14–15, 31
Maurice, Thomas 170
Mercier, L.-S. 157
Milizia, Francesco 51
Milton, John 88, 110–11, 127–31
Mithras 177, 182
Monboddo, James Burnett, Lord 188
Montfaucon, Bernard de, *Antiquity Explained* 104
monuments, national and commemorative 19, 41–44, 139, 147
More, Thomas 171
Morris, Robert 45, 188
Mudie, Robert 156
museums, imaginary 194–95
mythography 170–71, 180–82

Nash, John, 124–25, 138, 142, 146, 147, 154, 158; remodeling of Buckingham Palace 144, 161
neo-Platonism 98, 122
Noah's ark 177–81, 195

Opie, John 43
Ossian 125
Ottley, William Young 31, 44

Paestum, Temple of Poseidon 63, 65, 128
Panini, G. P. 138
Panorama of London, Regent Street Coliseum 73, 143, 158
Pansophy 171
Papworth, John 113, 119
Pasquin, Anthony (John Williams) 12

Pausanias 90–92, 97–98, 102, 107
Peacock, James, OIKIDIA, or Nutshells 46, 138
Peacock, Thomas 189
Pennethorne, James 105
Perry, James 167
perspective rendering 11, 36, 84–87, 94–95, 182–83
Pether, William 10
Pickersgill, Henry, Portrait of Joseph Gandy 10, 2
Picturesque, the 23, 44–49, 80, 114, 192
Piranesi, Francesco 23
Piranesi, G. B. 8, 18, 19, 83, 87, 112, 132, 157, 159
Pistocchi, Giuseppe 51
Pitt, William, the Younger 14, 47
Playfair, James 46
Plympton House, Plympton St. Maurice 200
Pocock, W. F. 119
Poe, Edgar Allan 124
Pope, Alexander 119
Porro, Girolamo, Tomb of Merlin 122, 137
Praed, William, 38
Price, Uvedale, Essay on Architecture 22–23, 44, 49–50
Priestley, Joseph 27
Prout, Samuel 73
Pugin, A. C. 73
Pugin, A. W. N. 76, 196–97

Quatremère de Quincy, A.-C. 168, 186

Radcliffe, Ann 200
Reform Bill Debate 165–66, 181
Rennie, James, Insect Architecture 192, 199
Repton, Humphry 46
Reynolds, Joshua 12, 14, 24, 200
Richardson, Margaret 163
Riego, General Rafael del 43–44
Rickman, Thomas 78
Robert, Hubert 95, 138
Robinson, G. J. 155
Rome, French sacking of 30
Rosslyn Chapel 74–76, 122–23, 177
Royal Academy Council 44, 59, 104

Rudofsky, Bernard 201
Ruskin, John 149, 156

Saint-Non, Abbé Richard de, Voyage pittoresque, ou description des Royaumes de Naples et de Sicile 88–90
Schinkel, K. F. 8
Scott, Sir Walter 68, 74
scenography 36, 105–07, 111
Sedlmayr, Hans 55
Seheult, F.-L. 51
Servandoni, G. N. 22
Seth, columns of 185
Shakespeare, William 14, 105; The Tempest 165–67, 200
Shaw, Simeon 192
Shelley, P. B. 10
Shepherd, George 74
Sinclair, John 47
Smirke, Robert 58, 156
Smith, Charles 162
Soane, George 167, 200
Soane, John 10, 19, 36–41, 46, 56–58, 60, 62, 63, 82, 86–87, 91, 112, 128, 131, 132–44, 149, 156–67, 181, 195, 199–200
– as Royal Academy Professor of Architecture 39–41, 86–87, 132, 152–54, 171–73
– criticism of Soane in the press 134–36, 138, 156, 160, 166–67, 200
– Sir John Soane's Museum 6, 156–61, 174–75

– Buildings and designs by:
Architectural Pasticcio, Sir John Soane's Museum 174–76, 181
Architectural Ruins—a Vision (Bank of England in ruins) 163–66, 176
Architectural Visions of Early Fancy 138–139, 156
Bird's-Eye View of the Bank of England 161–63, 175
Bird's-Eye View of a Design for a Royal Residence 142–43, 157
Bird's-Eye View of a Design for a Royal Palace 143–44, 160
Bridge and Gate Lodge at Tyringham 38, 35
Design for a Mausoleum 37, 34
Design for a National Entrance into the Metropolis 154–55, 168
Interior of Cricket Lodge 132–34, 152
Interior of a Town House (Soane Museum) 158–59, 171
Interior of the Edifice Devoted to Freemasonry 166–67, 178
Library of Pitzhanger 132–34, 151
Multiple Views of the Soane Museum 159–60, 172–73
Sepulchral Church (Tyringham) 38, 36–37
View from the Monk's Parlor, Soane Museum 161, 174
View in the Portico for a Royal Residence 143, 159
View of the Dome of the Soane Museum at Night 157–58, 150
View of the Dome of the Soane Museum 157, 170

Soane, John, Junior, Design for a Public Bath 70–71, 158, 69
Society of Dilettanti 98
Sophocles 107, 200
Spence, Thomas 48
Spiller, James 82
Stanfield, Clarkson 105
Starobinski, Jean 55
Staël, Madame de: Corinne, or Italy 88
Stephanoff, James, Assemblage of Works of Art 195, 203
Stothard, Thomas 41
Sublime, the 12, 21–22, 111, 127, 131, 160, 201
Summerson, John 8, 16, 32, 139, 160, 166
Swedenborg, Emanuel, Heaven and Hell 118–19

Tafuri, Manfredo 8
Tatham, C. H. 16, 30, 146, 159
Taylor, Thomas 91, 97, 98, 122
Thelwall, John 73
Thompson, E. P. 29
Thomson, Henry 59
Thomson, James 149
Toland, John 171
Tristan, Flora 198
Turner, J. M. W. 8, 84–86; Interior of Brocklesby Mausoleum 84, 93; Interior of a Prison 84, 91, 95, 104, 94; vignette to Pilgrim's Progress 127, 162, 188, 143

Valenciennes, P.-H. 25, 90–91; Ancient City of Agrigentum 101
Vanbrugh, John 24
Vesuvius 28
Viel de Saint-Maux, J.-L. 184, 186
Villalpando, J. B. 73
Volney, Comte de, Les ruins de l'empire 157, 181–82

Waagen, G. F. 157
Wallis, George Augustus 24–25, Landscape near Rome 25, 30, 31, 44, 19
Wailly, Charles de 111
Walpole, Horace 88, 119
Washington, D. C., urban plan for 29
Watts, Alaric 10
Webb, Eleanor 56
Webster, Sir Godfrey 28–29
Wellington, Duke of 146–47
Westmacott, Richard 18, 59
Whiston, William 171
White, John 146
White's Club 14, 16, 19, 31
Wightwick, George 11, 131; Palace of Architecture 195–96, 202
Wilkins, William 72
Wilson, John 67, 68
Wilson, Thomas, The Pyramid 198
Wood, John the Younger 46
Woodley, Charles 73
Wordsworth, William 10, 45, 68, 199
Wren, Christopher 188
Wright, Thomas 45–46
Wyatt, Benjamin Dean 146
Wyatville (Wyatt), Jeffry 72, 91; Imaginary Architectural Composition 91, 98
Wyatt, James 14, 15, 18, 23, 58, 84, 91, 144

– Buildings by:
London, Oxford Street Pantheon 18, 71, 113
Lincolnshire, Brocklesby Mausoleum 21, 84, 15